Peterson's

MASTER THE
CLEP®

12th Edition

PETERSON'S
Publishing

About Peterson's Publishing

To succeed on your lifelong educational journey, you will need accurate, dependable, and practical tools and resources. That is why Peterson's is everywhere education happens. Because whenever and however you need education content delivered, you can rely on Peterson's to provide the information, know-how, and guidance to help you reach your goals. Tools to match the right students with the right school. It's here. Personalized resources and expert guidance. It's here. Comprehensive and dependable education content— delivered whenever and however you need it. It's all here.

For more information, contact Peterson's, 2000 Lenox Drive, Lawrenceville, NJ 08648; 800-338-3282 Ext. 54229; or find us online at www.petersonspublishing.com.

Bernadette Webster, Director of Publishing; Mark D. Snider, Editor; Ray Golaszewski, Publishing Operations Manager; Linda M. Williams, Composition Manager

ISBN-13: 978-0-7689-3380-2
ISBN-10: 0-7689-3380-3

Printed in the United States of America

10 9 8 7 6 5 4 3 2 1   13 12 11

Twelfth Edition

By printing this book on recycled paper (40% post-consumer waste) 104 trees were saved.

Petersonspublishing.com/publishingupdates

Check out our Web site at www.petersonspublishing.com/publishingupdates to see if there is any new information regarding the test and any revisions or corrections to the content of this book. We've made sure the information in this book is accurate and up-to-date; however, the test format or content may have changed since the time of publication.

OUR PROMISE
SCORE HIGHER. GUARANTEED.

Peterson's Publishing, a Nelnet company, focuses on providing individuals and schools with the best test-prep products—books and electronic components that are complete, accurate, and up-to-date. In fact, we're so sure this book will help you improve your score on this test that we're guaranteeing you'll get a higher score. If you feel your score hasn't improved as a result of using this book, we'll refund the price you paid.

Guarantee Details:

If you don't think this book helped you get a higher score, just return the book with your original sales receipt for a full refund of the purchase price (excluding taxes or shipping costs or any other charges). Please underline the book price and title on the sales receipt. Be sure to include your name and mailing address. This offer is restricted to U.S. residents and to purchases made in U.S. dollars. All requests for refunds must be received by Peterson's within 120 days of the purchase date. Refunds are restricted to one book per person and one book per address.

Send to:
Peterson's Publishing, a Nelnet company
Customer Service
2000 Lenox Drive
Lawrenceville, NJ 08648

Contents

PART III: COLLEGE MATHEMATICS

PART IV: HUMANITIES

SPECIAL ADVERTISING SECTION

Saint Louis University John Cook School of Business
St. Mary's University Bill Greehey School of Business
Thomas Jefferson University School of Population Health
University of Medicine & Dentistry of New Jersey
The Winston Preparatory Schools

Before You Begin

HOW THIS BOOK IS ORGANIZED

The College-Level Examination Program (CLEP) may be a good choice for non-traditional students who are looking to begin a college career without taking the SAT Reasoning Test or the ACT, as most soon-to-be college students do. The CLEP can also be useful for current college students looking to save on the overwhelming cost of earning a degree.

The CLEP is designed to allow prospective, non-traditional college students the opportunity to demonstrate that they have the academic abilities to be successful in a college classroom. It is also designed to help students already enrolled in college to potentially test out of certain courses. This book was carefully researched and written to help you prepare for the CLEP. The chapters in this book explain what the CLEP is all about and review important material that is likely to appear on the various tests included in the CLEP. Completing the many practice exercises and practice tests in this book will help you pass these tests.

To get the most out of this book, take the time to read each section carefully and thoroughly.

- **Part I** serves as an introduction to the CLEP. In this part, you will find a basic overview of the CLEP, a brief introduction to the CLEP general examinations on which this book is based, a look at the extensive range of subject-specific CLEP exams, tips for registering and preparing for the CLEP, a guide to interpreting your scores, and more.

- **Parts II–VI** will provide you with a comprehensive guide to the five CLEP general examinations, which include the College Composition test, the College Mathematics test, the Humanities test, the Social Sciences and History test, and the Natural Sciences test. Each part is devoted to a specific exam and is composed of a pretest, an overview, and a posttest. We recommend that you begin your review of each part by taking the appropriate pretest. This 50-question test will help you to become familiar both with the types of questions you will likely encounter on the real CLEP exams and with the material each test covers. The pretest will also help you to evaluate your current skill level in each subject and can help you to pinpoint any areas in which you might need extra preparation. Once you have completed the pretest, read through the overview that follows. Each overview will provide you with a helpful guide to the material that is included on each exam. The information contained within each overview will help you to focus the direction of your studies in anticipation of taking the CLEP. Finally, each part concludes with a posttest designed to help you gauge how much progress you have made since you began your studies.

- The **Appendix** offers a test-by-test breakdown of the CLEP subject exams (Composition and Literature, World Languages, History and Social Sciences, Science and Math, and Business) for students interested in taking a more subject-specific test. The tests covered in this section include American Literature, Analyzing and Interpreting Literature, College Composition

Modular, English Literature, French Language, German Language, Spanish Language, American Government, Human Growth and Development, Introduction to Educational Psychology, Introduction to Psychology, Introduction to Sociology, Principles of Macroeconomics, Principles of Microeconomics, History of the United States I: Early Colonization to 1877, History of the United States II: 1856 to the Present, Western Civilization I: Ancient Near East to 1648, Western Civilization II: 1648 to the Present, Biology, Calculus, Chemistry, College Algebra, Precalculus, Financial Accounting, Introductory Business Law, Information Systems and Computer Applications, Principles of Management, and Principles of Marketing.

SPECIAL ADVERTISING SECTION

At the end of this book, don't miss the special section of ads placed by Peterson's preferred clients. Their financial support helps make it possible for Peterson's Publishing to continue to provide you with the highest-quality test-prep, educational exploration, and career-preparation resources you need to succeed on your educational journey.

YOU ARE WELL ON YOUR WAY TO SUCCESS

You have made the decision to make the most of your college career by taking the CLEP and have taken a very important step in that process. *Peterson's Master the CLEP®* will help you increase your score on any CLEP tests you take and prepare you for everything you need to know on the day of the exam and beyond it. Good luck!

FIND US ON FACEBOOK®

Join the CLEP conversation on Facebook® at www.facebook.com/petersonspublishing and receive additional test-prep tips and advice. Peterson's resources are available to help you do your best on these important exams—and others in your future.

GIVE US YOUR FEEDBACK

Peterson's publishes a full line of books—test prep, career preparation, education exploration, and financial aid. Peterson's publications can be found at high school guidance offices, college libraries and career centers, and your local bookstore and library. Peterson's books are now also available as eBooks.

We welcome any comments or suggestions you may have about this publication. Your feedback will help us make educational dreams possible for you—and others like you.

HUMANITIES PHOTO CREDITS

All images used in PART IV: Humanities are in the public domain.

Chapter 8: Pretest

Leonardo da Vinci, *The Last Supper*, 1495–1498. DaVinci LastSupper high res 2 nowatmrk.jpg, scanned by http://www.haltadefinizione.com, p.258.

Georges Seurat, *A Sunday on La Grande Jatte*, 1884–1886. A Sunday on La Grande Jatte, Georges Seurat, 1884.jpg; Art Institute of Chicago (Chicago, IL); p. 259.

Flemish harpsichord. Photo by Nick Michael, Flemish harpsichord.jpg, 2005, p. 260.

Chapter 9: Overview

The Acropolis (Athens, Greece). Photo by Adam Carr, Acropolis3.JPG, 27 April 2002, p. 283.

Pyramid (Egypt). Photo by Jon Bodsworth, 01_khafre_north.jpg, http://www.egyptarchive.co.uk, p. 283.

The Parthenon (Athens, Greece). Karen J. Hatzigeorgiou (host), *Parthenon: In the Time of Pericles*, http://karenswhimsy.com/parthenon.shtm, p. 284.

Notre Dame Cathedral (Paris, France). Photo by Tom S., NotreDame1.jpg, http://en.wikipedia.org/wiki/Image:NotreDame1.jpg, April 2007, p. 284.

Hagia Sophia (Istanbul, Turkey). Made available under Creative Commons CC0 1.0 Universal Public Domain Dedication. İstanbul-Ayasofya.JPG, 3 September 2009, p. 284.

The Pantheon (Rome, Italy). Karen J. Hatzigeorgiou (host), *Pantheon: Exterior View*, http://karenswhimsy.com/pantheon.shtm, p. 285.

Westminster Abbey (London, England). Photo by Ellocharlie, Westminster Abbey - West Door.jpg, 18 November 2006, p.285.

Florence Cathedral (Florence, Italy). Photo by Enne, Santa Maria del Fiore.jpg, 29 June 2006, p. 286.

Basilica di San Vitale (Rome, Italy). Photo by Lalupa, San Vitale 051112-20.JPG, 18 December 2005, p. 286.

St. Peter's Basilica (Vatican City). Photo by Wolfgang Stuck, Petersdom von Engelsburg gesehen.jpg, September 2004, p. 286.

Palace of Versailles (Versailles, France). Pierre Patel, *Le Château de Versailles en 1668*, 1668, p. 287.

Leonardo da Vinci, *The Last Supper*, 1495–1498. DaVinci LastSupper high res 2 nowatmrk.jpg, scanned by http://www.haltadefinizione.com, p.289.

Leonardo da Vinci, *Mona Lisa*, 1503. New version of .jpeg image in Public Domain. Mona Lisa. PNG, p. 289.

Michelangelo Buonarroti, *Creation of Adam*, c. 1511. From English Wikipedia, CreationofAdam. jpg, p. 290.

Sandro Botticelli, *The Birth of Venus,* c. 1486. From Google Art Project, Sandro Botticelli - La nascita di Venere - Google Art Project.jpg, p. 290.

Vincent van Gogh, *The Starry Night,* 1889. From Google Art Project, Van Gogh - Starry Night - Google Art Project.jpg, Museum of Modern Art (online database), p. 291.

Georges Seurat, *A Sunday on La Grande Jatte,* 1884–1886. A Sunday on La Grande Jatte, Georges Seurat, 1884.jpg; Art Institute of Chicago (Chicago, IL); p. 291.

Rembrandt van Rijn, *The Storm on the Sea of Galilee,* 1633. Transferred from en.wikipedia, Rembrandt Christ in the Storm on the Lake of Galilee.jpg, p. 292.

Peter Paul Rubens, *The Elevation of the Cross,* 1610–1611. Peter Paul Rubens 068.jpg, The Yorck Project: *10.000 Meisterwerke der Malerei,* DVD-ROM, 2002, p. 292.

Johannes Vermeer, *Girl With the Pearl Earring,* 1665. From Wikimedia Commons, Johannes Vermeer (1632-1675) - The Girl With The Pearl Earring (1665).jpg, p. 293.

Chapter 10: Posttest

Vincent van Gogh, *Self-portrait,* 1889. Vincent Willem van Gogh 106.jpg, The Yorck Project: *10.000 Meisterwerke der Malerei,* DVD-ROM, 2002, p. 305.

Raffaello (Raphael) Sanzio, *School of Athens,* 1505. From Wikimedia Commons, Raphael School of Athens.jpg, p. 308.

Auguste Rodin, *The Thinker,* 1902. Photo by AndrewHorne, Rodin.jpg, 11 Mar 2010, p. 311.

PART I

INTRODUCTION TO THE COLLEGE-LEVEL EXAMINATION PROGRAM (CLEP)

CHAPTER 1   The College-Level Examination Program (CLEP)

The College-Level Examination Program (CLEP)

WHAT IS THE CLEP?

Colleges and universities across the nation have long relied on standardized assessment tests such as the SAT Reasoning Test and the ACT to judge students' academic abilities and preparedness for college. These tests have served students who follow a traditional educational path—elementary school, secondary school, postsecondary education—quite well. But not all students gain their education in a traditional way. Some learn through hands-on training, independent study, or professional development programs. How do these students get their foot in the door at colleges and universities and prove that they have the academic chops to make it in a college classroom? The answer is the College-Level Examination Program, or CLEP.

The CLEP is a collection of thirty-three exams sponsored by the College Board. The exams, which are developed by college faculty across the nation, are designed to indicate college-level mastery of course content in a wide range of subject areas. The CLEP is an advantageous alternative for many students, as it helps to shorten the length of time required to earn a degree and lowers the cost of a college education. When taking CLEP exams, students rely on knowledge they have acquired through various means, not only what they have learned in a formal classroom setting. Those who earn a qualifying score have the opportunity to earn college credits and even bypass certain college classes, thereby allowing them to advance to higher levels of academic study at a faster rate and earn their degrees in less time.

The various CLEP exams will be discussed in more detail later, but the exams fall into five general content categories:

1. Composition and Literature
2. World Languages
3. History and Social Sciences
4. Science and Math
5. Business

Most of the tests are composed mainly of multiple-choice questions and last about 90 minutes. A few exams include other question types or optional essays. The tests are administered on computers, but for some of the tests, paper-and-pencil exams are available for those who cannot take the computerized exam.

WHO TAKES THE CLEP?

Tests such as the SAT Reasoning Test and the ACT are geared toward high school students about to enter college, but people of all ages and skill levels can take the CLEP. From the college student who wants to earn his or her degree at a fraction of the cost to the working parent who must balance school with work and family responsibilities to the professional looking to change careers, the CLEP is a flexible alternative that gives people the chance to put their college-level knowledge and abilities to the test.

CLEP GENERAL EXAMINATIONS

The CLEP includes both general examinations, which test a broad subject area, and subject examinations, which focus on one particular area of study and usually correspond to a particular college course. The following are the five general CLEP examinations:

1. College Composition
2. College Mathematics
3. Humanities
4. Social Sciences and History
5. Natural Sciences

College Composition

Added in 2010, the College Composition exam replaced the English Composition with Essay exam. The College Composition exam is a 120-minute test that includes fifty multiple-choice questions and two mandatory essays. The multiple-choice questions focus on conventions of Standard Written English, revision skills, the ability to use source materials, and rhetorical analysis. The essays assess argumentation, analysis, and synthesis skills.

College Mathematics

The College Mathematics exam is a 90-minute test that includes about sixty multiple-choice questions. About half are straightforward problems, while the other half require more extensive knowledge of underlying skills and concepts. Topics covered in the College Mathematics exam include math sets, logic, the real number system, functions and their graphs, probability and statistics, algebra, and geometry.

Humanities

The Humanities exam is a 90-minute test that includes 140 multiple-choice questions about literature and the arts. Half of the questions focus on literature, including fiction, nonfiction, poetry, and dramatic works. The other half focus on the arts, including visual arts such as painting, sculpture, and architecture and performing arts such as music, theater, dance, and film. The test covers periods from classical to contemporary, and some questions are cross-cultural in scope.

Social Sciences and History

The Social Sciences and History exam is a 90-minute test that includes 120 multiple-choice questions. About 40 percent of the test questions focus on history, including U.S. history, world history, and

Western civilization. The remaining questions are drawn from subject areas including anthropology, economics, geography, government/political science, psychology, and sociology.

Natural Sciences

The Natural Sciences exam is a 90-minute test that includes 120 multiple-choice questions. The Natural Sciences exam is generally used to fulfill general education science requirements. The test questions split evenly between two subject areas: biology and physical science.

CLEP SUBJECT EXAMS

In addition to the five general exams, the CLEP offers numerous exams in a variety of subject areas. The following is a brief overview of these exams, divided by content category and subject. For more detailed information about the CLEP and its various exams, visit http://clep.collegeboard.org. You can also contact the College Board:

P.O. Box 6600
Princeton, NJ
08541-6600
800-257-9558 (phone)
610-628-3726 (fax)
clep@info.collegeboard.org (e-mail)

Composition and Literature

American Literature

The American Literature exam is a 90-minute test with about 100 multiple-choice questions. It includes an optional essay section that some colleges and universities require. This section includes two essays to be answered in an additional 90-minute period. The essays are not graded by the College Board; they are graded by the college or university that requests them.

Analyzing and Interpreting Literature

The Analyzing and Interpreting Literature exam is a 90-minute test with about eighty multiple-choice questions. It includes an optional essay section that some colleges and universities require. This section includes two essays to be answered in an additional 90-minute period. The essays are not graded by the College Board; they are graded by the college or university that requests them.

College Composition Modular

The College Composition Modular has replaced two former tests: English Composition (not to be confused with English Composition with Essay) and Freshman College Composition. This is a 90-minute test with about ninety multiple-choice questions. It also includes an essay section, which may be provided by the college or university or by the CLEP; in either case, the essays are scored by the college or university. If the college or university chooses the essay provided by the CLEP, students have 70 minutes to answer two essays.

English Literature

The English Literature exam is a 90-minute test with about ninety-five multiple-choice questions. It includes an optional essay section that some colleges and universities require. This section requires students to respond to two of three essays in an additional 90-minute period. The essays are not graded by the College Board; they are scored by faculty at the colleges and universities to which students send their reports.

World Languages

French Language (Levels 1 and 2)

The French Language exam is a 90-minute test with about 121 multiple-choice questions. The test is divided into three sections, which are timed separately. Two sections focus on listening, and a third focuses on reading.

German Language (Levels 1 and 2)

The German Language exam is a 90-minute test with about 120 multiple-choice questions. The test is divided into three sections, which are timed separately. Two sections focus on listening, and a third focuses on reading.

Spanish Language (Levels 1 and 2)

The Spanish Language exam is a 90-minute test with about 120 multiple-choice questions. The test is divided into three sections, which are timed separately. Two sections focus on listening, and a third focuses on reading.

History and Social Sciences

American Government

The American Government exam is a 90-minute test with about ninety multiple-choice questions. Topics covered on the test include the presidency, bureaucracy, Congress, federal courts, civil liberties, civil rights, political parties, political beliefs, and the Constitution.

Human Growth and Development

The Human Growth and Development exam is a 90-minute test with about ninety multiple-choice questions. Topics covered on the test include theoretical perspectives; research strategies and methodology; biological, perceptual, cognitive, language, social, and atypical development throughout life; intelligence; family, home, and society; personality and emotion; learning; and schooling, work, and interventions.

Introduction to Educational Psychology

The Introduction to Educational Psychology exam is a 90-minute test with about 100 multiple-choice questions. Topics covered on the test include educational aims and philosophies, cognitive perspective, behavioral perspective, development, motivation, individual differences, testing, pedagogy, and research design and analysis.

Introduction to Psychology

The Introduction to Psychology exam is a 90-minute test with about ninety-five multiple-choice questions. Topics covered on the test include history, approaches, and methods of psychology; biological bases of behavior; sensation and perception; states of consciousness; learning; cognition; motivation and emotion; developmental psychology; personality; psychological disorders and health; treatment; social psychology; and statistics, tests, and measurement.

Introduction to Sociology

The Introduction to Sociology exam is a 90-minute test with about 100 multiple-choice questions. Topics covered on the test include institutions, social patterns, social processes, social stratification, and the sociological perspective.

Principles of Macroeconomics

The Principles of Macroeconomics exam is a 90-minute test with about eighty multiple-choice questions. Topics covered on the test include basic economic concepts; measurement of economic performance; national income and price determination; the financial sector; inflation, unemployment, and stabilization policies; economic growth and productivity; international trade; and finance.

Principles of Microeconomics

The Principles of Microeconomics exam is a 90-minute test with about eighty multiple-choice questions. Topics covered on the test include basic economic concepts, the nature and functions of product markets, factor markets, and market failure and the role of government.

History of the United States I: Early Colonization to 1877

The History of the United States I: Early Colonization to 1877 exam is a 90-minute test with about 120 multiple-choice questions. About 30 percent of the test focuses on the period from 1500 to 1789, while the remaining 70 percent focuses on 1790 to 1877. Topics covered include political institutions; political developments, behavior, and public policy; social developments; economic developments; cultural and intellectual developments; and diplomacy and international relations.

History of the United States II: 1865 to the Present

The History of the United States II: 1865 to the Present exam is a 90-minute test with about 120 multiple-choice questions. About 30 percent of the test focuses on the period from 1865 to 1914, while the remaining 70 percent focuses on 1915 to present. Topics covered include political institutions; political developments, behavior, and public policy; social developments; economic developments; cultural and intellectual developments; and diplomacy and international relations.

Western Civilization I: Ancient Near East to 1648

The Western Civilization I: Ancient Near East to 1648 exam is a 90-minute test with about 120 multiple-choice questions. Topics covered include the ancient Near East, ancient Greece and Hellenistic civilization, ancient Rome, medieval history, the Renaissance, the Reformation, and early modern Europe from 1560–1648.

Western Civilization II: 1648 to the Present

The Western Civilization II: 1648 to the Present exam is a 90-minute test with about 120 multiple-choice questions. Topics covered include absolutism and constitutionalism, 1648–1715; competition for empire and economic expansion; the scientific view of the world; the period of Enlightenment; revolution and Napoleonic Europe; the Industrial Revolution; political and cultural developments, 1815–1848; politics and diplomacy in the Age of Nationalism, 1850–1914; economy, culture, and imperialism, 1850–1914; the First World War; the Russian Revolution; Europe between the wars; the Second World War; and contemporary Europe.

Science and Math

Biology

The Biology exam is a 90-minute test with about 115 multiple-choice questions. Topics covered include molecular and cellular biology, organismal biology, and population biology.

Calculus

The Calculus exam is a 90-minute test with about forty-four multiple-choice questions. The test is divided into two timed sections, one lasting 50 minutes and the other lasting 40 minutes. Topics covered include limits, differential calculus, and integral calculus.

Chemistry

The Chemistry exam is a 90-minute test with about seventy-five multiple-choice questions. Topics covered include structure of matter, states of matter, reaction types, equations and stoichiometry, equilibrium, kinetics, thermodynamics, descriptive chemistry, experimental chemistry.

College Algebra

The College Algebra exam is a 90-minute test with about sixty multiple-choice questions. Topics covered include algebraic operations, equations and inequalities, functions and their properties, and number systems and operations.

Precalculus

The Precalculus exam is a 90-minute test with about forty-eight multiple-choice questions. The test is divided into two timed sections, one lasting 50 minutes and the other lasting 40 minutes. Topics covered include algebraic expressions, equations, and inequalities; concepts, properties, and operations of functions; symbolic, graphical, and tabular representations of functions; analytic geometry; trigonometry and its applications; and functions as models.

Business

Financial Accounting

The Financial Accounting exam is a 90-minute test with about seventy-five multiple-choice questions. Topics covered include general accounting principles, business ethics, income statements, balance sheets, and statements of cash flow.

Introductory Business Law

The Introductory Business Law exam is a 90-minute test with about 100 multiple-choice questions. Topics covered include history and sources of American law/constitutional law, American legal systems and procedures, contracts, legal environment, and torts.

Information Systems and Computer Applications

The Information Systems and Computer Applications exam is a 90-minute test with about 100 multiple-choice questions. Topics covered include information systems; office application software in organizations; hardware and systems technology; information systems software development; programming concepts and data management; and business, social, and ethical implications and issues.

Principles of Management

The Principles of Management exam is a 90-minute test with about 100 multiple-choice questions. Topics covered include organization and human resources, operational aspects of management, functional aspects of management, and international management and contemporary issues.

Principles of Marketing

The Principles of Marketing exam is a 90-minute test with about 100 multiple-choice questions. Topics covered include the role of marketing in society, the role of marketing in a firm, target marketing, product and service management, branding, pricing policies, distribution channels and logistics, integrated marketing communications, and e-commerce.

GETTING COLLEGE CREDIT

How would you like to take one 90-minute exam and earn the same amount of college credit that you would get if you spent a semester—or even a year—in the equivalent college class? Across the nation, about 2,900 colleges and universities grant credit for certain CLEP exams. Each college or university is different, however, so be sure to check your college or university's CLEP policy.

CHECK YOUR COLLEGE'S CLEP POLICY

Each college and university establishes its own CLEP policy. Some may grant credit for any and all CLEP exams, while others are selective in granting credit. Many institutions set limits on the amount of credits students can earn through CLEP exams. In addition, most institutions have set minimum qualifying scores for each exam. To earn credit, students must earn a score that is equivalent to or higher than the minimum qualifying score. Some colleges and universities may allow you to apply CLEP credits to satisfy the requirements of a particular course. Others may simply apply CLEP credits toward students' general education requirements. Because each college or university's CLEP policy varies so much, it is important to investigate each and every institution's policy to determine the one that works for you.

REGISTERING FOR THE CLEP

Registering to take one or more CLEP exams is relatively easy. The first step is to contact one of the 1,600 CLEP Test Centers found throughout the United States and abroad. To find a CLEP Test Center near you, visit http://apps.collegeboard.com/cbsearch_clep/searchCLEPTestCenter.jsp. After locating a convenient site for your test, contact the Test Center and ask about its registration process, testing schedule, and service fees. In addition, fill out a registration form and send it, along with your examination fee (which is separate from the center's administration/service fee) to the test center. If you require any type of special accommodations or if you are unable to take the test on a computer and require a traditional paper-and-pencil exam, be sure to make this known during the registration process.

One important note about registration: You may register to retake any CLEP exam, as long as you have not taken that same test at any point within the preceding six months.

PREPARING FOR THE TESTS

The type and depth of preparation required for a CLEP test depends largely on the individual. The tests are designed to assess your knowledge of information you have learned outside a traditional classroom setting; however, you may find that you need more than a quick brush-up on the material that will be covered in the exam. The College Board recommends studying the textbook that the college uses for the course that corresponds to the exam you plan to take. A number of online resources offer free study resources and sample questions. In addition, you can prepare by purchasing CLEP study guides.

Another helpful tool to help you prepare to take CLEP tests is the *CLEP Sampler*. You can download this free tutorial from the College Boards' Web site (http://www.collegeboard.com/student/testing/clep/prep_hint_e.html) to familiarize yourself with the software of the computerized CLEP exams. Many colleges that serve as CLEP Test Centers also have this software available on the public computers in their libraries. While this helpful tool does not include sample questions, it does explain the different types of questions and the instructions you will encounter on the exam.

- **Make a plan and stick to it.** Determine the areas where you need the most work. Then, set daily, weekly, or monthly goals that will help push you to succeed.

- **Set up a schedule.** Trying to cram for a CLEP exam the night before the test is a bad idea. Be sure to give yourself plenty of time to learn the material. By setting study times for yourself, you will be less likely to stray from your schedule.

- **Find a good place to study.** Look for a place free of distractions, where you can concentrate and maintain your focus.

- **Review, review, review.** It is not enough to study material one time. Be sure to review the material every week or two to keep the information fresh in your mind.

- **Know what to expect.** Familiarize yourself with the exam by learning the number and types of questions on the test and the time allotted for the test. Also, make sure you know exactly where to go on test day (this includes knowing the building and room number, where to park your car, and so on).

INTERPRETING YOUR SCORES

As mentioned previously, colleges and universities set their own policies when it comes to CLEP tests, CLEP scores, and awarding college credit. Therefore, the same score can have different outcomes at different schools. However, some standardization does exist, as the College Board recommends that colleges and universities refer to the guidelines created by the American Council on Education when they create their CLEP policies.

CLEP exams that involve only multiple-choice questions are scored by computer, so you will receive your score immediately upon completion of the exam. Tests with essays are graded differently, and it takes a few weeks to generate the score report.

How Your Scores Are Computed

Total scores for CLEP tests are generated from a formula score, which is converted to a scaled score. The formula score is determined by the number of questions you answer correctly. Each correct answer adds one point to your raw score. No points are deducted for skipped or incorrect answers. The formula score is then correlated to a scaled score between 20 and 80. A score of 20 is the lowest, and a score of 80 is the highest. The scaled score is the score that appears on your final score report.

How Your Essays Are Graded

Tests with mandatory essays, such as College Composition, are scored by college professors selected by the College Board. Two professors score each essay, and the two scores are added together. The essay score and the multiple-choice score are then combined, resulting in a formula score, which is converted to a scaled score between 20 and 80. The scaled score is the score that appears on your final score report, which is mailed to you a few weeks after the test.

Some tests have optional essays, which are scored by the college or university that requires them. These essays are not scored by the College Board. Optional essays are sent with the score report from the multiple-choice portion of the exam to the college or university that you select when you take your test.

You may choose to have your scores sent to the college or university of your choice, or you may choose to hold off on sending your score report until you have seen your score. If you choose the second option, you have ninety days to request the sending of your essay(s) to the college or university of your choice.

PART II
COLLEGE COMPOSITION

PRETEST ANSWER SHEET

Part I

1. Ⓐ Ⓑ Ⓒ Ⓓ Ⓔ	11. Ⓐ Ⓑ Ⓒ Ⓓ Ⓔ	21. Ⓐ Ⓑ Ⓒ Ⓓ Ⓔ	31. Ⓐ Ⓑ Ⓒ Ⓓ Ⓔ	41. Ⓐ Ⓑ Ⓒ Ⓓ Ⓔ
2. Ⓐ Ⓑ Ⓒ Ⓓ Ⓔ	12. Ⓐ Ⓑ Ⓒ Ⓓ Ⓔ	22. Ⓐ Ⓑ Ⓒ Ⓓ Ⓔ	32. Ⓐ Ⓑ Ⓒ Ⓓ Ⓔ	42. Ⓐ Ⓑ Ⓒ Ⓓ Ⓔ
3. Ⓐ Ⓑ Ⓒ Ⓓ Ⓔ	13. Ⓐ Ⓑ Ⓒ Ⓓ Ⓔ	23. Ⓐ Ⓑ Ⓒ Ⓓ Ⓔ	33. Ⓐ Ⓑ Ⓒ Ⓓ Ⓔ	43. Ⓐ Ⓑ Ⓒ Ⓓ Ⓔ
4. Ⓐ Ⓑ Ⓒ Ⓓ Ⓔ	14. Ⓐ Ⓑ Ⓒ Ⓓ Ⓔ	24. Ⓐ Ⓑ Ⓒ Ⓓ Ⓔ	34. Ⓐ Ⓑ Ⓒ Ⓓ Ⓔ	44. Ⓐ Ⓑ Ⓒ Ⓓ Ⓔ
5. Ⓐ Ⓑ Ⓒ Ⓓ Ⓔ	15. Ⓐ Ⓑ Ⓒ Ⓓ Ⓔ	25. Ⓐ Ⓑ Ⓒ Ⓓ Ⓔ	35. Ⓐ Ⓑ Ⓒ Ⓓ Ⓔ	45. Ⓐ Ⓑ Ⓒ Ⓓ Ⓔ
6. Ⓐ Ⓑ Ⓒ Ⓓ Ⓔ	16. Ⓐ Ⓑ Ⓒ Ⓓ Ⓔ	26. Ⓐ Ⓑ Ⓒ Ⓓ Ⓔ	36. Ⓐ Ⓑ Ⓒ Ⓓ Ⓔ	46. Ⓐ Ⓑ Ⓒ Ⓓ Ⓔ
7. Ⓐ Ⓑ Ⓒ Ⓓ Ⓔ	17. Ⓐ Ⓑ Ⓒ Ⓓ Ⓔ	27. Ⓐ Ⓑ Ⓒ Ⓓ Ⓔ	37. Ⓐ Ⓑ Ⓒ Ⓓ Ⓔ	47. Ⓐ Ⓑ Ⓒ Ⓓ Ⓔ
8. Ⓐ Ⓑ Ⓒ Ⓓ Ⓔ	18. Ⓐ Ⓑ Ⓒ Ⓓ Ⓔ	28. Ⓐ Ⓑ Ⓒ Ⓓ Ⓔ	38. Ⓐ Ⓑ Ⓒ Ⓓ Ⓔ	48. Ⓐ Ⓑ Ⓒ Ⓓ Ⓔ
9. Ⓐ Ⓑ Ⓒ Ⓓ Ⓔ	19. Ⓐ Ⓑ Ⓒ Ⓓ Ⓔ	29. Ⓐ Ⓑ Ⓒ Ⓓ Ⓔ	39. Ⓐ Ⓑ Ⓒ Ⓓ Ⓔ	49. Ⓐ Ⓑ Ⓒ Ⓓ Ⓔ
10. Ⓐ Ⓑ Ⓒ Ⓓ Ⓔ	20. Ⓐ Ⓑ Ⓒ Ⓓ Ⓔ	30. Ⓐ Ⓑ Ⓒ Ⓓ Ⓔ	40. Ⓐ Ⓑ Ⓒ Ⓓ Ⓔ	50. Ⓐ Ⓑ Ⓒ Ⓓ Ⓔ

answer sheet

Part II

Essay 1

answer sheet

Essay 2

answer sheet

Pretest

PART I

50 minutes • 50 questions

Conventions of Standard Written English

> **Directions:** The following sentences test your knowledge of grammar, diction (choice of words), and idioms. Some sentences are correct. No sentence contains more than one error.
>
> You will find that the error, if there is one, is underlined and lettered. Assume that elements of the sentence that are not underlined are correct and cannot be changed. In choosing answers, follow the requirements of Standard Written English.
>
> If there is an error, select the one underlined part that must be changed to make the sentence correct and fill in the corresponding oval on your answer sheet. If there is no error, select answer (E).

Example: SAMPLE ANSWER

Ⓐ ● Ⓒ Ⓓ Ⓔ

Highway road construction <u>and</u> slow
                              A

moving traffic <u>decreases</u> your <u>chances</u>
                   B   C

of enjoying smooth, <u>relaxed</u> holiday
                        D

travel. <u>No error.</u>
          E

Since the compound subject *highway road construction and slow moving traffic* is plural, the verb *decreases* should also be written in plural form as *decrease*. **The correct answer is (B).**

1. Chef Martin, <u>has all the ingredients</u> for
                 A   B

   <u>tonight's</u> dinner <u>been brought</u> to the
      C   D

   kitchen and prepared as you requested?

   <u>No error.</u>
      E

2. Although Tanya trained <u>hard</u> for her
                             A

   upcoming race, she also <u>took</u> plenty of
                              B

   time to rest, <u>remembering</u> that if you
                    C

   don't get enough rest, <u>she might</u> risk
                              D

   serious injury. <u>No error.</u>
                       E

21

3. As he raced <u>to work to</u> make it to the
    A   B

   big meeting on time, Arthur <u>realized</u> that
                               C

   he <u>forgotten</u> his briefcase at home.
        D

   <u>No error.</u>
     E

4. <u>Having pleaded</u> her case to the jury, the
       A

   defendant hoped <u>they would</u> understand
                    B

   her <u>predicament</u> and acquit <u>her</u> of all
         C   D

   charges. <u>No error.</u>
          E

5. <u>Exploring</u> far ahead of the others, Roger
     A

   <u>was clearly</u> the <u>less hesitant</u> of all his
      B   C

   traveling companions about the possible
   <u>dangers</u> of the jungle. <u>No error.</u>
     D   E

Revision Skills

Directions: Each of the following selections is an early draft of a student essay in which the sentences have been numbered for easy reference. Some parts of the selections need to be changed.

Read each essay and then answer the questions that follow. Some questions are about particular sentences and ask you to improve sentence structure and diction (choice of words). In making these decisions, follow the conventions of Standard Written English. Other questions refer to the entire essay or parts of the essay and ask you to consider organization, development, and effectiveness of language in relation to purpose and audience.

Questions 6–14 are based on the following draft of a student essay.

(1) After the fighting of World War II ceased, much of Europe was in shambles, and it seemed doubtful that the war-torn region could revive on its own. (2) In 1947, George C. Marshall, who was then the U.S. secretary of state, put forward an idea to use American money to help European nations rebuild themselves. (3) Marshall acted as secretary of defense during the Korean War. (4) The plan that Marshall created went on to help more than fifteen countries in Europe. (5) This successful plan—named after its creator— became known as the Marshall Plan.

(6) In the United States, opinions about the plan were mixed. (7) Some Americans thought that quickly rebuilding Europe would stop Communists from taking over the continent. (8) Other Americans, however, believed that the United States should not waste money on helping another continent rebuild themselves. (9) The plan eventually gained enough support in the government to be enacted. (10) On April 3, 1948, President Harry Truman signed the Foreign Assistance Act, which officially started the Marshall Plan.

(11) Most of the money meant for the Marshall Plan came in the form of grants for the participating European countries, some of the money also came in the form of loans. (12) Europe used the grants and loans to rebuilds lost infrastructure, develop trade, restore farming, and increase industry. (13) By 1950—the midpoint of the Marshall Plan— many countries involved in the plan had

reached their prewar levels of manufacturing and production.

(14) Despite spending millions of dollars on the plan, the United States gained financially from it. (15) Leaders from all over the world credited the Marshall Plan with preventing widespread poverty, famine, and political instability in Europe after World War II.

6. Which of the following would make the most logical title for the passage?

   (A) Americans' Reactions to the Marshall Plan

   (B) The Aftermath of World War II in Europe

   (C) The Cost of Rebuilding after a War

   (D) Rebuilding Europe with the Marshall Plan

   (E) The Life and Work of George Marshall

7. In context, which of the following is the best way to combine sentences 4 and 5?

   (A) The plan that Marshall created went on to help more than fifteen countries in Europe, and it was named after its creator.

   (B) The successful Marshall Plan was created by Marshall and helped more than fifteen countries in Europe.

   (C) Named after its creator, fifteen countries in Europe were helped by the successful plan that Marshall created.

   (D) After Marshall created it, more than fifteen countries in Europe were rebuilt by the Marshall Plan.

   (E) The Marshall Plan, which was named after its creator, went on to help rebuild more than fifteen European countries.

8. Which is the best revision of the underlined portion of sentence 8 (reproduced below)?

   Other Americans, however, believed that the United States should not waste money on helping another continent rebuild themselves.

   (A) Change "should" to "would."

   (B) Add "Thus" to the beginning of the sentence.

   (C) Change "themselves" to "itself."

   (D) Add "too" to the end of the sentence.

   (E) Change "another" to "other."

9. In context, which is best to add to the beginning of sentence 9?

   (A) Furthermore,

   (B) Additionally,

   (C) Nevertheless,

   (D) Consequently,

   (E) Therefore,

10. In context, which of the following versions of the underlined portion of sentence 11 (reproduced below) is best?

    Most of the money meant for the Marshall Plan came in the form of grants to the participating European countries, some of the money also came in the form of loans.

    (A) countries and some of the money

    (B) countries; therefore some of the money

    (C) countries but some of the money

    (D) countries; however, some of the money

    (E) countries, having some of the money

11. Deleting which of the following sentences would most improve the coherence of the passage?

    (A) Sentence 1

    (B) Sentence 3

    (C) Sentence 8

    (D) Sentence 11

    (E) Sentence 13

12. In context, which is the best replacement for "meant" in sentence 11?

(A) allocated

(B) fated

(C) devoted

(D) preordaine

(E) signified

13. In context, which of the following revisions must be made to sentence 12 (reproduced below)?

Europe used the grants and loans to rebuilds lost infrastructure, develop trade, restore farming, and increase industry.

(A) Add a colon after "to."

(B) Change "grants and loans" to "money."

(C) Add "international" before "trade."

(D) Change "rebuilds" to "rebuild."

(E) Change "farming" to "agriculture."

14. Which of the following sentences is best to add after sentence 14?

(A) In 1949, the United States government extended the Marshall Plan to cover more countries from different parts of the world.

(B) During the 1940s and 1950s, the United States exported many goods to Europe, and that area's increased financial stability encouraged the sale of more American goods.

(C) In all, the United States contributed roughly $13 billion of economic aid to Europe during the Marshall Plan, which lasted from 1948 to 1951.

(D) The countries involved in the Marshall Plan included the United Kingdom, France, Ireland, Italy, the Netherlands, Greece, Austria, Denmark, Belgium, and West Germany.

(E) The Soviet Union refused aid from the United States and condemned the Marshall Plan as an American effort to overtake the European economy.

15. Which of the following would be the best sentence with which to end the passage?

(A) Today, the Marshall Plan is widely respected by historians and policy makers, and leaders still use it as an example of successful foreign policy.

(B) The Marshall Plan was bipartisan as it was backed by a Democratic president and a Republican legislature.

(C) Thanks to the Marshall Plan, many countries in Western Europe had a 15 to 25 percent rise in their gross national products.

(D) One of the only Western European countries not invited to participate in the Marshall Plan was Spain, as it was ruled by dictator Francisco Franco.

(E) After George Marshall retired from office in 1951, he remained in the public eye and represented the United States in ceremonial activities.

Questions 16–25 are based on the following draft of a student essay.

(1) The emerald ash borer (EAB) is an invasive species of beetle that infects ash trees in the United States and Canada. (2) This insect originated in Asia and was first detected in the United States in 2002 in Michigan. (3) EAB is a serious threat to forests and urban trees in North America.

(4) In North America, the EAB infests only ash trees. (5) The female insects lay their eggs on ash trees in the spring, and the larvae borrow under the trees' bark and eat the tissue inside. (6) After a larva first infects a tree, it dies in three to five years.

(7) Ash trees infected with EAB usually show signs of infection before they die. (8) One of the first signs of infection is crown dieback, that is when the crown (or top) of the tree begins to die. (9) Another sign of EAB infestation is leaves sprouting from a tree's trunk. (10) If a tree manifests these symptoms, scientists or researchers might test the tree for EAB. (11) Trees that test positive for EAB

infection are destroyed. (12) Any ash trees within a specific area (usually a half-mile) are also destroyed.

(13) EAB and many other nonnative invasive species reek havoc in their new environments. (14) Other invasive species in the United States include the zebra mussel and the Asian long-horned beetle. (15) If EAB is not controlled, this insect could potentially kill off most of the ash trees in North America. (16) The death of these trees would impact biodiversity in the forest and could change the landscape of the United States' urban and rural woodlands.

16. Which of the following would make the most logical title for the passage?

   (A) The Threat of the Emerald Ash Borer
   (B) Invasive Species of the United States
   (C) Controlling Insect Populations
   (D) The Life Cycle of the Emerald Ash Borer
   (E) Michigan's Problem with Invasive Species

17. In context, which of the following is the best revision to sentence 6 (reproduced below)?

   After a larva first infects a tree, it dies in three to five years.

   (A) After an infection first occurs, it dies in three to five years.
   (B) It dies about three to five years after an infection first occurs.
   (C) The tree dies roughly three to five years after a larva first infects it.
   (D) A larva infects a tree, and it dies three to five years later.
   (E) Because of the infection, it dies roughly three to five year afterward.

18. Which of the following revisions is most needed in sentence 8 (reproduced below)?

   One of the first signs of infection is crown dieback, that is when the crown (or top) of the tree begins to die.

   (A) Add "slowly" before "begins."
   (B) Change "that" to "which."
   (C) Change the parentheses to commas.
   (D) Change "begins" to "starts."
   (E) Delete the comma.

19. Which would be the place to insert the following sentence?

   As it eats its way through an ash tree, an EAB larva creates a twisting pattern in the wood.

   (A) Immediately after sentence 2
   (B) Immediately after sentence 5
   (C) Immediately after sentence 9
   (D) Immediately after sentence 11
   (E) Immediately after sentence 13

20. Which of the following sentences is best to add after sentence 9?

   (A) Another negative effect of EAB infestation is the cost of removing damaged trees.
   (B) EAB infects healthy and unhealthy ash trees of all different ages and sizes.
   (C) Humans use ash trees to make products such as baseball bats and tool handles.
   (D) Each female EAB can lay between 60 and 90 eggs in her lifetime.
   (E) A third sign of infection is the splitting or chipping of a tree's bark.

21. In context, which of the following is the best way to combine sentences 11 and 12?

   (A) Trees that are positive for infection are destroyed; nevertheless, any ash trees within a specific area (usually a half-mile) are also destroyed.
   (B) Trees that are positive for infection are destroyed since any ash trees within a specific area (usually a half-mile) are also destroyed.

(C) Trees that are positive for infection are destroyed, so any ash trees within a specific area (usually a half-mile) are also destroyed.

(D) Trees that are positive for infection are destroyed; furthermore, any ash trees within a specific area (usually a half-mile) are also destroyed.

(E) Trees that are positive for infection are destroyed; therefore, any ash trees within a specific area (usually a half-mile) are also destroyed.

22. In context, which of the following versions of the underlined portion of sentence 13 (reproduced below) is best?

EAB and many other nonnative invasive species reek havoc in their new environments.

(A) Change "environments" to "habitats."

(B) Change "their" to "its."

(C) Delete "new."

(D) Add a comma after "havoc."

(E) Change "reek" to "wreak."

23. Which of the following revisions would most emphasize the purpose of sentence 16 (reproduced below)?

The death of these trees would impact biodiversity in the forest and could change the landscape of the United States' urban and rural woodlands.

(A) Change "trees" to "plants" and "urban" to "city."

(B) Insert "negatively" before "impact" and "forever" before "change."

(C) Change "forest" to "woods" and "United States'" to "country's."

(D) Insert "ash" before "trees" and "natural" before "landscape."

(E) Change "death" to "demise" and "change" to "alter."

24. Deleting which of the following sentences would most improve the coherence of the passage?

(A) Sentence 2

(B) Sentence 7

(C) Sentence 10

(D) Sentence 14

(E) Sentence 17

25. In context, which of the following would be the best sentence with which to end the passage?

(A) Before EAB was discovered in North America, people thought ash trees were dying from a different disorder.

(B) Therefore, monitoring and controlling EAB in North America is of the utmost importance.

(C) Invasive species often become pests because they have no natural enemies in their new habitats.

(D) One of the ways humans spread EAB is by moving infected firewood to a new area.

(E) However, solving the problem of the EAB might not be worth people's time and effort.

Ability to Use Source Materials

Directions: The following questions are designed to test your knowledge of basic research, reference, and composition skills. Some questions are self-contained, but other questions will ask you to refer to a passage. Read all of the answer choices before choosing the best answer for each question.

26. Johnson, Ashley. *Writing Your Own Story of Success.* Boston, MA: American Publishing, 2007.

    In the citation, which information is provided by "Boston, MA"?

    (A) The city where the book was published

    (B) The city where the most books sold

    (C) The city where the book was written

    (D) The city where the author lives

    (E) The city where the book was released

27. *The following excerpt is taken from a student's research paper.*

    In June of 1876, Lieutenant Colonel George Custer led his troops into battle against the Native Americans, whose forces were led by Sitting Bull (Bowman 2008, sec. 10).

    The phrase "sec. 10" indicates the

    (A) source was written in the tenth month of the year 2008

    (B) referenced material comes from the book's second printing

    (C) student used information from the source's tenth page

    (D) referenced material comes from the tenth section

    (E) student quoted ten words directly from author's work

28. Langford, Harriet. "George Washington." <http://www.historyoftheUSA.org> (accessed May 2, 2010).

    Which of the following is cited in this example?

    (A) An electronic database

    (B) A scholarly journal

    (C) An online newspaper

    (D) An electronic encyclopedia

    (E) A Web site

29. measure *n.* **1.** *a.* a sufficient amount or a reasonable degree; a set limit (happy beyond measure) *b.* the amount of something measured **2.** a tool or an instrument used for measuring; a unit of measuring **3.** the measuring process **4.** a plan or action (the senate proposed a measure to reduce legislative waste) **5.** *a.* a melody or a rhythm *b.* musical beats; musical meter (the flutist played the song's first measure) [Middle English mesure, from Late Latin *mensurare*, from Latin *mensura* "a measuring, a thing by which to measure."]

    Which of the following statements is NOT supported by the definition above?

    (A) One meaning of the word "measure" is the amount of something measured.

    (B) The word "measure" sometimes refers to a plan of action.

    (C) The word *mensurare* was used in Middle English.

    (D) The Latin word *mensura* is one of the roots of the word "measure."

    (E) The word "measure" can refer to beats of music.

Questions 30–37 refer to the following passage.

(1) Food is a vital part of human life; however, many people living in the United States and other Western countries see food merely as a cheap commodity. (2) Much of the food consumed in the United States and in other industrialized nations is grown on huge, industrial farms. (3) These industrial farms generally use large amounts of petroleum, pesticides, and other harmful chemicals. (4) Industrial farms are also notorious for practicing growing methods that are harmful to the environment (Collins 2003, A4). (5) Although industrial farming practices are still the norm in the United States, a new, sustainable agricultural movement is spreading throughout the country.

(6) Community-supported agriculture is a relatively new method of farming that is becoming more popular in the United States (Collins 2003, A4). (7) According to Neilson (2007, 240), "less than 2% of the American population grows the food that everyone eats." (8) Community-supported agriculture aims to get more people involved in the farming process.

(9) Community-supported agriculture programs (sometimes called CSAs) vary greatly, but they focus on members of the community becoming more involved in the food-growing process. (10) Many CSAs are set up so that members of the community pay a certain amount of money to a farmer, and in return receive products grown on the farm (Neilson 2007, 249). (11) Sometimes CSAs require their members to get involved in other ways, too.

(12) Besides getting the community more involved in food production, another goal of CSAs is to help small farmers make reasonable profits while maintaining their land (Neilson 2007, 235). (13) The farmers use the money they collect from CSA members to pay for their annual expenses. (14) Professor of agriculture Joan Wayne states, "When community members become part of a CSA, they take on some of the risks that farmers do, such as poor crop yields." (15) Because farmers are not alone in the risk, they have more opportunities to use sustainable growing methods. (16) Many CSA farms use organic or biodynamic growing methods (Collins 2003, A12).

References

Collins, Madeline. "CSA: The New Trend in Farming." *The New Observer*, A4, A12. November 25, 2003.

Neilson, Donald. *The Future of Agriculture: Farming in the New Millennium*. San Francisco, CA: USA Publishing, 2007.

30. Which of the following best describes the purpose of the first paragraph (sentences 1–5)?

   (A) It describes industrial farming, which the author sees as a problem.

   (B) It explains how to solve the problem of industrial farming.

   (C) It presents information to refute the argument made later in the passage.

   (D) It points out that the problem of industrial farming can be easily fixed.

   (E) It focuses on the causes of the industrial-farming problems.

31. Which of the following is cited in sentence 6?

   (A) A newspaper

   (B) A journal

   (C) A book

   (D) A pamphlet

   (E) A magazine

32. Which of the following pieces of information, if added to the second paragraph (sentences 6–8), would most effectively advance the writer's argument?

   (A) Along with offering fresh produce, some CSAs offer fresh meats, cheese, eggs, and honey.

   (B) As fewer people are involved in farming, the process becomes dirtier and worse for the environment.

   (C) Although some CSAs offer goods all year long, many operate during the major growing season (usually June through October).

(D) By using organic growing methods, farmers can preserve their land and use fewer chemicals on their crops.

(E) CSAs give farmers a chance to grow crops that may not sell well or for high prices in traditional farming.

33. The author of the passage quotes Neilson in sentence 7 most likely in order to

(A) commend the work being done by farmers in the United States

(B) emphasize the lack of most people's involvement in agriculture

(C) illustrate the need for new farming methods throughout the world

(D) elaborate on how CSAs began in the United States

(E) explain the difference between CSA and other types of agriculture

34. The third paragraph (sentences 9–11) could best be developed by

(A) explaining which members of the community most benefit from CSAs

(B) elaborating on other ways CSA members get involved

(C) adding information about the drawbacks CSAs can have

(D) expanding on the food-growing processes that many farmers use

(E) elaborating on the type of crops grown by CSAs

35. The information in parentheses in sentence 10 informs the reader that

(A) Neilson's book about community supported agriculture is more than 2,000 pages long

(B) information about different types of farming can be found in Neilson's book

(C) Neilson's book includes information about the structure of a typical CSA

(D) the sentence is taken directly from a book that Neilson wrote in 2007

(E) Neilson is a supporter of and a member of a local CSA

36. Which is best to do with sentence 14 (reproduced below)?

Professor of agriculture Joan Wayne states, "When community members become part of a CSA, they take on some of the risks that farmers do, such as poor crop yields."

(A) Explain at which institution the professor teaches.

(B) Add a counterargument made by another agriculture professor.

(C) Delete the information about Wayne's profession.

(D) Change the quotation to a paraphrase.

(E) Provide a citation that describes where the quotation came from.

37. The first item listed in the References section indicates all the following EXCEPT that

(A) "CSA: The New Trend in Farming" was written by Madeline Collins

(B) *The New Observer* is a periodical

(C) "CSA: The New Trend in Farming" is an article in a periodical

(D) *The New Observer* is published in California

(E) "CSA: The New Trend in Farming" is more than one page long

Rhetorical Analysis

Directions: Each of the following passages consists of numbered sentences. Because the passages are part of longer writing samples, they do not necessarily constitute a complete discussion of the issue presented.

Read each passage carefully and answer the questions that follow it. The questions test your awareness of a writer's purpose and of characteristics of prose that are important to good writing.

Questions 38–42 refer to the following paragraphs.

(1) After years of virtually ignoring the world energy crisis and growing environmental concerns, American automakers have finally begun to recognize the need for energy-efficient and environmentally friendly automobiles. (2) For quite some time, American car companies insisted on primarily producing oversized, gas-guzzling vehicles that wasted precious energy reserves and polluted the environment. (3) Faced with pressure to alter their approach, automakers have, at last, started to switch gears and turn their attention to smaller, energy-efficient vehicles and gas-electric hybrid cars. (4) With less emphasis on extravagant, wasteful cars, American roadways are quickly becoming greener than ever.

(5) The impetus for this considerable shift in focus was likely the impact of more forward-thinking competition and evolving consumer values. (6) Many overseas automakers were producing and marketing energy-efficient cars long before American car companies caught onto the trend. (7) The gradual influx of environmentally friendly foreign cars into the American market slowly increased consumer interest in more efficient vehicles. (8) Faced with strong overseas competition and growing consumer demand for a better domestic product, American car companies were left with no choice but to abandon many of their earlier designs and instead focus on more environmentally conscious models. (9) This change has marked a major turning point for the American automotive industry and may be a sign of additional innovations to come.

38. In sentence 2, the author most likely uses the phrase *for quite some time* in order to

   (A) support a previous statement
   (B) emphasize the longevity of a problem
   (C) qualify the assertions that follow it
   (D) stress the author's opinion about the subject
   (E) indicate the severity of a problem

39. In sentence 3, the author's use of the phrase *at last* is most likely meant to

   (A) imply the author's opinion
   (B) introduce a new assertion
   (C) link two separate thoughts
   (D) summarize the author's argument
   (E) clarify an unclear point

40. Which of the following best describes the function of sentence 4?

   (A) It illustrates an effect of the change described earlier.
   (B) It supports the author's claim regarding the cause of the change.
   (C) It reinforces the author's assertions about the auto industry.
   (D) It serves as a transition between the first and second paragraphs.
   (E) It provides a summary of the first paragraph.

41. The primary purpose of paragraph 2 is to

   (A) explain the methods used to produce energy-efficient cars
   (B) exemplify the types of cars that became popular
   (C) discuss the failure of American car companies

(D) explain the reasons for the change described earlier

(E) link consumer interest to foreign innovations

42. Sentence 9 primarily serves to

(A) support the author's claims about the influence of foreign competitors

(B) denote possible future implications of change in the auto industry

(C) compare the current state of the auto industry to its former state

(D) illustrate the importance of consumer values in the economic marketplace

(E) emphasize the need for energy-efficient and environmentally friendly cars

Questions 43–47 refer to the following paragraphs.

(1) The newspaper industry has survived the arrival of a number of different news mediums over the years, but none has presented more of a threat than the Internet. (2) In the early twentieth century, newspapers were virtually the only means of keeping up with current events. (3) A new invention called radio offered a faster way to deliver the news, but newspapers remained as popular as ever. (4) The advent of television certainly had an impact on the newspaper industry, but readership still remained relatively high. (5) Even as cable television and 24-hour news networks became commonplace, the newspaper still remained popular with consumers. (6) Despite overcoming so much previous adversity, however, the rise of the Internet has become a very serious threat to the health of the newspaper industry.

(7) At the time of its inception, the Internet was not an immediate threat to newspapers. (8) As use of the Internet became more widespread and various news agencies established online presences, people increasingly turned to the Web for their news. (9) The immediacy of Internet-based news was so great that no other medium, not even television, could compete. (10) This was particularly bad news for the newspaper

industry, as the stories it printed were often considered old news by the time their papers hit the streets.

(11) Adapting to the demands of Information Age has been difficult for newspapers. (12) While television news networks have maintained their audiences through a shift toward entertainment, newspapers have struggled to find ways to stay competitive. (13) Many newspapers have started their own Web sites, but that solution is flawed at best. (14) Most readers who visit a newspaper's Web site are probably not going to purchase the hard copy.

(15) Due to their inability to compete with Internet news sources, many newspapers are now faced with dwindling readership and reduced profits. (16) The future of the newspaper industry hangs in the balance and if some solution is not found soon, that future may be very bleak indeed.

43. In the context of the passage, which of the following transition words or phrases, if inserted at the beginning of sentence 8, would be the most logical?

(A) Therefore,

(B) Nonetheless,

(C) However,

(D) Regardless,

(E) Moreover,

44. In sentence 9, the phrase *not even television* is meant to address which of the following assumptions?

(A) Various news mediums transmit the news at different speeds.

(B) Broadcast news is timelier than printed news.

(C) News can be disseminated very quickly and efficiently through television.

(D) Modern news mediums are always more efficient than older ones.

(E) The Internet is the fastest of all presently available new mediums.

45. Which of the following best describes the function of sentence 12?

(A) It supports the idea that newspapers have not struggled to compete against the Internet.

(B) It draws the reader into a future conclusion based on prior knowledge.

(C) It suggests a possible solution for the problems the newspaper industry currently faces.

(D) It demonstrates that other mediums have managed to compete with online news.

(E) It connects the point of the paragraph with the overall point of the passage.

46. The primary purpose of sentence 14 is to

(A) introduce the final paragraph

(B) summarize the point of paragraph 4

(C) reiterate the author's opinion about the Internet

(D) illustrate how newspapers have adapted to the Internet

(E) clarify the failure of the previously mentioned solution

47. Which of the following best describes the organization of the passage as a whole?

(A) A problem is discussed and a solution is suggested.

(B) A theory is proposed and supported by evidence.

(C) A practice is defined and described in great detail.

(D) A method is analyzed and proven ineffective.

(E) A phenomenon is introduced and an explanation is presented.

Questions 48–50 refer to the following paragraphs.

(1) Born in 1872, Paul Laurence Dunbar was one of the first African American poets to gain national prominence. (2) Dunbar's parents were former slaves who moved north to Dayton, Ohio. (3) Dunbar was a stellar student and was the only black child in his class. (4) In school, Dunbar became the editor of a small, short-lived student newspaper. (5) By the time he was fourteen years old, Dunbar had already published poems in Dayton's newspaper, the *Dayton Herald*.

(6) Unfortunately, despite being a gifted student, Dunbar could not afford to attend college. (7) After high school, Dunbar worked as an elevator operator and wrote poems and stories in his free time. (8) In 1893, Dunbar published a collection of poetry called *Oak and Ivy* at his own expense. (9) Dunbar sold copies of his book to people who rode in his elevator.

48. In context, "stellar" (sentence 3) most nearly means

(A) astronomic

(B) excellent

(C) classic

(D) starry

(E) grand

49. The primary purpose of sentence 4 is to support which of the author's assumptions?

(A) Dunbar was one of the earliest recognized African American poets.

(B) Dunbar was the son of freed slaves from the south.

(C) Dunbar was the only African American student in his class.

(D) Dunbar was locally published from a very young age.

(E) Dunbar was an exceptional school student.

50. The word "Unfortunately" in sentence 6 is meant to address which of the following assumptions?

    (A) Tracking which students went to college in the 1800s was difficult.

    (B) In the 1800s, students who were not wealthy didn't go to college.

    (C) Going to college is an important experience for good students.

    (D) College academics are a challenge that few students can master.

    (E) Students who do well in high school do not necessarily do well in college.

PART II

70 minutes

The Essays

Essay 1

Sample Topic 1

Stories and storytelling are important to humanity and to society.

> **Directions:** Write an essay in which you discuss the extent to which you agree or disagree with the statement above. Support your discussion with specific reasons and examples from your reading, experience, or observations.

Essay 2

Sample Topic 2

> **Directions:** The following assignment requires you to write a coherent essay in which you synthesize the two sources provided. Synthesis refers to combining the sources and your position to form a cohesive, supported argument. You must develop a position and incorporate both sources. You must cite the sources whether you are paraphrasing or quoting. Refer to each source by the author's last name, by the title, or by any other means that adequately identifies it.

Introduction

For the past few decades, the popularity of alternative medicine has skyrocketed in the United States and other Western nations. Alternative medicine includes many different treatments such as aromatherapy, acupuncture, massage, reflexology, naturopathy, and yoga. Currently, some insurance companies in the United States and Europe pay for a few types of alternative medicines. Some people believe insurance companies should pay for all the alternative treatments that patients seek.

Assignment

Read the following sources carefully. Then write an essay in which you develop a position on whether insurance companies should pay for alternative treatments. Be sure to incorporate and cite both of the accompanying sources as you develop your position.

> Kipling, Michael A. "Alternative Medicine May Be Bad for Your Health." *Times-Tribune*, August 30, 2008.

The following passage is excerpted from an article in a newspaper.

    As alternative medicines become more popular, more people are turning to their insurance companies to pay for these treatments. Although some insurance companies have begun to cover some treatments, many are still hesitant to cover other types of alternative treatments—something many critics of alternative medicine are happy about.

Critics claim that alternative medicine can be dangerous and should not be paid for by insurance companies. These same critics, such as Dr. Janet White, believe that if insurance companies start paying for these treatments, patients may believe that companies endorse alternative medicines. White says, "If a patient learns that her insurance provider is paying for neuropathy, for example, she might think 'Hey, this must be a good treatment or my insurance company wouldn't pay for it.'"

White, who is a family doctor, has seen an increase in patients who are seeking alternative treatment. "I just don't see enough benefits to think alternative medicine is the way to go. In fact, one of my colleagues told me that he had patients contract Hepatitis C from dirty needles at an acupuncture clinic. That's very alarming."

Rawlings, Margot. "Beyond the Hype: The Real Benefits of Alternative Medicine." *The Truth of Alternative Medical Treatments*. <www.healthandlifestyles.org> (accessed December 31, 2008).

The following passage is excerpted from an article on a Web site.

Conventional medical treatments usually involve treating one aspect of a person's body, but alternative treatments usually aim to treat the body as a whole. This approach gives more opportunities for the body to heal itself. Furthermore, conventional treatments usually rely on harsh chemicals and dangerous procedures to help patients, but alternative treatments rely on natural products and mostly noninvasive procedures.

Even though colleges and universities have published reports extolling the benefits of various alternative medicine treatments, many of these treatments are still not covered by health insurance. A few procedures, such as massage and yoga, are covered by some insurance companies, but most alternative procedures are not covered. Insurance companies claim that alternative treatments have not yet been proven to work, but this is not the case. One needs to look at only a handful of recent studies to see the truth.

Although all medical treatments pose risks, the benefits of alternative medicines far outweigh the dangers. It's time for the American public to insist that their voices be heard so that insurance companies begin paying for alternative treatments.

ANSWER KEY AND EXPLANATIONS

Part I

1. A	11. B	21. D	31. A	41. D
2. D	12. A	22. E	32. B	42. B
3. D	13. D	23. B	33. B	43. C
4. E	14. B	24. D	34. B	44. C
5. C	15. A	25. B	35. C	45. D
6. D	16. A	26. A	36. E	46. E
7. E	17. C	27. D	37. D	47. E
8. C	18. B	28. E	38. B	48. B
9. C	19. B	29. C	39. A	49. E
10. D	20. E	30. A	40. A	50. C

1. **The correct answer is (A).** Choice (A) is incorrect because the verb *has* is used incorrectly. It should be written in the present perfect tense as *have*.

2. **The correct answer is (D).** Choice (D) is incorrect because the sentence shifts from the second-person *you* to the third-person *she*. To be grammatically correct, *she* should be replaced with *you*.

3. **The correct answer is (D).** Choice (D) is incorrect because the verb *forgotten* requires the helping verb *had* to be grammatically correct.

4. **The correct answer is (E).** This sentence contains no errors.

5. **The correct answer is (C).** Choice (C) is incorrect because the sentence compares Rodger with a number of people, so the adjective *less,* which is used to compare only two subjects, should be replaced with *least.*

6. **The correct answer is (D).** The main focus of the passage is the way the Marshall Plan helped European nations rebuild after World War II. The title that best expresses this idea is *Rebuilding Europe with the Marshall Plan,* which is choice (D). Choices (A) and (E) are incorrect because they are too specific. Choices (B) and (C) are incorrect because they are too general.

7. **The correct answer is (E).** Choices (A) and (B) are incorrect because they are too repetitive. Choices (C) and (D) are false because they begin with modifying clauses with meanings that are unclear. Choice (E) has a clear meaning and is not repetitive; therefore, it is the correct answer.

8. **The correct answer is (C).** The antecedent *continent* is singular so the singular reflexive pronoun *itself,* which is choice (C), is correct.

9. **The correct answer is (C).** The information in sentence 9 contrasts with the information in sentence 8. Choice (C) is correct because the word *Nevertheless* indicates that the idea of the sentence contrasts the information that came before it.

10. **The correct answer is (D).** Choices (A) and (C) are incorrect because the conjunctions *and* and *but* do not properly connect the two independent clauses. Choice (B) is incorrect because the word *therefore* indicates a cause-and-effect relationship that is not present.

11. **The correct answer is (B).** Choice (B) is a sentence that is unrelated to the Marshall Plan, and removing this sentence makes the passage clearer. Choices (A), (C), (D), and (E) are incorrect because those sentences deal with the Marshall Plan and add supporting details to the essay's main idea.

12. **The correct answer is (A).** Choice (A) is correct because in context the word *meant* means *set aside for a specific purpose* or *allocated*.

13. **The correct answer is (D).** Choice (D) is correct because the infinitive phrase in the sentence should be *to rebuild* rather than *to rebuilds*. Choice (A) is incorrect because a colon would make the sentence's structure awkward. Choices (B) and (E) are incorrect because they merely replace words from the sentence with synonyms and do not change the sentence's meaning or structure. Choice (C) is incorrect because the word *international* adds little information to the sentence, and it is not a necessary change.

14. **The correct answer is (B).** Choice (B) is correct because sentence 14 says that the United States benefited from the Marshall Plan, and choice (B) describes how the country benefited. Choices (A), (C), (D), and (E) are incorrect because, although they add information about the Marshall Plan, they do not support the main idea of the paragraph.

15. **The correct answer is (A).** Choice (A) is correct because it concludes the passage by giving a reason for why the essay's topic is important and influential. Choices (B), (C), (D), and (E) are incorrect because they add more details about the topic, but do not properly conclude the essay.

16. **The correct answer is (A).** Choices (B), (C), and (E) are incorrect because they are too general. Choice (D) is incorrect because it is too specific. Choice (A) is correct because it captures the main idea of the essay without being too narrow or too broad in scope.

17. **The correct answer is (C).** The sample sentence needs revision because the pronoun *it* does not have a clear antecedent. Choice (C) is correct because this choice removes the pronoun and clarifies the author's meaning.

18. **The correct answer is (B).** Choice (B) is correct because the word *which*, rather than the word *that*, should be used to introduce the restrictive clause.

19. **The correct answer is (B).** Choice (B) is correct because sentence 5 describes how larvae get into the tree, and the example sentence describes what larvae do once they are inside the tree. The other choices are incorrect because the example sentence does not support the main ideas of the other paragraphs.

20. **The correct answer is (E).** Choice (E) is correct because sentences 7 and 8 describe effects of EAB on trees and so does the sentence in choice (E). Choices (A), (B), (C), and (D) are incorrect because they do not support the main idea of the paragraph.

21. **The correct answer is (D).** Choice (D) is correct because the two clauses are properly connected, and the word *furthermore* indicates that the second part of the sentence elaborates on the first part, which it does.

22. **The correct answer is (E).** Choice (E) is correct because the word *reek* means *stink* or *smell*; the word *wreak* means *to cause*, which is the meaning the author intended.

23. **The correct answer is (B).** The author wants readers to know that EABs have real effects on the environment, and choice (B) emphasizes these negative and long-lasting effects.

24. **The correct answer is (D).** Choice (D) is correct because sentence 14 describes other invasive species and is not related to the essay's main idea.

25. **The correct answer is (B).** Choice (B) is correct because it tells readers why the information in the essay is important.

26. **The correct answer is (A).** Choice (A) is correct because the publisher location is the only location information included in most references.

27. **The correct answer is (D).** In in-text citations, *sec.* means *section;* therefore, you can determine that the referenced material comes from the source's tenth section.

28. **The correct answer is (E).** Choice (E) is correct because the citation lists all the major pieces of a Web site citation (including a Web address, an access date, and a title).

29. **The correct answer is (C).** Choice (C) is correct because the word *mensurare* was used in Late Latin, rather than Middle English.

30. **The correct answer is (A).** Choice (A) is correct because the first paragraph describes industrial farming in a negative way, indicating the author thinks industrial farming is a negative thing.

31. **The correct answer is (A).** The full citation for the work that Collins wrote is included at the end of the passage. Choice (A) is correct because the full citation includes an author, an article title, a publication title, a date of publication, and page numbers—which together indicate a newspaper.

32. **The correct answer is (B).** The second paragraph discusses how a small amount of people grow most of the country's food. The author believes this is a negative thing. Choice (B) is correct because that sentence adds information on the same topic.

33. **The correct answer is (B).** Choice (B) is correct because it deals with the topic of the quotation.

34. **The correct answer is (B).** The third paragraph states that CSA members can get involved in different ways, but the paragraph never describes the ways members get involved. Choice (B) is correct because it describes other ways members can get involved, which gives the paragraph more clarification.

35. **The correct answer is (C).** Choice (C) is correct because the citation indicates the source is a book and because the sentence describes CSA structure.

36. **The correct answer is (E).** Choice (E) is correct because when using direct quotations from other sources, writers should include where they got the information.

37. **The correct answer is (D).** Choice (D) is correct because although the book in the reference section was published in California, the references do not indicate where the newspaper was published.

38. **The correct answer is (B).** Choice (B) is correct because the phrase suggests that the problem in question had been ongoing for a lengthy period of time.

39. **The correct answer is (A).** Choice (A) is correct because the phrase is specifically used to express the author's opinion that the change in the auto industry should have happened sooner.

40. **The correct answer is (A).** Choice (A) is correct because the sentence addresses the effects of the change in the auto industry described in the preceding paragraph.

41. **The correct answer is (D).** Choice (D) is correct because paragraph 2 clearly provides an explanation of the reasons for the changes in the American auto industry described in paragraph 1.

42. **The correct answer is (B).** Choice (B) is correct because the sentence discusses possible future implications of the recent changes in the auto industry.

43. **The correct answer is (C).** Choice (C) is correct because the word however would fit most logically at the beginning of the sentence.

44. **The correct answer is (C).** Choice (C) is correct because the phrase implies that television is a very rapid means of disseminating news. None of the other choices accurately reflects the implications of the phrase in question.

45. **The correct answer is (D).** Choice (D) is correct because the sentence indicates a means through which the television news media has adapted to compete with the Internet.

46. **The correct answer is (E).** Choice (E) is correct because it provides additional information that further explains the author's assertions about the ineffectiveness of newspaper Web sites in the previous sentence.

47. **The correct answer is (E).** Choice (E) is correct because the passage introduces and explains the phenomenon that has occurred as the newspaper industry had to deal with the arrival of the Internet.

48. **The correct answer is (B).** Choice (B) is correct because clues from the sentence indicate that Dunbar was an excellent student.

49. **The correct answer is (E).** Choice (E) is correct because sentence 4, which states that Dunbar served as editor of a student newspaper, suggests that he was an exceptional student.

50. **The correct answer is (C).** Choice (C) is the best answer because the word *unfortunately* addresses that assumption.

Part II

Essay 1

Scoring Guide: College Composition Examination for Essay 1
Readers will assign scores based on the following scoring guide.

6—A 6 essay demonstrates a high degree of competence and sustained control, although it may have a few minor errors.

A typical essay in this category

- addresses all elements of the writing task effectively and insightfully
- develops ideas thoroughly, supporting them with well-chosen reasons, examples, or details
- is well focused and well organized
- demonstrates superior facility with language, using effective vocabulary and sentence variety
- demonstrates general mastery of the standard conventions of grammar, usage, and mechanics but may have minor errors

---

5—A 5 essay demonstrates a generally high degree of competence, although it will have occasional lapses in quality.

A typical essay in this category

- addresses the writing task effectively
- is well developed, using appropriate reasons, examples, or details to support ideas
- is generally well focused and well organized
- demonstrates facility with language, using appropriate vocabulary and some sentence variety
- demonstrates strong control of the standard conventions of grammar, usage, and mechanics but may have minor errors

---

4—A 4 essay demonstrates clear competence, with some errors or lapses in quality.

A typical essay in this category

- addresses the writing task competently
- is adequately developed, using reasons, examples, or details to support ideas
- is adequately focused and organized
- demonstrates competence with language, using adequate vocabulary and minimal sentence variety
- generally demonstrates control of the standard conventions of grammar, usage and mechanics but may have some errors

3—A 3 essay demonstrates limited competence.

A typical essay in this category exhibits ONE OR MORE of the following weaknesses:

- addresses only some parts of the writing task
- develops unevenly and often provides assertions but few relevant reasons, examples, or details
- is poorly focused and/or poorly organized
- displays frequent problems in the use of language
- demonstrates inconsistent control of grammar, usage, and mechanics

2—A 2 essay is seriously flawed.

A typical essay in this category exhibits ONE OR MORE of the following weaknesses:

- is unclear or seriously limited in addressing the writing task
- is seriously underdeveloped, providing few reasons, examples, or details
- is unfocused and/or disorganized
- displays frequent serious errors in the use of language that interfere with meaning
- contains frequent serious errors in grammar, usage, and mechanics that may interfere with meaning

1—A 1 essay is fundamentally deficient.

A typical essay in this category exhibits ONE OR MORE of the following weaknesses:

- provides little or no evidence of the ability to develop an organized response to the writing task
- is underdeveloped
- contains severe writing errors that persistently interfere with meaning

0—Off topic.

Provides no evidence of an attempt to respond to the assigned topic, is written in a language other than English, merely copies the prompt, or consists of only keystroke characters.

Sample Essay

Note: Errors in the sample essays are intentionally reproduced.

This essay is scored at a 6.

I agree with the statement that stories and storytelling are important to humanity and to society. Throughout history, humans have created stories and used these stories to make sense of and deal with the world. These stories have helped humans understand who they are, why they are here, and what is important to their society or culture.

Stories are so important to humanity that even early humans found ways to tell stories. Although records cannot tell us if early humans told oral stories, early humans did paint pictures in caves. The cave paintings, just like many other stories from throughout history, tell about the lives of the people who created them. Many cave paintings depict animals and weapons—signifying the humans' hunting for food. Other cave paintings show people, nature, and religious ceremonies. These pictures tell stories about early humans' lives. Although no one knows for sure why humans created these pictures, many different cultures from around the world created similar images on the walls of caves. I believe that early humans created these pictures because they felt the need to tell their stories.

As soon as humans began recording history, they also began recording the stories they told. Many ancient civilizations created stories to make sense of the world around them. These stories helped them form societies in which people held similar beliefs. For example, the ancient Greeks created stories about gods and goddesses; these stories gave explanations for the weather, nature, love, and even death. As the Greeks passed stories through the generations, they created a coherent society that used the stories to teach lessons about the world and life.

One Greek story describes why the word has bad things such as hardship, illness, and toil. In the story, the king of the gods, Zeus, created a woman named Pandora. He also created a jar that held evil things (such as toil and illness) as well as hope. Pandora was a curious women, so she opened the jar and allowed all the evil things, as well as hope, to enter the world. Although Pandora tried to close the jar to keep the evil from escaping, she was too late. This story taught the Greek people a lesson about being too curious, and it served to explain why humans must endure pain and suffering in life. This story helped the Greeks understand themselves better and create societal norms.

Another example of an ancient culture that used stories as a basis for its society is ancient Egypt. Although Egypt and Greece were relatively far apart, both societies developed stories to explain how the earth was created and what happens to people when they die. The ancient Egyptians' stories also helped them understand their world. For example, the Nile River flooded Egypt every year, and the Egyptians formed a story about a goddess, Hapi, who caused the flood. This story and stories like it were an integral part of ancient Egyptian society.

In modern society, people use stories for many of the same reasons that our ancestors did. The stories people tell today relay information about how we live and what we value. Stories also give our societies meanings and rules. For example, for hundreds of years children have listened to and read Aesop's fables, which contain morals and lessons about the best ways to live life. One of Aesop's famous fables is about the tortoise and the hare. Most people living in the United States have heard the tale and know its moral: Slow and steady wins the race. Because this story is known throughout American society, it shows that even our society is influenced by stories.

The drive to tell stories—both true and untrue—seems to be a human characteristic that has remained unchanged for centuries.

Essay 2

Scoring Guide: College Composition Examination for Essay 2
Readers will assign scores based on the following scoring guide.

6—A 6 essay demonstrates a high degree of competence and sustained control, although it may have a few minor errors.

A typical essay in this category:

- cites sources appropriately

- develops a position effectively and insightfully, using well-chosen reason, examples, or details for support

- synthesizes* both sources effectively with an effective and convincing link between the sources and the position

- is well focused and well organized

- demonstrates superior facility with language, using effective vocabulary and sentence variety

- demonstrates general mastery of the standard conventions of grammar, usage, and mechanics but may have minor errors

---

5—A 5 essay demonstrates a generally high degree of competence, although it will have occasional lapses in quality.

A typical essay in this category:

- cites sources appropriately

- develops a position consistently, using appropriate reasons, examples, or details for support

- synthesizes both sources clearly, with a clear link between the sources and the position

- is generally well focused and well organized

- demonstrates facility with language, using appropriate vocabulary and some sentence variety

- demonstrates strong control of the standard conventions of grammar, usage, and mechanics but may have minor errors

---

4—A 4 essay demonstrates competence, with some errors and lapses in quality.

A typical essay in this category:

- cites sources appropriately

- develops a position adequately, using reasons, examples, or details for support

- synthesizes both sources adequately, using reasons, examples, or details for support

- is adequately focused and organized

- demonstrates competence with language, using adequate vocabulary and minimal sentence variety

- generally demonstrates control of the standard conventions of grammar, usage, and mechanics but may have some errors

3—A 3 essay demonstrates limited competence.

A typical essay in this category exhibits ONE OR MORE of the following weaknesses:

- develops a position unevenly, often using assertions rather than relevant reasons, examples, or details for support
- synthesizes one source only or two sources inadequately, or establishes an inadequate link between the source(s) and the position
- displays problems in citing sources: citations are confusing or incomplete
- is poorly focused and/or poorly organized
- displays frequent problems in the use of language
- demonstrates inconsistent control of grammar, usage, and mechanics

2—A 2 essay is seriously flawed.

A typical essay in this category exhibits ONE OR MORE of the following weaknesses:

- is seriously underdeveloped, providing few or no relevant reasons, examples, or details for support
- synthesizes only one source weakly or establishes a very weak link between the source(s) and the position
- does not cite any source
- is unfocused and/or disorganized
- displays frequent serious errors in the use of language that may interfere with meaning
- contains frequent serious errors in grammar, usage, and mechanics that may interfere with meaning

1—A 1 essay is fundamentally deficient.

A typical essay in this category exhibits ONE OR MORE of the following weaknesses:

- does not develop a position
- fails to synthesize the source(s) used or uses no sources at all
- contains severe writing errors that persistently interfere with meaning

0—Off topic

Provides no evidence of an attempt to respond to the assigned topic, is written in a language other than English, merely copies the prompt, or consists of only keystroke characters.

*For the purpose of scoring, synthesis refers to combining sources and writer's position to form a cohesive, supported argument.

Sample Essay

Note: Errors in the sample essays are intentionally reproduced.

This essay is scored a 6.

America is a country that prides itself on the freedoms of its citizens, and most people living in the United States believe they have the right to choose the medical treatments that best fit their wants and needs. Having a choice in medical procedures is important, and I believe health insurance companies should help Americans choose the treatment options they want by paying for alternative medicines.

The popularity of alternative medical treatments is on the rise in the United States. As more people decide to seek these alternative treatments, they look to their insurance companies to pay for them (Rawlings). Although most Americans expect their insurance companies to pay for all or most of their treatments, those looking for the insurance companies to pay for alternative medicine might be disappointed. Insurance companies in the United States currently do not pay for most alternative medicine treatments, but some do pay for procedures such as yoga and massage (Rawlings). I believe insurance companies in the United States should pay for all or most of their clients' alternative treatments.

Although, as journalist Michael Kipling points out in a 2008 article, some people have contracted illnesses or have been similarly harmed by alternative treatments, other people are harmed by conventional treatments all the time. American doctors are required to have liability insurance because they can make mistakes and harm people. Furthermore, in their commercials, pharmaceutical companies are required to list the many possible risks and side effects their products can cause. Despite these risks, insurance companies see nothing wrong with paying for these traditional treatments

Society should not judge alternative medication on whether there are risks involved, because there are. Rather, society should judge these treatments on whether the risks outweigh the benefits. If the benefits are greater than the potential for risks, then alternative medicines should be considered viable alternatives to traditional medicines. In fact, many alternative medicines treat patients' entire bodies, giving them what some might say is a more complete treatment (Rawlings).

According to Rawlings, a number of colleges and universities have published studies describing the positive results of different alternative treatments. If insurance companies are willing to pay for traditional doctors and large pharmaceutical companies for treatments that are effective but hold some risks, then insurance companies should also be willing to pay alternative medicine practitioners for their work.

In his article, Kipling states that one reason the critics of alternative healthcare do not want insurance companies funding alternative treatments is because patients will believe the insurance companies endorse what they fund. However, an insurance company's financial support does not equal its approval. Insurance companies must remain unbiased. They cannot offer to pay for one drug for arthritis over another drug for arthritis just because they don't like the side effects of one. It should be the same for alternative and conventional medical treatments. If patients choose to have their arthritis treated with homeopathy, rather than a chemical, the insurance company should respect the patient's wishes just as though the patient chose one pill over another.

In conclusion, patients in America should have the right to choose the form of treatment they believe best helps them stay healthy and happy. Insurance companies exist to help people pay for the care they need to make their lives longer and more enjoyable. American society is moving away from conventional treatments and toward alternative treatments. The insurance companies should change with the times and give their customers what they want.

OVERVIEW ANSWER SHEET

Conventions of Standard Written English

1. Ⓐ Ⓑ Ⓒ Ⓓ Ⓔ   4. Ⓐ Ⓑ Ⓒ Ⓓ Ⓔ   7. Ⓐ Ⓑ Ⓒ Ⓓ Ⓔ   9. Ⓐ Ⓑ Ⓒ Ⓓ Ⓕ   11. Ⓐ Ⓑ Ⓒ Ⓓ Ⓔ

2. Ⓐ Ⓑ Ⓒ Ⓓ Ⓔ   5. Ⓐ Ⓑ Ⓒ Ⓓ Ⓔ   8. Ⓐ Ⓑ Ⓒ Ⓓ Ⓔ   10. Ⓐ Ⓑ Ⓒ Ⓓ Ⓔ   12. Ⓐ Ⓑ Ⓒ Ⓓ Ⓔ

Revision Skills

1. Ⓐ Ⓑ Ⓒ Ⓓ Ⓔ   5. Ⓐ Ⓑ Ⓒ Ⓓ Ⓔ   9. Ⓐ Ⓑ Ⓒ Ⓓ Ⓔ   13. Ⓐ Ⓑ Ⓒ Ⓓ Ⓔ   17. Ⓐ Ⓑ Ⓒ Ⓓ Ⓔ

2. Ⓐ Ⓑ Ⓒ Ⓓ Ⓔ   6. Ⓐ Ⓑ Ⓒ Ⓓ Ⓔ   10. Ⓐ Ⓑ Ⓒ Ⓓ Ⓔ   14. Ⓐ Ⓑ Ⓒ Ⓓ Ⓔ   18. Ⓐ Ⓑ Ⓒ Ⓓ Ⓔ

3. Ⓐ Ⓑ Ⓒ Ⓓ Ⓔ   7. Ⓐ Ⓑ Ⓒ Ⓓ Ⓔ   11. Ⓐ Ⓑ Ⓒ Ⓓ Ⓔ   15. Ⓐ Ⓑ Ⓒ Ⓓ Ⓔ   19. Ⓐ Ⓑ Ⓒ Ⓓ Ⓔ

4. Ⓐ Ⓑ Ⓒ Ⓓ Ⓔ   8. Ⓐ Ⓑ Ⓒ Ⓓ Ⓔ   12. Ⓐ Ⓑ Ⓒ Ⓓ Ⓔ   16. Ⓐ Ⓑ Ⓒ Ⓓ Ⓔ   20. Ⓐ Ⓑ Ⓒ Ⓓ Ⓔ

Ability to Use Source Materials

1. Ⓐ Ⓑ Ⓒ Ⓓ Ⓔ   4. Ⓐ Ⓑ Ⓒ Ⓓ Ⓔ   7. Ⓐ Ⓑ Ⓒ Ⓓ Ⓔ   9. Ⓐ Ⓑ Ⓒ Ⓓ Ⓔ   11. Ⓐ Ⓑ Ⓒ Ⓓ Ⓔ

2. Ⓐ Ⓑ Ⓒ Ⓓ Ⓔ   5. Ⓐ Ⓑ Ⓒ Ⓓ Ⓔ   8. Ⓐ Ⓑ Ⓒ Ⓓ Ⓔ   10. Ⓐ Ⓑ Ⓒ Ⓓ Ⓔ   12. Ⓐ Ⓑ Ⓒ Ⓓ Ⓔ

Rhetorical Analysis

1. Ⓐ Ⓑ Ⓒ Ⓓ Ⓔ   4. Ⓐ Ⓑ Ⓒ Ⓓ Ⓔ   7. Ⓐ Ⓑ Ⓒ Ⓓ Ⓔ   10. Ⓐ Ⓑ Ⓒ Ⓓ Ⓔ   12. Ⓐ Ⓑ Ⓒ Ⓓ Ⓔ

2. Ⓐ Ⓑ Ⓒ Ⓓ Ⓔ   5. Ⓐ Ⓑ Ⓒ Ⓓ Ⓔ   8. Ⓐ Ⓑ Ⓒ Ⓓ Ⓔ   11. Ⓐ Ⓑ Ⓒ Ⓓ Ⓔ   13. Ⓐ Ⓑ Ⓒ Ⓓ Ⓔ

3. Ⓐ Ⓑ Ⓒ Ⓓ Ⓔ   6. Ⓐ Ⓑ Ⓒ Ⓓ Ⓔ   9. Ⓐ Ⓑ Ⓒ Ⓓ Ⓔ

Essay 1

Essay 2

answer sheet

Overview

This section provides an overview of the material that will appear on the CLEP College Composition examination. This test is designed to assess students' analysis, argumentation, synthesis, usage, and research skills in an effort to determine how they will perform in a first-year college composition course.

The College Composition examination consists of two parts. The first part contains fifty multiple-choice questions that the student must answer in 50 minutes. This portion of the exam covers four subject areas: Conventions of Standard Written English, Revision Skills, Ability to Use Source Materials, and Rhetorical Analysis.

SUBJECT AREA OVERVIEW

The following provides a brief overview of the skills assessed by each subject area:

Conventions of Standard Written English

This section makes up 10 percent of the multiple-choice questions you will encounter on the exam.

This section includes several stand-alone questions in which you must locate the error, if one exists, within a sentence. Some of the sentences contain no errors, and no sentence contains more than one error.

Questions in this section assess your ability to recognize errors relating to grammar, sentence structure, and logic. This may include, but is not limited to, errors in syntax, sentence boundaries, agreement, and punctuation. Some questions will also test students' awareness of diction (choice of words), idiom, active/passive voice, and logical agreement.

Revision Skills

This section makes up 40 percent of the multiple-choice questions you will encounter on the exam.

In this section, you will read several passages that are designed to look like early drafts of essays or editorials. You must then answer questions about how to best revise various portions of these essays and editorials.

These questions will assess your organization skills, ability to evaluate evidence, and your awareness of audience, tone, and purpose. They also measure your ability to recognize errors in coherence between sentences and paragraphs, consistency of point of view, and transitions.

Ability to Use Source Materials

This section makes up 25 percent of the multiple-choice questions you will encounter on the exam.

This section includes stand-alone questions as well as passage-based questions that assess your knowledge of basic reference and research skills. The passage-based questions may also test some of the skills listed under Revision Skills and Rhetorical Analysis.

Generally, the questions in this section measure your familiarity with the use of reference materials and their ability to evaluate and document sources. You should note that documentation styles may include, but are not limited to, MLA, APA, and Chicago manuals of style.

Rhetorical Analysis

This section makes up 25 percent of the multiple-choice questions you will encounter on the exam.

In this section, you will read several passages and answer questions that test your ability to analyze writing. These questions will test your knowledge of tone, organization/structure, rhetorical effects, and use of language. This section also measures your ability to evaluate evidence, think critically, and recognize the author's purpose.

WRITING ASSIGNMENTS

The second part of the College Composition exam includes two timed writing assignments. You will have a total of 70 minutes to complete both assignments.

In one of the assignments, you are provided with a statement and asked to write an essay that discusses the extent to which you agree or disagree with the statement. You must use examples from your readings, experiences, or observations to support your positions.

The other assignment asks you to read two sources that discuss a single topic. You must then take a position and construct an argument by synthesizing the two sources, which you must also cite.

All essays must be typed on a computer.

A well-written and well-organized essay will address all aspects of the writing assignment in a coherent and intelligent manner while also demonstrating a high degree of competence, a clear understanding of conventions of Standard Written English, and the effective use of vocabulary and sentence variety.

SCORING

One point is given for each multiple-choice question that is answered correctly. No points are awarded or subtracted when the question is answered incorrectly or not at all. This raw score is then converted to a scaled score before being combined with the scores from the essays. Two readers score each essay independently. The combined score of the two essays is weighted approximately equally with your score on the multiple-choice section. These two scores are combined to produce your total score, which is reported as a single scaled score between 20 and 80. College Board does not provide separate scores for the multiple-choice and essay sections.

If you are interested in retesting, you must wait six months from the original test date to retake the test.

COLLEGE COMPOSITION MODULAR

College Board also offers a College Composition Modular examination. This test allows college administrators to either provide and score their own writing assignments or use the essay section provided by CLEP and score it themselves. This test gives the college more control over the writing assignments on the test. The exam contains a multiple-choice section with 90 questions that must be completed in 90 minutes and, depending on the option chosen, two essays that must be completed in 70 minutes.

This book, however, will focus on the College Composition examination, which includes many of the same elements tested on the College Composition Modular.

COLLEGE COMPOSITION DIRECTIONS

The following sections will provide you with an overview and explanation of the different types of questions that appear on the College Composition examination. Read the directions for each section carefully and consider memorizing them, so that you will understand what you are being asked to do when it's time to take the actual test.

Each set of directions is followed by sample questions and explanations. You will then have the opportunity to test your skills by completing a number of practice exercises. *Peterson's Master the CLEP* also includes additional exams for further practice and review.

CONVENTIONS OF STANDARD WRITTEN ENGLISH

As explained in the overview, questions in this section test your ability to recognize errors relating to grammar, sentence structure, and logic. These types of questions may contain errors in agreement, punctuation, word choice, and syntax.

The following discusses the type of question that you will encounter in this section of the test. After that, you will read some practice questions and answer explanations. Lastly, you will complete review questions. Be sure to read the answer explanation, so you are certain that you understand the correct answer.

Typically, the question is written like this:

Many <u>people</u> around <u>the world</u> call New York City <u>their</u> <u>hometown</u>. <u>No error</u>.
    A   B   C   D   E

Choices (A), (B), (C), and (D) refer to underlined parts of the sentence that may or may not contain an error. Choice (E) indicates that there is no error in the sentence. Remember, each sentence contains only one error, if there is one. This sentence does not contain an error. **The correct answer is (E).**

The best way to answer these types of questions is to first consider the individual parts of the sentence. Determine if there is an error. If not, try reading the sentence as a whole. This may help you decide where the error is, or if the sentence is correct as written.

CONVENTIONS OF STANDARD WRITTEN ENGLISH: REVIEW QUESTIONS

Directions: The following sentences test your knowledge of grammar, diction (choice of words), and idioms. Some sentences are correct. No sentence contains more than one error.

You will find that the error, if there is one, is underlined and lettered. Assume that elements of the sentence that are not underlined are correct and cannot be changed. In choosing answers, follow the requirements of Standard Written English.

If there is an error, select the one underlined part that must be changed to make the sentence correct and fill in the corresponding oval on your answer sheet. If there is no error, select answer (E).

Example 1:   **SAMPLE ANSWER**

Ⓐ Ⓑ ● Ⓓ Ⓔ

Many <u>countries</u> around the world
              A

<u>have adopted</u> English as <u>its</u> official
       B   C

<u>language</u>. <u>No error.</u>
     D   E

The pronoun *its* does not agree in number with the subject, *countries*. **The correct answer is (C).**

Example 2:   **SAMPLE ANSWER**

Ⓐ Ⓑ Ⓒ Ⓓ ●

In <u>the event</u> of a winter storm, the
        A

<u>holiday</u> concert will be <u>pushed</u> back
     B   C

to <u>December</u> fifteenth. <u>No error.</u>
        D   E

There is no error in this sentence. **The correct answer is (E).**

The following sentences will give you a chance to practice. Read each sentence carefully, mark your answers, and then check them against the answers and explanations that appear at the end of this overview.

1. <u>Between</u> the three of <u>them</u>, they did not
        A   B

   <u>have</u> enough money <u>for</u> a new basketball.
    C   D

   <u>No error.</u>
       E

2. We <u>were</u> <u>suppose</u> to see a movie at the
          A   B

   drive-in, <u>but</u> it started raining just as we
                C

   were <u>about</u> to leave. <u>No error.</u>
          D   E

3. On <u>Memorial Day</u>, the <u>president</u> will <u>lay</u>
           A   B   C

   a wreath <u>at</u> the Tomb of the Unknown
              D

   Soldier. <u>No error.</u>
                 E

4. <u>Although</u> they had <u>already</u> left the house,
       A   B

   his <u>Mother</u> insisted that they <u>return</u> so she
          C   D

   could grab a sweater. <u>No error.</u>
                              E

5. The <u>National Weather Service</u> could
        A

    not <u>predict</u> how many people would be
            B

    <u>effected</u> by the <u>powerful</u> winter storm.
        C   D

    <u>No error.</u>
        E

6. To <u>register</u> for the test, <u>you must</u> pay a fee
        A   B

    and <u>provide</u> proof of residency,
            C

    <u>which is about 50 dollars.</u> <u>No error.</u>
                D   E

7. The <u>beloved</u> king <u>rained</u> over his people
        A   B

    with great <u>benevolence</u> for many years
                    C

    before <u>passing the throne</u> to his only son.
                    D

    <u>No error.</u>
        E

8. <u>Covered in cat hair,</u> <u>Bethany wondered</u> if
            A   B

    the couch <u>would ever</u> be clean <u>again.</u>
                    C   D

    <u>No error.</u>
        E

9. The student center <u>comprises</u> four
                        A

    distinctive <u>areas;</u> a recreation room,
                B

    <u>a study longue,</u> a dining hall, and a
            C

    student government office. <u>No error.</u>
            D   E

10. <u>With</u> a look of satisfaction <u>on her face,</u>
        A   B

    the teacher <u>handed back</u> the <u>students</u>
                    C   D

    papers. <u>No error.</u>
                E

11. The <u>cheerleading</u> association <u>reported</u> that
            A   B

    there were <u>less</u> serious injuries this year
                C

    <u>than</u> last year. <u>No error.</u>
        D   E

12. <u>Without her assistance,</u> the <u>committee</u>
            A   B

    would <u>not have</u> finished the proposal
                C

    <u>on time.</u> <u>No error.</u>
        D   E

REVISION SKILLS

Revision skills questions measure your ability to revise and organize early drafts of essays. Each passage is numbered for easy reference. The questions in this section may ask how to rearrange sentences, delete unnecessary statements, and improve transitions between paragraphs.

The following discusses the types of questions that you are most likely to encounter in this section of the test. After that, there are review questions. Be sure to check the answers and explanations at the end of this chapter.

Sentence Revisions

Typically, the question is written like this:

In context, which is the best replacement for "X" in sentence 1?

OR

Which is the best revision of the underlined portion of sentence 5 (reproduced below)?

OR

In context, which of the following is the best revision to sentence 3 (reproduced below)?

OR

In context, which is best to add to the beginning of sentence 7?

These types of questions ask you to determine which revision would most improve the clarity of each sentence. In some cases, this involves changing a word or adding punctuation. For some questions, the best answer is to leave the sentence as it is.

Many times, you can eliminate obviously incorrect answers by reading each choice carefully. Before selecting your final answer, think about how the change would affect the entire sentence. This will help you choose the best option.

Organization

Typically, questions about organization are written like this:

Which of the following sentences is best to add after sentence 1?

OR

In context, where should the following sentence be placed?

These types of questions ask you to consider how the placement of a sentence affects the rest of the passage. To answer these questions correctly, you must not only consider the sentence's placement within the passage, but also its placement within a paragraph. Be sure that rearranging a sentence does not interrupt the flow of ideas.

You can eliminate obviously incorrect answers by ignoring choices that would interfere with the logic of the paragraph or passage.

Adding/Deleting Sentences

Questions about adding or deleting sentences are usually written like this:

Which of the following sentences is best to add after sentence 8?

OR

The passage as a whole could be clarified by adding which of the following before the first sentence?

OR

Deleting which of the following sentences would most improve the coherence of the passage?

These types of questions ask you to consider the organization of the passage as well as the logical flow of ideas. To correctly answer these types of questions, consider how the other sentences in the paragraph would be affected by the deletion or addition of a sentence. Carefully read the sentences around the sentence in the question to determine if any change would affect the clarity of the paragraph or the passage.

Eliminate obviously incorrect choices before selecting the best possible answer.

Combining Sentences

Combining sentence questions are written like this:

In context, which of the following is the best way to combine sentences 1 and 2?

These types of questions ask you to consider how combining two sentences might improve a paragraph or passage. Remember that the correct answer should follow conventions of Standard Written English. You can eliminate obviously incorrect choices by looking for errors in punctuation, grammar, and agreement.

REVISION SKILLS: REVIEW QUESTIONS

Directions: Each of the following selections is an early draft of a student essay in which the sentences have been numbered for easy reference. Some parts of the selections need to be changed.

Read each essay and then answer the questions that follow. Some questions are about particular sentences and ask you to improve sentence structure and diction (choice of words). In making these decisions, follow the conventions of Standard Written English. Other questions refer to the entire essay or parts of the essay and ask you to consider organization, development, and effectiveness of language in relation to purpose and audience.

Example Selection

(1) Running a marathon requires dedication and strength and endurance. (2) These skills must be cultivated over time. (3) This is why it is important to train slowly. (4) Don't try to run 26 miles on your first day! (5) Start off running a few miles every day. (6) As you become stronger, you can add more miles to your run.

Example 1:   **SAMPLE ANSWER**

Which is the best revision of the underlined portion of sentence 1 (reproduced below)?
Running a marathon requires dedication and strength and endurance.

(A) requires dedication, strength, endurance
(B) requires dedication, strength, and endurance
(C) requires dedication; strength; and endurance
(D) requires dedication, as well as strength, and endurance
(E) requires dedication, and strength, and endurance

Choice (A) is incorrect because the conjunction *and* is required. Choice (C) includes incorrect use of semicolons. Choices (D) and (E) are too wordy. **The correct answer is (B).**

Example 2:   **SAMPLE ANSWER**

In context, which of the following is the best way to combine sentences 5 and 6?

(A) As you become stronger, you can add more miles to your everyday run, but you should start off running a few miles a day.
(B) Start off, running a few miles every day, and, as you become stronger, add more miles to your run.
(C) Start off running, every day, a few miles, and add more miles to your run, once you become stronger.
(D) Every day, start off running a few miles, you can add more miles to your run as you become stronger.
(E) Start off running a few miles every day, and add more miles to your run as you become stronger.

Choices (A), (B), and (C) are awkward and confusing. Choice (D) is a run-on sentence. Choice (E) successfully combines both sentences without changing the original meaning. **The correct answer is (E).**

The following selections and questions will give you a chance to practice your revision skills. Read each selection carefully before attempting to answer the questions. Mark your answers and then check them against the answers and explanations that appear at the end of this overview.

Questions 1–10 are based on a draft of a student's essay.

(1) Although actors and actresses are the ones who appear on movie posters, it's important to remember that there are many people working behind the scenes on every movie set. (2) Hundreds of men and women work long hours securing the perfect props, fixing the lighting, and create sound effects. (3) Without these people, there would not be any costumes, sets, or special effects. (4) A movie cannot be made without a crew.

(5) Members of a film crew typically include a gaffer and his best boy, a boom operator, a foley artist, a greensman, a propsmaster, and a set dresser. (6) Working closely with teams of other crewmembers, these men or women handle the minute details that help brings movies to life. (7) For example, a gaffer is in charge of all the electricity on a set. (8) A best boy is the gaffer's assistant. (9) A grip's main concern is lighting, still he works closely with both the gaffer and the best boy. (10) A strong foley artist is also a critical component: this person is responsible for the sound effects. (11) Greensmen, propsmasters, and set dressers rarely are seen, but they create the world of the film threw their handling of the plants, props, and set details.

(12) One crewmember that is easy to recognize is the boom operator. (13) This person is responsible for recording all of the dialogue in a scene. (14) On a movie set, you can locate the boom operator by looking for the person who is holding a giant, padded microphone above the actors.

(15) Without the dedicated men and women that fill these positions, movies would not be the same. (16) Scenes would be poorly set, props would fall apart, and the dialogue would be difficult to hear. (17) So, next time you sit down to watch a film, think about all of the invisible people who had a hand in making the movie. (18) Also, all of the crewmembers' names are listed in the credits.

1. Deleting which of the following sentences would most improve the coherence of the passage?
   (A) Sentence 6
   (B) Sentence 8
   (C) Sentence 12
   (D) Sentence 14
   (E) Sentence 18

2. In context, which of the following revisions must be made to sentence 2 (reproduced below)?

   Hundreds of men and women work long hours securing the perfect props, fixing the lighting, and create sound effects.

   (A) Change "long" to "lengthy."
   (B) Add "of" before "women."
   (C) Change "create" to "creating."
   (D) Add "and" before "fixing."
   (E) Change "effects" to "affects."

3. In context, which is best to add to the beginning of sentence 4?
   (A) Because,
   (B) Obviously,
   (C) In addition,
   (D) However,
   (E) On the other hand,

4. Which is the best revision of the underlined portion of sentence 6 (reproduced below)?

   Working closely with teams of other crewmembers, these men or women handle the minute details that help brings movies to life.

   (A) the minute details, which help brings movies to life

   (B) the minute details that help bring movies to life

   (C) the minute details that help brought movies to life

   (D) the minute details that help brings movies to lives

   (E) the minute details, and that help brings movies to life

5. In context, which of the following is the best way to combine sentences 7 and 8?

   (A) For example, the gaffer is in charge of all the electricity on a set; the gaffer's assistant is the best boy.

   (B) The gaffer, for example, and his assistant, called the best boy, are in charge of all the electricity on a set.

   (C) The gaffer and the best boy, who is the gaffer's assistant, are in charge of all the electricity on a set, for example.

   (D) For example, the gaffer and his assistant, called the best boy, are in charge of all the electricity on a set.

   (E) For example, the people in charge of all the electricity on a set are the gaffer and the best boy, his assistant.

6. In context, after which sentence should the following sentence be placed?

   A skilled boom operator will catch even the barest of whispers without allowing the microphone to fall into the shot.

   (A) Sentence 10

   (B) Sentence 11

   (C) Sentence 12

   (D) Sentence 13

   (E) Sentence 14

7. In context, which of the following revisions must be made to sentence 11 (reproduced below)?

   Greensmen, propsmasters, and set dressers are rarely seen, but they create the world of the film threw their handling of the plants, props, and set details.

   (A) Change "threw" to "through."

   (B) Delete the comma after "props."

   (C) Delete the comma after "seen."

   (D) Change "but" to "also."

   (E) Place "handling" after "details."

8. Which is the best revision of the underlined portion of sentence 10 (reproduced below)?

   A strong foley artist is also a critical component: this person is responsible for the sound effects.

   (A) component, this person

   (B) component; this person

   (C) component because this person

   (D) component, however, this person

   (E) component, still this person

9. In context, which is the best replacement for "that" in sentence 15?

   (A) who

   (B) whom

   (C) which

   (D) they

   (E) have

10. Which of the following would make the most logical title for the passage?

    (A) Invisible Workers

    (B) People Behind the Scenes

    (C) How Movies Are Made

    (D) Occupations in Hollywood

    (E) How to Make a Movie

Questions 11–20 are based on a draft of a student's essay.

(1) Many people might be surprised to learn that the Post-it® note was not an intentional invention. (2) It was a mistake—a failure of sorts.

(3) While working at 3M's research lab in 1968, Spencer Silver attempted to create a glue that was stronger then any other adhesive in the company's arsenal of products. (4) When he tested the product, he was disappointed to find that the glue easily peeled away. (5) Instead of tossing the product and destroying the formula, Silver files it and restarted his research.

(6) In the early 1970s, 3M employee Arthur Fry came across Silver's weak glue while searching for something to make his bookmark stick to the page of his hymnal. (7) An avid member of his church's choir, Fry had grown mad when the bookmark that was holding his spot kept falling out of the book. (8) He needed something to help the bookmark stick to the page while simultaneously keeping the page intact and clean. (9) Familiar with Silver's "failed" glue, Fry placed a bit of the adhesive on the back of his bookmark and was pleased to find that it stuck without damaging the page.

(10) Fry shared his discovery with other 3M employees, who adapted Silver's glue for their own needs. (11) They used the glue on small pieces of paper and stuck the notes in convenient areas where they would notice them later on, on book covers, doorframes, and desks. (12) 3M marketed the product as Post-it® notes in 1977, they became a household name by 1979. (13) You probably have Post-it® notes in your own home. (14) What began as a perceived failure quickly became one of the most popular office supplies to date.

11. In context, which is best to add to the beginning of sentence 2?
    (A) In fact,
    (B) In addition,
    (C) Although
    (D) Or,
    (E) Obviously,

12. In context, which of the following revisions must be made to sentence 3 (reproduced below)?

    While working at 3M's research lab in 1968, Spencer Silver attempted to create a glue that was stronger then any other adhesive in the company's arsenal of products.

    (A) Change "3M's" to "3Ms'."
    (B) Add "had" before "attempted."
    (C) Add "the" before "3M."
    (D) Change "then" to "than."
    (E) Change "company's" to "companies."

13. Which is the best revision of the underlined portion of sentence 5 (reproduced below)?

    Instead of tossing the product and destroying the formula, Silver files it and restarted his research.

    (A) destroying the formula; Silver filed it and restarted
    (B) destroying the formula Silver files it and restarted
    (C) destroying the formula, and Silver filed it and restarted
    (D) destroying the formula, Silver filed it and restarted
    (E) destroyed the formula, Silver files it and restarted

14. In context, which is the best replacement for "mad" in sentence 7?
    (A) angered
    (B) mean
    (C) frustrated
    (D) upset
    (E) tired

15. Deleting which of the following sentences would most improve the coherence of the passage?

    (A) Sentence 1
    (B) Sentence 4
    (C) Sentence 8
    (D) Sentence 10
    (E) Sentence 13

16. Which of the following should be done with the underlined portion of sentence 8 (reproduced below)?

    He needed something to help the bookmark stick to the page while simultaneously keeping the page intact and clean.

    (A) Leave it as it is.
    (B) the page; while simultaneously
    (C) the page: while simultaneously
    (D) the page, but while simultaneously
    (E) the page, and while simultaneously

17. Which would be the best place to insert the following sentence?

    Today, Post-it® notes are one of the most frequently purchased office supplies around the world.

    (A) After Sentence 1
    (B) After Sentence 6
    (C) After Sentence 8
    (D) After Sentence 10
    (E) After Sentence 12

18. Which of the following revisions would most emphasize the purpose of sentence 10 (reproduced below)?

    Fry shared his discovery with other 3M employees, who adapted Silver's glue for their own needs.

    (A) Insert "however" at the beginning of the sentence.
    (B) Change "for their own needs" to "for themselves."
    (C) Insert "amazing" before "discovery" and "quickly" before "adapted."
    (D) Change "employees" to "workers" and "glue" to "adhesive."
    (E) Change "other" to "several" and "who" to "whom."

19. Which of the following revisions is most needed in sentence 11 (reproduced below)?

    They used the glue on small pieces of paper and stuck the notes in convenient areas where they would notice them later on, on book covers, doorframes, and desks.

    (A) Change "they" to "employees."
    (B) Add "office" before "desks."
    (C) Change the period to an exclamation point.
    (D) Change the comma after "on" to a colon.
    (E) Add a comma after "paper."

20. Which of the following versions of the underlined portion of sentence 12 (reproduced below) is best?

    3M marketed the product as Post-it® notes in 1977, they became a household name by 1979.

    (A) notes in 1977, but they became
    (B) notes in 1977, and they became
    (C) notes in 1977, also they became
    (D) notes in 1977, however, they became
    (E) notes in 1977 they became

ABILITY TO USE SOURCE MATERIALS

This section of the test assesses your ability to use source materials and recognize the basic elements found in research papers, including in-text citations and reference lists. The passages you encounter in this section are often samples of student research papers. For this reason, the passages may contain errors in logic or may fail to properly cite sources.

It's important to remember that the test does not adhere to only one style of documentation. You may encounter sources that are documented according to MLA, APA, or Chicago manuals of style. If you are unfamiliar with a particular style, think about how another style would set up a reference or citation. This could help you determine the correct answer.

The questions in this section not only ask about various parts of references, but also require you to evaluate the sources that the author uses. For these questions, you may be asked why an author uses a particular source. Other questions may ask you to think about how the author could improve a particular section by adding a quote or citation.

In addition to passage-based questions, this section includes several stand-alone questions. Some questions may ask you to evaluate information obtained from reference materials, such as dictionaries or encyclopedias. Other questions will test your knowledge of in-text citations and reference lists.

Remember to read each question carefully to ensure you are choosing the information that best answers the question.

The following discusses the types of questions you are most likely to encounter in this section of the test. After that, there are review questions.

Citations and References

Citations and reference questions are usually written like this:

In the citation, what information is provided by "X"?

OR

The second item in the References section indicates all of the following EXCEPT that

OR

Which of the following is cited in sentence 3?

These questions test your knowledge of source material and citations. Remember, the test does not always use the same style (MLA, APA, Chicago). Occasionally, you may come across a style with which you are unfamiliar. In these cases, use the knowledge you have to try to determine which part of the reference or citation is being discussed.

You can usually eliminate obviously incorrect choices quickly. For example, if the reference contains a Web site address, you can be fairly confident that the reference is not discussing a book or printed newspaper.

Passage Construction

Typically, the question is written like this:

The author of the passage uses "X" in sentence 3 most likely in order to

OR

The author of the passage quotes "X" in sentence 9 most likely in order to

These types of questions ask you to consider why the author included a specific piece of information. How does this information affect the rest of the paragraph, or even the rest of the passage? You can determine the purpose of certain sentences by thinking about what the author hopes to accomplish in this passage. With this in mind, choose the answer most likely to advance the author's argument or purpose.

Revision

Typically, the question is written like this:

Which is best to do with sentence 12 (reproduced below)?

OR

The final paragraph (sentences 14–16) could best be developed by

Remember, the passages in this section are often samples of student essays. This means that they may have errors in organization or proper use of citations and references. These types of questions ask you to think about the best way to revise certain sections of the passage.

This may involve adding additional information or including a citation. In some cases, the best answer is to leave the sentence or paragraph as it is. Remember to read each answer choice carefully before selecting the best answer.

ABILITY TO USE SOURCE MATERIALS: REVIEW QUESTIONS

Directions: The following questions are designed to test your knowledge of basic research, reference, and composition skills. Some questions are self-contained, but other questions will ask you to refer to a passage. Read all of the answer choices before choosing the best answer for each question.

Example Selection

(1) The emperor penguin is the largest species of penguin in the world. (2) These magnificent birds somehow manage to survive on Antarctica's frozen tundra. (3) According to the World Wildlife Fund (WWF), "climate change and habitat loss pose the greatest risk" to the emperor penguins. (4) However, the animals are not currently part of the federal government's list of endangered species.

References

U.S. Fish and Wildlife Service. "Endangered Species Program." U.S. Fish and Wildlife Service Web site. http://www.fws.gov/endangered/wildlife.html (accessed June 1, 2010).

World Wildlife Fund. "Emperor Penguin Facts." World Wildlife Fund Web site. http://www.worldwildlife.org/ogc/species_SKU.cfm?cqs=CTEP (accessed June 1, 2010).

Example 1:   **SAMPLE ANSWER**

The author of the passage uses quotes in sentence 3 most likely in order to

(A) suggest that emperor penguins are endangered

(B) show the importance of the emperor penguin

(C) describe how the emperor penguins survive

(D) explain the threats to emperor penguins

(E) provide information about other penguins

Choice (A) is incorrect because the author later says that the birds are not endangered. Choice (B) is also wrong because the species' importance is not discussed in the quoted text. Choice (C) is incorrect because the quote does not explain how the birds survive. Choice (E) is not correct because the quote does not discuss other penguins. **The correct answer is (D).**

Example 2:   **SAMPLE ANSWER**

The second item in the References section indicates all of the following EXCEPT that the

(A) information was originally published on June 1, 2010

(B) World Wildlife Fund is listed as the author of this information

(C) information was accessed by the author of the passage on June 1, 2010

(D) information was originally published on the World Wildlife Fund Web site

(E) "Emperor Penguins Facts" is a part of the World Wildlife Fund Web site

The only piece of information not indicated by the reference is that the information was originally published on June 1, 2010. This is the date that the information was accessed by the author of the passage. **The correct answer is (A).**

The following selections and questions will give you a chance to practice your ability to use source materials. Some questions refer to passages, while other questions are self-contained. Read each selection carefully before attempting to answer the questions. Mark your answers, and then check them against the answers and explanations that appear at the end of this overview.

1. **withered.** *v.* **1.** To become dry and sapless; especially: to shrivel from or as if from loss of bodily moisture. **2.** To lose vitality, force, or freshness. **3.** To cause to wither. **4.** To make speechless or incapable of action. See synonyms at **stun**. [Middle English *widren,* probably akin to *weder,* weather.]

   Which of the following statements is NOT supported by the definition above?

   (A) *Widren* was a word used in Middle English.

   (B) The word "wither" always has to do with speech.

   (C) One meaning of "withered" has negative connotations.

   (D) The word "withered" has both abstract and concrete meanings.

   (E) The word "stun" is sometimes used as a synonym for "wither."

2. Kennedy, Allison. *The Loss of North America's Honeybees.* Harrison University, Biology Dept., 2007. Web. 27 Jan. 2010. <http://harrisonu.edu/resources/honeybees/index.html>.

   In the citation, what information is provided by "2007"?

   (A) The date the information was accessed on the Internet

   (B) The date that the author finished her research

   (C) The date that the article was submitted to the college

   (D) The date that the article was published on the Internet

   (E) The date that North American honeybees started dying

3. *The following excerpt is taken from a student's research paper.*

   Scientists believe that vaccines could help in the fight against cancer. Vaccines against several forms of cancer could be available "within the next 10 years," according to a study completed at the Garrison Medical Center (Louis, Forthcoming, 206).

   The word "forthcoming" means that the

   (A) quote could not be verified

   (B) study has not been completed yet

   (C) study has not been published yet

   (D) vaccine is not available yet

   (E) vaccine has not been tested yet

4. Hansen, Gretta. 2009. *All My Yesterdays: Poems.* Trans. William Bishop. New York: Sheppard Publishing.

   In the citation, what information is provided by "Trans. William Bishop"?

   (A) The name of the collection's editor

   (B) The name of the collection's illustrator

   (C) The name of the collection's co-author

   (D) The name of the collection's publisher

   (E) The name of the collection's translator

<u>Questions 5–12</u> refer to the following passage.

(1) In August 2006, the International Astronomical Union (IAU) came to a disheartening decision: Pluto would no longer be considered a planet. (2) Instead, scientists would refer to Pluto as a as dwarf planet.

(3) According to Fraser Cain, publisher of *Universe Today*, "Pluto was first discovered in 1930 by Clyde W. Tombaugh at the Lowell Observatory in Flagstaff Arizona" (2008). (4) Tombaugh was 22 years old at the time and had originally named the solar system's newest addition Planet X. (5) Later, a suggestion by an 11-year-old elementary school student would lead scientists to name the planet Pluto, after a Roman god.

(6) From 1930 to 2006, students in elementary and middle schools all over the world learned the names of the nine planets in the solar system: Mercury, Venus, Earth, Mars, Jupiter, Saturn, Uranus, Neptune, and Pluto. (7) When the IAU announced that Pluto would lose its status as a planet, many people began questioning the institution's criteria for what constitutes a planet.

(8) Alan Boyle, author of *The Case for Pluto: How a Little Planet Made a Big Difference*, claims that the definition of a planet is no longer clear. (9) "Today, the term covers a wide spectrum of worlds, and that spectrum is certain to get wider as more discoveries are made. (10) That doesn't mean the word itself is spoiled…. (11) It's only natural that a concept so fundamental to an entire field of science should be so broad" (Boyle, 2009, 202).

(12) According to Cain, for a mass to be considered a planet, the mass must orbit the sun, contain a particular amount of gravity, and be the biggest mass in its orbit. (13) Pluto is surrounded by other, larger masses, making it ineligible for planet status.

(14) However, Cain says that Pluto can regain its status, but the tiny mass must work for it. (15) "There are still many objects with similar size and mass to Pluto jostling around in its orbit. (16) And until Pluto crashes into many of them and gains mass, it will remain a dwarf planet," Cain explains.

References

Boyle, Alan. 2009. *The Case for Pluto: How a Little Planet Made a Big Difference*. Hoboken, New Jersey: John Wiley and Sons, Inc.

Cain, Fraser. 2008. "Why is Pluto Not a Planet?" *Universe Today* (April 10, 2008), <http://www.universetoday.com/2008/04/10/why-pluto-is-no-longer-a-planet/> (accessed June 1, 2010).

5. Which of the following is cited in sentence 3?
   (A) A Web site article
   (B) A newspaper
   (C) A search engine
   (D) A magazine
   (E) An encyclopedia

6. The information in parentheses in sentence 3 informs the reader that
   (A) Cain's article can be found on page 2008
   (B) Cain's article is 2,008 pages long
   (C) the IAU said Pluto was not a planet in 2008
   (D) Cain's article was published in 2008
   (E) information about Pluto became available in 2008

7. The author of the passage quotes Boyle in sentence 9 most likely in order to
   (A) describe Pluto's history as a planet
   (B) point out that Earth doesn't meet the IAU's criteria
   (C) emphasize the effect of the IAU's decision
   (D) provide information on other former planets
   (E) suggest that the criteria for a planet is imprecise

8. Which is best to do with sentence 12 (reproduced below)?

   According to Cain, for a mass to be considered a planet, the mass must orbit the sun, contain a particular amount of gravity, and be the biggest mass in its orbit.

   (A) Leave it as it is.

   (B) Provide Cain's academic credentials.

   (C) Include a page number for the reference.

   (D) Add quotation marks around the sentence.

   (E) Add information in parentheses explaining Cain's claim.

9. Which of the following pieces of information, if added to the fourth paragraph (sentences 8–11), would most effectively advance the writer's argument?

   (A) A critical review of Alan Boyle's book

   (B) Biographical information on Alan Boyle

   (C) A comparison of how the term "planet" has changed over time

   (D) Information on how other planets meet the IAU's requirements

   (E) Specific figures on the IAU's requirements for a mass to be considered a planet

10. Which of the following best describes the purpose of the final paragraph (sentences 14–16)?

    (A) It details the IAU's criteria for a mass to be considered a planet.

    (B) It presents information to refute the IAU's argument.

    (C) It suggests that scientists need to reopen the debate.

    (D) It explains how Pluto might become a planet again.

    (E) It elaborates on why Pluto is no longer a planet.

11. The final paragraph (sentences 14–16) could best be developed by

    (A) adding information about how Pluto was first discovered

    (B) discussing why the IAU's decision angered so many people

    (C) elaborating on the likelihood of Pluto regaining planet status

    (D) explaining how scientists devised the criteria for planet status

    (E) adding information on how Pluto's new status affected school children

12. The first item listed in the References section indicates all of the following EXCEPT that

    (A) the book was published in 2009

    (B) the book was written in Hoboken, New Jersey

    (C) Alan Boyle is the author of this book

    (D) the publisher is located in Hoboken, New Jersey

    (E) John Wiley and Sons is the publisher of this book

RHETORICAL ANALYSIS

In this section, you will read a set of passages and answer questions based on these passages. Each passage is numbered for easy reference. Often, these passages are portions of larger writing samples and do not constitute a complete discussion of the topics presented. This requires you to infer how the original passage was most likely presented. This section assesses your ability to recognize the key components of a writing sample, including the main idea, purpose, content, and style of the passage. Other questions ask about the function of certain sentences, organization of the passage, and areas where revision is needed.

The following discusses the types of questions that you are most likely to encounter in this section of the test. After that, there is a practice with questions and answers.

Purpose

Typically, the question is written like this:

The passage is primarily concerned with

OR

The author's primary purpose in mentioning "X" in sentence 5 is

This type of question is asking you about the author's motivation. Why did the author write this passage? The main idea of the passage might be about school uniforms, but you want to determine why the author is writing about the subject. Does the author want to persuade the audience to support the idea of school uniforms? Does the author believe that school uniforms are the solution to a larger problem?

The best way to determine purpose is to determine what sort of essay you are reading. This is where you must infer what the entire essay looks like. After you decide what sort of essay you are reading, you can think about why a person would write this style of essay. This will help you determine the author's purpose.

The second version of this question asks you why the author included a specific piece of information. To correctly answer this question, you will have to decide how the specific information relates to the author's larger purpose. How does including this information support the author's overall argument? Consider how the passage might be different if this information was omitted.

Content

A content question is usually written like this:

According to the passage, "X" led to

This type of question is asking you to consider the details that make up the content of the passage. These types of questions ask you to consider why or how something took place. You may also be asked to think about how specific details in the passage relate to the main idea. These types of questions test your ability to read critically. To answer these questions correctly, you must first read the question carefully to ensure that you know what is being asked. If you have trouble, refer back to the passage to try to locate the answer.

Word Choice and Vocabulary

Typically, the question is written like this:

The word "X" in sentence 2 is meant to address which of the following assumptions?

OR

In context, "X" most nearly means

Authors choose their words carefully. You can assume that there is a reason that the author chooses one word over another. For these questions, your job is to determine why the author chose a specific word or phrase and how this choice affects a sentence, paragraph, or passage.

To answer these questions effectively, it is necessary to consider the other words and sentences surrounding the word or phrase in question. This helps you understand the context in which the word is being used.

Organization

A question about organization is usually written like this:

Which of the following best describes the organization of the passage as a whole?

These types of questions are designed to test your ability to recognize how and why the author organized ideas, sentences, and paragraphs in a particular manner. Understanding the purpose of the passage can help you determine why the author organized the passage in a specific style or format. If the author is arguing for a particular solution to a problem, then he might decide to present the problem first and then explain how the solution would work to resolve this issue.

In many cases, you can eliminate several obviously incorrect answer choices quickly. This will help you to focus on the choices that make the most sense in the context of the passage.

Functions of Sentences

Typically, the question is written like this:

Sentence 1 serves to

OR

Which of the following best describes sentence 1?

These types of questions again ask you to consider the author's purpose and the overall organization of the passage. Just as authors choose their words carefully, they also place sentences in certain spots for strategic purposes. A sentence that introduces the main idea of the passage would most likely be located in the first paragraph. However, it might not always be the first sentence. In such an instance, think about why the author might wait to introduce the main idea. How does this affect the rest of the paragraph?

Remember to consider the context of the sentence. Read the other sentences that surround the sentence in question. Think about how this sentence fits in with the other sentences. This will help you determine why the author chose to include this sentence in the passage.

RHETORICAL ANALYSIS: REVIEW QUESTIONS

Directions: Each of the following passages consists of numbered sentences. Because the passages are part of longer writing samples, they do not necessarily constitute a complete discussion of the issue presented.

Read each passage carefully and answer the questions that follow it. The questions test your awareness of a writer's purpose and of characteristics of prose that are important to good writing.

Example Selection

(1) Besides being extremely beautiful, sunflowers are also very useful. (2) Sunflower seeds are a delicious treat, consumed by both people and animals. (3) Sunflower oil is often used in cooking, and sunflower butter (made from crushed seeds) is a popular alternative to peanut butter. (4) Strangely, many farmers consider sunflowers weeds because they often grow alongside other crops like corn and soy.

Example 1:   **SAMPLE ANSWER**

The passage is primarily concerned with

(A) describing the different parts of the sunflower

(B) explaining the many ways that sunflowers are useful

(C) refuting the claim that sunflowers are beautiful

(D) exploring the history of sunflowers in North America

(E) illustrating the different opinions about sunflowers

The passage is mainly about how sunflowers are useful. Choice (A) is incorrect because the passage does not describe the different parts of the sunflower. Choice (C) is wrong because the author believes that sunflowers are beautiful. Choice (D) is incorrect because the history of sunflowers is not discussed. Choice (E) is wrong because, while another opinion of sunflowers is discussed, this is not the focus of the passage. **The correct answer is (B).**

Example 2:   **SAMPLE ANSWER**

The word "Strangely" in sentence 4 is meant to address which of the following assumptions?

(A) Sunflower oil can be used in cooking.

(B) Sunflower seeds are a delicious treat.

(C) People and animals can eat sunflower seeds.

(D) Sunflowers are extremely beautiful and very useful.

(E) Sunflower seeds can be used to make sunflower butter.

"Strangely" is used to address the original statement about the beauty and usefulness of sunflowers in sentence 1. The author of this passage can't imagine farmers thinking of sunflowers as a weed. **The correct answer is (D).**

The following selections and questions will give you a chance to practice your rhetorical analysis skills. Read each selection carefully before attempting to answer the questions. Mark your answers and then check them against the answers and explanations that appear at the end of this overview.

Questions 1–3 refer to the following paragraph.

(1) Today, many people know Jane Austen as the author of such classics as *Pride and Prejudice, Emma,* and *Sense and Sensibility.* (2) Her works have been read in school, performed on stage, and immortalized on the silver screen. (3) Austen was unknown to her fans during the nineteenth century because her works were published anonymously. (4) Her identity was only revealed after her death, when her brother Henry wrote a touching biography of his sister for the publications of *Persuasion* and *Northanger Abbey*.

1. Which of the following best describes sentence 1?
   (A) It introduces readers to the subject of the passage.
   (B) It discusses the reasons for why some literary works endure.
   (C) It explores the connections between literature and film.
   (D) It describes opposing views of a particular author.
   (E) It states the thesis of the discussion to follow.

2. Which of the following transition words or phrases, if inserted at the beginning of sentence 3 (reproduced below), would be most logical in the context of the passage?

   Austen was unknown to her fans during the nineteenth century because her works were published anonymously.

   (A) Of course,
   (B) In fact,
   (C) Surprisingly,
   (D) Therefore,
   (E) Likewise,

3. The author's primary purpose in mentioning *Persuasion* and *Northanger Abbey* is to
   (A) show readers why Austen's work is still read
   (B) suggest that Austen was not a popular author
   (C) compare Austen's last books to her first
   (D) explain how Austen's identity was revealed
   (E) describe how Austen's work changed over time

Questions 4–8 refer to the following passage.

(1) When high school students near the end of their senior year, many look ahead to a two- or four-year undergraduate education at the college or university of their choice. (2) They picture themselves graduating with a degree in their selected field after many hours of studying and researching.

(3) Not every student views the world this way. (4) Talented basketball players hoping to play professionally upon graduating from high school were once able to skip college and go straight to the National Basketball Association (NBA). (5) In 2005, the NBA players' union changed many high school basketball players' plans when they accepted a rule affectionately referred to as "one and done." (6) This rule prevented American players from joining the league until the age of 19.

(7) While some coaches and fans feel this rule is unfair, many educators support the NBA's decision. (8) An off year between high school and the pros enables many young players to receive at least one year of higher education. (9) A full year of college would ensure that many players complete some of the required core classes, which educators see as fundamental to producing well-rounded adults.

(10) Although many educators would support a rule that calls for professional basketball players to earn a degree before entering the league, they have accepted that this will most likely never occur. (11) Instead, professors do what they can to support student-athletes who enter their schools with dreams of the NBA. (12) If students find an area of study that interests them while they attend college during that one year, perhaps they will return to finish their degrees someday.

4. Sentence 2 primarily serves to

   (A) reveal the reasons for the NBA's ruling

   (B) defend a student's right not to attend college

   (C) highlight the problems with the "one and done" rule

   (D) describe the various fears that high school graduates experience

   (E) contrast the hopes of many graduates with the hopes of basketball players

5. According to the passage, the NBA's ruling led to

   (A) an increase in the number of players admitted to the draft

   (B) many colleges refusing to admit basketball players

   (C) many players only attending one year of college

   (D) a decrease in the number of college athletes

   (E) tougher requirements for first-year students

6. The discussion of core classes in sentence 9 primarily serves to

   (A) explain why many students leave college

   (B) demonstrate the importance of higher education

   (C) describe how college can improve a player's skills

   (D) indicate that the NBA made a mistake in its ruling

   (E) counter the claim that every player should attend college

7. In context, "fundamental" (sentence 9) most nearly means

   (A) basic

   (B) easy

   (C) important

   (D) necessary

   (E) difficult

8. The passage is primarily concerned with

   (A) explaining a recent phenomenon

   (B) arguing for a particular view of a topic

   (C) detailing the issues that professional athletes face

   (D) exploring the connections between sports and higher education

   (E) explaining why people have misconceptions of basketball players

Questions 9–13 refer to the following passage.

(1) Knowing how to defend yourself and stay safe is important, no matter where you live. (2) Regardless of a given city or town's crime rate, every high school student across the country should be required to enroll in a self-defense class. (3) Whether the class is offered outside of school or as part of a physical education program, students should be required to complete a specific number of training hours before graduation.

(4) Although knowing how to defend yourself from physical attack is important, taking a self-defense class could actually help reduce your chances of becoming involved in violent crime in the first place.

(5) Self-defense courses teach people to recognize the characteristics of a potentially dangerous situation or area, allowing them to leave before anything negative occurs.

(6) Completing a self-defense course would give high school students the confidence to handle challenging situations and provide them with skills that could someday save their lives. (7) The outside world is sometimes a scary and dangerous place. (8) It is our duty as educators, parents, and friends to give young people all of the tools they need to survive and thrive once they leave high school.

9. Which of the following best describes the organization of the passage as a whole?

   (A) A procedure is introduced and then described in more detail.

   (B) An approach is presented and backed up with support.

   (C) A phenomenon is described and an explanation is provided.

   (D) A problem is presented and a solution is detailed.

   (E) An opinion is offered and then refuted by the author.

10. According to the passage, taking self-defense classes leads to

   (A) an increase in violent crime

   (B) more aggressive students

   (C) a drop in school violence

   (D) the ability to save the lives of others

   (E) an ability to recognize unsafe situations

11. In context, "characteristics" (sentence 5) most nearly means

   (A) facts

   (B) signs

   (C) manners

   (D) locations

   (E) personalities

12. Which of the following transition words or phrases, if inserted at the beginning of sentence 8 (reproduced below), would be the most logical in the context of the passage?

   It is our duty as educators, parents, and friends to give young people all of the tools they need to survive and thrive once they leave high school.

   (A) Similarly,

   (B) Of course,

   (C) However,

   (D) Therefore,

   (E) In fact,

13. This passage is primarily concerned with

   (A) arguing for a particular course of action

   (B) exploring the link between crime and location

   (C) describing the various methods of self-defense

   (D) detailing the unique aspects of a particular program

   (E) explaining how high school prepares students for the real world

THE TWO ESSAYS

The College Composition examination contains two timed mandatory essays that must be completed within 70 minutes.

For the first essay, you will read a statement and write an essay that discusses the extent to which you agree or disagree with the statement. You must use examples from your readings, experiences, or observations to support your position in this essay.

For the second essay, you will read two sources that discuss a single topic. Then, you will be asked to take a position and construct an argument by synthesizing and citing the two sources in a coherent essay.

All essays must be typed on a computer.

The following provides information for writing a well-organized and thoughtful essay. Then, you will find two sample essay assignments. Complete the assignments and check your work against the sample essays that appear at the end of this overview.

HOW TO WRITE AN ESSAY

An essay is a way to express your ideas in writing rather than by speaking. To do so effectively, you need to focus on a specific topic, roughly organize your ideas, and write as clearly and logically as possible in the time allotted.

Elements of a Good Essay

A good essay contains the following elements:
- Content
- Cogency
- Clarity
- Coherence
- Correctness

Let's discuss each element separately.

Content

People read an article to the end only if they find it interesting, surprising, or informative. However, in the context in which you are writing an essay, and the fact that the readers must read each essay to the end, use your common sense. Don't try too hard to be unique in your perspective or reasoning, but, on the other hand, avoid clichés and well-worn expressions. Try to avoid melodrama and under-statement. In other words, take the subject seriously, respond honestly, and use examples from your own experience, the experience of people you know personally, or your reading. This approach will take care of ensuring both the individuality of your essay and the reader's interest.

Cogency

If you express your thoughts and point of view about the subject in the context of what you know and believe at the time of writing, you will have no difficulty in being convincing. Remember, no one expects you to be an expert on the subject of the topic since you will have no prior knowledge of what the topic will be. If you use a voice that is not yours, not only will the reader find it difficult to understand you, but also the quality of your writing will suffer.

Clarity

Time is important here, for both you and the readers. Avoid vague, general words, such as thing, and try to use concrete, specific examples and language to avoid wordiness.

Coherence

Even though you explore several ideas in your essay, they should all be related or connected. It is important, therefore, that as you move from one idea to another, you make clear the connecting link between them. These connecting links can express opposition or contrast, addition or amplification, cause or effect, relations in time or place, and time sequence, to name a few. Coherence focuses on the importance of transitional words and phrases, which you need to link or connect paragraphs effectively.

Correctness

If you are taking a test like CLEP, chances are that you have more than a basic command of the English language. You must, however, write under the pressure of time, and it is likely that you will make some mistakes in your essay. Sometimes, as you read over the essay, you will discover that you can express the same idea or information more succinctly. In other instances, you will find that you have inadvertently made an error in grammar or punctuation. Try to familiarize yourself with the more common sentence errors.

The Process of Writing the Essay

You will be provided with a "prompt"—or topic—about which to write. Be sure that you read the topic carefully, preferably twice. Then take a few minutes to organize your ideas and begin to write. Don't spend too much time on organizing a rough outline; more ideas may occur to you as you write. While the CLEP readers realize that you have a limited amount of time in which to write, you are expected to write logically and clearly.

Four basic steps to writing an essay follow:

1. Read (about 2–3 minutes)
2. Plan (about 3–4 minutes)
3. Write (about 20–25 minutes)
4. Proofread and edit (about 5 minutes)

Typically, an essay has three parts: introduction, body, and conclusion. Writing the introduction is sometimes the most difficult part of the writing process. Professional writers often write the introduction *after* they have completed the body and conclusion of a piece of writing. You may want to leave some blank space at the top of the page when you write your CLEP essay so that you can come back after finishing your essay and write an effective introduction.

Introduction

This part of the essay introduces your topic and establishes your focus—that is, the point you want to prove about this topic. While it is possible to write any number of different kinds of opening paragraphs, given the time limit you will have for this CLEP essay, you should strive to be concise and clear. You may want to let your thesis serve as your introduction. In that case, the introduction will be brief, perhaps only a sentence or two. Be sure that your first sentence responds *directly* to the topic. You should begin your discussion as quickly as possible.

Body

This is the substance, or main content, of your essay. In this section of your essay, you will discuss the topic, offer supporting examples, and draw conclusions—in other words, prove your point. In this main part of your essay, you must be careful to develop your ideas as logically and smoothly as possible.

Fluency of expression and sentence variety are two areas the CLEP readers will evaluate when they read your essay. These skills are best developed by practicing; the more you write, the better you will become at expressing your ideas clearly and effectively. Another important quality necessary for a successful essay is sufficient evidence. Be sure that you have included enough support to prove your point. Each of these supporting details requires discussion to show its significance. You must demonstrate the worth of each point or piece of information. A brief explanation, then, of every supporting example is necessary.

Another very important consideration involves demonstrating your mastery of the basics of English composition. Try to avoid major composition errors such as comma splices and sentence fragments. Comma splices occur when a writer attempts to connect two independent clauses with only a comma to join them. To connect these independent clauses correctly, a writer must use a coordinating conjunction, such as *and* or *but,* and a comma, or the writer may use a semicolon instead of a comma. Of course, a third choice is to treat the two independent clauses as two separate, complete sentences. The CLEP readers will not unduly penalize you for careless mistakes, such as a few spelling errors, but you must strive to write as well as you can.

Conclusion

This is the final section of your essay, the place in which you remind your reader of the point you set out to prove. This last part may be only a sentence, or it could be several sentences. Just as there are a number of ways to write the opening paragraph or introduction, the conclusion can take many forms. Reemphasizing your focus is the main purpose of this section.

The Step-By-Step Essay

Follow these seven steps while writing your essay.

1. **Read the topic or question "prompt."** Read it at least twice. Be sure that you understand the topic. Do not write on any other topic.

2. **Take a few minutes to generate some ideas.** This process is sometimes called "brainstorming." Your goal here is to think of as many possibly relevant ideas as you can. Think quickly, but carefully consider your ideas. Choose one idea that appeals the most to you and about which you know the most.

3. **Compose a thesis, which is a statement of the topic and your focus.** In other words, craft the point you are setting out to prove in your essay. For instance, if the topic is the value of single-sex education, you may choose to agree or to disagree with this approach. Your thesis, then, could be one of these: Single-sex education benefits students more than it limits them. In this thesis, your focus is "benefits." In your essay, you are setting out to prove that the benefits outweigh the limitations. You could, however, write an essay that supports the opposite position. Here is a possible thesis for such an essay: Single-sex education is not beneficial to either gender.

4. **Begin the introduction (or save it for last).** Give an overview of the topic; include your thesis in this opening section. Try to move into the body as quickly as possible.

5. **Write the body of the essay.** While other forms of exposition are touted today, the five-paragraph theme is still alive and well. You can choose to compose three body paragraphs, but you are not restricted to three. *The actual number of paragraphs is not so important as the content in the body.* Each of these body paragraphs should include a strong topic sentence that clearly establishes the main idea of the paragraph; each paragraph is designed to help you build an effective discussion of your topic and focus.

6. **Write the conclusion or closing section of your essay.** Remind the reader of what you set out to prove—your focus. Did you succeed in defending your approach?

7. **Take a few minutes to review and proofread your essay.** Next to planning, this is perhaps the most critical part of the process of writing your essay. Read the essay carefully; check for grammar errors and misspellings. Change any words or phrases that you do not think express your ideas clearly.

Now, try part of this process with a sample topic.

Topic or Question Prompt

With all of the choices available today in secondary education, each student can decide whether a small college or a large university is the right choice for him or her. Choose to defend one position: small colleges are better for students or large universities are better for students. Develop your response into a well-written essay.

Sample 1: Reasons for a Large University

    Large universities offer students more for their money today. Because the cost of higher education rises dramatically every year, more students are choosing large universities.

    In recent years, more college students seem to flock to large universities because of a number of important factors. The multiplicity of offerings or opportunities, both academic and social, is attractive. At a large university, a student often has contact with outstanding educators, nationally recognized experts, such as poets or scientists, who are on the faculty at the university. The library holdings are extensive; usually, the school plant is spacious and well maintained. Security is provided so that students feel safe on campus. A large endowment and operating budget provide access to well-equipped labs for science and languages. A student has many opportunities to be involved in campus life—from social clubs to civic organizations to intramural sports. College athletics for schools at this level are tremendously popular and competitive. Attending a large college or university provides a better value for the dollar. Students concerned about costs and expenses, however, are best advised to determine which qualities in a college or university are the most important to them. The tuition and fees are just one aspect of a much larger whole.

In this sample essay, the writer offers a quick overview of some important benefits of attending a large university. The first, underlined sentence in the opening serves as the thesis, with *more* as the focus.

On the other hand, a student can argue in favor of small colleges.

Sample 2: Reasons for a Small College

Small colleges offer more benefits to students eager to enter the job market. Because of the competitiveness in the job market today, more students are choosing a small college instead of a large university. At a small college, a student finds the enrollment more limited in his or her classes, so that regular participation in class discussions is possible. The instructor or professor actually knows each student by name. A small college provides more opportunities for students to gain the confidence necessary to polish their speaking and writing skills, both of which are essential for successful job applications and interviews.

Campus life is rewarding because the size of the enrollment increases the possibility of close friendships. Although a large university library provides a virtually endless source of information, with the world practically at our fingertips because of the Web and cyberspace, students can access information from almost anywhere, not just in their college library. Students who choose small colleges contend that their choice stems from a desire to be more than a number or a face in the crowd. They believe they will be better prepared to face today's job market because they will have gained the composure and confidence that participating in small classes ensures.

In this part of the essay, the first sentence serves as the thesis, with *more benefits* as the focus.

Sample Essay Topics

Choose one of these and write a practice essay:

The role of technology in our lives today: Have we become too dependent?

The censorship of books and music (the rating of TV shows and movies): Is it ever appropriate?

"Education means developing the mind, not stuffing the memory." (Anon.) Respond to this quotation. Do you agree or disagree? Why?

Single-sex education: Is it more beneficial than coed education?

Qualities of a hero: What are the most important? Why?

The aging of America: What problems are we facing?

Role of violence in society today: How can we reduce the level?

USAGE REVIEW: PARTS OF SPEECH

Noun

A NOUN is the name of a person (actor), place (city), or thing (lamp).

There are three kinds of nouns, according to the type of person, place, or thing the noun names.

1. A *common* noun refers to a general type: girl, park, army.

2. A *proper* noun refers to a particular person, place, or thing, and always begins with a capital letter: Mary, Central Park, U.S. Army.

3. A *collective* noun signifies a number of individuals organized into one group: team, crowd, Congress.

Singular/Plural

Every noun has number. That means every noun is either singular or plural. The singular noun means only one; the plural noun means more than one. There are four ways to form the plurals of nouns:

1. by adding *s* to the singular (horses, kites, rivers)

2. by adding *es* to the singular (buses, churches, dishes, boxes, buzzes)

3. by changing the singular (*man* becomes *men, woman* becomes *women, child* becomes *children, baby* becomes *babies, alumnus* becomes *alumni*)

4. by leaving the singular as it is (*moose, deer,* and *sheep* are all plural as well as singular)

Note: When forming the plural of letters and numbers, add *s:* As, 150s.

Case

Nouns also have case, which indicates the function of the noun in the sentence. There are three cases—the nominative case, the objective case, and the possessive case.

1. **Nominative Case**

   A noun is in the nominative case when it is the subject of a sentence:

   > The *book* fell off the table.

   > The *boys* and *girls* ran outside.

   The subject of a sentence is the person, place, or thing that the sentence is about. Thus, the book fell off the table is about the book.

   A noun is in the nominative case when it is a predicate noun. This is a noun used after a linking verb. In such cases, the predicate noun means the same as the subject.

   > Einstein was a *scientist.* (Einstein = scientist)

   > Judith was a brilliant *scholar* and gifted *teacher.* (Judith = scholar and teacher)

   A noun is in the nominative case when it is used in direct address. A noun in direct address shows that someone or something is being spoken to directly. This noun is set off by commas.

   > *Claudel,* please answer the phone.

   > Go home, *Fido,* before you get hit by a car.

   A noun is in the nominative case when it is a nominative absolute. This is a noun with a participle (see verbs) that stands as an independent idea but is part of a sentence.

The *rain* having stopped, we went out to play.

The *bike* having crashed, the race was stopped.

A noun is in the nominative case when it is a nominative in apposition. This is one of a pair of nouns. Both nouns are equal in meaning and are next to each other. The noun in apposition is set off from the rest of the sentence by commas.

Steve, *my son*, is going to college.

That man is Syd, the *musician*.

2. Objective Case

A noun is in the objective case when it is the direct object of a verb. A direct object is the receiver of the action of a verb. A verb that has a direct object is called a transitive verb.

The team elected *David*.

The team won the *game*.

A noun is in the objective case when it is the indirect object of a verb. This is a noun that shows *to* whom or *for* whom the action is taking place. The words *to* and *for* may not actually appear in the sentence, but they are understood. An indirect *object* must be accompanied by a direct object.

Pedro threw *Mario* the ball. (Pedro threw the ball to Mario).

Anya bought her *mother* a gift. (Anya bought a gift for her mother).

A noun is in the objective case when it is an objective complement. An objective complement is a noun that explains the direct object. The word *complement* indicates that this noun *completes* the meaning of the direct object.

The team elected Terry *captain*.

A noun is in the objective case when it is an objective by apposition. An objective by apposition is very much like a nominative in apposition. Again we have a pair of nouns that are equal in meaning and are next to each other. The noun in apposition explains the other noun, but now the noun being explained is in the objective case. Therefore, the noun in apposition is called the objective by apposition. The objective by apposition is set off from the rest of the sentence by commas.

The bully pushed Steve, the little *toddler*, into the sandbox.

He gave the money to Sam, the *banker*.

A noun is in the objective case when it is an adverbial objective. This is a noun that denotes distance or time.

The storm lasted an *hour*.

The troops walked five *miles*.

A noun is in the objective case when it is an object of a preposition.

The stick fell into the *well*. (*Into* is the preposition.)

The picture fell on the *table*. (*On* is the preposition.)

See the section on prepositions.

3. Possessive Case

A noun is in the possessive case when it shows ownership. The correct use of the possessive case is often tested on the exam. The following seven rules will help you answer such questions correctly.

1. The possessive case of most nouns is formed by adding an apostrophe and *s* to the singular.

    The *boy's* book

    Emile's coat

2. If the singular ends in *s,* add an apostrophe, or apostrophe *s*.

    The *bus's* wheels

    OR

    The *bus'* wheels

    Charles' books

    OR

    Charles's books

3. The possessive case of plural nouns ending in *s* is formed by adding just an apostrophe.

    The *dogs'* bones

    Note: If *dog* was singular, the possessive case would be *dog's*.

4. If the plural noun does not end in *s,* then add an apostrophe and *s*.

    The *children's* toys

    The *men's* boots

5. The possessive case of compound nouns is formed by adding an apostrophe and *s* to the last word if it is singular, or by adding an *s* and an apostrophe if the word is plural.

    My *brother-in-law's* house

    My *two brothers'* house

6. To show individual ownership, add an apostrophe and *s* to each owner.

    Joe's and *Jim's* boats (They each own their own boat.)

7. To show joint ownership, add an apostrophe and *s* to the last name.

    Joe and *Jim's* boat (They both own the same boat.)

Pronouns

A pronoun is used in place of a noun. The noun for which a pronoun is used is called the antecedent. The use of pronouns, particularly the relationship between a pronoun and its antecedent, is one of the most common items found on the test. Always make sure a pronoun has a clear antecedent.

    John had a candy bar and a cookie. He ate *it* quickly. (Ambiguous) (What is the antecedent of *it—candy bar* or *cookie?*)

    The boy rode his bike through the hedge, *which* was very large. (Ambiguous) (What was very large—the *bike* or the *hedge?*)

    The captain was very popular. *They* all liked him. (Ambiguous) (Who liked him? *They* has no antecedent.)

There are ten kinds of pronouns:

1. **Expletive pronoun.** The words *it* and *there* followed by the subject of the sentence are expletive pronouns.

    There were only a few tickets left.

    It was a long list of chores

    When using an expletive, the verb agrees with the subject.

    There *remains* one *child* on the bus.

    There *remain* many *children* on the bus.

2. **Intensive pronoun.** This is a pronoun, ending in *self* or *selves,* which follows its antecedent and emphasizes it.

    He *himself* will go.

    The package was delivered to the boys *themselves.*

3. **Reflexive pronoun.** This is a pronoun, ending in *self* or *selves,* which is usually the object of a verb or preposition or the complement of a verb.

    I hate *myself.*

    They always laugh at *themselves.*

    Myself, yourself, himself, herself, and *itself* are all singular. *Ourselves, yourselves,* and *themselves* are all plural. There is no such pronoun as hisself or theirselves. Do not use *myself* instead of *I* or *me.*

4. **Demonstrative pronoun.** This is used in place of a noun and points out the noun. Common demonstrative pronouns are *this, that, these,* and *those.*

    I want *those.*

5. **Indefinite pronoun.** This pronoun refers to any number of persons or objects. Following is a list of some singular and plural indefinite pronouns.

    SINGULAR

    anybody, anyone, each, everybody, everyone, no one, nobody, none, somebody, someone

    PLURAL

    all, any, many, several, some

    If the singular form is used as a subject, the verb must be singular.

    Everyone of *them* sings. (One person sings.)

    If the singular form is used as an antecedent, its pronoun must be singular.

    Did *anybody* on any of the teams lose *his* sneakers? (One person lost *his* sneakers.)

6. **Interrogative pronoun.** This pronoun is used in asking a question. Such pronouns are *who, whose, whom, what,* and *which. Whose* shows possession. *Whom* is in the objective case. *Whom* is used only when an object pronoun is needed.

7. **Reciprocal pronoun.** This pronoun is used when referring to mutual relations. The reciprocal pronouns are *each other* and *one another.*

    They love *one another.*

    They often visit *each other's* houses.

    Note that the possessive is formed by an *'s* after the word *other.*

8. **Possessive pronoun.** This pronoun refers to a noun that owns something. The possessive pronouns are as follows:

> SINGULAR
>
> mine (my), yours, his, hers, its
>
> PLURAL
>
> ours, yours, theirs

Notice that possessive pronouns do not use an *'s*. *It's* is a contraction meaning *it is; its* denotes possession.

9. **Relative pronoun**.

> Nominative case—who, that, which
>
> Objective case—whom, that, which
>
> Possessive case—whose

A relative pronoun used as the subject of a dependent clause is in the nominative case.

> I know who stole the car.
>
> Give the prize to whoever won it.

A relative pronoun used as the object of a dependent clause is in the objective case.

> He is the thief whom I know. (Object of verb know)

Note that the difficulty always comes between choosing who or whom. Remember that who is in the nominative case and is used for the appropriate situations discussed under nominative case in the section on nouns. Whom is in the objective case and is used for the appropriate situations discussed under objective case in the section on nouns.

> Who is coming? (Who is the subject.)
>
> Whom are you going with? (Whom is the object of the preposition with.)

The relative pronoun in the possessive case is whose. Notice there is no apostrophe in this word. The contraction who's means who is.

> I know whose book it is. (Denotes possession)
>
> I know who's on first base. (Who's means who is.)

10. **Personal pronoun.**

	SINGULAR	PLURAL
NOMINATIVE CASE		
First person	I	we
Second person	you	you
Third person	he, she, it	they
OBJECTIVE CASE		
First person	me	us
Second person	you	you
Third person	him, her, it	them

	SINGULAR	PLURAL
POSSESSIVE CASE		
First person	mine (my)	ours (our)
Second person	yours (your)	yours (your)
Third person	his, hers, its (his, her, its)	theirs (their)

Personal pronouns denote what is called person. First-person pronouns show the person or thing that is speaking.

> I am going. (First person speaking)

Second-person pronouns show the person or thing being spoken to.

> You are my friend. (Second person spoken to)

Third-person pronouns show the person or thing being spoken about.

> Bea did not see her. (Third person spoken about)

Important for the Exam

Pronouns must agree with their antecedents in person, number, and gender.

Who refers to persons only.

Which refers to animals or objects.

That refers to persons, animals, or objects.

> I don't know *who* the actor is. (Person)
>
> They missed their dog, *which* died. (Animal)
>
> I finished the book, *which* (or *that*) you recommended. (Object)
>
> They are the people *who* started the fight. (Person)
>
> That is the tiger *that* ran loose. (Animal)
>
> The light *that* failed was broken. (Object)

Note that the singular indefinite antecedents always take a singular pronoun.

> *Everyone* of the girls lost *her* hat.
>
> *None* of the boys lost *his*.

Note that collective singular nouns take singular pronouns; collective plural nouns take plural pronouns.

> The choir sang *its* part beautifully.
>
> The choirs sang *their* parts beautifully.

Note that two or more antecedents joined by *and* take a plural pronoun.

> Dave *and* Steve lost *their* way.

Note that two or more singular antecedents joined by or or nor take a singular pronoun.

> Tanya *or* Charita may use *her* ball.
>
> Neither Tanya *nor* Charita may use *her* ball.

If two antecedents are joined by *or* or *nor*, and if one is plural and the other is singular, the pronoun agrees in number with the nearer antecedent.

> Neither the *ball* nor the *rackets* were in *their* place.

Case

Remember that pronouns must also be in one of the three correct cases: nominative, objective, or possessive.

1. A pronoun must be in the nominative case when it is the subject of a sentence.

   > James and *I* went to the airport.
   >
   > *We* freshmen helped the seniors.
   >
   > Peter calls her more than *I* do.
   >
   > Peter calls her more than *I*. (Here, the verb *do* is understood, and *I* is the subject of the understood verb *do*.)

2. A pronoun is in the objective case when it is a direct object of the verb.

   > Leaving James and *me*, they ran away.
   >
   > John hit *them*.
   >
   > The freshmen helped *us* seniors.

   A pronoun is in the objective case when it is the indirect object of a verb.

   > Give *us* the ball.

   A pronoun is in the objective case when it is an object of a preposition.

   > To Ben and *me*
   >
   > With Sheila and *her*
   >
   > Between you and *them*

3. A pronoun is in the possessive case when it shows ownership.

   > *Her* car broke down.
   >
   > *Theirs* did also.

   A pronoun is in the possessive case when it appears before a gerund (see verbals).

   > *His* going was a sad event.

For a more detailed analysis of the three cases, see the section on the cases of nouns.

Adjectives

An adjective describes or modifies a noun or a pronoun. An adjective usually answers the question which one? Or what kind? Or how many? There are a number of types of adjectives you should know. Here are five.

1. Articles (a, an, the) must agree in number with the noun or pronoun they modify.

   > *A* boy
   >
   > *An* apple
   >
   > *The* girls

If the noun or pronoun begins with a consonant, use *a*. If the noun or pronoun begins with a vowel, use *an*.

> *A* pear
>
> *An* orange

2. Limiting adjectives point out definite nouns or tell how many there are.

> *Those* books belong to John.
>
> The *three* boys didn't see *any* birds.

3. Descriptive adjectives describe or give a quality of the noun or pronoun they modify.

> The *large* chair
>
> The *sad* song

4. Possessive, demonstrative, and indefinite adjectives look like the pronouns of the same name. However, the adjective does not stand alone. It describes a noun or pronoun.

> *This* is *mine*. (Demonstrative and possessive pronouns)
>
> *This* book is *my* father's. (Demonstrative and possessive adjectives)

5. Interrogative and relative adjectives look the same, but they function differently. Interrogative adjectives ask questions.

> *Which* way should I go?
>
> *Whose* book is this?
>
> *What* time is John coming?

Relative adjectives join two clauses and modify some word in the dependent clause.

> I don't know *whose* book it is.

Important for the Exam

An adjective is used as a predicate adjective after a linking verb. If the modifier is describing the verb (a nonlinking verb), we must use an adverb.

> The boy is *happy*. (Adjective)
>
> Joe appeared *angry*. (Adjective)
>
> The soup tasted *spicy*. (Adjective)
>
> Joe looked *angrily* at the dog. (Adverb—*angrily* modifies *looked*)

Positive, Comparative, and Superlative Adjectives

The *positive* degree states the quality of an object.

The *comparative* degree compares two things. It is formed by using less or more or adding er to the positive.

The *superlative* degree compares three or more things. It is formed by using least or most or adding est to the positive.

POSITIVE	COMPARATIVE	SUPERLATIVE
easy	easier, more easy, less easy	easiest, most easy, least easy
pretty	prettier, more pretty, less pretty	prettiest, least pretty, most pretty

DO NOT USE TWO FORMS TOGETHER

> She is the most prettiest. (Incorrect)
>
> She is the prettiest. (Correct)
>
> She is the most pretty. (Correct)

Verbs

A verb either denotes action or a state of being. There are four major types of verbs: transitive, intransitive, linking, and auxiliary.

Transitive and Intransitive Verbs

1. Transitive verbs are action words that must take a direct object. The direct object, which receives the action of the verb, is in the objective case.

   > Joe *hit* the ball. (*Ball* is the direct object of *hit*.)
   >
   > Joe *hugged* Rita. (*Rita* is the direct object of *hugged*.)

2. Intransitive verbs denote action but do not take a direct object.

   > The glass *broke*.
   >
   > The boy *fell*.

Important for the Exam

Set, lay, and *raise* are always transitive and take an object. *Sit, lie*, and *rise* are always intransitive and do not take a direct object.

> *Set* the book down, *lay* the pencil down, and *raise* your hands. (*Book, pencil*, and *hands* are direct objects of *set, lay*, and *raise*.)
>
> *Sit* in the chair.
>
> She *lies* in bed all day.
>
> The sun also *rises*.

The same verb can be transitive or intransitive, depending on the sentence.

> The pitcher *threw* wildly. (Intransitive)
>
> The pitcher *threw* the ball wildly. (Transitive)

Linking and Auxiliary Verbs

3. Linking verbs have no action. They denote a state of being. Linking verbs mean "equal." Here are some examples: *is, are, was, were, be, been, am* (any form of the verb *to be*), *smell, taste, feel, look, seem, become*, and *appear*.

   Sometimes, these verbs are confusing because they can be linking verbs in one sentence and action verbs in another. You can tell if the verb is a linking verb if it means "equal" in the sentence.

   > He felt nervous. (*He* equals *nervous*.)
   >
   > He felt nervously for the door bell. (*He* does not equal *door bell*.)

Linking verbs take a predicate nominative or predicate adjective. (See sections on nouns, pronouns, and adjectives.)

> It *is I*.

> It *is she*.

4. Auxiliary verbs are sometimes called "helping" verbs. These verbs are used with an infinitive verb (to plus the verb) or a participle to form a verb phrase.

The common auxiliary verbs are:

> All forms of *to be, to have, to do*, and *to keep*.

> The verbs *can, may, must, ought to, shall*,

> He *has to go*. (Auxiliary *has* plus the infinitive *to go*)

> He *was going*. (Auxiliary *was* plus the present participle *going*)

> He *has gone*. (Auxiliary *has* plus the past participle *gone*)

There is no such form as *had ought*. Use *ought to have* or *should have*.

> He *ought to have gone*.

> He *should have gone*.

Every verb can change its form according to five categories. Each category adds meaning to the verb. The five categories are: *tense, mood, voice, number*, and *person*.

Tense

Tense indicates the *time*, or *when*, the verb occurs. There are six tenses. They are:

present	past	future
present perfect	past perfect	future perfect

Three principal parts of the verb—the present, the past, and the past participle—are used to form all the tenses.

The *present tense* shows that the action is taking place in the present.

> The dog *sees* the car and *jumps* out of the way.

The present tense of a regular verb looks like this:

	SINGULAR	PLURAL
First person	I jump	We jump
Second person	You jump	You jump
Third person	He, she, it jumps	They jump

Notice that an *s* is added to the third-person singular.

The *past tense* shows that the action took place in the past.

> The dog *saw* the car and *jumped* out of the way.

The past tense of a regular verb looks like this:

	SINGULAR	PLURAL
First person	I jumped	We jumped
Second person	You jumped	You jumped
Third person	He, she, it jumped	They jumped

Notice that *ed* is added to the verb. Sometimes just *d* is added, as in the verb *used*, for example. In regular verbs the past participle has the same form as the past tense, but it is used with an auxiliary verb.

The dog *had jumped*.

The *future tense* shows that the action is going to take place in the future. The future tense needs the auxiliary verbs *will* or *shall*.

The dog *will see* the car and *will jump* out of the way.

The future tense of a regular verb looks like this:

	SINGULAR	PLURAL
First person	I shall jump	We shall jump
Second person	You will jump	You will jump
Third person	He, she, it will jump	They will jump

Notice that *shall* is used in the first person of the future tense.

To form the three *perfect tenses,* the verb *to have* and the past participle are used.

The present tense of *to have* is used to form the *present perfect*.

The dog *has seen* the car and *has jumped* out of the way.

The present perfect tense shows that the action has started in the past and is continuing or has just been implemented in the present.

The past tense of *to have* is used to form the *past perfect*.

The dog *had seen* the car and *had jumped* out of the way.

The past perfect tense shows that the action had been completed in the past.

The future tense of *to have* is used to form the *future perfect*.

The dog *will have seen* the car and *will have jumped* out of the way.

The future perfect tense shows that an action will have been completed before a definite time in the future.

The following table shows the present, past, and future tenses of *to have.*

	PRESENT TENSE	
	SINGULAR	PLURAL
First person	I have	We have
Second person	You have	You have
Third person	He, she, it has	They have

	PAST TENSE	
	SINGULAR	PLURAL
First person	I had	We had
Second person	You had	You had
Third person	He, she, it had	They had

	FUTURE TENSE	
	SINGULAR	PLURAL
First person	I shall have	We shall have
Second person	You will have	You will have
Third person	He, she, it will have	They will have

The perfect tenses all use the past participle. Therefore, you must know the past participle of all the verbs. As we said, the past participle usually is formed by adding *d* or *ed* to the verb. However, there are many irregular verbs. Following is a table of the principal parts of some irregular verbs.

PRESENT	PAST	PAST PARTICIPLE
arise	arose	arisen
awake	awoke, awaked	awoke, awaked, awakened
awaken	awakened	awakened
be	was	been
bear	bore	borne
beat	beat	beaten
become	became	become
begin	began	begun
bend	bent	bent
bet	bet	bet
bid (command)	bade, bid	bidden, bid
bind	bound	bound
bite	bit	bitten
bleed	bled	bled
blow	blew	blown
break	broke	broken
bring	brought	brought
build	built	built
burn	burned	burned, burnt
burst	burst	burst
buy	bought	bought
catch	caught	caught
choose	chose	chosen
come	came	come
cost	cost	cost
dig	dug	dug
dive	dived, dove	dived
do	did	done
draw	drew	drawn
dream	dreamed	dreamed
drink	drank	drunk
drive	drove	driven
eat	ate	eaten
fall	fell	fallen
fight	fought	fought
fit	fitted	fitted
fly	flew	flown
forget	forgot	forgotten, forgot
freeze	froze	frozen
get	got	got, gotten
give	gave	given
go	went	gone
grow	grew	grown
hang (kill)	hanged	hanged
hang (suspended)	hung	hung
hide	hid	hidden
hold	held	held
know	knew	known
lay	laid	laid
lead	led	led
lend	lent	lent

PRESENT	PAST	PAST PARTICIPLE
lie (recline)	lay	lain
lie (untruth)	lied	lied
light	lit	lit
pay	paid	paid
raise (take up)	raised	raised
read	read	read
rid	rid	rid
ride	rode	ridden
ring	rang	rung
rise (go up)	rose	risen
run	ran	run
saw (cut)	sawed	sawed
say	said	said
see	saw	seen
set	set	set
shake	shook	shaken
shine (light)	shone	shone
shine (to polish)	shined	shined
show	showed	shown, showed
shrink	shrank	shrunk, shrunken
sing	sang	sung
sit	sat	sat
slay	slew	slain
speak	spoke	spoken
spend	spent	spent
spit	spat, spit	spat, spit
spring	sprang	sprung
stand	stood	stood
steal	stole	stolen
swear	swore	sworn
swim	swam	swum
swing	swung	swung
take	took	taken
teach	taught	taught
tear	tore	torn
throw	threw	thrown
wake	waked, woke	waked, woken
wear	wore	worn
weave	wove, weaved	woven, weaved
weep	wept	wept
win	won	won
write	wrote	written

Another aspect of tense that appears on the test is the *correct sequence* or *order of tenses*. Be sure if you change tense you know why you are doing so. Following are some rules to help you.

When using the perfect tenses remember:

The present perfect tense goes with the present tense.

> present
> As Dave *steps* up to the mound,

> present perfect
> the pitcher *has thrown* the ball to

> present perfect
> first, and I *have caught* it.

The past perfect tense goes with the past tense.

> past
> Before Dave *stepped* up to the

> past perfect
> mound, the pitcher *had thrown*

> past perfect
> the ball to first, and I *had caught* it.

The future perfect goes with the future tense.

> future
> Before Dave *will step* up to the mound, the pitcher

> future perfect
> *will have thrown* the ball to first,

> future perfect
> and I *shall have caught* it.

The present participle (verb + *ing*) is used when its action occurs at the same time as the action of the main verb.

> John, *answering* the bell, *knocked* over the plant. (*Answering* and *knocked* occur at the same time.)

The past participle is used when its action occurs before the main verb.

> The elves, *dressed* in costumes, will *march* proudly to the shoemaker. (The elves dressed *before* they will march.)

Mood

The mood or mode of a verb shows the manner of the action. There are three moods.

1. The *indicative mood* shows the sentence is factual. Most of what we say is in the indicative mode.

2. The *subjunctive mood* is used for conditions contrary to fact or for strong desires. The use of the subjunctive mood for the verb *to be* is a test item.

Following is the conjugation (list of forms) of the verb *to be* in the subjunctive mood:

PRESENT TENSE

	SINGULAR	PLURAL
First person	I be	We be
Second person	You be	You be
Third person	He, she, it be	They be

PAST TENSE

	SINGULAR	PLURAL
First person	I were	We were
Second person	You were	You were
Third person	He, she, it were	They were

If I *be* wrong, then punish me.

If he *were* king, he would pardon me.

Also, *shall* and *should* are used for the subjunctive mood.

If he *shall* fail, he will cry.

If you *should* win, don't forget us.

3. The *imperative mood* is used for commands.

Go at once!

If strong feelings are expressed, the command ends with an exclamation point. In commands, the subject *you* is not stated but is understood.

Voice

There are two voices of verbs. The *active* voice shows that the subject is acting upon something or doing something *to* something else. The active voice has a direct object.

      subject   object
The *car* hit the *box*.

The *passive* voice shows that the subject is acted upon *by* something. Something was done *to* the subject. The direct object becomes the subject. The verb *to be* plus the past participle is used in the passive voice.

      subject
The *box* was hit by the car.

Number

This, as before, means singular or plural. A verb must agree with its subject in number.

The *list was* long. (Singular)

The *lists were* long. (Plural)

Nouns appearing between subject and verb do not change subject/verb agreement.

The *list* of chores *was* long. (Singular)

The *lists* of chores *were* long. (Plural)

Subjects joined by *and* are singular if the subject is one person or unit.

> My *friend and colleague has* decided to leave. (Singular)
>
> *The Five and Dime is a popular name for general stores.* (Singular)
>
> *Tea and milk is* my favorite drink. (Singular)

Singular subjects joined by *or, either-or,* and *neither-nor* take singular verbs.

> Either Alvin or Lynette *goes* to the movies.

If one subject is singular and one is plural, the verb agrees with the nearer subject.

> Either Alvin or the girls *go* to the movies.

The use of the expletive pronouns *there* and *it* do not change subject/verb agreement.

> There *is no one* here.
>
> There *are snakes* in the grass.
>
> Think: No one is there; snakes are in the grass.

A relative pronoun takes a verb that agrees in number with the pronoun's antecedent.

> It is the *electrician who suggests* new wiring. (Singular)
>
> It is the *electricians who suggest* new wiring. (Plural)

Singular indefinite pronouns take singular verbs.

> Everybody *buys* tickets.

It is hard to tell if some nouns are singular. Following is a list of tricky nouns that take singular verbs.

> Collective nouns—*army, class, committee, team*
>
> Singular nouns in plural form—*news, economics, mathematics, measles, mumps, politics*
>
> Titles, although plural in form, refer to a single work—*The New York Times*, Henry James's *The Ambassadors*
>
> The *army is* coming.
>
> *News travels* fast.
>
> *Jaws is* a good movie.

Don't (do not) is incorrect for third-person singular. *Doesn't (does not)* is correct.

> He *doesn't* agree.

Person

Person, as before, refers to first person (speaking), second person (spoken to), and third person (spoken about). A verb must agree with its subject in person.

> I study. (First person)
>
> He studies. (Third person)

Intervening nouns or pronouns do not change subject/ verb agreement.

> *He* as well as she *is* going. (Third person)

If there are two or more subjects joined by *or* or *nor*, the verb agrees with the nearer subject.

> Either John or *we are* going. (First-person plural)

Adverbs

An adverb describes or modifies a verb, an adjective, or another adverb. Adverbs usually answer the questions *why?, where?, when?, how?* and *to what degree?* Many adverbs end in *ly*. There are two types of adverbs similar in use to the same type of adjective.

1. *Interrogative adverbs* ask questions.

    Where are you going?

    When will you be home?

2. *Relative adverbs* join two clauses and modify some word in the dependent clause.

    No liquor is sold *where* I live.

As with adjectives, there are three degrees of comparison for adverbs and a corresponding form for each.

1. The *positive* degree is often formed by adding *ly* to the adjective.

    She was *angry*. (Adjective)

    She screamed *angrily*. (Adverb)

2. The *comparative* is formed by using *more* or *less* or adding *er* to the positive.

3. The *superlative* is formed by using *most* or *least* or adding *est* to the positive.

Here are two typical adverbs:

POSITIVE DEGREE	COMPARATIVE DEGREE	SUPERLATIVE DEGREE
easily	easier, more easily, less easily	easiest, most easily, least easily
happily	happier, more happily, less happily	happiest, most happily, least happily

Conjunctions

Conjunctions connect words, phrases, or clauses. Conjunctions can connect equal parts of speech.

    and

    but

    for

    or

Some conjunctions are used in pairs:

    either...or

    neither...nor

    not only...but also

Here are some phrases and clauses using conjunctions:

    John *or* Mary (Nouns are connected.)

On the wall *and* in the window (Phrases are connected.)

Mark had gone, *but* I had not. (Clauses are connected.)

Either you go, *or* I will. (Clauses are connected.)

If the conjunction connects two long clauses, a comma is used in front of the coordinating conjunction:

Julio went to the game in the afternoon, but Pedro decided to wait and go to the evening game.

Some conjunctions are transitional:

therefore

however

moreover

finally

nevertheless

These conjunctions connect the meaning of two clauses or sentences.

Important for the Exam

Be aware of *comma splices*. Comma splices occur when one connects two independent clauses with a comma rather than with a semicolon or with a comma followed by a coordinating conjunction. An independent clause is a clause that can stand alone as a complete sentence.

His bike was broken; therefore, he could not ride. (Correct)

His bike was broken. Therefore, he could not ride. (Correct)

His bike was broken, and, therefore, he could not ride. (Correct)

His bike was broken, therefore, he could not ride. (Incorrect)

He found his wallet, however he still left the auction. (Incorrect)

The last two sentences are comma splices and are incorrect. *Remember, two independent clauses cannot be connected by a comma.*

Prepositions

A preposition shows the relationship between a noun or pronoun and some other word in the sentence.

The following are all prepositions:

about	for	through
above	in	to
across	inside	under
around	into	up
behind	of	upon
beneath	off	within
during	over	without

Sometimes groups of words are treated as single prepositions. Here are some examples:

according to

ahead of

in front of

in between

The preposition, together with the noun or pronoun it introduces, is called a prepositional phrase.

Under the table

In front of the oil painting

Behind the glass jar

Along the waterfront

Beside the canal

Very often on the test, idiomatic expressions are given that depend upon prepositions to be correct. Following is a list of idioms showing the correct preposition to use:

Abhorrence of: He showed an *abhorrence of* violence.

Abound in (or *with*): The lake *abounded with* fish.

Accompanied by (a person): He was *accompanied by* his friend.

Accompanied with: He *accompanied* his visit *with* a house gift.

Accused by, of: He was *accused by* a person *of* a crime.

Adept in: He is *adept in* jogging.

Agree to (an offer): I *agree to* the terms of the contract.

Agree with (a person): I *agree with* my son.

Agree upon (or *on*) (a plan): I *agree upon* that approach to the problem.

Angry at (a situation): I was *angry at* the delay.

Available for (a purpose): I am *available for* tutoring.

Available to (a person): Those machines are *available to* the tenants.

Burden with: I won't *burden* you *with* my problems.

Centered on (or *in*): His efforts *centered on* winning.

Compare to (shows difference): An orange can be *compared to* a grapefruit.

Compare with (shows similarity): An orange can't be *compared with* a desk.

Conform to (or *with*): He does not *conform to* the rules.

Differ with (an opinion): I *differ with* his judgment.

Differ from (a thing): The boss's car *differs from* the worker's car.

Different from: His book is *different from* mine. (Use *different than* with a clause.)

Employed at (salary): He is *employed at* $25 a day.

Employed in (work): He is *employed in* building houses.

Envious of: She is *envious of* her sister.

Fearful of: She is *fearful of* thunder.

Free of: She will soon be *free of* her burden.

Hatred of: He has a *hatred of* violence.

Hint at: They *hinted at* a surprise.

Identical with: Your dress is *identical with* mine.

Independent of: I am *independent of* my parents.

In search of: He went in *search of* truth.

Interest in: He was not *interested in* his friends.

Jealous of: He was *jealous of* them.

Negligent of: He was *negligent of* his responsibilities.

Object to: I *object to* waiting so long.

Privilege of: He had the *privilege of* being born a millionaire.

Proficient in: You will be *proficient in* grammar.

Wait for: We will *wait for* them.

Wait on (service): The maid *waited on* them.

Like is used as a preposition. He wanted his dog to act *like* Lassie.

Verbals

Sometimes verbs can change their form and be used as nouns, adverbs, or adjectives. These forms are called verbals.

The infinitive is formed by adding *to* in front of the verb. The infinitive may act as a noun, adjective, or adverb.

> I love *to sing*. (Noun)
>
> Music *to sing* is my favorite kind. (Adjective)
>
> He went *to sing* in the choir. (Adverb)

An infinitive phrase is used as a noun, adjective, or adverb.

> I love *to sing songs*. (Noun)
>
> Music *to sing easily* is my favorite. (Adjective)
>
> He went *to sing very often*. (Adverb)

The participle can be either present or past. The present participle is usually formed by adding *ing* to a verb. The past participle is usually formed by adding *n, en, d,* or *ed* to a verb. The participle is used as an adjective.

> The *swaying* crane struck the *fallen* boy. (*Swaying* is a present participle; *fallen* is a past participle.)

A participle phrase is used as an adjective.

> *Blowing the crane fiercely*, the wind caused much danger.

Important for the Exam

Beware of dangling participle phrases.

> *Blowing the crane fiercely*, the crowd ran. (The wind is blowing the crane, not the crowd.)

The gerund is formed by adding *ing* to a verb. Although the gerund may look like a present participle, it is used only as a noun.

> *Seeing* clearly is important for good *driving*. (*Seeing* is the subject; *driving* is the object of the preposition *for*.)

A participle phrase is used as a noun.

> *Seeing traffic signals* is important for good driving.

Phrases

A prepositional phrase begins with a preposition. A prepositional phrase can also be a noun phrase, an adjective phrase, or an adverbial phrase.

> *"Over the hill"* was the slogan of the geriatric club. (Noun phrase)
>
> The top *of the statue* was broken. (Adjective phrase)
>
> The owl sat *in the nest*. (Adverbial phrase)

See the previous section on *verbals* for infinitive phrases, participle phrases, and gerund phrases.

Important for the Exam

A dangling or misplaced modifier is a word or phrase acting as a modifier that does not refer clearly to the word or phrase it modifies.

> A bright light blinded his eyes *over the door*. (Misplaced modifier—his eyes were not over the door.)
>
> *Blowing the crane fiercely*, the crowd ran. (Misplaced participle phrase—the crowd was not blowing the crane.)
>
> *Watching television*, cookies were eaten. (Dangling gerund phrase—cookies were not watching television.)
>
> *Not able to stop*, the man jumped out of my way. (Dangling infinitive phrase—is it the man who could not stop?)

The following modifying phrases clearly show what they modify.

> A bright light over the door blinded his eyes. Because the wind was blowing the crane fiercely, the crowd ran.

Watching television, Laura ate the cookies. Since I was not able to stop, the man jumped out of my way.

Clauses

Clauses are groups of words that contain a subject and a predicate (verb part of the sentence). There are two main kinds of clauses. One kind is the *independent clause*, which makes sense when it stands alone. Independent clauses are joined by coordinating conjunctions.

> I know how to clean silver, *but* I never learned how to clean copper.

The two independent clauses could stand alone as complete sentences.

> I know how to clean silver. I never learned how to clean copper.

The other kind of clause is a *dependent* or *subordinate clause*. Although this type of clause has a subject and a predicate, it cannot stand alone.

> When I learn to clean copper, I will keep my pots sparkling.

When I learn to clean copper, by itself, does not make sense. Dependent clauses are always used as a single part of speech in a sentence. They function as nouns or adjectives or adverbs. When they function as nouns, they are called *noun clauses*. When they function as adjectives, they are called *adjective clauses*. When they are adverbs, they are called *adverbial clauses*. Since a dependent or subordinate clause cannot stand alone, it must be joined with an independent clause to make a sentence. A *subordinating conjunction* does this job. A relative pronoun (*who, that, which, what, whose*, and *whom*) may act as the subordinating conjunction. For adjective and adverbial clauses, a relative adverb (*while* and *when*) may act as the subordinating conjunction.

> I noticed *that he was very pale*.

That he was very pale is a noun clause—the object of the verb *noticed. That* is the subordinating conjunction.

> *Who was guilty* is not known.

Who was guilty is a noun clause—the subject of the verb *is. Who* is the subordinating conjunction.

> She lost the belt, *which was a present*.

Which was a present is an adjective clause describing *belt. Which* is the subordinating conjunction.

> She lost the belt *when she dropped the bag*.

When she dropped the bag is an adverbial clause answering the question *when* about the predicate. *When* is the subordinating conjunction.

Clauses should refer clearly and logically to the part of the sentence they modify.

> We bought a dress at Bloomingdale's, *which was expensive*.
> (Misplaced adjective clause. Did the writer mean Bloomingdale's was expensive?)

Correct: We bought a dress, *which was expensive,* at Bloomingdale's.

> *When finally discovered*, not a sound was heard.
> (Misplaced adverbial clause. Who or what is discovered?)

Correct: *When finally discovered*, the boys didn't make a sound.

Sentences

A sentence is a group of words that expresses a complete thought. An independent clause can stand by itself and may or may not be a complete sentence.

> Beth and Terry rode the Ferris wheel; they enjoyed the ride. (Two independent clauses connected by a semicolon)
> Beth and Terry rode the Ferris wheel. They enjoyed the ride. (Two independent clauses— each is a sentence)

A *simple sentence* has one independent clause. A dependent clause is never a sentence by itself. Here are some simple sentences:

> John and Fred played.
> John laughed and sang.
> John and Fred ate hot dogs and drank beer.

The following is not an independent clause:

> Fred said. (Incorrect—*said* is a transitive verb. It needs a direct object.)
> Fred said hello. (Correct)

A *compound sentence* has at least two independent clauses.

> *Darryl bought the meat*, and *Laverne bought the potatoes*.

A *complex sentence* has one independent clause and at least one dependent clause.

> Because she left early, she missed the end. (*Because she left early* is the dependent clause. *She missed the end* is an independent clause.)

A *compound-complex sentence* has two independent clauses and one or more dependent clauses.

> You prefer math, and I prefer music, although I am the math major.

> (*You prefer math* and *I prefer music* are the independent clauses. The dependent clause is *although I am a math major.*)

Common Sentence Errors

Sentence Fragments

These are parts of sentences that are incorrectly written with the capitals and punctuation of a sentence.

> Around the corner. Because she left early. Going to the movies. A terrible tragedy.

Remember that sentences must have at least a subject and a verb.

Run-on Sentences

These are sentences that are linked incorrectly.

> The rain was heavy, lightning was crackling he could not row the boat. (Incorrect)

> Because the rain was heavy and lightning was crackling, he could not row the boat. (Correct)

> The rain was heavy. Lightning was crackling. He could not row the boat. (Correct)

Faulty Parallelism

Elements of equal importance within a sentence should have parallel structure or similar form.

> To sing, *dancing*, and to laugh make life happy. (Incorrect)

> To sing, to dance, and to laugh make life happy. (Correct)

> He wants health, wealth, and *to be happy*. (Incorrect)

> He wants health, wealth, and happiness. (Correct)

WATCH ARBITRARY TENSE SHIFTS

> He *complained* while his father *listens*. (Incorrect)

> He *complained* while his father *listened*. (Correct)

WATCH NOUN-PRONOUN AGREEMENTS

> A *person* may pass if *they* study. (Incorrect)

> A *person* may pass if *he* studies. (Correct)

WATCH THESE DON'TS

> DON'T use *being that*; use *since* or *because*.

> DON'T use *could of, should of, would of*; use *could have, should have, would have*.

> DON'T use the preposition *of* in the following: off *of* the table, inside *of* the house.

> DON'T use *this here* or *that there*; use just *this* or *that*.

> DON'T misuse *then* as a coordinating conjunction; use *than* instead.

He is better *then* he used to be. (Incorrect)

He is better *than* he used to be. (Correct)

Capitalization

Capitalize all proper nouns.

Capitalize names of specific people, places, things, peoples, and their languages: *Americans, America, Spanish*.

Note: Henry takes Spanish three times a week. Henry takes math three times a week.

Capitalize religions and holy books.

Islam

Koran

Bible

Capitalize calendar words.

Monday

April

Capitalize historical periods and events.

Renaissance

Civil War

Always capitalize the first word in a sentence.

It is Henry.

Capitalize the first word in a letter salutation.

Dear John,

Dear Sir,

Capitalize the first word of a letter closing.

Very truly yours,

Capitalize the first word in a direct quote.

He said, "Go away."

Capitalize the first, last, and important words in titles.

The Man Without a Country

Note: *A, an, and,* and *the* are usually not capitalized unless they are the first word.

Note also that conjunctions and prepositions with fewer than five letters are usually not capitalized.

Capitalize words used as part of a proper noun.

Hudson Street

Uncle Fritz

Capitalize specific regions.

I want to move to the South.

Capitalize abbreviations of capitalized words.

> D. B. Edelson

Capitalize acronyms formed from capitalized words.

> NASA
>
> NATO

Capitalize the pronoun *I*.

> I beseech you to hear my prayer.

Note that capitals are not used for seasons (summer, winter). Note that capitals are not used for compass directions (east, northeast).

Note that capitals are not used for the second part of a quote: "I see," she said, "how smart Henry is."

Punctuation

The Period

Use the period to end full sentences.

> Harry loves candy.
>
> Although John knew the course was difficult, he did not expect to fail.

Use the period with abbreviations.

> Mr.
>
> Ph.D.

The Question Mark

Use the question mark to end a direct question.

> Are you going to the store?

Note that indirect questions end with a period.

> He asked how Sue knew the right answer.

The Exclamation Point

Use the exclamation point to denote strong feeling.

> Act now!

The Colon

The colon can introduce a series or an explanation, but it must always follow an independent clause.

> The following sciences are commonly taught in college: biology, chemistry, and physics. (Correct)
>
> The sciences are: biology, chemistry, and physics. (Incorrect)

The sciences are is not an independent clause.

The colon is used after the salutation in a business letter.

> Dear Sir:

The colon is used to express the time.

> It is 1:45.

The Semicolon

The semicolon is used to link related independent clauses not linked by *and, but, or, nor, for, so,* or *yet.*

> No person is born prejudiced; prejudice must be taught.

The semicolon is used before conjunctive adverbs and transitional phrases placed between independent clauses.

> No person is born prejudiced; however, he has been taught well.

> No person is born prejudiced; nevertheless, he has always appeared bigoted.

The semicolon is used to separate a series that already contains commas. The team had John, the pitcher; Paul, the catcher; and Peter, the shortstop.

The Comma

The comma is used before long independent clauses linked by *and, but, or, nor, for, so,* or *yet.*

> No person is born prejudiced, but some people learn quickly.

The comma is used following clauses, phrases, or expressions that introduce a sentence.

> As I was eating, the waiter cleared the table.

> In a great country like ours, people enjoy traveling.

The comma is used with nonrestrictive, or parenthetical, expressions (not essential to the meaning of the main clause).

> He pulled the ice-cream sundae, topped with whipped cream, toward him.

> John is afraid of all women who carry hand grenades. *Notice there is no comma.* John is not afraid of all women. He is afraid of all women who carry hand grenades (restrictive clause).

Use commas between items in a series.

> Beth loves cake, candy, cookies, and ice cream.

Use the comma in direct address.

> Pearl, come here.

Use the comma before and after terms in apposition.

> Give it to Pearl, our good friend.

Use the comma in dates or addresses.

> June 3, 1996 Freeport, Long Island

Use the comma after the salutation in a friendly letter.

> Dear Henry,

Use the comma after the closing in letters.

> Sincerely yours,

Use a comma between a direct quotation and the rest of the sentence.

> "Our fudge," the cook bragged, "is the best in town."

Be sure to use two commas when needed.

> A good dancer, generally speaking, loves to dance.

Do not separate subjects and verbs with a comma.

> Students and teachers, receive rewards. (Incorrect)

Do not separate verbs and their objects with a comma.

> He scolded and punished, the boys. (Incorrect)

The Apostrophe

Use the apostrophe to denote possession (see nouns).

> John's friend

Use the apostrophe in contractions.

> didn't (did not)
>
> there's (there is)

Do not use an apostrophe with *his, hers, ours, yours, theirs,* or *whose.*

Use an apostrophe with *its* if *its* is a contraction.

> The dog chewed *its* bone; *it's* hard for a little dog to chew such a big bone. (*It's* means it is; *its* is a pronoun that denotes possession.)

Quotation Marks

Use quotation marks in direct quotes.

> "Get up," she said.

Use single quotes for a quote within a quote.

> Mark said, "Denise keeps saying 'I love you' to Ralph."

Parentheses

Use parentheses to set off nonrestrictive or unnecessary parts of a sentence.

> This book (an excellent review tool) will help students.

The Dash

Use the dash instead of parentheses.

> This book—an excellent review—will help students.

Use the dash to show interruption in thought.

> There are eight—remember, eight—parts of speech.

Rhetorical Review

Style

Good writing is clear and economical.

AVOID AMBIGUOUS PRONOUN REFERENCES

Tom killed Jerry. I feel sorry for *him*. (Who is *him*? Tom? Jerry?)

Burt is a nice man. I don't know why *they* insulted him. (Who does *they* refer to?)

AVOID CLICHÉS

Betty is *sharp as a tack*. The math exam was *easy as pie*. It will be *a cold day in August* before I eat dinner with Louisa again.

AVOID REDUNDANCY

Harry is a man who loves to gamble. (Redundant—we know that Harry is a man.)

Harry loves to gamble. (Correct)

Claire is a strange one. (Redundant—one is not necessary.)

Claire is strange. (Correct)

This July has been particularly hot in terms of weather. (Redundant—*in terms of weather* is not necessary.)

This July has been particularly hot. (Correct)

AVOID WORDINESS

The phrases on the left are wordy. Use the words on the right.

WORDY	PREFERABLE
the reason why is that	because
the question as to whether	whether
in a hasty manner	hastily
be aware of the fact that	know
due to the fact that	because
in light of the fact that	since
regardless of the fact that	although
for the purpose of	to

AVOID VAGUE WORDS OR PHRASES

It is always preferable to use specific, concrete language rather than vague words and phrases.

The reality of the situation necessitated action. (Vague)

Bill tied up the burglar before the burglar could tie up him. (Specific)

BE ARTICULATE: USE THE APPROPRIATE WORD OR PHRASE

The following are words or phrases that are commonly misused:

Accept:	to receive or agree to (verb)
	I *accept* your offer.
Except:	preposition that means to leave out
	They all left *except* Dave.
Adapt:	to change (verb)
	We must *adapt* to the new ways.
Adopt:	to take as one's own, to incorporate (verb)
	We will *adopt* a child.
Affect:	to influence (verb)
	Their attitude may well *affect* mine.
Effect:	result (noun)
	What is the *effect* of their attitude?
Allusion:	a reference to something (noun)
	The teacher made an *allusion* to Milton.
Illusion:	a false idea (noun)
	He had the *illusion* that he was king.
Among:	use with more than two items (preposition)
	They pushed *among* the soldiers.
Between:	use with two items (preposition)
	They pushed *between* both soldiers.
Amount:	cannot be counted (noun)
	Sue has a large *amount* of pride.
Number:	can be counted (noun)
	Sue bought a *number* of apples.
Apt:	capable (adjective)
	She is an *apt* student.
Likely:	probably (adjective)
	We are *likely* to receive the prize.
Beside:	at the side of (preposition)
	He sat *beside* me.
Besides:	in addition to (preposition)
	There were others there *besides* Joe.
Bring:	toward the speaker (verb)
	Bring that to me.
Take:	away from the speaker (verb)
	Take that to him.
Can:	to be able to (verb)
	I *can* ride a bike.
May:	permission (verb)
	May I ride my bike?
Famous:	well known (adjective)
	He is a *famous* movie star.
Infamous:	well known but not for anything good (adjective)
	He is the *infamous* criminal.
Fewer:	can be counted (adjective)
	I have *fewer* pennies than John.

Less:	cannot be counted (adjective)
	I have *less* pride than John.
Imply:	the speaker or writer is making a hint or suggestion (verb)
	He *implied* in his book that women were inferior.
Infer:	to draw a conclusion from the speaker or writer (verb)
	The audience *inferred* that he was a woman-hater.
In:	something is already there (preposition)
	He is *in* the kitchen.
Into:	something is going there (preposition)
	He is on his way *into* the kitchen.
Irritate:	to annoy (verb)
	His whining *irritated* me.
Aggravate:	to make worse (verb)
	The soap *aggravated* his rash.
Teach:	to provide knowledge (verb)
	She *taught* him how to swim.
Learn:	to acquire knowledge (verb)
	He *learned* how to swim from her.
Uninterested:	bored (adjective)
	She is *uninterested* in everything.
Disinterested:	impartial (adjective)
	He wanted a *disinterested* jury at his trial.

Organization

A paragraph, like an essay, must have some organization plan. Each paragraph should represent the development of some point the author is making. Learn to recognize topic sentences, which often come at the beginning or end of a paragraph. Topic sentences tell the reader the main point of the paragraph.

Here are some sample topic sentences:

De Tocqueville is also concerned with the conflict between individual liberty and equality.

Another of the social institutions that leads to disaster in *Candide* is the aristocracy.

The Fortinbras subplot is the final subplot that points to Hamlet's procrastination.

Example

Read the following paragraph and answer the appropriate questions.

(1) *Throughout history, writers and poets have created countless works of art.* (2) *The result is Paul's failure to pursue Clara and establish a meaningful relationship with her.* (3) *Paul's mother loves him, but the love is smothering and overprotective.* (4) *Although Paul feels free to tell his mother almost everything, he fails to tell her he is sexually attracted to Clara.* (5) *His feelings for Clara obviously make him feel he is betraying his mother.*

(6) *Paul Morel's relationship with his mother in* Sons and Lovers *interferes with his relationship with Clara.*

1. Which sentence(s) does NOT belong in the paragraph?
   (A) 3,6
   (B) 1
   (C) 4
   (D) 2
   (E) 5

The correct answer is (B). The first sentence is inappropriate to the idea of the paragraph, which concerns Paul's relationship with his mother and with Clara. The first sentence is also vague and virtually meaningless. Obviously, many works of art have been created throughout history.

2. Unscramble the paragraph and put the sentences in the correct order.
   (A) 2,4,3,6,5
   (B) 6,5,2,4,3
   (C) 3,4,5,6,2
   (D) 6,3,4,5,2
   (E) 2,5,4,3,6

The correct answer is (D). Obviously, sentence 1 does not fit the paragraph. Sentence 6 mentions Paul by his full name, the name of the work, and his relationships with both women, all of which are covered in the paragraph. It is the topic sentence. Sentence 2 sums up the paragraph; the clue is in the phrase "the result is." Logically, sentence 2 should end the paragraph. Since the paragraph concerns Paul's relationship with his mother and its effect on his relationship with Clara, the other sentences should fall in place.

Summary

This section has covered a lot of the basic rules of grammar. It is primarily a reference section, and you will not be expected to know everything on the exam. However, we suggest you use this section as a handy guide to help you understand many of the answers that might involve certain grammar principles with which you may not be familiar. Feel free to highlight certain portions of these principles so you can go back to them from time to time, especially when confronted with more difficult explanations of some of the problems in the exams in this book.

THE ESSAYS

First Essay

Sample Topic 1

Competition is essential for a person's healthy development.

> **Directions:** Write an essay in which you discuss the extent to which you agree or disagree with the statement above. Support your discussion with specific reasons and examples from your reading, experience, or observations.

Second Essay

Sample Topic 2

> **Directions:** The following assignment requires you to write a coherent essay in which you synthesize the two sources provided. Synthesis refers to combining the sources and your position to form a cohesive, supported argument. You must develop a position and incorporate both sources. You must cite the sources whether you are paraphrasing or quoting. Refer to each source by the author's last name, the title, or by any other means that adequately identifies it.

Introduction

Adolescence is a time of self-discovery. For this reason, many students, parents, and even some educators feel that the enforcement of strict dress codes or the requirement of school uniforms stifles students' creativity and limits their ability to express their individuality. Conversely, others argue that dress codes and school uniforms help limit distractions and promote equality among the student body, which improves the educational environment.

Assignment

Read the following sources carefully. Then write an essay in which you develop a position on whether or not dress codes improve the educational environment. Be sure to incorporate and cite both of the accompanying sources as you develop your position.

> Cannon, Katrina. (2010, June 01). "Strict dress codes cause more problems than they solve." *The Daily Observer*, pp. 11A.

The following passage is excerpted from an editorial in a local newspaper.

Although many schools across the nation have adopted dress codes, many people still believe that such restrictions violate the rights of individuals. Many students, with the support of their parents, have spoken out against the strict dress codes in their school districts. While these students acknowledge the benefits of school uniforms and dress codes, their chief complaint is that such policies strip students of their individuality.

Many teenagers express their personalities through the clothes and accessories they wear. These items often indicate a student's musical taste or favorite colors. Many kids also wear attire that shows their support for certain organizations, such as the school's basketball team or the local library. Clothing often leads to conversations between students, and allows them to form unique social bonds with their classmates. The clothing that students choose to wear is often an expression of who they are.

Of course, every school should have policies that prohibit overtly sexual or offensive attire, but they do not need to be so restrictive as to completely stamp out any sense of individuality. While most students understand that flip-flops are more of a safety risk than sneakers and can recognize why the school might restrict such footwear, many do not believe that enforcing strict dress codes will reduce outside distractions. Besides, forcing a teen to wear a uniform he doesn't feel comfortable in won't improve his chances of understanding algebra.

Turner, Marissa. (2010, May 05). "Dress codes lead to less fighting, more learning." *Today's Teachers*, 7.4, 31.

The following passage is excerpted from an article in a magazine for educators.

After enforcing strict dress codes or requiring uniforms, educators across the country have noticed a decrease in school violence and classroom disruption. Many school officials claim that a decrease in bullying and harassment in regards to personal property (clothing, jewelry, handbags, etc.) has lead to fewer physical altercations.

Requiring a particular code of dress has not only cut down on inappropriate and offensive attire in some schools, but has also created a gray area between the social classes. Many dress codes require khakis and polo shirts for both male and female students. Because of this, students do not stand out among their classmates just because their parents can or cannot afford to buy them designer clothes. Students now appear to each other as equals. This gives them the opportunity to develop friendships based on common interests that have nothing to do with their socioeconomic backgrounds.

The enforcement of dress codes or uniforms also decreases distractions caused by certain pieces of attire. When students look alike, less time is spent scrutinizing or praising classmates' fashion choices. This gives students more time to focus on their studies.

ANSWERS AND EXPLANATIONS

Conventions of Standard Written English

1. A	4. C	7. B	9. B	11. C
2. B	5. C	8. A	10. D	12. E
3. E	6. D			

1. **The correct answer is (A).** *Between* is used only to compare two people or items. *Among* should be used in instances when there are more than two people or items.

2. **The correct answer is (B).** The word *were* indicates that the sentence is in the past tense. Therefore, *supposed* is needed.

3. **The correct answer is (E).** There is no error in this sentence.

4. **The correct answer is (C).** In this sentence, *Mother* follows the possessive pronoun *his*. In such cases, *mother* should not be capitalized. If, however, you were addressing your mother, then you would capitalize the word.

5. **The correct answer is (C).** *Affect* and *effect* are often confused. *Affect* is usually a verb, while *effect* is usually a noun. In this case, the author is saying that the National Weather Service doesn't know how many people will be *affected*, or influenced, by the winter storm.

6. **The correct answer is (D).** This clause is modifying *proof of residency*, when it should be modifying *fee*. The sentence should read: To register for the test, you must pay a fee, which is about 50 dollars, and provide proof of residency.

7. **The correct answer is (B).** *Reign* is sometimes confused with *rain*. *Reign* means "to exercise authority," while *rain* refers to a form of precipitation. *Reign* is to the correct word for the sentence.

8. **The correct answer is (A).** This is a case of a misplaced modifier. The participle phrase *covered in cat hair* describes the *couch*, not *Bethany*.

9. **The correct answer is (B).** In this sentence, a semicolon is used to join two independent clauses. The second part of this sentence cannot stand on its own as an independent clause. Therefore, a colon should be used.

10. **The correct answer is (D).** The *papers* belong to the *students*. Therefore, *students'* must be used to show possession.

11. **The correct answer is (C).** *Less* and *fewer* are often confused. *Fewer* is used when referring to count nouns, and *less* is used when referring to mass nouns. Because injuries can be counted, *fewer* should replace *less* in this sentence.

12. **The correct answer is (E).** There is no error in this sentence.

Revision Skills

1. E	5. D	9. A	13. D	17. E
2. C	6. E	10. B	14. C	18. C
3. B	7. A	11. A	15. E	19. D
4. B	8. B	12. D	16. A	20. B

1. **The correct answer is (E).** This sentence makes very little sense at the end of the passage. It creates an awkward conclusion, and it would be best to delete it.

2. **The correct answer is (C).** It's necessary to change *create* to *creating* to fix the error in parallelism.

3. **The correct answer is (B).** The best transition word is *obviously*. Choices (A), (C), (D), and (E) do not provide a proper introduction to the sentence.

4. **The correct answer is (B).** *Bring* must be changed to agree with *movies*. Choices (A), (D), and (E) do not correct the original problem. Choice (C) uses the wrong form of *bring*.

5. **The correct answer is (D).** Choices (A), (B), (C), and (E) are all awkward and confusing. The only choice that effectively combines the two sentences while maintaining their original meaning is choice (D).

6. **The correct answer is (E).** Choices (A), (B), (C), and (D) would make the paragraph awkward. The best place for the sentence is immediately after sentence 14.

7. **The correct answer is (A).** The word *threw* means to have thrown something, such as a ball. *Through* is correct in this sentence. Choice (B) is incorrect because the serial comma is necessary. Choice (C) would make the sentence incorrect. Choice (D) would make the sentence a run-on sentence. Choice (E) would change the original meaning of the sentence.

8. **The correct answer is (B).** Choice (A) would create a run-on sentence. Choice (C) is awkward. Choices (D) and (E) use the wrong transition. Since the two sentences are closely related, they should be separated with a semicolon.

9. **The correct answer is (A).** Because *men and women* refers to people, the proper word to use is *who*.

10. **The correct answer is (B).** *People Behind the Scenes* is the title that best describes what the entire passage is about.

11. **The correct answer is (A).** Choices (B), (C), (D), and (E) do not fit in the context of the sentence.

12. **The correct answer is (D).** Choice (A) shows the plural possessive form, which is incorrect in this case. Choices (B) and (C) add unnecessary words to the sentence. Choice (E) is incorrect because the sentence is talking about one company.

13. **The correct answer is (D).** Choice (A) incorrectly uses a semicolon. Choice (B) does not correct the original error. Choice (C) unnecessarily adds the word *and*. Choice (D) uses the incorrect tense of *destroy*.

14. **The correct answer is (C).** Choice (C) is the most precise word choice in the context of this sentence.

15. **The correct answer is (E).** Choice (E) interrupts the flow of the paragraph with an unnecessary sentence.

16. **The correct answer is (A).** There is no need to add any punctuation before *while* in this sentence.

17. **The correct answer is (E).** Choices (A), (B), (C), and (D) would confuse the reader and make the passage awkward. Choice (E) places the sentence in the best possible spot in the passage.

18. **The correct answer is (C).** The author wants to emphasize the fact that the rediscovery of the glue was important to Fry and the other 3M employees. Choices (A), (B), (D), and (E) make unnecessary changes to the sentence.

19. **The correct answer is (D).** The comma after *on* needs to be a colon. The other changes are unnecessary.

20. **The correct answer is (B).** Choices (A), (C), and (E) create an awkward sentence. Choice (E) creates a run-on sentence. Choice (B) is the best revision.

Ability to Use Source Materials

1. B	4. E	7. E	9. C	11. C
2. D	5. A	8. A	10. D	12. B
3. C	6. D			

1. **The correct answer is (B).** Choice (A) is incorrect because *widren* was a word used in Middle English. Choice (B) is wrong because *withered* can have negative connotations. Choice (C) is incorrect because the word can refer to losing vitality, which is an abstract idea, as well as to losing moisture, which is a concrete idea. Choice (E) is wrong because *stun* is a synonym for *wither*.

2. **The correct answer is (D).** Choice (A) is wrong because the article was accessed on January 27, 2010. Choices (B) and (C) are incorrect because references do not require authors to list the date that the author finished her research or submitted it to the college. Choice (E) is wrong because this information would most likely be found in the article itself, not in the reference.

3. **The correct answer is (C).** In a citation, the word "forthcoming" refers to a work that has not been published yet.

4. **The correct answer is (E).** The abbreviation "trans." refers to "translator." Choice (E) is the only correct option.

5. **The correct answer is (A).** The quote comes from Fraser Cain's article, which was originally published on the *Universe Today* Web site.

6. **The correct answer is (D).** The information in parentheses refers to the date the article was published. Choices (A) and (B) are incorrect because they refer to page length and page numbers. Although the IAU did say that Pluto was not a planet in 2008, this has nothing to do with the information found in parentheses. Therefore, choice (C) is wrong.

Choice (E) is incorrect because there was information on Pluto before 2008.

7. **The correct answer is (E).** Choice (A) is incorrect because the sentence isn't describing Pluto's history. Choices (B) and (D) are incorrect because the author doesn't talk about Earth or any other planet specifically. Choice (C) is wrong because the sentence doesn't discuss the effect of the IAU's decision.

8. **The correct answer is (A).** There is no need to include the date in parentheses because it was already cited earlier in the passage. Choice (B) is incorrect because Cain's credentials are discussed earlier in the passage. Choice (C) is wrong because the article was published on a Web site. Choice (D) is incorrect because the author of the passage is paraphrasing Cain's work. Choice (E) is also wrong because the information in the sentence is self-explanatory.

9. **The correct answer is (C).** The fourth paragraph discusses how *planet* is now a broad term without clear parameters. Choices (A) and (B) would not add to the discussion of this issue. Choice (D) is wrong because it is unnecessary to show how other planets meet the IAU's requirements. Choice (E) is incorrect because specific figures would not help the reader understand how the term *planet* became so broad. A comparison of how the definition has changed over time would allow readers to see why Boyle now describes it as broad.

10. **The correct answer is (D).** Choices (A) and (E) are incorrect because these concepts were discussed earlier in the passage. Choices

(B) and (C) are wrong because the author doesn't want to refute the IAU's argument or suggest that the debate be reopened.

11. **The correct answer is (C).** Choice (A) is incorrect because this was discussed earlier in the passage. Choices (B), (D), and (E) are wrong because these ideas have little relevance to the information in the paragraph.

12. **The correct answer is (B).** Hoboken, New Jersey refers to the publisher's location, not the author's. The other choices present information that is indicated in the citation.

Rhetorical Analysis

1. A	4. E	7. D	10. E	12. D
2. C	5. C	8. A	11. B	13. A
3. D	6. B	9. B		

1. **The correct answer is (A).** Choice (B) is wrong because the sentence does not discuss the endurance of Austen's work. Choice (C) is incorrect because the sentence does not mention film. Sentence 1 does not offer more than one view of Austen; therefore, choice (D) is wrong. Choice (E) is incorrect because the author doesn't offer a thesis statement.

2. **The correct answer is (C).** Choice (C) is the best answer because Austen's anonymous status in the nineteenth century would likely surprise many of today's readers who know her as one of the most popular authors of all time.

3. **The correct answer is (D).** The author mentions these books because it was because of these novels that Austen's brother revealed her identity after her death.

4. **The correct answer is (E).** The sentence talks about high school graduates imagining the day when they will graduate from college. This is in direct contrast to the hopes that many basketball players have for their future.

5. **The correct answer is (C).** The NBA's ruling lead to the "one and done" rule, meaning player generally only attend one year of college before signing up for the draft. This did not affect the number of players admitted to the draft or the number of student athletes. Therefore, choices (A) and (D) are incorrect. The ruling also did not cause colleges to refuse to admit basketball players or create tougher requirements for first-year students. This makes choices (B) and (E) incorrect as well.

6. **The correct answer is (B).** Sentence 9 says that educators feel that core classes are fundamental to producing well-rounded adults. The author is using this sentence to show readers the importance of higher education.

7. **The correct answer is (D).** In this case, *fundamental* means *necessary*. Choice (A) is wrong because although *fundamental* can mean *basic*, this definition does not fit the context of the sentence. Choices (B), (C), and (E) are not synonyms for *fundamental* and do not fit the context of the sentence.

8. **The correct answer is (A).** Choice (B) is wrong because the passage doesn't argue for or against the NBA's ruling. Choice (C) is incorrect because while the passage mentions professional athletes, it doesn't discuss the issues they face. Although sports and higher education are both discussed, the author doesn't explore the connections between these two areas. Therefore, Choice (D) is wrong. Choice (E) is incorrect because the author never discusses people's misconceptions of basketball players.

9. **The correct answer is (B).** Choices (A) and (C) are incorrect because the passage does not describe a procedure or phenomenon. Choice (D) is wrong because the author isn't talking about a specific problem, but rather discussing a broad issue that affects many people. Choice (E) is incorrect because the author is not refuting an opinion. The author is offering an approach to the issue of preparing students for the dangers of the real world through self-defense classes.

10. **The correct answer is (E).** The author states that self-defense classes help students recognize potentially dangerous situations.

Choices (A), (B), and (C) are incorrect because taking self-defense classes does not lead to an increase in violent crime, more aggressive students, or a drop in school violence. While self-defense classes can help students protect themselves, the passage does not discuss saving others. Therefore, choice (D) is wrong.

11. **The correct answer is (B).** In the context of this sentence, *characteristics* refers to *signs*. Taking a self-defense class helps students recognize the signs of a dangerous situation.

12. **The correct answer is (D).** The word *therefore* connects this sentence to the previous sentence, which discusses the dangers of the outside world.

13. **The correct answer is (A).** This passage is making the argument that required self-defense classes would provide students with practical skills to help them survive in the outside world.

The Essays

Essay 1

Scoring Guide: College Composition Examination for Essay 1

Readers will assign scores based on the following scoring guide.

6—A 6 essay demonstrates a high degree of competence and sustained control, although it may have a few minor errors.

A typical essay in this category

- addresses all elements of the writing task effectively and insightfully
- develops ideas thoroughly, supporting them with well-chosen reasons, examples, or details
- is well focused and well organized
- demonstrates superior facility with language, using effective vocabulary and sentence variety
- demonstrates general mastery of the standard conventions of grammar, usage, and mechanics but may have minor errors

---

5—A 5 essay demonstrates a generally high degree of competence, although it will have occasional lapses in quality.

A typical essay in this category

- addresses the writing task effectively
- is well developed, using appropriate reasons, examples, or details to support ideas
- is generally well focused and well organized
- demonstrates facility with language, using appropriate vocabulary and some sentence variety
- demonstrates strong control of the standard conventions of grammar, usage, and mechanics but may have minor errors

---

4—A 4 essay demonstrates clear competence, with some errors or lapses in quality.

A typical essay in this category

- addresses the writing task competently
- is adequately developed, using reasons, examples, or details to support ideas
- is adequately focused and organized
- demonstrates competence with language, using adequate vocabulary and minimal sentence variety
- generally demonstrates control of the standard conventions of grammar, usage and mechanics but may have some errors

3—A 3 essay demonstrates limited competence.

A typical essay in this category exhibits ONE OR MORE of the following weaknesses:

- addresses only some parts of the writing task
- develops unevenly and often provides assertions but few relevant reasons, examples, or details
- is poorly focused and/or poorly organized
- displays frequent problems in the use of language
- demonstrates inconsistent control of grammar, usage, and mechanics

2—A 2 essay is seriously flawed.

A typical essay in this category exhibits ONE OR MORE of the following weaknesses:

- is unclear or seriously limited in addressing the writing task
- is seriously underdeveloped, providing few reasons, examples, or details
- is unfocused and/or disorganized
- displays frequent serious errors in the use of language that interfere with meaning
- contains frequent serious errors in grammar, usage, and mechanics that may interfere with meaning

1—A 1 essay is fundamentally deficient.

A typical essay in this category exhibits ONE OR MORE of the following weaknesses:

- provides little or no evidence of the ability to develop an organized response to the writing task
- is underdeveloped
- contains severe writing errors that persistently interfere with meaning

0—Off topic.

Provides no evidence of an attempt to respond to the assigned topic, is written in a language other than English, merely copies the prompt, or consists of only keystroke characters.

Sample Essay

Note: Errors in the sample essays are intentionally reproduced.

This essay is scored at a 6.

I agree with the statement "competition is essential for a person's healthy development." Although competition can sometimes be intimidating and makes completing tasks more difficult, it can still be beneficial. There are, however, restrictions to this statement.

For example, too much or too little competition in early childhood can affect a person's development.

Children who are not challenged may grow up believing that they can always get their way. This will leave many children ill prepared for the inevitable disappointments that they will encounter as young adults. If a child constantly has everything handed to him throughout his formative years, he might be surprised when he doesn't get the first job he applies to or feel extremely dejected when a college rejects his application.

Healthy competition challenges children to perform duties or tasks to the best of their abilities. It teaches them that hard work is valued and, often, rewarded. Also, children who engage in athletic or academic competitions learn important lessons about team work and playing by the rules. These are vital social skills that are easily demonstrated through challenging competitions.

Of course, too much competition can negatively affect children. As previously mentioned, competition can be intimidating. Constantly throwing children into competitive environments could cause unnecessary anxiety. This could cause some children to develop an irrational fear of failure. In some cases, children may opt to forgo the task completely rather than risk failing. On the other hand, too much competition could also make children overly aggressive. These children might then view everything as a competition and forget that winning isn't everything.

This drive to be the best at just about everything can be dangerous. From my own personal experiences, I have noticed that extremely competitive people are rarely satisfied. These people are not happy with second place and they never accept defeat. This sort of behavior quickly becomes exhausting for the individual and the people around him.

It is easy to see how competition can become negative, but a healthy level of competition often produces positive results. Competition encourages people to work for what they want. It helps people develop the drive needed to accomplish challenging tasks. Many people think of competition as something negative, simply because there always has to be a loser. However, in a healthy competition, both winners and losers accept their fates and learn from their experiences. For this reason, I believe that a moderate amount of competition is necessary for person to develop into a well-rounded individual.

Essay 2

Scoring Guide: College Composition Examination for Essay 2
Readers will assign scores based on the following scoring guide.

6—A 6 essay demonstrates a high degree of competence and sustained control, although it may have a few minor errors.

A typical essay in this category:

- cites sources appropriately
- develops a position effectively and insightfully, using well-chosen reasons, examples, or details for support
- synthesizes* both sources effectively with an effective and convincing link between the sources and the position
- is well focused and well organized
- demonstrates superior facility with language, using effective vocabulary and sentence variety
- demonstrates general mastery of the standard conventions of grammar, usage, and mechanics but may have minor errors

---

5—A 5 essay demonstrates a generally high degree of competence, although it will have occasional lapses in quality.

A typical essay in this category:

- cites sources appropriately
- develops a position consistently, using appropriate reasons, examples, or details for support
- synthesizes both sources clearly, with a clear link between the sources and the position
- is generally well focused and well organized
- demonstrates facility with language, using appropriate vocabulary and some sentence variety
- demonstrates strong control of the standard conventions of grammar, usage, and mechanics but may have minor errors

---

4—A 4 essay demonstrates competence, with some errors and lapses in quality.

A typical essay in this category:

- cites sources appropriately
- develops a position adequately, using reasons, examples, or details for support
- synthesizes both sources adequately, using reasons, examples, or details for support
- is adequately focused and organized
- demonstrates competence with language, using adequate vocabulary and minimal sentence variety
- generally demonstrates control of the standard conventions of grammar, usage, and mechanics but may have some errors

3—A 3 essay demonstrates limited competence.

A typical essay in this category exhibits ONE OR MORE of the following weaknesses:

- develops a position unevenly, often using assertions rather than relevant reasons, examples, or details for support
- synthesizes one source only or two sources inadequately, or establishes an inadequate link between the source(s) and the position
- displays problems in citing sources: citations are confusing or incomplete
- is poorly focused and/or poorly organized
- displays frequent problems in the use of language
- demonstrates inconsistent control of grammar, usage, and mechanics

2—A 2 essay is seriously flawed.

A typical essay in this category exhibits ONE OR MORE of the following weaknesses:

- is seriously underdeveloped, providing few or no relevant reasons, examples, or details for support
- synthesizes only one source weakly or establishes a very weak link between the source(s) and the position
- does not cite any source
- is unfocused and/or disorganized
- displays frequent serious errors in the use of language that may interfere with meaning
- contains frequent serious errors in grammar, usage, and mechanics that may interfere with meaning

1—A 1 essay is fundamentally deficient.

A typical essay in this category exhibits ONE OR MORE of the following weaknesses:

- does not develop a position
- fails to synthesize the source(s) used or uses no sources at all
- contains severe writing errors that persistently interfere with meaning

0—Off topic

Provides no evidence of an attempt to respond to the assigned topic, is written in a language other than English, merely copies the prompt, or consists of only keystroke characters.

*For the purpose of scoring, synthesis refers to combining sources and writer's position to form a cohesive, supported argument.

Sample Essay

Note: Errors in the sample essays are intentionally reproduced.

This essay is scored a 6.

Although the idea of following strict dress codes or having to wear uniforms upsets or irritates some students, the benefits of these policies appear to outweigh any negative effects that may arise.

While the desire to express oneself through clothing and accessories is easy to understand, this expression is unnecessary in an educational environment. Dress codes and school uniforms aren't an attack on students' individuality, they are an attempt to limit distractions and help students focus on their studies. One of the added benefits of such policies is a decrease in school violence and distractions created by material possessions.

In high school, many students are bullied because of the way they dress. While many students are able to brush off such harassment, others grow upset and eventually confront their bullies. According to an article by Marissa Turner for Today's Teachers, "a decrease in bullying and harassment in regards to personal property (clothing, jewelry, handbags, etc.) has lead to fewer physical altercations" in high school hallways (2010, p. 31). When students are dressed the same, there is less of a chance that any one student will stand out from the crowd.

Dress codes may also help students focus on their studies by eliminating the gossip that certain fashion choices tend to generate.

While sitting in class, students may be distracted by whispering or note passing, but funky socks, crazy hairpieces, or offensive graphic tees will no longer steal their attention. "When students look alike, less time is spent scrutinizing or praising classmates' fashion choices," said Turner (2010, p. 31).

In "Strict Dress Codes Cause More Problems than They Solve," Katrina Cannon points out that students' "chief complaint is that such policies strip [them] of their individualism" (2010, p. 11A). She argues that particular items of clothing express various personality traits. Enforcing a dress code limits students' ability to make a statement about who they are. While this point is valid, there are many other ways that students can express themselves. Instead of expressing themselves through their clothing, they can gain a reputation as a stellar student or a star athlete. Clothes don't have to define a person.

It may be difficult for students to adapt to a dress code, but they will soon become accustomed to it. Students can find other ways to express themselves through their schoolwork and extracurricular activities. Without fighting over material possessions or judging people on appearances, students will be able to focus on the most important part of going to school: getting an education.

POSTTEST ANSWER SHEET

Part I

1. Ⓐ Ⓑ Ⓒ Ⓓ Ⓔ   11. Ⓐ Ⓑ Ⓒ Ⓓ Ⓔ   21. Ⓐ Ⓑ Ⓒ Ⓓ Ⓕ   31. Ⓐ Ⓑ Ⓒ Ⓓ Ⓔ   41. Ⓐ Ⓑ Ⓒ Ⓓ Ⓔ
2. Ⓐ Ⓑ Ⓒ Ⓓ Ⓔ   12. Ⓐ Ⓑ Ⓒ Ⓓ Ⓔ   22. Ⓐ Ⓑ Ⓒ Ⓓ Ⓔ   32. Ⓐ Ⓑ Ⓒ Ⓓ Ⓔ   42. Ⓐ Ⓑ Ⓒ Ⓓ Ⓔ
3. Ⓐ Ⓑ Ⓒ Ⓓ Ⓔ   13. Ⓐ Ⓑ Ⓒ Ⓓ Ⓔ   23. Ⓐ Ⓑ Ⓒ Ⓓ Ⓔ   33. Ⓐ Ⓑ Ⓒ Ⓓ Ⓔ   43. Ⓐ Ⓑ Ⓒ Ⓓ Ⓔ
4. Ⓐ Ⓑ Ⓒ Ⓓ Ⓔ   14. Ⓐ Ⓑ Ⓒ Ⓓ Ⓔ   24. Ⓐ Ⓑ Ⓒ Ⓓ Ⓔ   34. Ⓐ Ⓑ Ⓒ Ⓓ Ⓔ   44. Ⓐ Ⓑ Ⓒ Ⓓ Ⓔ
5. Ⓐ Ⓑ Ⓒ Ⓓ Ⓔ   15. Ⓐ Ⓑ Ⓒ Ⓓ Ⓔ   25. Ⓐ Ⓑ Ⓒ Ⓓ Ⓔ   35. Ⓐ Ⓑ Ⓒ Ⓓ Ⓔ   45. Ⓐ Ⓑ Ⓒ Ⓓ Ⓔ
6. Ⓐ Ⓑ Ⓒ Ⓓ Ⓔ   16. Ⓐ Ⓑ Ⓒ Ⓓ Ⓔ   26. Ⓐ Ⓑ Ⓒ Ⓓ Ⓔ   36. Ⓐ Ⓑ Ⓒ Ⓓ Ⓔ   46. Ⓐ Ⓑ Ⓒ Ⓓ Ⓔ
7. Ⓐ Ⓑ Ⓒ Ⓓ Ⓔ   17. Ⓐ Ⓑ Ⓒ Ⓓ Ⓕ   27. Ⓐ Ⓑ Ⓒ Ⓓ Ⓔ   37. Ⓐ Ⓑ Ⓒ Ⓓ Ⓔ   47. Ⓐ Ⓑ Ⓒ Ⓓ Ⓔ
8. Ⓐ Ⓑ Ⓒ Ⓓ Ⓔ   18. Ⓐ Ⓑ Ⓒ Ⓓ Ⓔ   28. Ⓐ Ⓑ Ⓒ Ⓓ Ⓔ   38. Ⓐ Ⓑ Ⓒ Ⓓ Ⓔ   48. Ⓐ Ⓑ Ⓒ Ⓓ Ⓔ
9. Ⓐ Ⓑ Ⓒ Ⓓ Ⓔ   19. Ⓐ Ⓑ Ⓒ Ⓓ Ⓔ   29. Ⓐ Ⓑ Ⓒ Ⓓ Ⓔ   39. Ⓐ Ⓑ Ⓒ Ⓓ Ⓔ   49. Ⓐ Ⓑ Ⓒ Ⓓ Ⓔ
10. Ⓐ Ⓑ Ⓒ Ⓓ Ⓔ   20. Ⓐ Ⓑ Ⓒ Ⓓ Ⓔ   30. Ⓐ Ⓑ Ⓒ Ⓓ Ⓔ   40. Ⓐ Ⓑ Ⓒ Ⓓ Ⓔ   50. Ⓐ Ⓑ Ⓒ Ⓓ Ⓔ

answer sheet

Part II

Essay 1

_____

(blank lined answer sheet)

answer sheet

Essay 2

answer sheet

Posttest

PART I

50 minutes • 50 questions

Conventions of Standard Written English

Directions: The following sentences test your knowledge of grammar, diction (choice of words), and idioms. Some sentences are correct. No sentence contains more than one error.

You will find that the error, if there is one, is underlined and lettered. Assume that elements of the sentence that are not underlined are correct and cannot be changed. In choosing answers, follow the requirements of Standard Written English.

If there is an error, select the one underlined part that must be changed to make the sentence correct and fill in the corresponding oval on your answer sheet. If there is no error, select answer (E).

Example: **SAMPLE ANSWER**

Ⓐ Ⓑ ● Ⓓ Ⓔ

The <u>school's</u> literary magazine contains
    A

a treasury of <u>student-composed</u> poetry
           B

and <u>offered</u> a collection of short stories
   C

<u>written</u> by the faculty. <u>No error.</u>
  D   E

This verb tense in this sentence is inconsistent. The verbs *contains* and *offered* should be written in the same tense. To correct this problem, *offered* should be written as *offers*. **The correct answer is (C).**

1. At our current rate, <u>our</u> supply of
                A

 gasoline <u>will have</u> run out <u>by the time</u>
         B   C

 we <u>reached</u> our destination. <u>No error.</u>
     D   E

2. <u>Having failed</u> to <u>have thought</u> of it
    A   B

 earlier, we now realize that we should
 <u>has purchased</u> insect repellant
    C

 <u>in anticipation</u> of our hike. <u>No error.</u>
    D   E

3. <u>Following</u> the interview, the reporter
    A

 <u>remarked</u> that he <u>had found</u> the heiress
    B   C

 to be an incredibly <u>vein</u>, arrogant
              D

 woman. <u>No error.</u>
      E

4. Its not often in this day and age that you
   A   ,   B

   can find a truly honest person who can be
             C   D

   trusted unconditionally. No error.
                              E

5. We firmly believe that the crown prince
                 A

   would have made an excellent king,
        B   C

   had he lived to take the throne. No error.
     D   E

Revision Skills

Directions: Each of the following selections is an early draft of a student essay in which the sentences have been numbered for easy reference. Some parts of the selections need to be changed.

Read each essay and then answer the questions that follow. Some questions are about particular sentences and ask you to improve sentence structure and diction (choice of words). In making these decisions, follow the conventions of Standard Written English. Other questions refer to the entire essay or parts of the essay and ask you to consider organization, development, and effectiveness of language in relation to purpose and audience.

Questions 6–15 are based on a draft of an editorial in a school newspaper.

(1) Over the last few years, misbehavior among students has become more and more of a problem. (2) Incidents such as vandalism, bullying, and fighting has become increasingly common. (3) The classes of the teachers are constantly being disrupted by unruly students. (4) Many students are being disrespectful to his or her peers, elders, and others. (5) To permit this kind of behavior is completely unacceptable, and we firmly believe that something must be done about it immediately.

(6) We believe that the solution to the ongoing behavior problem is simple. (7) The current discipline system must be revised. (8) We believe that the current disciplinary code, which usually involves little more than detention, does not adequately discourage the bad behavior of the students. (9) Punishing misbehaving students by forcing them to spend an extra hour at school has not had any positive effect on their demeanor. (10) Suspensions have also been ineffective because they serve only as a way for students to get themselves out of school.

(11) In response to our school's behavioral problems, we suggest that the discipline policy be redesigned to take a more proactive approach to encouraging good behavior. (12) We recommend finding creative alternatives to detention and suspension that will increase the awareness of the students of the effects of their actions and deter misbehavior. (13) We believe that if such alternatives are instated; student behavior will improve school-wide. (14) Ultimately, a student body that is more well-behaved will make our school a better place to learn.

6. Which of the following is the best way to revise the underlined portion of sentence 2 (reproduced below)?

   Incidents such as vandalism, bullying, and fighting has become increasingly common.

   (A) had become
   (B) have had become
   (C) has became
   (D) have become
   (E) will have become

7. Which is the best revision of sentence 3 (reproduced below)?

   The classes of the teachers are constantly being disrupted by unruly students.

   (A) Unruly students are constantly disrupting the classes of the teachers.

   (B) Teachers' classes are constantly being disrupted by unruly students.

   (C) Constantly, teachers' classes are being disrupted by students who are unruly.

   (D) Disrupted by unruly students, teachers' classes are constantly.

   (E) The unruly students are constantly disrupting the teachers' classes.

8. Which is the best revision of the underlined portion of sentence 4 (reproduced below)?

   Many students are being disrespectful to his or her peers, elders, and others.

   (A) our

   (B) his

   (C) they

   (D) we

   (E) their

9. In context, which is the best replacement for "to permit this kind of behavior" in sentence 5?

   (A) Permitting this behavior

   (B) The permission of this behavior

   (C) Giving permission of this behavior

   (D) To be permitting this behavior

   (E) The permitting of this behavior

10. In context, which of the following is the best way to combine sentences 6 and 7?

    (A) We believe that the solution to the ongoing behavior problem is simple, the current discipline system must be revised.

    (B) We believe that the solution to the ongoing behavior problem is simple; the current discipline system must be revised.

    (C) We believe that the solution to the ongoing behavior problem is simple: the current discipline system must be revised.

    (D) We believe that the solution to the ongoing behavior problem is simple the current discipline system must be revised.

    (E) We believe, that the solution to the ongoing behavior problem is simple, the current discipline system must be revised.

11. Which is the best revision of the underlined portion of sentence 8 (reproduced below)?

    We believe that the current disciplinary code, which usually involves little more than detention, does not adequately discourage the bad behavior of the students.

    (A) the student's bad behavior.

    (B) behavior of the bad students.

    (C) student's bad behavior.

    (D) the students bad behavior.

    (E) students' bad behavior

12. In context, which is best to add to the beginning of sentence 9?

    (A) Nonetheless,

    (B) However,

    (C) Fortunately,

    (D) Therefore,

    (E) Clearly,

13. In context, which is the best replacement for "awareness of the students" in sentence 12?

    (A) students awareness

    (B) students' awareness

    (C) student's awareness

    (D) students's awareness

    (E) student awareness

14. In context, which of the following versions of the underlined portion of sentence 13 (reproduced below) is best?

We believe that if such alternatives are instated; student behavior will improve school-wide.

(A) instated; student behavior

(B) instated student behavior

(C) instated, student behavior

(D) instated: student behavior

(E) instated. Student behavior

15. Which is the best revision of sentence 14 (reproduced below)?

Ultimately, a student body that is more well-behaved will make our school a better place to learn.

(A) A student body that is more well-behaved will make our school a better place to learn.

(B) Ultimately, a more well-behaved student body will make our school a better place to learn.

(C) Ultimately, a student body that is more behaved will make our school a better place to learn.

(D) Ultimately, a well-behaved student body will make our school a better place to learn.

(E) Ultimately, our school will be made a better place to learn by a well-behave student body.

Questions 16–25 are based on a draft of an editorial for a local newspaper.

(1) The school board recently announced plans to amend the district's graduation requirements. (2) This new amendment requiring students to complete 75 hours of community service before graduation. (3) This requirement would overburden an already overextended student population.

(4) The school board members forget just how busy many students are these days. (5) In addition to schoolwork, many students participate in extracurricular activities, such as sports and academic clubs, and artistic programs. (6) Other students have afterschool or weekend jobs that allow them to save money for college. (7) Older students may also have family responsibilities, such as watching younger siblings after school, that would conflict with volunteer work. (8) Asking students to commit such a large block of time to volunteering seem unfair. (9) Students are already working as hard as they can.

(10) It's true that many college admissions counselors look for volunteer work on a prospective student's application. (11) This factor alone doesn't usually affect whether or not the student is accepted. (12) In fact, volunteering could actually take time away from a student's most important job, studying. (13) With test scores at an all-time low, we can't ask students to give up precious studying time to volunteer.

(14) The school board should take these issues into consideration before making their decision. (15) It seems that parents, teachers, and community members are asking more and more of young people. (16) These hardworking kids do their best to please everyone. (17) Asking them to complete 75 hours of community service before graduation won't necessarily turn teens into well-rounded individuals. (18) It might just add to the already mounting pressure they feel to succeed.

16. Which of the following should be done with the underlined portion of sentence 2 (reproduced below)?

This new amendment requiring students to complete 75 hours of community service before graduation.

(A) has required

(B) will require

(C) requires

(D) has required

(E) required

17. In context, which of the following is the best revision to sentence 5 (reproduced below)?

    In addition to schoolwork, many students participate in extracurricular activities, such as sports and academic clubs, and artistic programs.

    (A) Delete the "and" after "sports" and replace it with a comma.

    (B) Delete the comma after "schoolwork."

    (C) Change "participate" to "participating."

    (D) Change "In addition to" to "Besides."

    (E) Change "such as" to "like."

18. Which of the following versions of the underlined portion of sentence 8 (reproduced below) is best?

    Asking students to commit such a large block of time to volunteering seem unfair.

    (A) seems

    (B) will seem

    (C) seeming

    (D) seemed

    (E) have seemed

19. In context, which of the following is the best way to combine sentence 10 and 11?

    (A) It's true that many college admissions counselors look for volunteer work on a prospective student's application: this factor alone doesn't usually affect whether or not the student is accepted.

    (B) It's true that many college admissions counselors look for volunteer work on a prospective student's application, this factor alone, however, doesn't usually affect whether or not the student is accepted.

    (C) It's true that many college admissions counselors look for volunteer work on a prospective student's application, but this factor alone doesn't usually affect whether or not the student is accepted.

    (D) It's true that many college admissions counselors look for volunteer work on a prospective student's application, and this factor alone doesn't usually affect whether or not the student is accepted.

    (E) It's true that many college admissions counselors look for volunteer work on a prospective student's application, since this factor alone doesn't usually affect whether or not the student is accepted.

20. In context, which of the following revisions must be made to sentence 12 (reproduced below)?

    In fact, volunteering could actually take time away from a student's most important job, studying.

    (A) Delete "In fact."

    (B) Delete "actually."

    (C) Change "could" to "would."

    (D) Change "student's" to "students'."

    (E) Change the comma after "job" to a colon.

21. In context, which of the following is the best revision to sentence 13 (reproduced below)?

    With test scores at an all-time low, we can't ask students to give up precious studying time to volunteer.

    (A) Leave it as is.

    (B) Change "test" to "testing."

    (C) Change the comma to a semicolon.

    (D) Begin the sentence with "In addition."

    (E) Change "volunteer" to "volunteering."

22. Which of the following versions of the underlined portion of sentence 14 (reproduced below) is best?

The school board should take these issues into consideration before making their decision.

(A) making its decision

(B) to make their decision

(C) making their decisions

(D) their decision is made

(E) while making their decision

23. Which of the following would make the most logical title for the editorial?

(A) Community Service Could Help Students Get into College

(B) Community Service Could Do More Harm Than Good

(C) Students Should Limit Extracurricular Activities

(D) Students Should Concentrate on Studying

(E) Students Need More Free Time

24. In context, which of the following is the best way to combine sentence 17 and 18?

(A) Asking them to complete 75 hours of community service before graduation, it just might add to the already mounting pressure they feel to succeed and won't necessarily turn teens into well-rounded individuals.

(B) This won't necessarily turn teens into well-rounded individuals; completing 75 hours of community service before graduation might just add to the already mounting pressure they feel to succeed.

(C) Asking them to complete 75 hours of community service before graduation won't necessarily turn teens into well-rounded individuals; it might just add to the already mounting pressure they feel to succeed.

(D) Having to complete 75 hours of community service before graduation will only add, to the already mounting pressure they feel to succeed.

(E) Asking them to complete 75 hours of community service before graduation won't necessarily turn teens into well-rounded individuals, as a result, it might just add to the already mounting pressure they feel to succeed.

25. Which would be the best place to insert the following sentence?

Students should concentrate on raising their test scores instead of worrying if they have enough community service hours.

(A) After Sentence 9

(B) After Sentence 11

(C) After Sentence 13

(D) After Sentence 15

(E) After Sentence 17

Ability to Use Source Materials

Directions: The following questions are designed to test your knowledge of basic research, reference, and composition skills. Some questions are self-contained, but other questions will ask you to refer to a passage. Read all of the answer choices before choosing the best answer for each question.

26. slug *n.* **1.** sluggard (a habitually lazy person) **2.** A plastic or metal disk, lump, or cylinder of material such as *a.* A musket ball. *b.* A bullet. **3.** Any of numerous chiefly terrestrial pulmonate gastropods (order Stylommatophora) that are found in most parts of the world where there is a reasonable supply of moisture and are closely related to land snails but are long and wormlike and have only a rudimentary shell often buried in the mantle or entirely absent. **4.** *a.* A quantity of liquor drunk in one swallow. *b.* A detached mass of fluid that causes impact (as in a circulating system). [Middle English *slugge,* of Scandinavian origin; akin to Norwegian dial. *slugga* to walk sluggishly.]

    Which of the following statements is NOT supported by the definition above?

    (A) Some slugs are related to snails.

    (B) The word "slug" can refer to a bullet.

    (C) *Slugge* is a word of Scandinavian origin.

    (D) One meaning of "slug" has negative connotations.

    (E) All "slugs" are made of metal.

27. Gilbert, Natasha. "Britain Hits a Hurdle in Replacing Key Animal-Pathogen Facility," *Nature* (February 10, 2009). <http://www.nature.com/news/2009/090211/full/457769a.html> (accessed May 20, 2010).

    In the citation, what information is provided by "February 10, 2009"?

    (A) The date the article was accessed online

    (B) The date the event in the article occurred

    (C) The date the Web site was last updated

    (D) The date the article was published online

    (E) The date the author submitted her story

28. *The following excerpt is taken from a student's research paper.*

    Hammerhead sharks are certainly one of the strangest-looking creatures in the sea. However, the unique shape of their heads may have something to do with their having one of the largest brains of all species of sharks (Yopak et al., 2007).

    The phrase "et al." means

    (A) "additional information"

    (B) "alternate edition"

    (C) "alternate source"

    (D) "all included"

    (E) "and others"

29. James, Francis, 2001. *Selected Poems*. Ed. Janice Matthews. New York: Sheppard Publishing.

    In the citation, what information is provided by "Ed. Janice Matthews"?

    (A) The name of the collection's editor

    (B) The name of the collection's translator

    (C) The name of the collection's illustrator

    (D) The name of the collection's co-author

    (E) The name of the collection's publisher

Questions 30–37 refer to the following passage.

(1) The Salem witch trials were some of the most fascinating and terrifying events in American history. (2) In 1692, fear gripped the people of Salem Village, located in what was then the Massachusetts Bay Colony, when a doctor diagnosed two young girls as being "bewitched." (3) This led to an investigation and subsequent trial that resulted in the deaths of 20 people and ruined the lives and reputations of countless others. (4) Although the governor of the colony put an end to the trials in 1693 and the state of Massachusetts formally apologized for the tragedy in 1957, the causes of this tragic event still captivate historians more than 300 years later.

(5) Right before the trials, Salem Village saw an influx of new colonists, searching for refuge from the first of the French and Indian Wars. (6) This strained the resources of the village and caused tension among several groups, which contributed to the spread of gossip and suspicion throughout the area (King, 2002, 89). (7) However, this alone wasn't the cause of the widespread panic that led to accusations of witchcraft. (8) As scholar Aisha Whitmore explains, "The Puritans of Salem had a strong belief in evil—they were certain that anyone who deviated from the norms of Puritanical society must be practicing witchcraft."

(9) While these factors certainly created something of a powder keg in Salem, the hysteria didn't start until two young girls experienced strange muscle spasms, vomiting, and delusions that the local doctor could not explain. (10) After being questioned by adults, the girls accused three women of bewitching them. (11) From this point on, the people of Salem lived in fear, both of witchcraft and of the possibility of being labeled a witch. (12) For years, many scholars tried but failed to explain the strange symptoms of "bewitchment" the victims experienced. (13) However, in the 1970s, psychologist Linnda Caporael noted that all these symptoms could be explained by the ergot fungus, which can contaminate rye and other grains. (14) If the village doctor had only known about ergot poisoning, then this tragedy could have been avoided.

References

Caporael, Linnda. "Ergotism: The Satan Loosed in Salem?" *Science* 192 (1976): 21–26.

King, Jeffery. "How War Lead to the Salem Witch Trials." *Historians Online Magazine,* (March 2002). <http://historiansonlinemag.com/> (accessed May 20, 2010).

30. Which of the following is cited in sentence 6?
    (A) A book
    (B) A newspaper
    (C) An online magazine
    (D) An e-mail message
    (E) A scientific journal

31. The information in parentheses in sentence 6 informs the reader that
    (A) the sentence is a direct quote from a work written by King
    (B) King conducted research on the causes of the Salem witch trials in 2002
    (C) information about other witch trials in the United States can be found in a source written by King
    (D) King has written a work that provides information on how the new settlers affected life in Salem
    (E) information on how gossip led to the Salem witch trials can be found on page 2002 of a work by King

32. The author of the passage quotes Whitmore in sentence 8 most likely in order to

(A) point out that the people of Salem did not have modern medical technology

(B) explain why the people of Salem were susceptible to the hysteria over witchcraft

(C) emphasize the effect that new settlers had on the social groups of Salem Village

(D) provide information on other cases where societal beliefs lead to paranoia

(E) suggest that the people of Salem were not responsible for their actions

33. Which is best to do with sentence 8 (reproduced below)?

As scholar Aisha Whitmore explains, "The Puritans of Salem had a strong belief in evil—they were certain that anyone who deviated from the norms of Puritanical society must be practicing witchcraft."

(A) Add a citation indicating the source of the quotation from Whitmore.

(B) Add information in parentheses explaining Whitmore's quote.

(C) Paraphrase Whitmore's comment rather than quote it directly.

(D) Provide a list of Whitmore's scholarly credentials.

(E) Leave it as is.

34. Which of the following pieces of information, if added to the second paragraph (sentences 5–8), would most effectively advance the writer's argument?

(A) A comparison of how the new settlers differed from established colonists

(B) A description of how the people of Salem treated their neighbors

(C) Specific figures on the number of new settlers

(D) Biographical information on Aisha Whitmore

(E) Additional information about the Puritan belief system

35. Which of the following best describes the purpose of the final paragraph (sentences 9–14)?

(A) It describes the reasons people moved to Salem.

(B) It points out what the people of Salem did wrong.

(C) It elaborates on the causes of the young girls' illness.

(D) It explains why the Salem Witch Trials still interest people today.

(E) It details several ways that the trials could have been prevented.

36. The final paragraph (sentence 9–14) could best be developed by

(A) elaborating on the idea that fear can motivate people into taking action

(B) explaining the differences between the new and established settlers living in Salem

(C) describing the character of the women accused of bewitching the girls

(D) adding information about Linnda Caporael's academic credentials

(E) adding information about other fungi that can affect the mind

37. The first item listed in the References section indicates all of the following EXCEPT that

(A) "Ergotism: The Satan Loosed in Salem?" is about six pages long

(B) "Ergotism: The Satan Loosed in Salem?" was first published in 1976

(C) "Ergotism: The Satan Loosed in Salem?" was written by Linnda Caporael

(D) "Ergotism: The Satan Loosed in Salem?" was included in volume 192 of Science

(E) "Ergotism: The Satan Loosed in Salem?" is an article that was originally published online

Rhetorical Analysis

Directions: Each of the following passages consists of numbered sentences. Because the passages are part of longer writing samples, they do not necessarily constitute a complete discussion of the issue presented.

Read each passage carefully and answer the questions that follow it. The questions test your awareness of a writer's purpose and of characteristics of prose that are important to good writing.

Questions 38–42 refer to the following paragraphs.

(1) Countless events in European history have shaped what we know today as the modern world. (2) Few of these events, however, had as much of an impact of the formation of modern society as the French Revolution. (3) Many historians, in fact, view the French Revolution as the very dawn of modern society. (4) The changes brought on by the revolution had a profound effect on life in France, Europe, and, eventually, around the world. (5) The fundamental shift in thinking spurred on by the French Revolution sparked a worldwide revolution that led to the modern era.

(6) In the eighteenth century, French society was divided into three classes called estates. (7) The First and Second Estates were comprised of the clergy and aristocracy, while the Third Estate was comprised of the country's common people. (8) By the last quarter of the century, conditions had become all but unbearable for the Third Estate. (9) Financial instability led to widespread poverty among the lower class and drastically deficient food supplies meant many people were starving. (10) In addition, the First and Second Estates appears to be completely indifferent to the sufferings of the Third Estate. (11) Eventually, the Third Estate could take no more and, in 1789, the revolution began. (12) Within just a few years, the monarchy was overthrown and history was made.

(13) The fall of the French monarchy marked a significant change in the European way of life. (14) Traditional beliefs about government were transformed and the idea of monarchial rule was dispatched in favor of more balanced forms of government. (15)

Enlightenment ideals such as citizenship and inalienable rights swept across Europe and radically altered life all over the continent. (16) The transformation of Europe inspired similar transformation across the globe and, eventually, yielded today's modern world.

38. In context, sentences 9 and 10 serve to
    (A) explain the effects of the French Revolution
    (B) illustrate the conditions that sparked the French Revolution
    (C) explain the point of view held by the First and Second Estates
    (D) imply that the French Revolution was imitated under false pretenses
    (E) describe the state of affairs in Europe before the revolution began

39. In the context of the passage, which of the following transition words or phrases, if inserted at the beginning of sentence 16, would be the most logical?
    (A) Although,
    (B) Regardless,
    (C) Notwithstanding,
    (D) Moreover,
    (E) Nonetheless,

40. Which of the following best describes the function of paragraph 2?

(A) It suggests a theory about the impact of the French Revolution.

(B) It describes the resultant global effects of the French Revolution.

(C) It explains the circumstances and events of the French Revolution.

(D) It provides supporting evidence for a theory about the French Revolution.

(E) It offers an alternative explanation for the results of the French Revolution.

41. In context, sentence 3 serves to

(A) support a claim made in the previous sentence

(B) suggest a reason for an assertion made by the author

(C) provide a link between two separate thoughts in the paragraph

(D) disprove an alternative theory that differs from the author's

(E) introduce an idea to follow later in the paragraph

42. Which of the following best describes the function of sentence 13?

(A) It summarizes the information presented about the French Revolution in paragraph 2.

(B) It links the events described in paragraph 2 with the assertions about its effects in paragraph 3.

(C) It refutes the theory suggested in paragraph 1 and supports a new one in paragraph 3.

(D) It illustrates the author's hypothesis about the revolution suggested in paragraph 2.

(E) It further explains the causes of the French Revolution as stated in paragraph 2.

Questions 43–47 refer to the following passage.

(1) For more than a century, the Statue of Liberty has been an enduring symbol of freedom for people around the world. (2) Although this green lady has welcomed many visitors to our shores, most people are surprised to learn that the Statue of Liberty was originally the color bronze. (3) So, what gives this statue its famous green hue? (4) The answer may surprise you.

(5) The Statue of Liberty is made of copper, a malleable metal that has a variety of uses. (6) Copper is commonly used to make coins, pipes, wires, and even musical instruments. (7) In most cases, copper metal starts out as a bronze color. (8) However, if left exposed to the elements, copper can turn a pale green color through a process called patina. (9) Patina occurs when copper reacts with water and oxygen in the atmosphere. (10) Over time, the copper develops a thin layer of patina, which actually protects the copper underneath from environmental damage.

43. Which of the following best describes the organization of the passage as a whole?

(A) A procedure is introduced and then described in more detail.

(B) A problem is presented and a solution is evaluated.

(C) A question is asked and then an answer is presented.

(D) A fact is presented and then discussed in detail.

(E) An approach is presented and proved to be reliable.

44. Which of the following best describes sentence 1?

(A) It gives the thesis of the passage.

(B) It discusses a well-known American symbol.

(C) It gives the color of a well-known American symbol.

(D) It describes an opposing view of a famous symbol.

(E) It explores the connections between symbols and freedom.

45. The author's primary purpose in mentioning the original color of the Statue of Liberty in sentence 2 is to

(A) show that the color of the statue has remained the same

(B) identify the material used to construct the statue

(C) argue that the status is now in need of repair

(D) explain that the statue looks different today

(E) make a point about the low quality of copper

46. In context, sentence 4 serves to

(A) act as a transition between the first paragraph and the second paragraph

(B) provide an answer to a question that was previously asked

(C) highlight the importance of the information just stated

(D) defend a common point of view about the Statue of Liberty

(E) show that most people don't know the Statue of Liberty's original color

47. In context, "commonly" (sentence 6) most nearly means

(A) painstakingly

(B) friendly

(C) annually

(D) simply

(E) usually

Questions 48–50 refer to the following passage.

(1) Every day, millions of people around the world start their mornings with a steaming cup of fresh coffee. (2) In fact, many people find it nearly impossible to get going without a cup of morning Joe. (3) Americans spend billions of dollars on coffee every year, making it the second most profitable natural commodity in the world, behind petroleum. (4) Although coffee is now one of the most popular beverages across the globe, it only became known to the Western world during the seventeenth century.

(5) According to legend, an Ethiopian goat herder was the first person to discover the simulative properties of the coffee bean. (6) One day, a goat herder named Kaldi noticed that his goats were leaping excitedly after eating the berries from a coffee bush. (7) Curious, Kaldi tried a few and quickly realized the energizing powers of the berries. (8) Soon, people across Africa and the Middle East were using the beans inside the berries to brew a broth, which was the precursor to what we now call coffee. (9) Eventually, people began roasting the tiny beans to create a stronger beverage.

(10) Europeans discovered coffee when a Venetian merchant traveled to Turkey and brought coffee back to Italy with him. (11) From here, the bold beverage spread across Europe like wildfire.

48. The passage is primarily concerned with

(A) refuting a common legend

(B) detailing the history of coffee

(C) explaining the popularity of coffee

(D) arguing for a particular point of view

(E) exploring how certain beverages are made

49. According to the passage, the goats' behavior led to the

(A) sale of coffee throughout Europe

(B) use of coffee as a morning beverage

(C) discovery of coffee's energizing properties

(D) feeding of other berries to animals

(E) dependence of people on caffeine

50. The discussion of the popularity of coffee in sentence 3 serves to

(A) describe the concerns of the coffee industry

(B) extend on a metaphor from sentence 1

(C) introduce the main topic for discussion

(D) summarize the history of coffee

(E) emphasize the importance of caffeine to Americans

PART II

70 minutes

The Essays

Essay 1

Sample Topic 1

It's foolish to try to change someone's mind.

Directions: Write an essay in which you discuss the extent to which you agree or disagree with the statement above. Support your discussion with specific reasons and examples from your reading, experience, or observations.

Essay 2

Sample Topic 2

Directions: The following assignment requires you to write a coherent essay in which you synthesize the two sources provided. Synthesis refers to combining the sources and your position to form a cohesive, supported argument. You must develop a position and incorporate both sources. You must cite the sources whether you are paraphrasing or quoting. Refer to each source by the author's last name, by the title, or by any other means that adequately identifies it.

Introduction

One of the most controversial topics in today's society is whether United States immigrants should be required to learn English. Although many people believe that all citizens of this country should speak English, others argue that the melting pot of different cultures and languages is one of the things that makes American unique.

Assignment

Read the following sources carefully. Then write an essay in which you develop a position on whether immigrants to the United States should be required to learn English. Be sure to incorporate and cite both of the accompanying sources as you develop your position.

Albert, George. "The English Issue." *America Monthly,* May 20, 2010, 18–19.

The following passage is excerpted from an article in a news magazine.

There are many practical reasons why United States immigrants should be required to learn English. The first, and possibly most important, reason that immigrants should learn the language is that a basic understanding of English is necessary to pass the citizenship test. Of course, certain factors allow some immigrants to be exempt from English testing. These immigrants should still learn English because this is the language that most of the American population speaks. Many immigrants come to our shores in search of the American dream. If part of that dream includes obtaining a higher level of education and finding a good job, then learning English isn't just important, it's necessary.

Some people worry that this requirement is a form of discrimination, but this couldn't be further from the truth. Requiring immigrants to learn English will help them to easily assimilate into our culture. This doesn't mean that immigrants would be barred from speaking their native tongues. It simply means that they would be required to have a basic understanding of the English language so that they could communicate with their neighbors, coworkers, and customers. This requirement isn't meant to punish immigrants; it's designed to help them succeed.

Jameson, McKenna. *America: The Melting Pot.* Chicago: Westside Press, 2009.

The following passage is excerpted from a book on American culture.

Surprisingly, most Americans don't know that the United States doesn't have an official language. While English has been the *de facto* language of the land since first being colonized by Great Britain, there is no legal document proclaiming English as our national tongue. Efforts in the past to institute English as the national language have been rejected. In 1780, the Continental Congress quickly dismissed John Adams's proposal to use English as the national language, fearing that such action would infringe on the personal liberties of American citizens.

With this information in mind, it seems unfair to require immigrants to learn English, which isn't even the official language of this country. Many of our ancestors came to these shores without knowing a single word of English. Some of them learned the language later, while others continued to speak, read, and write in their native tongues. The point is, most of them got along just fine, whether they learned English or not. In fact, many of these immigrants made important contributions to our culture. Many foreign words and phrases have become a part of the English language because of their frequent use by immigrants.

ANSWER KEY AND EXPLANATIONS

Part I

1. D	11. E	21. A	31. D	41. A
2. C	12. E	22. A	32. B	42. B
3. D	13. B	23. B	33. A	43. C
4. A	14. C	24. C	34. E	44. B
5. E	15. D	25. C	35. C	45. D
6. D	16. B	26. E	36. C	46. A
7. B	17. A	27. D	37. E	47. E
8. E	18. A	28. E	38. B	48. B
9. A	19. C	29. A	39. D	49. C
10. C	20. E	30. C	40. C	50. C

1. **The correct answer is (D).** The sentence is written in the future perfect tense, so the verb *reached* should be written in the present tense as *reach*.

2. **The correct answer is (C).** The word *we* is plural, so the plural verb *have purchased* is needed.

3. **The correct answer is (D).** *Vein* is used incorrectly in this sentence. *Vein* refers to a blood vessel. The correct word to use in this case would be *vain*, which means to exhibit excessive pride in oneself.

4. **The correct answer is (A).** The word *its* is used incorrectly in this sentence. *Its* is a possessive pronoun and should be replaced with *it's*, which is a contraction for *it is*.

5. **The correct answer is (E).** This sentence contains no errors.

6. **The correct answer is (D).** The subject of this sentence, *incidents*, is plural. Therefore, a plural helping verb is required.

7. **The correct answer is (B).** The best revision is *Teachers' classes are constantly being disrupted by unruly students*. The other choices have awkward sentence construction or contain grammatical errors.

8. **The correct answer is (E).** The subject of the sentence, *students*, is plural, but the pronouns *his or her* are singular. *His or her* should be replaced with the plural pronoun *their*.

9. **The correct answer is (A).** The phrase *to permit this kind of behavior* is wordy. A more concise way to write the phrase is permitting this behavior.

10. **The correct answer is (C).** Choice (C) is the most appropriate option because a colon is used to separate an explanation from a preceding independent clause. The independent clause in this sentence is *We believe that the solution to the ongoing behavior problem is simple* and the solution is *the current discipline system must be revised*.

11. **The correct answer is (E).** The phrase *students' bad behavior* is the best choice to replace the underlined portion of the sentence because it isn't wordy or awkward.

12. **The correct answer is (E).** The world *clearly* would best be used at the beginning of sentence 9 because it implies that forcing student to spend an extra hour at school has obviously not had any effect.

13. **The correct answer is (B).** The phrase *awareness of students* is wordy and awkward. It would best be replaced by *students' awareness,* which is clearer and correctly uses the plural possessive form of *student.*

14. **The correct answer is (C).** The two portions of sentence 13 (*We believe that if such alternatives are instated* and *student behavior will improve school-wide*) form a single, complete thought and, as such, should be separated by a comma.

15. **The correct is answer is (D).** The best revision to this sentence is *Ultimately, a well-behaved student body will make our school a better place to learn.* The other choices have awkward, wordy sentence construction.

16. **The correct answer is (B).** The amendment has not been passed yet, so the correct verb form is *will require.*

17. **The correct answer is (A).** Choice (B) is incorrect because a comma should precede an introductory phrase. Choice (C) would not match the tense of the sentence. Choices (D) and (E) would be too informal for an editorial in the local newspaper.

18. **The correct answer is (A).** The subject of this sentence is the gerund phrase *Asking students to commit such a large block of time to volunteering.* This phrase should be following by the singular verb *seems.*

19. **The correct answer is (C).** Choice (C) is correct because the conjunction *but* properly combines the two ideas.

20. **The correct answer is (E).** Choice (E) is correct because the colon would improve the audience's comprehension of the sentence.

21. **The correct answer is (A).** The sentence is correct as is.

22. **The correct answer is (A).** The *school board* is a collective noun; therefore, it needs a singular pronoun; choice (A) is the best answer because *its* is a singular pronoun.

23. **The correct answer is (B).** None of the other choices describe what the entire editorial is about. They only refer to certain parts of the editorial. The best title for this passage is "Community Service Could Do More Harm Than Good," choice (B), because this title captures the main idea of the essay.

24. **The correct answer is (C).** This is the only choice that combines the two sentences without changing the original meaning of either. Some of the sentences in the answer choices also have awkward construction.

25. **The correct answer is (C).** Choice (C) is the best answer because the previous sentence discusses test scores.

26. **The correct answer is (E).** Choice (E) is the only statement that cannot be supported by the definition. The definition says that a slug can be made of plastic or metal.

27. **The correct answer is (D).** Choice (D) is correct because the date the article was published is a required part of the citation.

28. **The correct answer is (E).** The phrase "Et al." is used to tell the reader that multiple authors worked on this paper; therefore, you know that choice (E), *and other,* is correct.

29. **The correct answer is (A).** The abbreviation "Ed." means "editor" when it is used in a reference. Choice (A) is correct because "Ed." indicates the editor of the collection.

30. **The correct answer is (C).** The Web site address should alert the reader that this is an online journal, which is choice (C). Choices (A), (B), (D), and (E) are incorrect because these publications do not require Web addresses in their citations.

31. **The correct answer is (D).** Choice (D) is correct because the information in the parentheses indicates it is an in-text citation for a work that King wrote about the Salem witch trials.

32. **The correct answer is (B).** The best answer is choice (B) because the quotation discusses how the Puritans' belief in evil caused them to react the way they did.

33. **The correct answer is (A).** While the author uses the quote, he or she does not indicate the source of the quote; a full reference is not included for Aisha Whitmore. Therefore, you can determine that the author should add a citation indicating the source of the quotation from Whitmore, which is choice (A).

34. **The correct answer is (E).** Choice (E) is the right answer because only information about the Puritan belief system would explain why the rumors lead to the Salem witch trials.

35. **The correct answer is (C).** Choice (C) is correct because the first paragraph mentions the two girls who were thought to be "bewitched," and this idea is further described in the last paragraph.

36. **The correct answer is (C).** The paragraph mentions only that the girls accused three women of bewitching them; it does not give any information about these women. Choice (C) is the most closely related to the subject matter of the third paragraph.

37. **The correct answer is (E).** All of the answer choices are correct EXCEPT for choice (E). Authors who include articles that were originally published online must include Web addresses for the sites where these articles first appeared.

38. **The correct answer is (B).** Choice (B) is correct because sentences 9 and 10 describe the severe conditions under which the people of the Third Estate were forced to live prior to the revolution. The other choices are all incorrect based on the information in the paragraph.

39. **The correct answer is (D).** Sentence 16 adds information that builds on the previous sentence's assertion about the effects of the French Revolution. Use of the word *moreover* would suggest an extension of the author's previous thought, so choice (D) is correct. None of the other choices would logically fit into the sentence.

40. **The correct answer is (C).** Choice (C) is the best answer because paragraph 2 clearly serves only to provide a specific explanation of the circumstances that led to the French Revolution and its direct result.

41. **The correct answer is (A).** Choice (A) is the correct answer because sentence 3 offers information that supports the author's previous claim that the French Revolution had a significant impact on modern society.

42. **The correct answer is (B).** Choice (B) is the correct answer because the sentence connects the fall of the French monarch with the author's assertions about this event that follow.

43. **The correct answer is (C).** Choice (C) is correct because in the first paragraph, the author asks a question, and in the rest of the article the author answers that question.

44. **The correct answer is (B).** Choice (B) is correct because the sentence talks about the Statue of Liberty, which is a well-known American symbol.

45. **The correct answer is (D).** Choice (D) is correct because the author says that the statue used to be the color bronze but is currently green; therefore, the author wants the audience to know the statue looks different today.

46. **The correct answer is (A).** Choice (A) is correct because the sentence hints that the rest of the essay will answer the question posed in the first part of the essay.

47. The correct answer is (E). In context, the word "commonly" is referring to something that is done regularly or often, so you can determine the word most nearly means "usually," which is choice (E). The other choices do not fit within the context of the sentence.

48. The correct answer is (B). Choice (B) is the best answer because the essay discusses coffee's history.

49. The correct answer is (C). While choices (A), (B), (D), and (E) eventually took place, the initial result of the goats' behavior was the discovery of coffee's energizing properties, which is choice (C).

50. The correct answer is (C). Choice (C) is the best answer because the sentence states that millions of people drink coffee, indicating to the audience that essay will most likely be about coffee.

Part II

Essay 1

Scoring Guide: College Composition Examination for Essay 1
Readers will assign scores based on the following scoring guide.

6—A 6 essay demonstrates a high degree of competence and sustained control, although it may have a few minor errors.

A typical essay in this category

- addresses all elements of the writing task effectively and insightfully
- develops ideas thoroughly, supporting them with well-chosen reasons, examples, or details
- is well focused and well organized
- demonstrates superior facility with language, using effective vocabulary and sentence variety
- demonstrates general mastery of the standard conventions of grammar, usage, and mechanics but may have minor errors

---

5—A 5 essay demonstrates a generally high degree of competence, although it will have occasional lapses in quality.

A typical essay in this category

- addresses the writing task effectively
- is well developed, using appropriate reasons, examples, or details to support ideas
- is generally well focused and well organized
- demonstrates facility with language, using appropriate vocabulary and some sentence variety
- demonstrates strong control of the standard conventions of grammar, usage, and mechanics but may have minor errors

---

4—A 4 essay demonstrates clear competence, with some errors or lapses in quality.

A typical essay in this category

- addresses the writing task competently
- is adequately developed, using reasons, examples, or details to support ideas
- is adequately focused and organized
- demonstrates competence with language, using adequate vocabulary and minimal sentence variety
- generally demonstrates control of the standard conventions of grammar, usage and mechanics but may have some errors

---

3—A 3 essay demonstrates limited competence.

A typical essay in this category exhibits ONE OR MORE of the following weaknesses:

- addresses only some parts of the writing task
- develops unevenly and often provides assertions but few relevant reasons, examples, or details
- is poorly focused and/or poorly organized
- displays frequent problems in the use of language
- demonstrates inconsistent control of grammar, usage, and mechanics

2—A 2 essay is seriously flawed.

A typical essay in this category exhibits ONE OR MORE of the following weaknesses:

- is unclear or seriously limited in addressing the writing task
- is seriously underdeveloped, providing few reasons, examples, or details
- is unfocused and/or disorganized
- displays frequent serious errors in the use of language that interfere with meaning
- contains frequent serious errors in grammar, usage, and mechanics that may interfere with meaning

1—A 1 essay is fundamentally deficient.

A typical essay in this category exhibits ONE OR MORE of the following weaknesses:

- provides little or no evidence of the ability to develop an organized response to the writing task
- is underdeveloped
- contains severe writing errors that persistently interfere with meaning

0—Off topic.

Provides no evidence of an attempt to respond to the assigned topic, is written in a language other than English, merely copies the prompt, or consists of only keystroke characters.

Sample Essay

Note: Errors in the sample essays are intentionally reproduced.

This essay is scored at a 6.

I disagree with the statement that it's foolish to try to change someone's mind. While I agree that changing someone's opinion on a certain topic or belief can be difficult, it's not impossible. People have the right to their own opinions, but, in some cases, it is necessary to try to influence their thoughts to enact positive change.

Think about how the world would be different if people didn't try to create change by influencing others. If everyone agreed that it's foolish to try to change people's minds, then nothing would ever get accomplished. Some of the most important events in history would not have taken place.

One example of this is the fight to end slavery in the United States. For years, abolitionists worked to end slavery by writing letters, giving speeches, and protesting the sale of slaves throughout the United States. The ability of such actions to influence others is clearly seen in the work of abolitionists such as William Lloyd Garrison and Lydia Maria Child.

For more than thirty years, Garrison published The Liberator, an antislavery newspaper that called for the immediate release of all slaves, as well as their assimilation into American society. This idea was certainly not popular when Garrison started publishing in the 1830s, yet he continued writing and speaking about these ideas over the years. Eventually, Garrison's work influenced Lydia Maria Child to devote her life to abolitionism. Child would go on to pen a book about abolition and to fight for the rights of slaves for the rest of her life.

People like Garrison and Child were highly influential in the passage of the Emancipation Proclamation. After the Civil War broke out, President Abraham Lincoln's major concern was ending the fighting and preserving the Union. He believed in emancipation, but he also worried about losing the support of border slave states that had sided with the Union. Abolitionists, however, wanted the president to abolish slavery throughout the country. The president received countless letters from both prominent abolitionists and regular citizens calling for an emancipation proclamation. This strategy worked, and Lincoln eventually issued the proclamation. Without people like Garrison and Child working to change the opinions of others, slavery might have continued.

Of course, you don't need to look to history to see an example of how people can change the minds of others; the evidence for this can be found in every school across America. Organizations like Students Against Destructive Decisions (S.A.D.D.) and Drug Abuse Resistance Education (D.A.R.E) work to help students make positive decisions in various aspects of their lives. If these organizations can change one student's mind about taking drugs or drinking and driving, then their efforts have not been in vain. It is certainly not foolish to try to show students the consequences of participating in such destructive behaviors.

In our everyday lives, we often encounter people who have strong opinions about certain political or social issues. In these cases, yes, it might be foolish to try to change one person's mind in the course of a single conversation. Many times, these types of communications deteriorate into shouting matches between the two parties. However, this doesn't mean that we should all keep our thoughts and opinions to ourselves because we're never going to change the opinions of others. The free expression of different opinions is the only way that real change ever occurs.

In conclusion, trying to change someone's mind isn't foolish, it's necessary if we are to continue to evolve as a society. In the grand scheme of things, it would be more foolish to not attempt to change people's minds, especially when the issue at hand involves the well-being of all.

Essay 2

Scoring Guide: College Composition Examination for Essay 2
Readers will assign scores based on the following scoring guide.

6—A 6 essay demonstrates a high degree of competence and sustained control, although it may have a few minor errors.

A typical essay in this category:

- cites sources appropriately
- develops a position effectively and insightfully, using well-chosen reasons, examples, or details for support
- synthesizes* both sources effectively with an effective and convincing link between the sources and the position
- is well focused and well organized
- demonstrates superior facility with language, using effective vocabulary and sentence variety
- demonstrates general mastery of the standard conventions of grammar, usage, and mechanics but may have minor errors

---

5—A 5 essay demonstrates a generally high degree of competence, although it will have occasional lapses in quality.

A typical essay in this category:

- cites sources appropriately
- develops a position consistently, using appropriate reasons, examples, or details for support
- synthesizes both sources clearly, with a clear link between the sources and the position
- is generally well focused and well organized
- demonstrates facility with language, using appropriate vocabulary and some sentence variety
- demonstrates strong control of the standard conventions of grammar, usage, and mechanics but may have minor errors

---

4—A 4 essay demonstrates competence, with some errors and lapses in quality.

A typical essay in this category:

- cites sources appropriately
- develops a position adequately, using reasons, examples, or details for support
- synthesizes both sources adequately, using reasons, examples, or details for support
- is adequately focused and organized
- demonstrates competence with language, using adequate vocabulary and minimal sentence variety
- generally demonstrates control of the standard conventions of grammar, usage, and mechanics but may have some errors

3—A 3 essay demonstrates limited competence.

A typical essay in this category exhibits ONE OR MORE of the following weaknesses:

- develops a position unevenly, often using assertions rather than relevant reasons, examples, or details for support
- synthesizes one source only or two sources inadequately, or establishes an inadequate link between the source(s) and the position
- displays problems in citing sources: citations are confusing or incomplete
- is poorly focused and/or poorly organized
- displays frequent problems in the use of language
- demonstrates inconsistent control of grammar, usage, and mechanics

2—A 2 essay is seriously flawed.

A typical essay in this category exhibits ONE OR MORE of the following weaknesses:

- is seriously underdeveloped, providing few or no relevant reasons, examples, or details for support
- synthesizes only one source weakly or establishes a very weak link between the source(s) and the position
- does not cite any source
- is unfocused and/or disorganized
- displays frequent serious errors in the use of language that may interfere with meaning
- contains frequent serious errors in grammar, usage, and mechanics that may interfere with meaning

1—A 1 essay is fundamentally deficient.

A typical essay in this category exhibits ONE OR MORE of the following weaknesses:

- does not develop a position
- fails to synthesize the source(s) used or uses no sources at all
- contains severe writing errors that persistently interfere with meaning

0—Off topic

Provides no evidence of an attempt to respond to the assigned topic, is written in a language other than English, merely copies the prompt, or consists of only keystroke characters.

*For the purpose of scoring, synthesis refers to combining sources and writer's position to form a cohesive, supported argument.

Sample Essay

Note: Errors in the sample essays are intentionally reproduced.

This essay is scored a 6.

For hundreds of years, Americans have used English as our primary form of communication. Both the Declaration of Independence and the Constitution, two of our most important historical documents, are in English. Our street signs, emergency warning systems, and historical landmarks all use the English language to communicate with the public. English is a part of our everyday lives, and, therefore, immigrants to this country should be required to have at least a basic understanding of the language.

As George Albert points out in his article "The English Issue," immigrants should learn English because "a basic understanding of English is necessary in order to pass the citizenship test." Since English is an important part of becoming a citizen, asking immigrants to learn the language doesn't seem like it should cause so much controversy. However, "[s]ome people worry that this requirement is a form of discrimination" (Albert). Some people wonder if asking immigrants to learn English is an attack on foreign cultures. As Albert suggests, asking immigrants to learn English doesn't bar them from "speaking their native tongues." This requirement is designed to help immigrants assimilate into American society, which is the goal of many new citizens.

McKenna Jameson, however, disagrees with Albert's point of view. In her book America: The Melting Pot, Jameson notes that the United States does not actually have an official langudge the way that many other countries do. The author argues that it is hypocritical of us to ask immigrants to learn English when it is not this country's official language. Jameson does point out that English is our country's "de facto language." This

is an important distinction. The term "de facto" means "being such in effect though not formally recognized." Often for something to become de facto, a majority of the population must agree to it. This means that a large portion of the American public feels that English is the country's official language, no matter what the law actually says.

Jameson also points out that many of our ancestors did not know English when they immigrated to the United States. She believes that "most of them got along just fine, whether they learned English or not." While this may be true, Jameson forgets that many of these immigrants settled in ethnic communities where knowing English wasn't necessary to survive and thrive. Though these communities still exist in larger urban areas, there are not as many as there once were. Many modern immigrants are likely to live in areas of the country were English is the predominant language.

Jameson also seems to think that requiring immigrants to learn English will somehow diminish the wonderful contributions that immigrants make to our society and our language. Again, it is important to point out requiring immigrants to learn English isn't an effort to stamp out their cultural heritage. This is a country of immigrants, and our people often celebrate the traditions of various cultures. As Albert believes, the English requirement "isn't meant to punish immigrants; it's designed to help them succeed."

In conclusion, this country was founded on the idea that people could settle here and be free from the political and religious restrictions forced on them by other countries. Requiring immigrants to learn English doesn't go against this idea. Learning English will help immigrants thrive and will allow them to contribute new ideas and traditions to our society, just as our ancestors did long ago.

PART III
COLLEGE MATHEMATICS

PRETEST ANSWER SHEET

1. Ⓐ Ⓑ Ⓒ Ⓓ	11. Ⓐ Ⓑ Ⓒ Ⓓ	21. Ⓐ Ⓑ Ⓒ Ⓓ	31. Ⓐ Ⓑ Ⓒ Ⓓ	41. Ⓐ Ⓑ Ⓒ Ⓓ
2. Ⓐ Ⓑ Ⓒ Ⓓ	12. Ⓐ Ⓑ Ⓒ Ⓓ	22. Ⓐ Ⓑ Ⓒ Ⓓ	32. Ⓐ Ⓑ Ⓒ Ⓓ	42. Ⓐ Ⓑ Ⓒ Ⓓ
3. Ⓐ Ⓑ Ⓒ Ⓓ	13. Ⓐ Ⓑ Ⓒ Ⓓ	23. Ⓐ Ⓑ Ⓒ Ⓓ	33. Ⓐ Ⓑ Ⓒ Ⓓ	43. Ⓐ Ⓑ Ⓒ Ⓓ
4. Ⓐ Ⓑ Ⓒ Ⓓ	14. Ⓐ Ⓑ Ⓒ Ⓓ	24. Ⓐ Ⓑ Ⓒ Ⓓ	34. Ⓐ Ⓑ Ⓒ Ⓓ	44. Ⓐ Ⓑ Ⓒ Ⓓ
5. Ⓐ Ⓑ Ⓒ Ⓓ	15. Ⓐ Ⓑ Ⓒ Ⓓ	25. Ⓐ Ⓑ Ⓒ Ⓓ	35. Ⓐ Ⓑ Ⓒ Ⓓ	45. Ⓐ Ⓑ Ⓒ Ⓓ
6. Ⓐ Ⓑ Ⓒ Ⓓ	16. Ⓐ Ⓑ Ⓒ Ⓓ	26. Ⓐ Ⓑ Ⓒ Ⓓ	36. Ⓐ Ⓑ Ⓒ Ⓓ	46. Ⓐ Ⓑ Ⓒ Ⓓ
7. Ⓐ Ⓑ Ⓒ Ⓓ	17. Ⓐ Ⓑ Ⓒ Ⓓ	27. Ⓐ Ⓑ Ⓒ Ⓓ	37. Ⓐ Ⓑ Ⓒ Ⓓ	47. Ⓐ Ⓑ Ⓒ Ⓓ
8. Ⓐ Ⓑ Ⓒ Ⓓ	18. Ⓐ Ⓑ Ⓒ Ⓓ	28. Ⓐ Ⓑ Ⓒ Ⓓ	38. Ⓐ Ⓑ Ⓒ Ⓓ	48. Ⓐ Ⓑ Ⓒ Ⓓ
9. Ⓐ Ⓑ Ⓒ Ⓓ	19. Ⓐ Ⓑ Ⓒ Ⓓ	29. Ⓐ Ⓑ Ⓒ Ⓓ	39. Ⓐ Ⓑ Ⓒ Ⓓ	49. Ⓐ Ⓑ Ⓒ Ⓓ
10. Ⓐ Ⓑ Ⓒ Ⓓ	20. Ⓐ Ⓑ Ⓒ Ⓓ	30. Ⓐ Ⓑ Ⓒ Ⓓ	40. Ⓐ Ⓑ Ⓒ Ⓓ	50. Ⓐ Ⓑ Ⓒ Ⓓ

answer sheet

Pretest

75 minutes • 50 questions

Directions: Each of the questions or incomplete statements below is followed by four suggested answers or completions. Select the one that is best in each case.

1. How many factors are included in the prime factorization of 840?

   [   ]

2. Given $f(x) = x - 9$ and $g(x) = 2x - 7$,

   what is $g(f(x))$?

   (A) $2x - 16$

   (B) $2x - 32$

   (C) $2x - 2$

   (D) $2x - 25$

3. If $a \div b$, which of the following must be true?

   (A) $a \div (b + c)$

   (B) $a \div (b - c)$

   (C) $a \div bc$

   (D) $a \div c$

4. Which of the following truth table columns correctly represents $p \wedge \sim q$?

   (A)

$p \wedge \sim q$
F
T
F
F

   (B)

$p \wedge \sim q$
T
T
F
T

   (C)

$p \wedge \sim q$
F
T
T
F

   (D)

$p \wedge \sim q$
T
F
T
T

   7, 11, 4, 9, 13, 12, 8, 5, 10, 6, 3, 11

5. The number of dogs from a local pet shelter receiving homes each month is shown above. Which of the following best represents the standard deviation of the number of dogs receiving homes each month?

   (A) 3.28

   (B) 3.04

   (C) 3.48

   (D) 3.16

$$-3x + 18 = 12$$
$$4x - 9 = -1$$

6. Which of the following represents the solution to the system of linear equations shown above?

   (A) $x = -1$

   (B) $x = 3$

   (C) $x = 4$

   (D) $x = 2$

7. Which of the following rules can be used to determine if a number is divisible by 3?

   (A) If the digit in the ones place is divisible by 3, then the number is divisible by 3.

   (B) If the sum of the digits is divisible by 3, then the number is divisible by 3.

   (C) If the last two digits in the number are divisible by 3, then the number is divisible by 3.

   (D) If the product of the digits is divisible by 3, then the number is divisible by 3.

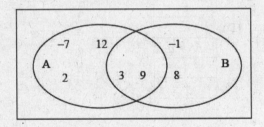

8. Given the Venn diagram above, which of the following represents $A \cap B$?

   (A) $\{-7, 2, 12, 3, 9, -1, 8\}$

   (B) $\varnothing$

   (C) $\{3, 9\}$

   (D) $\{-1, 8, -7, 2, 12\}$

9. Which of the following graphs represents the solution to the inequality $12x - 3y \geq 6$?

(A)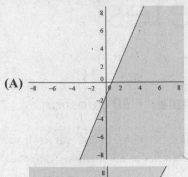

(B)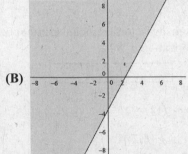

(C)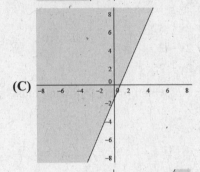

(D)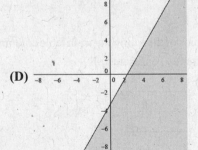

1028, 1056, 1011, 1046, 1019, 1041, 1058, 1022, 1051, 1096, 1021, 1047

10. The number of water bottles donated per month to a local charity is shown above. What is the median number of water bottles donated?

(A) 1041.5

(B) 1043.5

(C) 1047.5

(D) 1049.5

11. Elizabeth rolls a 6-sided die and flips a coin. What is the probability that she rolls a number less than 5 and gets tails?

(A) $\frac{1}{4}$

(B) $\frac{1}{3}$

(C) $\frac{1}{2}$

(D) $\frac{1}{8}$

12. Which of the following represents the product of $16i$ and $(3 + 2i)$?

(A) $32 - 48i$

(B) $-48 + 32i$

(C) $-32 + 48i$

(D) $48 - 32i$

13. Which of the following parent functions has a range of all real numbers?

(A) $f(x) = x$

(B) $f(x) = x^2$

(C) $f(x) = \frac{1}{x}$

(D) $f(x) = |x|$

14. Given the equation $\log_9(3x - 3) = 6$, write the solution for x.

[   ]

If Amanda drives to work, then it is a weekday.

15. Which of the following represents the inverse of the statement above?

(A) If it is not a weekday, then Amanda does not drive to work.

(B) If it is not a weekday, then Amanda drives to work.

(C) If Amanda does not drive to work, then it is not a weekday.

(D) If it is a weekday, then Amanda drives to work.

16. Which of the following is the correct simplification of $\log_8 512^x$?

(A) $2x$

(B) $12x$

(C) $6x$

(D) $3x$

17. The probability of having a conference call or having a conference call at 1:00 is 0.38. The probability of having a conference call is 0.29, and the probability of having a conference call at 1:00 is 0.18. What is the probability of having a conference call and having a conference call at 1:00?

[   ]

Student Classification	Coffee Shop A	Coffee Shop B
Freshman	21	28
Sophomore	32	19
Junior	13	17
Senior	28	32

18. The table above shows the number of college students who prefer Coffee Shop A and Coffee Shop B. What is the probability that a student who prefers Coffee Shop B is a junior?

(A) $\frac{17}{96}$

(B) $\frac{17}{94}$

(C) $\frac{17}{30}$

(D) $\frac{5}{16}$

19. Which of the following equations represents a stretching of the graph of the parent function $g(x) = x^2$ and a shift to the left?

(A) $g(x) = (2x - 2)^2$

(B) $g(x) = \left(\dfrac{1}{2}x + 2\right)^2$

(C) $g(x) = \dfrac{1}{2}x^2 + 2$

(D) $g(x) = 2x^2 - 2$

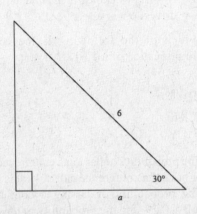

20. Given the triangle above, what is the length of side a?

(A) 3

(B) $2\sqrt{3}$

(C) $3\sqrt{2}$

(D) $3\sqrt{3}$

21. Four students define a rational number according to the following descriptions.
   I. A rational number is non-repeating and non-terminating.
   II. A rational number is repeating and terminating.
   III. A rational number can be expressed as the ratio, $\dfrac{a}{b}$, where $b \neq 0$.
   IV. A rational number is repeating or terminating.

Which of the descriptions are true?

(A) I and III only

(B) II and III only

(C) III only

(D) III and IV only

22. Which of the following statements are true?
   I. Only odd numbers may be prime.
   II. All even numbers are multiples of 2.
   III. The real number system is finite, in terms of numbers included.

(A) I only

(B) I and II only

(C) II only

(D) I, II, and III

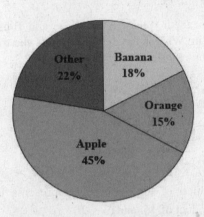

23. A total of 300 students are surveyed to determine their favorite fruit. The circle graph above shows the results of the survey. Based on the graphs, which of the following statements is true?

(A) 79 fewer students chose "Other" than "Apple."

(B) 20 fewer students chose "Orange" than "Other."

(C) 90 more students chose "Apple" than "Orange."

(D) 10 more students chose "Orange" than "Banana."

If Hannah mows the yard, then it is Tuesday.

24. Which of the following represents the negation of the statement above?

(A) Hannah does not mow the yard, and it is Tuesday.

(B) It is not Tuesday, and Hannah does not mow the yard.

(C) Hannah does not mow the yard, and it is not Tuesday.

(D) Hannah mows the yard, and it is not Tuesday.

25. Which of the following angles is coterminal with $-20°$?

    (A) $380°$

    (B) $-730°$

    (C) $340°$

    (D) $-400°$

26. Given $f(x) = \dfrac{1}{x-8}$ and $g(x) = x^2 + 2$, what is $f(g(x))$?

    (A) $\dfrac{1}{x^2 - 6}$

    (B) $x^2 - 6$

    (C) $\left(\dfrac{1}{x-8}\right)^2 + 2$

    (D) $\dfrac{1}{x^2 - 8}$

27. How many prime numbers can be found between 1 and 50?

28. Given the function $y = x^2 + 5$, which of the following represents the reflection of the function across the x-axis?

    (A) $y = -x^2 + 5$

    (B) $y = \sqrt{x - 5}$

    (C) $y = -x^2 - 5$

    (D) $y = x^2 - 5$

29. Which of the following equations is perpendicular to the line $y = \dfrac{1}{3}x + 6$ and passes through the point $(8, -2)$?

    (A) $y = -\dfrac{1}{3}x + 26$

    (B) $y = -3x + 22$

    (C) $y = -3x + 24$

    (D) $y = \dfrac{1}{3}x + 18$

30. Which of the following represents the inverse of the function $y = 17x + 8$?

    (A) $y = 17x - 8$

    (B) $y = \dfrac{17}{x} - 8$

    (C) $y = \dfrac{1}{17}x - \dfrac{8}{17}$

    (D) $y = \dfrac{1}{17}x - 8$

31. A total of 55 people apply to be included in a company's freelance pool. The company is hiring a group of 3 new freelancers. How many different 3-person freelance groups can the company select?

    (A) 18,915

    (B) 29,420

    (C) 157,410

    (D) 26,235

32. Given $A = \{2, -8, 9, 13, 7\}$ and $B = \{5, 2, -1, 3\}$, which of the following is NOT a subset of $A \times B$?

    (A) $\{(2,3), (2,7)\}$

    (B) $\{(-8,-1), (-8,3), (13,3), (7,3)\}$

    (C) $\{(-8,3), (9,5), (7,5)\}$

    (D) $\{(13,-1), (9,5), (13,5), (13,2)\}$

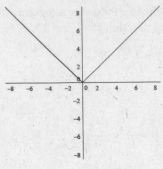

33. What is the domain of the function graphed above?

(A) All real numbers greater than or equal to 0

(B) All real numbers greater than or equal to 0 and less than or equal to 10

(C) All real numbers greater than or equal to −10

(D) All real numbers

34. A bag contains 4 yellow marbles, 7 green marbles, 9 red marbles, and 4 blue marbles. What is the probability that Elijah will select a red marble and then a green marble if the first marble is not replaced?

(A) $\dfrac{7}{64}$

(B) $\dfrac{27}{92}$

(C) $\dfrac{7}{128}$

(D) $\dfrac{21}{184}$

35. Which of the following sets is equivalent to but NOT equal to A = {−3, 14, 3, 26}?

(A) {−3, 14, 2, 8, 3, 26}

(B) {3, 26, 14, −3}

(C) {8, −12, 9, 2}

(D) {7, 3, 14, −18, 9}

36. Mandy spins a spinner with eight equally spaced sections labeled 1 through 8. What is the probability that the spinner lands on an even number or an even number less than 5?

(A) $\dfrac{1}{4}$

(B) $\dfrac{3}{8}$

(C) $\dfrac{2}{3}$

(D) $\dfrac{3}{4}$

37. Hannah must choose a set of winter accessories comprised of a hat, a scarf, and a pair of gloves. The store has 18 different-colored hats, 6 different-colored scarves, and 4 pair of different-colored gloves. How many different accessory sets can she select?

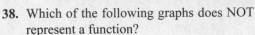

38. Which of the following graphs does NOT represent a function?

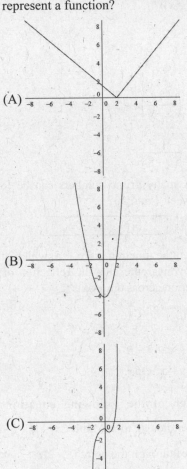

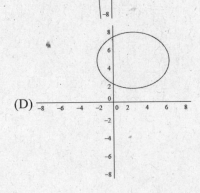

39. Aaron spins a spinner with eight equally spaced sections, labeled 1 through 8, and rolls a 6-sided die. What is the probability that Aaron either spins the spinner and it lands on a number less than 4 or rolls a number greater than 3?

(A) $\dfrac{2}{3}$

(B) $\dfrac{7}{8}$

(C) $\dfrac{7}{12}$

(D) $\dfrac{3}{16}$

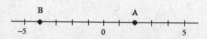

40. Given the number line shown above, which of the following absolute value expressions is true?

(A) $|A - B| < 0$

(B) $|AB| < 0$

(C) $|A + B| > 0$

(D) $\left|\dfrac{B}{A}\right| < 0$

41. If $A = \{-9, 3, 8, 2, -1\}$ and $B = \{7, 3, -1, 2, 4\}$, which of the following represents $A \cup B$?

(A) $\{-9, 8, 7, 4\}$

(B) $\{-9, 3, 8, 2, -1, 7, 4\}$

(C) $\{3, -1, 2\}$

(D) $\{-9, 3, -1, 7, 4, 8\}$

42. Which of the following functions does NOT have an inverse function?

(A) $g(x) = |x - 3|$

(B) $g(x) = x - 3$

(C) $g(x) = x^3 - 3$

(D) $g(x) = \dfrac{1}{x} - 3$

43. Which of the following expressions can be used to represent all odd numbers greater than or equal to 1, where $a \geq 1$?

(A) $2a + 1$

(B) $2a - 3$

(C) $2a$

(D) $2a - 1$

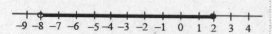

44. Which of the following inequality statements is represented by the graph above?

(A) $x < -8$ or $x \geq 2$

(B) $-8 < x \leq 2$

(C) $x > -8$ or $x \leq 2$

(D) $-8 \leq x < 2$

45. Twenty-six athletes are competing for first through sixth place in a state competition. How many ways can the athletes place first, second, third, fourth, fifth, and sixth?

(A) 165,765,600

(B) 895,600

(C) 135,255,800

(D) 45,385,225

46. Which of the following represents an irrational number less than 2?

(A) $\dfrac{19}{8}$

(B) $\sqrt{3}$

(C) $\dfrac{21}{11}$

(D) π

47. Given $A = \{x, y, z\}$ and $B = \{a, b, c, d\}$, how many ordered pairs are found in the cross-product from A to B?

48. Which of the following are inverse functions?

    (A) $f(x) = 3x - 8$ and $g(x) = \frac{1}{3}x + 8$

    (B) $f(x) = 2x - 12$ and $g(x) = \frac{1}{2}x + 6$

    (C) $f(x) = x^2$ and $g(x) = -x^2$

    (D) $f(x) = \frac{1}{x}$ and $g(x) = x$

If Kelsey writes an article, then it is autumn.

49. What is the contrapositive of the statement above?

    (A) If Kelsey does not write an article, then it is not autumn.

    (B) If it is autumn, then Kelsey writes an article.

    (C) If it is not autumn, then Kelsey does not write an article.

    (D) If it is autumn, then Kelsey does not write an article.

p: If it rains, then it is Friday.

q: It is not Friday.

50. Given the premises above, which of the following correctly represents the conclusion?

    (A) It does not rain.

    (B) It is a weekday.

    (C) It rains.

    (D) It is Saturday.

ANSWER KEY AND EXPLANATIONS

1. 6	11. B	21. D	31. D	41. B
2. D	12. C	22. C	32. A	42. A
3. C	13. A	23. C	33. D	43. D
4. A	14. 177,148	24. D	34. D	44. B
5. A	15. C	25. C	35. C	45. A
6. D	16. D	26. A	36. D	46. B
7. B	17. 0.09	27. 15	37. 432	47. 12
8. C	18. A	28. C	38. D	48. B
9. A	19. B	29. B	39. B	49. C
10. B	20. D	30. C	40. C	50. A

1. **The correct answer is (6).** The prime factorization of 840 can be written as $2 \cdot 2 \cdot 2 \cdot 3 \cdot 5 \cdot 7$, which includes 6 factors.

2. **The correct answer is (D).** The composition of the functions requires $f(x)$ to be evaluated within $g(x)$. Therefore, $x - 9$ must be substituted for x in the expression $2x - 7$. Doing so gives $2(x - 9) - 7$, which equals $2x - 18 - 7$, or $2x - 25$.

3. **The correct answer is (C).** If a divides b, then a also divides the product of b and some other integer, c. If $2 | 4$, then $2 | (4 \cdot 6)$.

4. **The correct answer is (A).** The conjunction of two sets includes all elements common to both sets. Thus, the conjunction of $p \wedge \sim q$ implies a truth value of "true" only when both values of p and $\sim q$ are true. The truth table is shown below:

p	q	$\sim q$	$p \wedge \sim q$
T	T	F	F
T	F	T	T
F	T	F	F
F	F	T	F

5. **The correct answer is (A).** The standard deviation can be calculated using the following $s_x = \sqrt{\dfrac{\Sigma \left(x - \overline{x}\right)^2}{n - 1}}$, where x represents each score, $\overline{x}$ represents the mean, and n represents the number of scores. Substituting the mean of 8.25, each score, and the sample size into the formula gives $s_x = \sqrt{\dfrac{118.25}{11}}$, which is approximately 3.28.

6. **The correct answer is (D).** Substitution of the x-value of 2 into each equation gives a true statement:

$$-3(2) + 18 = 12 \quad 4(2) - 9 = -1$$
$$-6 + 18 = 12 \quad 8 - 9 = -1$$
$$12 = 12 \quad -1 = -1$$

7. **The correct answer is (B).** A number is divisible by 3 if and only if the sum of the digits is divisible by 3. For example, 216 is divisible by 3 because $2 + 1 + 6 = 9$, and 9 is divisible by 3.

8. **The correct answer is (C).** The notation $A \cap B$ is read as "A intersects B" and denotes all elements common to Sets A and B. The elements 3 and 9 are common to both sets. Therefore, {3, 9} represents the intersection of the two sets.

9. **The correct answer is (A).** The inequality can be solved for y and rewritten as $-3y \geq -12x + 6$ or $y \leq 4x - 2$. The inequality has a slope of 4 and a y-intercept of -2. Substitution of a test point into the inequality will reveal where the shading should occur. Substitution of (0,0) into the inequality $y \leq 4x - 2$ gives $0 \leq 4(0) - 2$, or $0 \leq -2$, which is a false statement. Therefore, the side of the inequality not containing the point (0,0) should be shaded. The graph for choice (A) has the correct slope and y-intercept and is shaded below the line.

10. **The correct answer is (B).** The median of a data set is the middle value, or the average of the two middle values, when all data are arranged in ascending order. The number of water bottles donated per month can be written in the following ascending order: 1011, 1019, 1021, 1022, 1028, 1041, 1046, 1047, 1051, 1056, 1058, 1096. The middle two values are 1041 and 1046. The average of the two middle values is 1043.5; thus, the median is 1043.5.

11. **The correct answer is (B).** The probability of the events can be determined using the formula $P(A \text{ and } B) = P(A) \, P(B)$. Thus, the probability can be written as $P(A \text{ and } B) = \frac{4}{6} \cdot \frac{1}{2}$, which equals $\frac{4}{12}$, or $\frac{1}{3}$.

12. **The correct answer is (C).** The product can be written as $(16i)(3 + 2i)$, which equals $48i + 32i^2$. Since $i^2 = -1$, the expression can be simplified as $48i - 32$, or $-32 + 48i$.

13. **The correct answer is (A).** The line $f(x) = x$ has all real numbers as the range, or output values, $f(x)$. The range is not restricted in terms of output values.

14. **The correct answer is (177,148).** The logarithmic equation can be rewritten as $9^{\log_9(3x-3)} = 9^6$, which can be solved as follows:

$$3x - 3 = 531,441$$
$$3x = 431,444$$
$$x = 177,148$$

15. **The correct answer is (C).** The inverse of a statement is represented as $\sim p \rightarrow \sim q$. Thus, the inverse of the given statement requires the negation of the hypothesis p and the negation of the conclusion q. The inverse can be written as "If Amanda does not drive to work, then it is not a weekday."

16. **The correct answer is (D).** The logarithmic expression can be rewritten as $\log_8(8^3)^x$, which equals $\log_8 8^{3x}$, or $3x$.

17. **The correct answer is (0.09).** The probability of non-mutually exclusive events A or B can be determined using the formula $P(A \text{ or } B) = P(A) + P(B) - P(A \text{ and } B)$. Substituting the given probabilities allows you to write $0.38 = 0.29 + 0.18 - P(A \text{ and } B)$, which simplifies to $0.38 = 0.47 - P(A \text{ and } B)$ or $-0.09 = -P(A \text{ and } B)$. Dividing each side by -1 reveals $P(A \text{ and } B) = 0.09$. Thus, the probability of having a conference call and having a conference call at 1:00 is 0.09.

18. **The correct answer is (A).** The value of the event in question is 17; 17 juniors prefer Coffee Shop B. The total number of students who prefer Coffee Shop B is 96. Therefore, the probability that a student who prefers Coffee Shop B is a junior is $\frac{17}{96}$.

19. **The correct answer is (B).** A stretching of a graph requires a slope with a smaller absolute value. The given function has a slope of 1; therefore, a function with a slope of $\frac{1}{2}$ will indeed be stretched, showing a flatter/slower slope. A shift to the left is indicated by a change within the parenthesis, predicated by a positive shift. Thus, the function $g(x) = \left(\frac{1}{2}x + 2\right)^2$, represents a stretching of the parent function and a shift to the left of 2 units.

20. **The correct answer is (D).** The length of side a can be determined by finding the cosine of 30°. The following equation can be written $\cos 30° = \frac{a}{6}$. Multiplying each side by 6 allows you to solve for a, $6 \cdot \frac{\sqrt{3}}{2} = \frac{a}{6} \cdot 6$, which reduces to $\frac{6\sqrt{3}}{2}$, or $3\sqrt{3}$.

21. **The correct answer is (D).** A rational number can be expressed as the ratio of a to b, where b does not equal 0. A rational number is repeating or terminating. The definition for I pertains to an irrational number. The definition for II is incorrect because of the conjunction "and."

22. **The correct answer is (C).** The first statement is not correct because 2 is an even number and is prime. The last statement is not correct because the real number system is infinitely large. All even numbers are multiples of 2, by definition of an even number, as represented by the expression $2a$. Thus, only statement II is correct.

23. **The correct answer is (C).** The number of students who chose each fruit can be determined by multiplying each percentage by the total number of students surveyed, or 300. Thus, 135 students chose "Apple," while 45 students chose "Orange." Ninety more students chose "Apple" than "Orange."

24. **The correct answer is (D).** The negation of a conditional statement can be represented as $\sim (p \rightarrow q)$, or $p \wedge \sim q$. The negation of the conclusion, or q, can be written as "It is not Tuesday." Therefore, the negation of the given statement is "Hannah mows the yard and it is not Tuesday."

25. **The correct answer is (C).** Coterminal angles differ by a multiple of 360°; $-20° + 360° = 340°$. Thus, 340° is coterminal with $-20°$.

26. **The correct answer is (A).** The composition of the functions requires $g(x)$ to be evaluated within $f(x)$. Therefore, $x2 + 2$ must be substituted for x in the expression $\dfrac{1}{x-8}$.

Doing so gives $\dfrac{1}{(x^2 + 2) - 8}$, which can be simplified as $\dfrac{1}{x^2 - 6}$.

27. **The correct answer is (15).** The prime numbers between 1 and 50 are 2, 3, 5, 7, 11, 13, 17, 19, 23, 29, 31, 37, 41, 43, and 47. There are 15 prime numbers between 1 and 50.

28. **The correct answer is (C).** The reflection of a function across the x-axis requires a replacement of y with $-y$. Therefore, the reflected function can be written as $-y = x^2 + 5$. Dividing each side by -1 gives $y = -x^2 - 5$.

29. **The correct answer is (B).** A line perpendicular to another line has a negative reciprocal for the slope. Thus, the slope of a line perpendicular to the given line will have a slope of -3. To determine the equation of a line perpendicular to a given line that passes through a particular point, you must substitute the new slope and x- and y-values of the given point into the slope-intercept form of a line, or $y = mx + b$. Doing so allows you to write $-2 = -3(8) + b$, where $b = 22$. Thus, the equation of the line perpendicular to the given line is $y = -3x + 22$.

30. **The correct answer is (C).** The inverse of a function can be found by switching the x- and y-variables and solving for y. Doing so allows you to write $x = 17y + 8$. Solving for y gives: $y = \dfrac{x-8}{17}$, or $y = \dfrac{1}{17}x - \dfrac{8}{17}$.

31. **The correct answer is (D).** The problem involves a combination whereby order does not matter. The combination can be determined using the formula $\dfrac{n!}{r!(n-r)!}$, where n represents the number of subjects and r represents the number in each group. Substituting the given values allows you to write $\dfrac{55!}{3!(55-3)!}$, or $\dfrac{55!}{3!52!}$, which equals 26,235.

32. **The correct answer is (A).** The cross-product of A and B can be written as $\{(2,5),$ $(2,2), (2,-1), (2,3), (-8,5), (-8,2), (-8,-1),$ $(-8,3), (9,5), (9,2), (9, -1), (9,3), (13,5),$ $(13,2), (13,-1), (13,3), (7,5), (7,2), (7,-1),$ $(7,3)\}$. The ordered pair $(2,7)$ is not included in $A \times B$.

33. **The correct answer is (D).** The domain of the graphed function is all real numbers. All real numbers are allowed as input or x-values.

34. **The correct answer is (D).** The probability of one event and another event can be determined using the formula $P(A \text{ and } B) = P(A) \cdot P(B)$. The events described here are dependent. Therefore, the total sample space for the second draw will be 1 less than the sample space for the first draw. Thus, $P(A \text{ and } B) = \frac{9}{24} \cdot \frac{7}{23}$, or $\frac{63}{552}$, which reduces to $\frac{21}{184}$.

35. **The correct answer is (C).** Equivalent sets have the same number of elements. Equal sets have identical elements and the same number of elements.

36. **The correct answer is (D).** The probability of one event or another event can be determined using the formula $P(A \text{ or } B) = P(A) + P(B) - P(A \text{ and } B)$. Thus, $P(A \text{ or } B) = \frac{4}{8} + \frac{4}{8} - \frac{2}{8}$, which equals $\frac{6}{8}$, or $\frac{3}{4}$.

37. **The correct answer is (432).** The problem is a counting problem. The number of different accessory sets can be found by calculating the product of the number of all different-colored hats, all different-colored scarves, and all different-colored gloves: $18 \cdot 6 \cdot 4 = 432$. Thus, she can select 432 different accessory sets.

38. **The correct answer is (D).** The circle does not represent a function. Each x-value is mapped to more than one y-value. Notice that a vertical line drawn through the graph intersects the graph at more than one point.

39. **The correct answer is (B).** The probability of one event or another event, where the events are independent, can be determined by using the formula $P(A \text{ or } B) = P(A) + P(B)$. Thus, $P(A \text{ or } B) = \frac{3}{8} + \frac{3}{6}$, which equals $\frac{42}{48}$, or $\frac{7}{8}$.

40. **The correct answer is (C).** An absolute value sum will always be positive. For example, $|2 + (-4)| = |-2|$, which equals 2, and 2 is greater than 0. A counterexample cannot be found.

41. **The correct answer is (B).** The union indicates all elements in Set A or Set B. Therefore, $A \cup B = \{-9, 3, 8, 2, -1, 7, 4\}$.

42. **The correct answer is (A).** An inverse function does not have a y-value mapped to more than one x-value. The function $g(x) = |x - 3|$ has y-values that are mapped to more than one x-value. For example, the y-value of 1 is mapped to the x-values 2 and 4. A horizontal line test indicates that this absolute value function does not have an inverse function because it intersects the graph in more than one place.

43. **The correct answer is (D).** The expression $2a - 1$ represents all odd numbers greater than or equal to 1, where $a \geq 1$. Substitution of the value 1 for a reveals $2(1) - 1$, or 1. Substitution of the value 2 for a reveals $2(2) - 3$, or 3.

44. **The correct answer is (B).** The graph represents all real numbers greater than -8 and less than or equal to 2, written as $-8 < x \leq 2$.

45. **The correct answer is (A).** The problem involves a permutation because order matters. The permutation can be calculated using the formula $\frac{n!}{(n-r)!}$. Substituting the value of 26 for n and the value of 6 for r allows you to write: $\frac{26!}{(26-6)!}$, or $\frac{26!}{20!}$, which equals 165,765,600. Thus, there are 165,765,600 ways the 26 athletes can place first through sixth place.

46. **The correct answer is (B).** The number given for choice (B) is irrational and less than 2; it is approximately 1.732.

47. **The correct answer is (12).** The cross-product can be written as A × B = {(x,a), (x,b), (x,c), (x,d), (y,a), (y,b), (y,c), (y,d), (z,a), (z,b), (z,c), (z,d)}. The number of ordered pairs in the cross-product is equal to the product of the number of elements in Set A and the number of elements in Set B.

48. **The correct answer is (B).** The composition of any two functions that are inverse functions will equal x. The composition of $f(g(x))$ can be written as $f(g(x)) = 2\left(\frac{1}{2}x + 6\right) - 12$, which equals $x + 12 - 12$ or x. The composition of $g(f(x))$ can be written as $g(f(x)) = \frac{1}{2}(2x - 12) + 6$, which equals $x - 6 + 6$, or x. Thus, the functions, $f(x) = 2x - 12$ and $g(x) = \frac{1}{2}x + 6$, are indeed inverse functions.

49. **The correct answer is (C).** The contrapositive of a statement can be written as $\sim q \rightarrow \sim p$, where $\sim p$ represents the negation of the hypothesis and $\sim q$ represents the negation of the conclusion. Therefore, the contrapositive of the given statement is "If it is not autumn, then Kelsey does not write an article."

50. **The correct answer is (A).** The premise can be written as $p \rightarrow q$, followed by $\sim q$. Therefore, by the law of contraposition, the conclusion must be $\sim p$. Therefore, the conclusion can be written as "It does not rain."

OVERVIEW ANSWER SHEET

1. Ⓐ Ⓑ Ⓒ Ⓓ   5. Ⓐ Ⓑ Ⓒ Ⓓ   9. Ⓐ Ⓑ Ⓒ Ⓓ   13. Ⓐ Ⓑ Ⓒ Ⓓ   17. Ⓐ Ⓑ Ⓒ Ⓓ

2. Ⓐ Ⓑ Ⓒ Ⓓ   6. Ⓐ Ⓑ Ⓒ Ⓓ   10. Ⓐ Ⓑ Ⓒ Ⓓ   14. Ⓐ Ⓑ Ⓒ Ⓓ   18. Ⓐ Ⓑ Ⓒ Ⓓ

3. Ⓐ Ⓑ Ⓒ Ⓓ   7. Ⓐ Ⓑ Ⓒ Ⓓ   11. Ⓐ Ⓑ Ⓒ Ⓓ   15. Ⓐ Ⓑ Ⓒ Ⓓ   19. Ⓐ Ⓑ Ⓒ Ⓓ

4. Ⓐ Ⓑ Ⓒ Ⓓ   8. Ⓐ Ⓑ Ⓒ Ⓓ   12. Ⓐ Ⓑ Ⓒ Ⓓ   16. Ⓐ Ⓑ Ⓒ Ⓓ   20. Ⓐ Ⓑ Ⓒ Ⓓ

answer sheet

Overview

The CLEP College Mathematics test assesses your ability to solve the types of math problems you would solve in a basic, college math course for non-math majors. You don't need knowledge of advanced mathematical concepts to score well on this test.

The exam contains about 60 questions that you must answer in 90 minutes. The test doesn't contain questions that require calculations, so you don't need a calculator, but an online, non-graphing scientific calculator will be available to you.

The problems on the CLEP College Mathematics test can be grouped into two basic categories:

1. Routine, straightforward math problems (50 percent of the questions on the test)
2. Non-routine problems in which you must apply skills and concepts (50 percent of the questions on the test)

Questions on this CLEP test are about the following subjects:

Real Number System (20 percent or 12 questions)

- Even and odd numbers
- Prime and composite numbers
- Factors and divisibility
- Rational and irrational numbers
- Absolute value and order
- Open and closed intervals

Sets (10 percent or 6 questions)

- Union and intersection
- Subsets, disjoint sets, equivalent sets
- Venn diagrams
- Cartesian product

Probability and Statistics (25 percent or 15 questions)

- Counting problems, including permutations and combinations
- Computation of probabilities of simple and compound events
- Simple conditional probability
- Mean, median, mode, and range
- Concept of standard deviation
- Data interpretation and representation: tables, bar graphs, line graphs, circle graphs, pie charts, scatterplots, histograms

Logic (10 percent or 6 questions)

- Truth tables, negations, conjunctions, implications, and equivalents
- Conditional statements, hypotheses, conclusions, and counterexamples
- Necessary and sufficient conditions
- Converse, inverse, and contrapositive

Functions and Their Graphs (20 percent or 12 questions)

- Domain and range
- Properties and graphs of functions
- Composition of functions and inverse functions
- Simple transformations of functions: translations, reflections, symmetry

Additional Topics from Algebra and Geometry (15 percent or 9 questions)

- Complex numbers
- Logarithms and exponents
- Perimeter and area of plane figures
- Properties of triangles, circles, and rectangles
- The Pythagorean Theorem
- Parallel and perpendicular lines
- Algebraic equations, systems of linear equations, and inequalities
- Fundamental Theorem of Algebra, Remainder Theorem, Factor Theorem

REAL NUMBER SYSTEM

About 12 questions on the CLEP College Mathematics test will be about *real numbers*, numbers that appear on a number line. The real number system includes, but is not limited to, the following:

- Positive numbers
- Negative numbers
- Rational numbers
- Irrational numbers
- Decimals
- Fractions
- Square roots
- Cube roots
- Zero
- Pi (π)

Real numbers get their name because they are not imaginary numbers. An *imaginary number* is a number that when squared is a negative number. All real numbers when squared are positive, because a negative number multiplied by a negative number yields a positive number. A negative radicand is an example of a negative number:

$\sqrt{-a}$ where $a > 0$.

Even and Odd Numbers

Numbers can be grouped into many different sets. Perhaps the most basic way is to group numbers into even and odd numbers.

Even numbers: 0, 2, 4, 6, 8, 10....

Odd numbers: 1, 3, 5, 7, 9, 11....

Larger numbers are even if the number in the one's place is an even number and odd if the digit in the one's place is an odd number.

Even number: 1270

Odd number: 2391

Practice 1

Indicate whether each number is even or odd.

1. 15
2. 6230
3. 10,001
4. 17,256
5. 101,263

Prime and Composite Numbers

A *prime number* can be divided only by 1 and itself. The following numbers are some of the many prime numbers:

2, 3, 13, 17, 19, 43, 571, 829, 911

Numbers that aren't prime numbers are called *composite numbers*. A composite number can be divided by numbers other than 1 and itself. Here are some composite numbers:

6, 10, 12, 200, 525, 812, 915

Practice 2

Indicate whether each number is prime or composite.

   1. 127
   2. 602
   3. 811
   4. 1050
   5. 2234

Factors and Divisibility

The numbers by which a number can be divided are called factors. The number 6 may be divided by 1, 2, 3, and 6. These are factors of 6 because:

$1 \times 6 = 6$

$2 \times 3 = 6$

Negative numbers are also factors because two negatives multiplied together yield a positive number:

$-1 \times -6 = 6$

$-2 \times -3 = 6$

When a number can be divided by a factor, it's said to be *divisible* by that factor. For example, since 6 can be divided by 2 and 3, it's divisible by these numbers.

Practice 3

List the factors of each number.

   1. 8
   2. 14
   3. 21
   4. 32
   5. 45

Rational and Irrational Numbers

A *rational number* is a number that can easily be expressed as a fraction or a ratio. The numerator and denominator of a fraction are both integers. (Integers are the set of positive whole numbers, negative whole numbers, and zero.) Rational numbers can be ordered on a number line. The following are rational numbers:

$\dfrac{1}{3}$

3 or $\dfrac{3}{1}$

-3 or $-\dfrac{3}{1}$

A rational number written in decimal form may be non-terminating, meaning it may go on forever. However, as long as it can be written as a fraction, it's a rational number.

$$\frac{2}{3} = 0.0666666\overline{6}$$

An *irrational number*, on the other hand, cannot be expressed as a fraction or ratio. When expressed as a decimal, irrational numbers are non-repeating and non-terminal. Pi (π) is an irrational number. The following are also irrational numbers:

$\pi = 3.141592653589$ (and more...)

$e = 2.718281828459045$ (and more...)

$\varphi = 1.61803398874989$ (and more...)

Practice 4

Indicate whether each of the following numbers is rational or irrational.

1. $\frac{1}{2}$

2. 7

3. $\sqrt{2}$

Absolute Value and Order

The *absolute value* of a number is the positive distance between the number and zero on a number line. The absolute value of both positive and negative numbers is positive. Negative numbers are the opposite of positive numbers because they are found on opposite sides of zero on a number line. The absolute value symbol is two bars placed on either side of the number and is read "the absolute value of x."

$$|-3| = 3 \quad |8| = 8$$

The algebraic definition of absolute value is $|a| = \begin{cases} a \text{ if } a \geq 0 \\ -a \text{ if } a < 0 \end{cases}$.

Given x and y are real numbers, then the properties of absolute value are as follows:

- $|x| = |-x|$. A number and its opposite have the same absolute value.

- $|x| \geq 0$. The absolute value of a number is always nonnegative.

- $|x| = 0 \Leftrightarrow x = 0$. The absolute value of a number is zero if and only if the number is zero.

- $|x \cdot y| = |x| \cdot |y|$. The absolute value of the product is the product of the absolute values.

- $\left|\dfrac{x}{y}\right| = \dfrac{|x|}{|y|}$. The absolute value of the ratio is the ratio of the absolute values.

- $|x^n| = |x|^n$. If n is an integer, the absolute value of a number raised to a power is the absolute

value of the number raised to that power, as long as the power is an integer.

When comparing two negative integers, the one closer to zero on the number line is greater.

Practice 5

Write the absolute value for each example.

1. $|-10|$

2. $|-10 + 3|$

3. $|-3 \times 5|$

Order the integers from least to greatest.

4. -3, -10, 8, 0

5. 1, -1, 0, 5, -2

Open and Closed Intervals

Intervals are sets of real numbers that may include endpoints and are expressed as an ordered pair. Intervals include open, closed, and half-open intervals.

If a and b are real numbers, then the *open interval* of numbers between a and b is written as (a,b) using parentheses. The symbol $\in$ is read "is a member of."

$(a,b) = \{x \in \mathbb{R} \,|\, a < x < b\}$

Open intervals do not include where the variable is equal to the endpoint.

$(5,10) = \{6, 7, 8, 9\}$

If a and b are real numbers, then the *closed interval* is written as $[a, b]$ using braces.

$[a,b] = \{x \in \mathbb{R} \,|\, a \le x \le b\}$

A closed interval includes where the variable is equal to the endpoint.

$[5,10] = \{5, 6, 7, 8, 9, 10\}$

If a and b are real numbers, then *half-open intervals* are written as $(a, b]$ or $[a,b)$ using both parenthesis and braces.

$(a,b] = \{x \in \mathbb{R} \,|\, a < x \le b\}$

$[a,b) = \{x \in \mathbb{R} \,|\, a \le x < b\}$

If infinity or negative infinity is used as an endpoint, an open interval must be used because infinity has no exact value.

Practice 6

Write the set indicated by the interval.

1. $(6, 15)$
2. $[11, 18]$
3. $(33, 42]$
4. $[19, 23)$
5. $(-\infty, 12]$

SETS

About 6 questions on the CLEP College Mathematics test will be about *sets*, which are collections of objects. Sets can include numbers, letters, or words and are usually represented by capital letters and braces or brackets. Sets include, but are not limited to, the following:

- Unions
- Intersections
- Subsets
- Disjoint sets
- Equivalent sets
- Venn diagrams
- Cartesian products

Objects in a set are called *elements* or *members*.

If $A = \{37, 47, 57, 67, 77, 87\}$, $87 \in A$ (Eighty-seven is a member of Set A.)

Union and Intersection

A *union* of two sets results in a new set whose members include the members of each original set. The symbol for set union is $\cup$.

$A = \{1, 2, 3\}$
$B = \{2, 3, 4, 5\}$
$A \cup B = \{1, 2, 3, 4, 5\}$

There is no need to repeat numbers in the new set if there is a number contained in both the original sets.

An *intersection* of two sets results in a new set, which includes only the common members of the original sets. The symbol for set intersection is $\cap$.

$A = \{1, 2, 3\}$
$B = \{2, 3, 4, 5\}$
$A \cap B = \{2, 3\}$

Members 2 and 3 are contained in both Set A and Set B.

Empty brackets, {}, indicate an empty set or null set $\varnothing$.

Practice 7

Indicate the union or intersection for the given sets.

1. $A = \{r, s, t\}$
   $B = \{r, t, u\}$
   $A \cup B =$

2. $P = \{\}$
   $R = \{0, 3, 7, 10\}$
   $P \cap R =$

3. $O = \{1, 2, 3, 10\}$
   $P = \{1, 2, 9, 10\}$
   $O \cup P =$

4. $K = \{-5, -4, -1, 2\}$
   $J = \{\text{all negative numbers}\}$
   $K \cap J =$

5. $U = \{-3, -2, -1, 3, 4\}$
   $T = \{\text{all positive numbers}\}$
   $U \cap T =$

Subsets, Disjoint Sets, Equivalent Sets

A *subset* is a group of elements or members that belong to a larger set. The larger set is often referred to as the *superset*. The symbol for subset is $\subset$.

A set is actually a subset of itself. Therefore, $A \subset A$.

Sets are said to be *disjoint* if $A \cap B = \varnothing$. For example, $\{A, B, C\}$ and $\{D, E\}$ are *disjoint* because none of the elements in Set A appear in Set B.

Equivalent sets contain the same number of elements. *Equal sets* contain the same number of elements and the exact same elements.

Practice 8

Indicate whether each group of sets are subsets, disjoints, equals, or equivalents.

1. $A = \{2, 3, 4, 10, 15, 25, 30\}$

   $B = \{25\}$

2. $A = \{3, 5, 10\}$

   $B = \{5, 10, 12\}$

3. $A = \{12, 24, 36\}$

   $B = \{6, 18, 30\}$

4. $A = \{2, 4, 6, 8\}$

   $B = \{2, 4, 6, 8\}$

5. $A = \{r, s, t, u\}$

   $B = \{r, s\}$

Venn Diagrams

Venn diagrams are visual representations of sets.

A union and intersection are represented with a Venn diagram where overlap of the sets occurs.

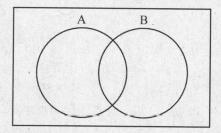

Practice 9

Use the Venn diagram to complete Questions 1–4.

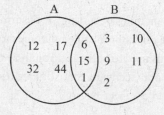

1. Set A includes: {   }

2. Set B includes: {   }

3. $A \cup B =$

4. $A \cap B =$

Cartesian Product

The *Cartesian product* forms ordered pairs of members from two sets represented by $A \times B$.

$A = \{3, 4, 5\}$ $B = \{13, 14\}$

$A \times B =$

(3, 13)   (4, 13)   (5, 13)

(3, 14)   (4, 14)   (5, 14)

Practice 10

Use the Cartesian product to find $A \times B$.

1. $A = \{2, 3\}$

     $B = \{5, 6, 7\}$

     $A \times B =$

PROBABILITY AND STATISTICS

About 15 questions on the CLEP College Mathematics test will be about probability and statistics. Probability and statistics includes, but is not limited to, the following:

- Counting
- Permutations
- Combinations
- Simple events
- Compound events
- Simple conditional probability
- Mean
- Median
- Mode
- Range
- Standard deviation
- Tables
- Bar graphs
- Line graphs
- Circle graphs
- Pie charts
- Scatterplots
- Histograms

Probability is the likelihood of something occurring; it describes events that do not occur with certainty and are represented as the ratio of probable outcomes to the total number of possible outcomes. *Statistics* are a set of methods used to collect and analyze data. A statistic is a fact or piece of information expressed as a number or percentage. Statistics are used in many occupations, including weather forecasting, economics, and engineering.

Statistical data can be analyzed using exploratory methods or confirmatory methods. Exploratory methods analyze what the data indicates and often involve the computation of averages or percentages. In addition, data is often displayed visually. Confirmatory methods use probability to attempt to answer specific questions.

Permutations and Combinations

The order of things is important in a *permutation,* but not in a *combination.*

The Fundamental Counting Principle allows us to find the number of possible outcomes. If an event has m possible outcomes, and another event has n possible outcomes, then there are mn possible outcomes for the two events.

If there are 3 shirts to choose from and 2 pairs of shorts, then there are 6 possible outfits that can be made: $3 \times 2 = 6$.

A *factorial* is the product of an integer and all the integers less than that integer. It is denoted by $n!$.

$4! = 4 \times 3 \times 2 \times 1 = 24$

When there are n number of athletes competing for a gold, silver, or bronze medal, the order the athletes finish is important. The following formula applies to permutations:

$$_nP_r = \frac{n!}{(n-r)!}$$

The total number of elements is represented by n, r is the size of the subgroup, and P is the permutation. If there are 6 athletes competing for 3 medals, to find the permutation:

$$_6P_3 = \frac{6!}{(6-3)!} = \frac{6 \times 5 \times 4 \times 3 \times 2 \times 1}{3 \times 2 \times 1} = \frac{720}{6} = 120$$

For very large numbers, simply multiply the number of digits equal to r.

$$_6P_3 = \frac{6!}{(6-3)!} = 6 \times 5 \times 4 = 120$$

A *combination* is an unordered grouping of a set; the order does not matter. The following formula is used to determine the number of combinations:

$$_nC_r = \frac{n!}{r!(n-r)!}$$

How many ways can you form a team of 3 people from a group of 7 people? The order does not matter, so we use the formula:

$$_7C_3 = \frac{7!}{3!(7-3)!} = \frac{7 \times 6 \times 5 \times 4 \times 3 \times 2 \times 1}{(3 \times 2 \times 1)(4 \times 3 \times 2 \times 1)} = \frac{5040}{6 \times 24} = \frac{5040}{144} = 35$$

There are 35 teams of 3 that can be formed given a group of 7 people.

Practice 11

Determine whether each example is a permutation or combination.

1. Choose a president, vice president, and secretary from a group of 5.

2. Choose 2 desserts from a menu of 7.

3. List your top 3 favorite movies from a list of 10.

4. Ways to arrange a row of 5 students from a group of 10.

5. Create 3-character serial numbers using all 26 letters of the alphabet where no letters can be repeated.

Computation of Probabilities of Simple and Compound Events

A *simple event* is an event that results in only one single outcome. Rolling a die is a simple event because only one outcome is possible.

A *compound event* is an event that consists of two or more simple events. Rolling two dice is an example of a compound event. To calculate the probability of a compound event, the outcomes must be equally likely.

If the outcome of one event does not influence the outcome of the second event, the events are *independent*. This is expressed by $P(A \text{ and } B) = P(A) \times P(B)$.

The probability of rolling two dice and rolling a 2 on each one is $P(2) \times P(2) = \frac{1}{6} \times \frac{1}{6} = \frac{1}{36}$.

If the outcome of one event affects the outcome of the second event, the events are *dependent*. This is expressed by $P(A \text{ and } B) = P(A) \times P(B \text{ following } A)$.

A bag contains the letters B, A, and T. What is the probability of first choosing the B and then, without replacing the B, choosing the A?

$$P(A) = \frac{1}{3} \qquad P(B \text{ following } A) = \frac{1}{2}$$

$$\frac{1}{3} \times \frac{1}{2} = \frac{1}{6}$$

If the events occur at the same time, they are *mutually exclusive*.

$$P(A \text{ or } B) = P(A) + P(B)$$

Practice 12

Indicate whether each is an independent or dependent event.

1. Two dice are rolled. What is the probability of rolling double sixes on the first roll?

2. What is the probability tossing a coin and it landing on heads and rolling a 3 on a die?

3. A bag contains 3 blue marbles, 2 red marbles, and 2 black marbles. What is the probability of first choosing a blue marble and then, without replacing the marble, choosing a black marble?

4. Two bags contain all 26 letters of the alphabet. What is the probability of choosing a vowel first from each bag?

5. A coin is tossed and a die is rolled. What is the probability that the coin landed on heads and the die landed on an even number?

Simple Conditional Probability

The *conditional probability* of an Event B in relationship to an Event A is the probability that Event B occurs given Event A has already occurred.

Conditional probability is noted as $P(B \mid A)$ and read, "the probability of B given A."

$$P(B \mid A) = \frac{P(A \text{ and } B)}{P(A)}$$

A math teacher only gives two tests each semester. Ninety percent of the students in a math class passed the first test of the semester. Seventy percent of the class passed the second. What is the probability that a student passed the second test given he or she passed the first?

$$P(B \mid A) = \frac{P(A \text{ and } B)}{P(A)} = \frac{0.7}{0.9} = 78\%$$

Practice 13

Solve each conditional probability problem.

1. The probability that a student is absent on Monday is 0.05. Assume there are 5 days in the school week. What is the probability that a student is absent given today is Monday?

2. A science teacher gave her class two tests. Seventy percent of the class passed the first test. Fifty percent of the class passed both tests. What is the probability that a student passed the second test given he or she passed the first?

3. Twenty-five percent of students at a school play sports and 12 percent play a sport and have a job. What is the probability that a student has a job given he or she plays a sport?

Mean, Median, Mode, and Range

The *mean* of a set of data is found by dividing the sum of the numbers in a group by the number of addends. It is also known as the average and represented by the symbol μ.

12, 6, 18, 21, 22, 1, 4 = 84

84 ÷ 7 = 12

The mean is 12.

When a set of data is arranged in order, the middle number is the *median*.

12, 13, 14, 15, 16, 17, 18, 19, 20, 21, 22

The median is 17.

The *mode* is the number that occurs most often in a set of data.

13, 2, 3, 6, 9, 8, 4, 8, 10, 10, 6, 5

The modes are 6, 8, and 10, because they all appear twice within the data set.

The difference between the least and greatest numbers in a set of data is the *range*.

In the data set 13, 2, 3, 6, 9, 8, 4, 8, 10, 10, 6, 5, the range is 11. (13 − 2 = 11).

Practice 14

Calculate.

66, 55, 15, 49, 60, 59, 59, 11, 91, 75

1. What is the mean?
2. What is the median?
3. What is the mode?
4. What is the range?

Concept of Standard Deviation

Standard deviation is a measure of how spread out the data in a set is and is represented by the symbol σ. To compute standard deviation, complete the following six steps:

1. Calculate the mean for a set of data.
2. Subtract the mean from each data value.
3. Square each difference.
4. Total the squared deviations.
5. Divide by one less than the sample size.
6. Take the square root of the quotient.

The mean of 73, 58, 67, 93, 33, 18, 147 is 69.9.

$73 - 69.9 = 3.1^2 = 9.61$

$58 - 69.9 = -11.9^2 = 141.61$

$67 - 69.9 = -2.9^2 = 8.41$

$93 - 69.9 = 23.1^2 = 533.61$

$33 - 69.9 = -36.9^2 = 1361.61$

$18 - 69.9 = -51.9^2 = 2693.61$

$147 - 69.9 = 77.1^2 = 5944.41$

$9.61 + 141.61 + 8.41 + 533.61 + 1361.61 + 2693.61 + 5944.41 = 10{,}692.87$

$10{,}692.87 \div 6 = 1782.15$

$\sqrt{1782.15} = 42.2$

This process is represented in the formula:

$$s = \sqrt{\frac{1}{n-1}\sum (x_i - \overline{x})^2}$$

A low standard deviation reflects a set of data that is clustered near the mean, and a high standard deviation reflects a set of data that is widely apart.

Practice 15

Determine the standard deviation for the set of data.

 1. Ages of group members in years: 14, 14, 29, 24, 20, 42, 21, 30, 14

Data Interpretation and Representation

Data can be represented visually in charts and graphs so that it is easier to understand.

Circle graphs are also known as pie charts. Smaller portions of the data are compared to the overall set.

Bar graphs use bars to compare quantities. There are several different styles of bar graphs.

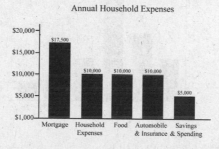

A *multiple bar graph* compares quantities in different subcategories.

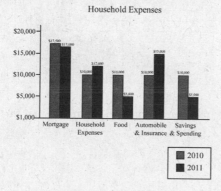

In a *stacked bar graph*, each bar is divided into subcategories but shows the overall total for each category.

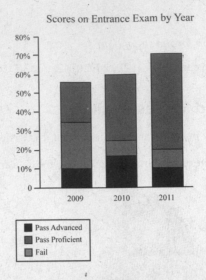

Scores on Entrance Exam by Year

A *histogram* is a vertical bar graph used to show data frequency within equal intervals.

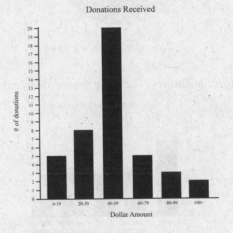

Donations Received

A *line graph* uses a line to show change over time.

XYZ Corp.

A *line plot* is used to show the frequency of data on a number line. An "x" is used to denote a piece of data at a given point.

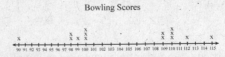

Bowling Scores

A *scatter plot* compares two different sets of data using a line and dots to determine if there is a relationship. A scatter plot is used to identify a negative trend, a positive trend, or no trend.

Negative trend: One set of data increases while the other decreases.

Positive trend: Both sets of data increase.

No trend: Points are scattered randomly showing no relationship.

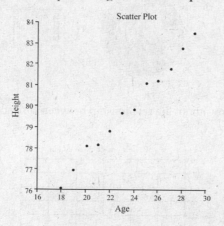

Practice 16

Interpret each chart or graph.

1. What is significant about 1990 compared to other years?

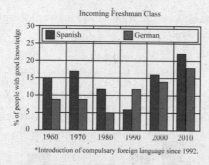

2. What was the value of XYZ Stock on January 21, 2011?

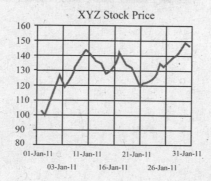

3. Which fruit generated the greatest sales in October?

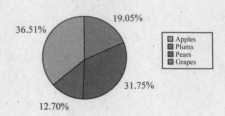

Percentage of Fruit Sales in October

4. What does this graph show about the relationship between flu vaccinations given and reported flu cases?

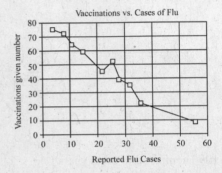

5. If a neighbor is considered to be an adult if he or she is over the age of 20, does Bill have more neighbors that are children or adults?

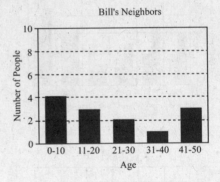

LOGIC

About 6 questions on the CLEP College Mathematics test will be about *logic*, which is the study of reasoning. Reasoning is expressed in arguments, which are declarative statements. These statements can either be true or false. The logic section of the test includes, but is not limited to, the following:

- Truth tables
- Conjunctions
- Disjunctions
- Implications
- Negations
- Conditional statements
- Necessary conditions

- Sufficient conditions
- Converse statements
- Inverse statements
- Contrapositive statements
- Hypotheses
- Conclusions
- Counterexamples

Truth Tables, Negations, Conjunctions, Implications, and Equivalents

Truth tables help determine the validity of an argument based on the truth or falsity of its parts. Symbols are used as connectives: $\sim, \wedge, \vee, \rightarrow, \leftrightarrow$.

P	$\sim P$
T	F
F	T

This table shows a simple *negation*. The $\sim$ symbol stands for "not." If P is true, then $\sim P$ (not P) is false. If P is false, then $\sim P$ is true.

A *conjunction* is a compound statement where two statements are joined with the conjunction "and." The $\wedge$ symbol stands for "and." The truth table below shows that P and Q are true when statements P and Q are true, but are otherwise false.

P: Ann is on the soccer team.

Q: Bill is on the lacrosse team.

Conjunction: Ann is on the soccer team and Bill is on the lacrosse team.

P	Q	$P \wedge Q$
T	T	T
T	F	F
F	T	F
F	F	F

A *disjunction* is a compound statement where two statements are joined with the conjunction "or." The symbol $\vee$ stands for ""or." The truth table below shows that if P or Q is true, then $P \vee Q$ is true.

P or Q is only false if P and Q are false. Note that in logic, the word "or" is used to mean either or both.

P	Q	P ∨ Q
T	T	T
T	F	T
F	T	T
F	F	F

Logistical implication leaves room for "if… then" changes. The symbol → means "implies."

P	Q	P → Q
T	T	T
T	F	F
F	T	T
F	F	T

The statement "If you win the race, then I will take you to dinner" is only true if the promise to take the winner to dinner is kept. Line 1 of the truth table below is true if you win the race and I take you to dinner, but Line 2 is false if you win the race and I don't take you to dinner. If you don't win the race, whether or not I take you to dinner is irrelevant. This is represented in the last two lines of the truth table below.

$P \leftrightarrow Q$ means that P and Q are *equivalent* because they have the same exact truth values. The statements are *biconditional*. Therefore, P and Q are only true if both P and Q are both true or both false.

P	Q	P ↔ Q
T	T	T
T	F	F
F	T	F
F	F	T

Practice 17

Complete each truth table.

1.

P	~P
T	
F	

2.

a	b	a ∨ b
T	T	
T	F	
F	T	
F	F	

3.

P	Q	P ∧ Q
T	T	
T	F	
F	T	
F	F	

4.

P	Q	~P	~P ∧ Q
T	T		
T	F		
F	T		
F	F		

5.

P	~P	~(~P)
T	F	
F	T	

Conditional Statements, Hypotheses, Conclusions, and Counterexamples

Conditional statements are symbolized by $P \rightarrow Q$ and are if–then statements.

A *hypothesis* is the ""if" part of the conditional statement, and the *conclusion* is the ""then" part of the conditional statement.

Given: *P:* I do my math homework.
           Q: I get an allowance.

Sentence: If I do my math homework, then I get an allowance.

A *counterexample* is an example that disproves a universal statement. Therefore, a valid argument is an argument that does not have a counterexample.

The Fundamental Principle of Logic states that an argument is valid if any argument with the same form is valid.

     All cats are animals.

     All dogs are animals.

     Therefore, all cats are dogs.

The argument has true premises, but the conclusion is false. One way to prove that this assertion is invalid is to provide a counterexample.

Practice 18

Identify the hypothesis and the conclusion for each example.

1. Given: *P:* Marty has a math assignment.
             Q: Pete has a soccer game.

2. Given: *P:* Three is an odd number.
             Q: Nine is composite.

3. Given: *P:* Darrel owns a car.
             Q: Ten is an even number.

Necessary and Sufficient Conditions

A *necessary condition* is something that must be present for something else to occur; without x, we won't have y. However, the presence of x does not necessarily guarantee y. For example, there must be gasoline in a car in order for it to start. However, having gasoline in the car does not guarantee that the car will start.

If a *sufficient condition* is present, then something is guaranteed to follow; the presence of x guarantees y. Receiving 98 points on an exam is sufficient to receive an A.

Practice 19

Indicate whether each statement is a necessary or a sufficient condition.

1. Is sunlight a necessary or sufficient condition for flowers to bloom?

2. Is being a female a necessary or sufficient condition for being a mother?

3. Is having oxygen in the earth's atmosphere a necessary or sufficient condition for sustaining human life?

4. Is placing a tray filled with water in the freezer a necessary or sufficient condition for making ice?

5. Is earning a final grade of 80 in a history class a necessary or sufficient condition for passing the class?

Converse, Inverse, and Contrapositive

Three types of statements can be made from conditional if–then statements: *converse, inverse,* and *contrapositive.*

To form a converse statement, interchange the hypothesis and the conclusion of the conditional statement:

> Conditional statement: If there is a noise, then the dog will bark.

> Converse statement: The dog will bark if there is a noise.

To form an inverse statement, use the negation of the hypothesis and the conclusion.

> Conditional statement: If there is a noise, then the dog will bark.

> Inverse statement: If there is no noise, then the dog will not bark.

To form a contrapositive statement, interchange the hypothesis and the conclusion of the inverse statement.

> Conditional statement: If there is a noise, then the dog will bark.

> Contrapositive statement: If the dog will not bark, then there is no noise.

Statement:	If P, then Q.
Converse:	If Q, then P.
Inverse:	If not P, then not Q.
Contrapositive:	If not Q, then not P.

If the original statement is true, then the contrapositive is also logically true. If the converse statement is true, then the inverse is also logically true.

Practice 20

Indicate the converse, inverse, and contrapositive for the statement

If the switch is up, then the light is on.

1. What is the converse?

2. What is the inverse?

3. What is the contrapositive?

FUNCTIONS AND THEIR GRAPHS

About 12 questions on the CLEP Mathematics test will be about functions and their graphs. A *function* is a relationship between two quantities (x,y), where one value depends on its relationship with another value. There is exactly one y for each x. Questions about functions and their graphs include, but are not limited to, the following:

- Properties of functions
- Graphs of functions
- Domain
- Range
- Composition of functions

- Inverse functions
- Translations
- Reflections
- Symmetry

Functions are also thought of as input and output or independent and dependent variables. Functions are written as $f(x)$, which is read "f of x."

Domain and Range

The first quantity, or input, is called the *domain*.

The *range* is the output or second quantity.

Given these points $\{(2,-3), (4,6), (3,-1), (6,6), (2,3)\}$, the domain are the x-values, or input values, and the range are the y-values, or the output values.

Domain: $\{2, 3, 4, 6\}$

Range: $\{-3, -1, 3, 6\}$

This relation is not a function because there are duplicate destinations for $x = 2$; (-3 and 3).

Practice 21

Determine the domain, range, and whether or not the relation is a function.

1. $\{(-3,4),(3,4), (-2,1), (5,6)$

2. $\{(1,1), (3,2), (7,7), (1,3)\}$

3. $\{(-3,5), (-2,5), (-1,5), (0,5), (1,5), (2,5)\}$

Properties of Functions and Graphs of Functions

Function relationships can be expressed in a table, as a rule, or in a graph.

Functions can be added, subtracted, multiplied, or divided.

$f(x) + g(x) = (f + g)(x)$

$f(x) - g(x) = (f - g)(x)$

$f(x)g(x) = (f \times g)(x)$

$\dfrac{f(x)}{g(x)} = \left(\dfrac{f}{g}\right)(x),$ where $g \neq 0$

Functions can be graphed on the coordinate plane using ordered pair values for (x, y).

A *linear function* produces a straight line when graphed; $y = x + 1$.

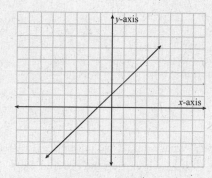

A *quadratic function* produces a curve pointing up or down when graphed; $y = x^2$.

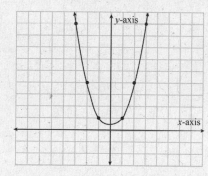

An *absolute value function* produces a "V-shape" pointing up or down on a graph; $y = |x| + 1$.

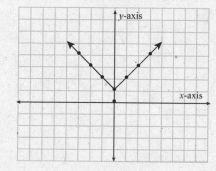

Practice 22

Identify how each function would look when graphed on a coordinate plane.

1. $y = 2x - 1$

2. $y = x^2 + 2x + 5$

3. $y = |x - 1| - 2$

Composition of Functions and Inverse Functions

A *composite function* uses two independent functions to form a *composition* of two functions that relate to one another. This is written as $f \circ g$ and is defined as $(f \circ g)(x) = f(g(x))$. It can also be written as $(g \circ f)(x) = (g(f(x))$. The inner function must be identified first and then solved through substitution.

Let $f(x) = x + 12$ and $g(x) = x^2 - 7$.

To find $(f \circ g)(x)$, the inner function g must first be evaluated.

$f(g(x)) = f(x^2 - 7) + 12$

$x^2 + 5$

The inverse of a function "undoes" what f did. If we define $f = \{(1,0), (4,5), (6,9)\}$, the inverse can be defined as $f^{-1} = \{(0,1), (5,4), (9,6)\}$ by inverting the ordered pairs.

To find the inverse of $f(x) = 2x + 3$. Write the function as an equation $y = 2x + 3$ and solve for x.

$x = \dfrac{(y - 3)}{2}$

$f^{-1}(x) = \dfrac{(x - 3)}{2}$

Practice 23

Evaluate each function.

1. Let $f(x) = -3x + 7$ and $g(x) = 4x - 9$.

   Evaluate $(f \circ g)(x)$.

2. Let $f(x) = \dfrac{x - 5}{20}$ and $g(x) = 3x$.

   Evaluate $(f \circ g)(-3)$.

3. Let $f(x) = 7x + 9$ and $g(x) = x^2$.

   Evaluate $(f \circ g)(4)$.

Simple Transformations of Functions: Translations, Reflections, Symmetry

A *transformation* of a graph moves according to a given rule. A graph can shift horizontally, vertically, or both. This is called a *translation*. When a graph flips over a line, it is a *reflection*, just like a mirror image.

The function $f(x)$ translates horizontally to $f(x + a)$ or $f(x - a)$. If $a > 0$, the graph slides to the right. If $a < 0$, then the graph slides to the left.

The function $f(x)$ translates vertically to $f(x) + a$. If $a > 0$, the graph slides upward. If $a < 0$, the graph slides downward.

If the function $f(x)$ reflects over the x-axis, the function is $-f(x)$. If the function $f(x)$ reflects over the y-axis, the function is $f(-x)$.

Symmetry means that you can pair the points such that the line is perpendicular to the segment joining the pair of points.

Symmetry can be tested several ways:

- Replace y with $-y$ in the equation. If you arrive at the same equation, it is symmetric to the x-axis.
$$x^2 + (-y)^2 = 9$$
$$x^2 + y^2 = 9$$

- Replace x with $-x$. If you arrive at the same, it is symmetric to the y-axis.
$$(-x)^2 + y^2 = 9$$
$$x^2 + y^2 = 9$$

- Interchange x and y. If the equation remains the same, it is symmetric to the line $y = x$.
$$y^2 + x^2 = 9$$
$$x^2 + y^2 = 9$$

- Replace x with $-x$ and y with $-y$. If the equation remains the same, it is symmetric to the origin.
$$(-x)^2 + (-y)^2 = 9$$
$$x^2 + y^2 = 9$$

Practice 24

Determine how the graphs will transform.

1. $g(x) = (x + 1)^2$

2. $y = f(x) + 2$

3. $y = (x + 4)^2 - 3$

4. $y = 3^x$ to $y = 3^{-x}$

ADDITIONAL TOPICS FROM ALGEBRA AND GEOMETRY

About 9 questions on the CLEP College Mathematics test will be about additional topics in algebra and geometry. Additional topics include, but are not limited to, the following:

- Complex numbers
- Logarithms and exponents
- Applications from algebra and geometry
- Perimeter and area of plane figures
- Properties of triangles, circles, and rectangles
- The Pythagorean Theorem
- Parallel and perpendicular lines

- Algebraic equations
- Systems of linear equations
- Inequalities
- Fundamental Theorem of Algebra
- Remainder Theorem
- Factor Theorem

Complex Numbers

A *complex number* is represented by $a + bi$, where a and b are real numbers and i is an imaginary unit. In the definition $a + bi$, a is called the real part of the complex number, and b is called the imaginary part.

$i = \sqrt{-1}$

Two complex numbers are equal if and only if their real and imaginary parts are equal: $a = c$ and $b = d$.

To add or subtract two complex numbers, add or subtract the real parts and the imaginary parts.

$(a + bi) + (c + di) = (a + c) + (b + d)i$

$(a + bi) - (c + di) = (a - c) + (b - d)i.$

To multiply complex numbers, use the formula below:

$(a + bi) \times (c + di) = (ac - bd) + (ad + bc)i$

The *conjugate* of a complex number is its opposite: $a + bi$ is $a - bi$.

A complex number becomes a real number when multiplied by its conjugate. It is also known as a *complex conjugate*.

$(a + bi)(a - bi) = (a^2 + b^2) + 0i = a^2 + b^2$

When dividing complex numbers, it is necessary to use the conjugate to produce a real number.

$$\frac{3 + 2i}{2 + 5i} = \frac{3 + 2i}{2 + 5i} \times \frac{2 - 5i}{2 - 5i}$$

$$= \frac{(3 + 2i)(2 - 5i)}{(2 + 5i)(2 - 5i)}$$

$$= \frac{16 - 11i}{29}$$

$$= \frac{16}{29} - \frac{11}{29}i$$

Practice 25

Solve each problem.

1. $(4 - 3i) + (5 + 4i) =$
2. $(5 - 4i) - (2 + 6i) =$
3. $(3 + 2i)(7 + 4i) =$
4. $(3 + 2i) \div (4 + 6i) =$
5. $(7 + 2i) \div (3 + 3i) =$

Logarithms and Exponents

Exponents are a short way of representing a number using a *base* and an exponent.

$3^4 = 3 \times 3 \times 3 \times 3$

$2^6 = 2 \times 2 \times 2 \times 2 \times 2 \times 2$

$10^5 = 100,000$

In the first example, 3 is the base and 4 is the exponent.

Properties of exponents:

- $a^m a^n = a^{m+n}$
- $(a^m)^n = a^{mn}$
- $(ab)^m = a^m b^m$
- $\dfrac{a^m}{a^n} = a^{m-n}, a \neq 0$
- $\left(\dfrac{a}{b}\right)^m = \dfrac{a^m}{b^m}, b \neq 0$
- $a^{-m} = \dfrac{1}{a^m}, a \neq 0$
- $a^{\frac{1}{n}} = \sqrt[n]{a}$
- $a^0 = 1, a \neq 0$
- $a^{\frac{m}{n}} = \sqrt[n]{a^m} = \left(\sqrt[n]{a}\right)^m$

Logarithms are exponents and are written $y = \log_a(x)$ if and only if $a^y = x$, where $a > 0$. $\log_5(25) = 2$ translates to $5^2 = 25$.

$\log_{10}(1) = 0$ translaters to $10^0 = 1$.

Properties for logarithms base a:

- $\log_a xy = \log_a x + \log_a y$
- $\log_a \dfrac{x}{y} = \log_a x - \log_a y$
- $\log_a x^y = y \cdot \log_a x$

- $\log_a a^x = x$
- $a^{\log_a x} = x$

Practice 26

Find the logarithms.

1. $\log_2 16 =$
2. $\log_4 2 =$
3. $\log_{10} 0.01 =$
4. $\log_7 343 =$
5. $\log_8 2 =$

Perimeter and Area of Plane Figures

The distance around a plane figure is its *perimeter*. The perimeter is found by finding the sum of lengths of all sides.

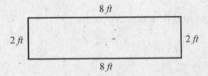

$2 + 2 + 8 + 8 = 20$ ft.

The perimeter of a circle is known as the *circumference*—the distance around the circle. The distance from the center of a circle to the outside is called the radius (*r*). The formula for circumference is $c = 2\pi r$.

Area is the measure of square units that cover a surface. Formulas are used to find the areas of various plane figures.

Triangle: $A = \frac{1}{2}bh$, where *b* is the base and *h* is the height.

Square: $A = s^2$, where *s* is the length of one side.

Rectangle: $A = bh$ or $A = lw$, where *b*, or *l*, is length and *h*, or *w*, is height.

Parallelogram: $A = bh$.

Circle: $A = \pi r^2$

Practice 27

Find the perimeter of each plane figure.

1.

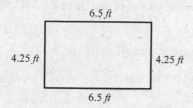

6.5 ft

4.25 ft   4.25 ft

6.5 ft

Find the area of each plane figure.

2.

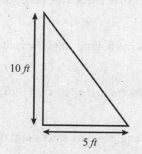

10 ft

5 ft

3.

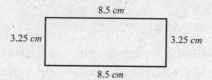

8.5 cm

3.25 cm   3.25 cm

8.5 cm

4.

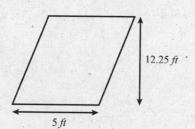

12.25 ft

5 ft

5.

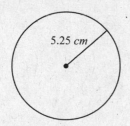

5.25 cm

Properties of Triangles, Circles, and Rectangles

A *triangle* is a three-sided polygon whose angles total 180 degrees. Triangles are classified by their sides and the measures of their angles. A triangle is named using a symbol and three capital letters: △*GHI* .

An *equilateral triangle* has all sides equal, all angles equiangular, and all angles acute.

An *isosceles triangle* has two equal sides, and two equiangular base angles.

A *scalene triangle* has no equal sides.

A *circle* is a closed-plane figure with all points measuring the same distance from the center point. One complete rotation equals 360 degrees.

The *diameter* or *chord* of a circle is the measure of any line segment passing through the center of the circle with endpoints on the circle.

The *radius* of a circle is the measure of any line segment with one endpoint in the center of the circle and another on the circle.

A *central angle* is an angle inside the circle, where the vertex of the angle is the center point of the circle.

An *arc* is part of a circle consisting of two endpoints on the circle.

A *rectangle* is a *quadrilateral*. A quadrilateral is a four-sided polygon whose interior angles equal 360 degrees. A rectangle is always a parallelogram, which always has opposite sides equal and congruent opposite angles. In a rectangle, all angles are right angles.

Practice 28

Identify each plane figure.

1. A plane figure that contains no angles
2. Interior angles that add up to 180 degrees
3. Includes a chord and a radius
4. Can be equilateral or scalene
5. A four-sided polygon whose angles total 360 degrees

The Pythagorean Theorem

Use the Pythagorean Theorem only with right triangles to find the missing length of either leg or the *hypotenuse*. The hypotenuse is the side opposite the right angle in a right triangle, while the other two sides are the legs.

$$a^2 + b^2 = c^2$$
$$4^2 + 3^2 = c^2$$
$$16 + 9 = c^2$$
$$25 = c^2$$
$$\sqrt{25} = 5$$
$$c = 5$$

Practice 29

Solve each equation.

1. $28^2 + 45^2 = c^2$
2. $a^2 + 21^2 = 29^2$
3. $16^2 + b^2 = 65^2$

Parallel and Perpendicular Lines

Lines are parallel if they never intersect. Parallel lines will have the same slope.

Lines are perpendicular if they intersect at a right angle and the product of their slopes is -1. Perpendicular lines also have slopes that are the negative reciprocals of each other. If one line has a slope of 5, the other will have a slope of $-\frac{1}{5}$.

Lines can be defined by their slopes.

$$\text{Slope} = \frac{\text{vertical change}}{\text{horizontal change}} = \frac{\text{change in } y}{\text{change in } x}$$

The formula for slope is $y = mx + b$, where m is the slope and b is the y-intercept.

Practice 30

Indicate whether the following are parallel or perpendicular lines.

1. $y = 2x + 1$
   $y = -0.5x + 4$
2. $y = 2x + 11$
   $2y - 4x = 1$
3. $y = \frac{2}{3}x + 7$
   $y = -1.5 + 4$

Algebraic Equations, Systems of Linear Equations, and Inequalities

Algebraic equations are mathematical sentences including numbers, variables (shown as letters), and an equal sign. Whatever operation is done on one side of the equal sign in an equation must be done on the opposite side as well. Equations can be one-step or multistep.

One step:

$$x + 3 = 9$$
$$ -3 \quad -3$$
$$x = 6$$

Multistep:

$$2x + 12 = 16$$
$$ -12 \quad -12$$
$$\frac{2x}{2} = \frac{4}{2}$$
$$x = 2$$

Two or more linear equations create a *system of linear equations*. Linear equations result in either one solution, many solutions, or no solutions and can be solved by graphing, adding, or subtracting or by substitution.

When there is only one solution, two lines will intersect at one point when graphed on the coordinate plane. When there is no solution, a set of parallel lines will result, and when there are many solutions, one line will result, because the solution set includes all points on the line.

Adding or subtracting:

$$3x - y = 3$$
$$\underline{x + y = 5}$$
$$4x = 8$$
$$x = 2$$

Substitute x for y in one equation.

$$2 + y = 5$$
$$y = 3$$

The solution set is (2,3).

When variables do not have opposite signs to cancel out, multiply one equation by -1 and then solve the equation.

Substitution:

$$2x + 3y = 12$$
$$x - y = 1$$

Solve for x in the second equation: $x = 1 + y.$

Substitute x in the first equation.

$$2(1 + y) + 3y = 12$$
$$2 + 2y + 3y = 12$$
$$2 + 5y = 12$$
$$5y = 10$$
$$y = 2$$

Substitute y into either equation to find a value for x.

$$2x + 3(2) = 12$$
$$2x + 6 = 12$$
$$2x = 6$$
$$x = 3$$

The solution set is (3,2).

When an equation includes $\neq, <, \leq, >,$ or $\geq,$ instead of $=,$ a mathematical *inequality* is formed. These are solved in the same manner as other equations except $\leq$ becomes $\geq$ and $\geq$ becomes $\leq$ when a negative variable results.

$$-5x + 10 < 15$$
$$-10 - 10$$
$$-5x \quad < 5$$
$$-x \quad < 1$$
$$x \quad > -1$$

Practice 31

Determine the solution set for the following equations.

1. $2x - 4y = -12$
   $2x + 5y = 6$
2. $3y + 2x = 11$
   $y - x = 4$
3. $2x + y = -18$
   $12x - 6y = 12$
4. $6x + 12 \leq 32$
5. $-3x + 18 \geq 3$

Fundamental Theorem of Algebra, Remainder Theorem, Factor Theorem

The Fundamental Theorem of Algebra states that any complex polynomial must have a complex root.

A *polynomial* is made up of terms that are only added, subtracted, or multiplied.

$3x^2 - 12$ will have two roots because the largest exponent is 2.

$$3x^2 - 12 = 0$$
$$3(x^2 - 4) = 0$$
$$x^2 = 4$$
$$x = \pm 2$$

The Remainder Theorem states when you divide a polynomial $f(x)$ by $x - c$, the remainder r will be $f(c)$.

$(2x^2 - 5x - 1) \div (x - 3)$

$f(3) = 2(3)^2 - 5(3) - 1 = 2$

The Factor Theorem states when $f(c) = 0$, then $x - c$ is a factor of the polynomial.

$2x^3 - x^2 - 7x + 2$

$f(2) \rightarrow 2(2)^3 - 2^2 - 7(2) + 2 = 0$

Therefore, $(x - 2)$ is a factor.

Practice 32

Find the remainder.

  1. $(2x^2 - 4x + 5) \div (x - 2)$

  2. $(6x^2 + 3x - 4) \div (x + 7)$

Determine if each is a factor.

  3. $2x^3 - x^2 - 21x + 18$

      $(x - 1)$

      $(x - 2)$

      $(x - 3)$

      $(x - 4)$

PRACTICE ANSWERS AND EXPLANATIONS

Real Number System

Practice 1

1. **The correct answer is odd.** A 5 appears in the one's place and is an odd number. Therefore, 15 is an odd number.

2. **The correct answer is even.** A 0 appears in the one's place and is an even number. Therefore, 6230 is an even number.

3. **The correct answer is odd.** A 1 appears in the one's place and is an odd number. Therefore, 10,001 is an odd number.

4. **The correct answer is even.** A 6 appears in the one's place and is an even number. Therefore, 17,256 is an even number.

5. **The correct answer is odd.** A 3 appears in the one's place and is an odd number. Therefore, 101,263 is an odd number.

Practice 2

1. **The correct answer is prime.**

2. **The correct answer is composite.**

3. **The correct answer is prime.**

4. **The correct answer is composite.**

5. **The correct answer is composite.**

Practice 3

1. **The correct answer is −8, −4, −2, −1, 1, 2, 4, and 8.** Two negative numbers must be multiplied together to yield 8. For example, $-1 \times -8 = 8$ and two positive numbers must be multiplied together to yield a positive product.

2. **The correct answer is −14, −7, −2, −1, 1, 2, 7, and 14.**

3. **The correct answer is −1, −3, −7, −21, 1, 3, 7, and 21.**

4. **The correct answer is −1, −2, −4, −8, −16, −32, 1, 2, 4, 8, 16, and 32.**

5. **The correct answer is −1, −3, −5, −9, −15, −45, 1, 3, 5, 9, 15, and 45.**

Practice 4

1. **The correct answer is rational.** Using division, $2 \div 1 = 0.5$. The number ends and is therefore rational.

2. **The correct answer is rational.** 7 is its own number.

3. **The correct answer is irrational.** The square root of 2 is 1.414213562373095 (and more...).

Practice 5

1. **The correct answer is 10.** Using a number line, −10 is 10 away from 0, therefore, the absolute value of −10 is 10.

2. **The correct answer is 7.** According to the order of operations, problems in brackets and parenthesis are solved first. Therefore, −10 + 3 = −7, and the absolute value of −7 is 7.

3. **The correct answer is 15.** According to the order of operations, problems in brackets and parenthesis are solved first. Therefore, −3 × 5 = −15, and the absolute value of −15 is 15.

4. **The correct answer is −10, −3, 0, 8.** Since −3 is closer to 0 on the number line, it is greater than −10.

5. **The correct answer is −2, −1, 0, 1, 5.** Since −1 is closer to 0 on the number line, it is greater than −2.

Practice 6

1. **The correct answer is {7, 8, 9, 10, 11, 12, 13, 14}.** The parenthesis indicate that this in an open set, and the endpoints are not included.

2. **The correct answer is {11, 12, 13, 14, 15, 16, 17, 18}.** The braces indicate that this is a closed set and the endpoints are included.

3. **The correct answer is {34, 35, 36, 37, 38, 39, 40, 41, 42}.** The parenthesis on the left indicates that 33 is not an endpoint, while the brace on the right indicates that 42 is an endpoint.

4. **The correct answer is {19, 20, 21, 22}.** The brace on the left indicates that 19 is an endpoint, while the parenthesis on the right indicates that 23 is not an endpoint.

5. **The correct answer is $x \leq 12$.** Negative infinity is an open interval because it includes all numbers less than or equal to 12, which is an endpoint, indicated by the brace on the right.

Sets

Practice 7

1. **The correct answer is {r, s, t, u}.** A union of two sets results in a new set whose members include the members of each original set. The member r is in Set A and Set B and does not need to be repeated.

2. **The correct answer is $\varnothing$.** An intersection of two sets includes only the common members of the original sets. Since one of the sets is empty, the result is a null set because no common members exist.

3. **The correct answer is {1, 2, 3, 9, 10}.** The union of Set O and Set P results in the new set. Members common to both sets are not repeated.

4. **The correct answer is {−5, −4, −1}.** The intersection requires you to look for common members of both sets. Since Set J contains all negative numbers, the intersection includes only the negative numbers from Set K.

5. **The correct answer is {3, 4}.** The intersection requires you to look for common members of both sets. Since Set T contains all positive numbers, the intersection includes only the positive numbers from Set U.

Practice 8

1. **The correct answer is subset.** A subset is a group of elements or members that belong to a larger set. Set B belongs to the larger Set A and is therefore a subset.

2. **The correct answer is equivalent.** Equivalent sets contain the same number of elements. Set A and Set B both contain three members.

3. **The correct answer is equivalent.** Equivalent sets contain the same number of elements. Set A and Set B both contain three members.

4. **The correct answer is equal.** Equal sets contain the same number of elements and the exact same elements. This is true of Sets A and B.

5. **The correct answer is subset.** Set B is a subset of Set A because the members of Set B are also contained in Set A.

Practice 9

1. **The correct answer is {1, 6, 12, 15, 17, 32, 44}.** In a Venn diagram, the elements contained in the intersection are members of both sets. Therefore, Set A includes the members in only A and the members in the intersection.

2. **The correct answer is {1, 2, 3, 6, 9, 10, 11, 15}.** The elements contained in the intersection are members of both sets. Therefore, Set B includes the members in only B and the members in the intersection.

3. **The correct answer is {1, 2, 3, 6, 9, 10, 11, 12, 15, 17, 32, 44}.** This problem asks for the union of Set A and Set B. The new set contains all of the members of both sets without repetition.

4. **The correct answer is {1, 6, 15}.** This problem asks for the intersection of Sets A and B. The intersection of two sets is easily seen in a Venn diagram and includes all the members in the intersection of the two sets.

Practice 10

1. **The correct answer is (2,5), (3,5), (2,6), (3,6), (2,7), (3,7).** The Cartesian product multiplies A times B, resulting in ordered pairs.

Probability and Statistics

Practice 11

1. **The correct answer is permutation.** The order in which the people are chosen matters, so this is an example of a permutation.

2. **The correct answer is combination.** The order in which the desserts are chosen doesn't matter, so this is an example of a combination.

3. **The correct answer is permutation.** The order in which the movies are listed matters, so this is an example of a permutation.

4. **The correct answer is combination.** The order in which the children are arranged in a row doesn't matter, so this is an example of a combination.

5. **The correct answer is combination.** The order in which the letters are arranged doesn't matter, so this is an example of a combination.

Practice 12

1. **The correct answer is independent.** This is an independent event because the second event is not dependent on the outcome of the first event. The formula for an independent event is used to solve this problem.

2. **The correct answer is independent.** Although there are two events, the outcome of the second event is not dependent on the first. Therefore, these events are independent, and the formula for an independent event is used to solve the problem.

3. **The correct answer is dependent.** The outcome of the second event is dependent on the first event. The first time a marble is drawn out of the bag, there is a 3:7 chance that a blue marble will be chosen. The probability of choosing a black marble the second time depends on the outcome of the first event.

4. **The correct answer is independent.** This is an independent event because the second event is not dependent on the outcome of the first event. The formula for an independent event is used to solve this problem.

5. **The correct answer is independent.** This is an independent event because the second event is not dependent of the outcome of the first event. The formula for an independent event is used to solve this problem.

Practice 13

1. **The correct answer is 25%.** $P(\text{Absent}|\text{Monday}) = \dfrac{P(\text{Monday and Absent})}{P(\text{Monday})} = \dfrac{0.05}{0.2} = 0.25$.

2. **The correct answer is 71%.** $P(\text{second}|\text{first}) = \dfrac{P(\text{first and second})}{P(\text{first})} = \dfrac{0.50}{0.70} = 0.71$.

3. **The correct answer is 48%.** $P(\text{job}|\text{sport}) = \dfrac{P(\text{job and sport})}{P(\text{sport})} = \dfrac{0.12}{0.25} = 0.48$.

Practice 14

1. **The correct answer is 54.** The mean is also known as the average. It is found by finding the sum of the addends, which is 540. We then divide 540 by 10, the number of addends, and arrive at 54.

2. **The correct answer is 59.** The median is the middle number or numbers in a set of data arranged in order. When arranged in order, the set of data is 11, 15, 49, 55, 59, 59, 60, 66, 75, 91. Both 59s are in the middle, but we only need to report the number once.

3. **The correct answer is 59.** The mode is the number that occurs most often in a set of data. In this set of data, 59 is the only number that occurs more than once.

4. **The correct answer is 80.** The range of a set of data is found by subtracting the smallest number in the data set from the largest: $91 - 11 = 80$.

Practice 15

1. **The correct answer is 9.4.** We first need to find the mean of the data: 23.1. We then subtract the mean from each data value and square each difference. Next, we find the sum of the squared deviations and divide this number by one less than the sample size; in this case 8. Finally, we take the square root of the quotient to arrive at 9.4. This data does not have a small standard deviation, therefore, the data are not clustered close to the mean.

Practice 16

1. **The correct answer is that 1990 is the only year where more people had a better knowledge of German compared to Spanish.** The multiple bar graph shows the percentage of incoming freshman with a good knowledge of Spanish and German. 1990 is the only year where the German bar is taller than the Spanish bar. Therefore, we can conclude that a greater percentage of incoming freshman had a good knowledge of German.

2. **The correct answer is 119.** First, we find the date January 21, 2011. Next, we see where the corresponding line falls on the graph. The line dips just below 120. Therefore, we can conclude that the value of the stock on January 21, 2011 was 119.

3. **The correct answer is apples.** The key to the right of the chart identifies what each color of the pie chart represents. By comparing the percentages labeling each section of the pie, we can conclude that apples generated the greatest sales in October.

4. **The correct answer is that there is a negative relationship.** By examining the dots on a scatter plot, we can determine the relationship between two variables. When connected, the dots form a line sloping downward from left to right. This indicates a negative relationship.

5. **The correct answer is children.** An adult is considered someone between the ages of 21 and 50. According to the histogram, Bill has 6 neighbors between the ages of 21 and 50 and 7 neighbors between the ages of 0 and 20.

Logic

Practice 17

1.

P	~P
T	F
F	T

2.

a	b	a ∨ b
T	T	T
T	F	T
F	T	T
F	F	F

3.

P	Q	P ∧ Q
T	T	T
T	F	F
F	T	F
F	F	F

4.

P	Q	~P	~P ∧ Q
T	T	F	F
T	F.	F	F
F	T	T	T
F	F	T	F

5.

P	~P	~(~P)
T	F	T
F	T	F

Practice 18

1. The hypothesis is "Marty has a math assignment." The conclusion is "Pete has a soccer game."

2. The hypothesis is "Three is an odd number." The conclusion is "nine is composite."

3. The hypothesis is "Darrel owns a car." The conclusion is "ten is an even number."

Practice 19

1. **The correct answer is necessary.** Without sunlight, flowers cannot bloom. Therefore, sunlight is a necessary condition.

2. **The correct answer is necessary.** One must be female in order to be a mother. Therefore, being a female is a necessary condition for being a mother.

3. **The correct answer is necessary.** Without oxygen, human life cannot be sustained. Therefore, oxygen is a necessary condition.

4. **The correct answer is sufficient.** If a tray filled with water is placed in a freezer, then the water is guaranteed to freeze. Therefore, placing water in the freezer is a sufficient condition.

5. **The correct answer is sufficient.** Earning a final grade of 80 in history guarantees a passing grade. Therefore, receiving a grade of 80 is a sufficient condition to passing the class.

Practice 20

1. **The correct answer is "If the light is on, then the switch is up."** The converse of an if P, then Q statement is if Q, then P.

2. **The correct answer is "If the switch is not up, then the light is not on."** The inverse of an if P, then Q statement is if not P, then not Q.

3. **The correct answer is "If the light is not on, then the switch in not up."** The contrapositive of an if P, then Q statement is if not Q, then not P.

Functions and Their Graphs

Practice 21

1. **The correct answer is domain $\{-3, 3, -2, 5\}$ and range $\{4, 1, 6\}$. This is a function.** The domain consists of the x-values in the ordered pairs, and the range consists of the y-values. Since each x-value has its own destination. This is a function.

2. **The correct answer is domain $\{1, 3, 7\}$ and range $\{1, 2, 7, 3\}$. This is not a function.** The domain consists of the x-values in the ordered pairs, and the range consists of the y-values. Since $x = 1$ has duplicate destinations (1 and 3), it is not a function.

3. **The correct answer is domain $\{-3, -2, -1, 0, 1, 2\}$ and range $\{5\}$. This is a function.** The domain consists of the x-values in the ordered pairs, and since 5 is the y-value in every ordered pair, it is the only range. Since each x-value has its own destination, this is a function.

Practice 22

1. **The correct answer is one diagonal line.** The equation is a linear function, and linear functions produce a straight line when graphed.

2. **The correct answer is curved.** The equation is a quadratic equation because it contains an exponent, and quadratic equations produce a curved line when graphed.

3. **The correct answer is "V-shaped."** The equation is an absolute function, and absolute functions produce a V-shaped line when graphed.

Practice 23

1. **The correct answer is $-12x + 34$.** We first define the inner function g and use the output of g as the input for f.

$$(f \circ g)(x) = f(g(x)) = f(4x - 9)$$
$$(f \circ g)(x) = -3(4x - 9) + 7$$
$$(f \circ g)(x) = -12x + 27 + 7$$
$$(f \circ g)(x) = -12 + 34$$

2. **The correct answer is -0.7.** We are given -3 as the value of the function, so we first substitute the value into g and use the output of g as the input for f.

$$g(-3) = 3(-3)$$
$$g(-3) = -9$$
$$f(-9) = \frac{-9 - 5}{20}$$
$$f(-9) = \frac{14}{20}$$
$$(f \circ g)(-3) = -0.7$$

3. **The correct answer is 121.** We first need to evaluate the inner function g using the output of g as the input for f.

$$g(4) = 4^2$$
$$g(4) = 16$$
$$f(16) = 7(16) + 9$$
$$f(16) = 121$$

Practice 24

1. **The correct answer is the graph will shift to the left by 1 unit.** The functions $f(x + a)$ or $f(x - a)$ define whether a graph will move horizontally or vertically. Since the function g is $+1$, it will shift to the left by 1 unit.

2. **The correct answer is the graph will shift up by 2 units.** The $f(x)$ determines if the graph will slide upward or downward. Since $y = f(x) + 2$, the graph will shift up by 2 units.

3. **The correct answer is the graph will shift to the left by 4 units and down by 3 units.** This combines the two functions $f(x + a)$ and $f(x)$ and results in the graph shifting left and down.

4. **The correct answer is the graph will be reflected in the y-axis.** If the function $f(x)$ reflects over the y-axis, the function is $f(-x)$.

Additional Topics from Algebra and Geometry

Practice 25

1. **The correct answer is 9 + 1i.** Add the real parts and the imaginary parts separately. $(4+5)+(-3+4)i$.

2. **The correct answer is 3 − 10i.** Subtract the real parts and the imaginary parts separately. $(5-2)-(-4-6)i$.

3. **The correct answer is 13 + 26i.** Use the formula $(ac-bd)+(ad+bc)i$. $(21-8)+(12+14)i$.

4. **The correct answer is $\dfrac{12-5i}{26}$.** Use the complex conjugate of the denominator to solve the problem.

   $$= \frac{3+2i}{4+6i}$$

   $$= \frac{(3+2i)(4-6i)}{(4+6i)(4-6i)}$$

   $$= \frac{(12+12)+(-18+8)i}{(16+36)+(-24+24)}$$

   $$= \frac{24-10i}{52}$$

   $$= \frac{12-5i}{26}$$

5. **The correct answer is $\dfrac{9-5i}{6}$.** Use the complex conjugate of the denominator to solve the problem.

   $$= \frac{(7+2i)}{(3+3i)}$$

   $$= \frac{(7+2i)(3-3i)}{(3+3i)(3-3i)}$$

   $$= \frac{(21+6)(-21+6)i}{(9+9)(9-9)i}$$

   $$= \frac{27-15i}{18}$$

   $$= \frac{9-5i}{6}$$

Practice 26

1. **The correct answer is 2^4.** We can think of this as 4^2 to help determine the answer. It is helpful to ask, "What squared will equal 16?"

2. **The correct answer is $\frac{1}{2}$.** It is helpful to think of a logarithm in missing parts: $4^? = 2$.

3. **The correct answer is –2.** It is helpful to think $10^? = 0.01$. $10^{-2} = 10^? = .01$. $\frac{1}{100}$, which is the same as 0.01.

4. **The correct answer is 7^3.**

5. **The correct answer is $\frac{1}{3}$.**

Practice 27

1. **The correct answer is 21.5 ft.** To find the perimeter of a rectangle, find the sum of all sides of a plane figure: $4.25 + 4.25 + 6.5 + 6.5 = 21.5$ ft.

2. **The correct answer is 25 ft.^{2}** To find the area of a triangle take half the base times the width:

   $$\frac{1}{2}(5) \times 10 = 2.5 \times 10 = 25 \text{ ft.}^2$$

3. **The correct answer is 27.625 cm.^{2}** To find the area of a rectangle multiply the length times the height: $8.5 \times 3.25 = 27.625$ cm.^{2}

4. **The correct answer is 61.25 ft.^{2}** To find the area of a parallelogram multiply the base times the height: $5 \times 12.25 = 61.25$ ft.^{2}

5. **The correct answer is 86.5 cm.^{2}** To find the area of a circle use the formula πr^2: $3.14(5.25)^2 = 86.5$ cm.^{2}

Practice 28

1. **The correct answer is circle.** A circle does not have any angles.

2. **The correct answer is triangle.** The three angles of a triangle sum to 180 degrees.

3. **The correct answer is circle.** A circle has a chord and a radius, which is half the diameter.

4. **The correct answer is triangle.** An equilateral triangle has all sides equal, while a scalene triangle has no equal sides.

5. **The correct answer is rectangle.** A rectangle has four sides, is a polygon, and its interior angles sum to 360 degrees.

Practice 29

1. **The correct answer is 53.** Using the formula $a^2 + b^2 = c^2$, we are able to find the missing hypotenuse.

$$28^2 + 45^2 = c^2$$
$$784 + 2025 = c^2$$
$$2809 = c^2$$
$$c = \sqrt{2809} = 53$$

2. **The correct answer is 20.**

$$a^2 + 21^2 = 29^2$$
$$a^2 + 441 = 841$$
$$a^2 = 841 - 441$$
$$a^2 = 400$$
$$a = \sqrt{400} = 20$$

3. **The correct answer is 63.**

$$16^2 + b^2 = 65^2$$
$$256 + b^2 = 4225$$
$$b^2 = 4225 - 256$$
$$b^2 = 3969$$
$$b = \sqrt{3969} = 63$$

Practice 30

1. **The correct answer is perpendicular.** The product of the slope of two perpendicular lines will be -1. $2 \times -0.5 = -1$.

2. **The correct answer is parallel.** Parallel lines will have the same slope. When we change the second equations to get y by itself, we see that both lines have a slope of 2.

3. **The correct answer is perpendicular.** The slope of perpendicular lines will be the negative reciprocal of the other. The negative reciprocal of $\frac{2}{3}$ is $-\frac{3}{2}$. When we divide 3 by 2, we get -1.5. Therefore, the lines are perpendicular.

Practice 31

1. **The correct answer is (–2,2).** Multiply one equation by -1 and then add and subtract the two equations to get a value for y. Substitute the value for y in one equation to solve for x.

2. **The correct answer is $\left(-\frac{1}{5}, 3\frac{4}{5} \right)$.** Solve the second equation for x or y and then substitute the value into the first equation.

3. **The correct answer is (–4,–20).** Multiply the first equation by 6 to eliminate the y variable, then substitute the value of x to determine y.

4. **The correct answer is $x \leq 3\frac{1}{3}$.** The variable x is not negative, so the sign remains the same.

5. **The correct answer is $x \leq 5$.** The variable x is not negative, so the sign changes.

Practice 32

1. **The correct answer is 5.** Substitute 2 for x. Use the order of operations and complete the exponents first before multiplying.

2. **The correct answer is 269.** Substitute -7 for x. Use the order of operations and complete the exponents first before multiplying.

3. **The correct answer is $(x - 3)$ is a factor.** When 3 is substituted for x, it is the only value that yields 0. Therefore, $(x - 3)$ is a factor.

COLLEGE MATHEMATICS: REVIEW QUESTIONS

1. Which one of the following linear equations is perpendicular to the graph of the linear equation $5y - 8x = 0$?

   (A) $y = x\dfrac{5}{8} - 6$

   (B) $y = -\dfrac{5}{8}x - 6$

   (C) $y = \dfrac{8}{5}x - 6$

   (D) $y = -\dfrac{8}{5}x - 6$

2. If $f(x) = x^2 - 3x + 5$, then $f(-3) =$

   (A) -13

   (B) 5

   (C) 8

   (D) 23

3. Which of the following statements is logically equivalent to the statement: "If it is going to rain, then I bring my umbrella."

   (A) If it is not going to rain, then I bring my umbrella.

   (B) If I bring my umbrella, then it is going to rain.

   (C) If I do not bring my umbrella, then it is not going to rain.

   (D) If I do not bring my umbrella, then it is going to rain.

4. If the mean of the numbers $w, x, y,$ and z is

   a, then $\dfrac{a}{w + x + y + z} =$

   (A) $a2$

   (B) $\dfrac{1}{4}$

   (C) 4

   (D) 2

5. In the Venn diagram below A, B, and C represent sets. Shade the regions representing $B \cup (A \cap C)$.

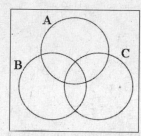

6. If m and n are real numbers, with $n < m$, which of the following must also be true?

   I. $|n| < |m|$

   II. $\dfrac{1}{n} > \dfrac{1}{m}$

   III. $\dfrac{m - n}{2} > 0$

   (A) I only

   (B) II and III

   (C) I and II

   (D) III only

7. If $f(x) = \dfrac{x}{1 - x}$ and $g(x) = \dfrac{1}{x^2}$, then

   $(f \circ g)(x) =$

   (A) $\dfrac{1 - 2x - x^2}{x^2}$

   (B) $\dfrac{1}{x - x^2}$

   (C) $\dfrac{x^2}{1 - x^2}$

   (D) $\dfrac{1}{x^2 - 1}$

8. What is the perimeter of the figure below?

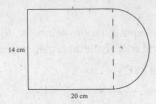

(A) $54 + 7\pi$

(B) $54 + 14\pi$

(C) $68 + 14\pi$

(D) $280 + 24.5\pi$

9. If x and y are prime numbers, what is the greatest common divisor of x^4y^6 and x^3y^8?

(A) x^4y^8

(B) x^7y^{14}

(C) xy^2xx

(D) x^3y^6

10. If $x - 2$ is a factor of $x^3 - kx^2 + 5x + 2$, what is the value of k?

(A) -2

(B) 2

(C) 5

(D) 6

11. A jar has exactly 7 blue marbles, 5 red marbles, and 4 green marbles. What is the probability that the first marble is blue and the second one is green, if the first marble is not replaced after it is selected?

(A) $\dfrac{7}{60}$

(B) $\dfrac{7}{64}$

(C) $\dfrac{11}{16}$

(D) $\dfrac{169}{240}$

12. Which of the following statements about an Event A are true?

I. The probability that Event A will occur can be negative.

II. The sum of the probability that Event A will occur and the probability that Event A will not occur is always equal to 1.

III. The probability of Event A must be between 0 and 1 inclusive.

(A) II and III

(B) I and II

(C) I and III

(D) II only

13. What is the value of x in the triangle below?

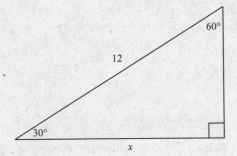

(A) 6

(B) $6\sqrt{2}$

(C) $8\sqrt{3}$

(D) $6\sqrt{3}$

14. For real numbers a and b, which of the following is equal to the maximum of a and b?

(A) $\dfrac{a + b - |a - b|}{2}$

(B) $\dfrac{a + b + |a - b|}{2}$

(C) $\dfrac{a + b + |a + b|}{2}$

(D) $\dfrac{a + b - |a + b|}{2}$

15. Out of 40 students, 14 are taking history and 29 are taking chemistry. If 5 students are in both classes, how many students are taking only history?

(A) 14

(B) 12

(C) 9

(D) 7

16. Which logical conclusion can be deduced from the following two premises?
   I. All informative things are useful.
   II. Some Web sites are not useful.

(A) Some Web sites are not informative.

(B) Some Web sites are useful.

(C) All informative things are not Web sites.

(D) All informative things are Web sites.

17. A car is purchased from a dealership for $40,000, and its price decreases linearly. If the car is worth $28,000 in 3 years, what expression represents the value (V) as a function of the number of years (t) since it was purchased?

(A) $V = 28,000 - 4000t$

(B) $V = 40,000 - 28,000t$

(C) $V = 40,000 + 4000t$

(D) $V = 40,000 - 4000t$

18. Which of the following is a root of $x^2 - 2x + 5 = 0$?

(A) $1 + 4i$

(B) $1 + 2i$

(C) $-1 + 4i$

(D) $-1 - 2i$

19. What is the sum of the mean and the median of the numbers 15, 21, 32, 15, 27?

(A) 43

(B) 51

(C) 54

(D) 131

20. What is the range of the following graph?

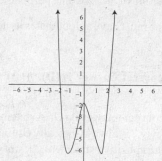

(A) $(-\infty, \infty)$

(B) $[-6, \infty)$

(C) $[-6, 6]$

(D) $(-\infty, 6]$

ANSWER KEY AND EXPLANATIONS

1. B	9. D	13. D	17. D
2. D	10. C	14. B	18. B
3. C	11. A	15. C	19. A
4. B	12. A	16. A	20. B

5.

6. D

7. D

8. A

1. **The correct answer is (B).** To find the slope, rewrite the equation as $y = \frac{8}{5}x$. This line has a slope of $\frac{8}{5}$. Any line perpendicular to this line must have a slope that is its negative reciprocal, $-\frac{5}{8}$.

2. **The correct answer is (D).** $f(-3) = (-3)^2 - 3(-3) + 5 = 9 + 9 + 5 = 23$.

3. **The correct answer is (C).** A statement, "If P, then Q," is always logically equivalent to its contrapositive statement, "If not Q, then not P."

4. **The correct answer is (B).** Since $\frac{w + x + y + z}{4} = a$, $w + x + y + z = 4a$ Thus, $\frac{a}{w + x + y + z} = \frac{a}{4a} = \frac{1}{4}$.

5. **The correct answer is** **.** The elements of $B \cup (A \cup C)$ are those that are either in B or in both A and C.

6. **The correct answer is (D).** Many counterexamples exist to show that Statements I and II are not always true. Statement III is always true since if $n < m$, then $0 < m - n$, and dividing both sides of the inequality by 2 yields $0 < \frac{m - n}{2}$.

7. **The correct answer is (D).**
$$f(g(x)) = f\left(\frac{1}{x^2}\right) = \frac{\frac{1}{x^2}}{1 - \frac{1}{x^2}} = \frac{1}{x^2 - 1}.$$

8. **The correct answer is (A).** The perimeter of the rectangular portion is $20 + 14 + 20 = 54$, and the circumference (perimeter) of the semicircular portion is $\frac{\pi d}{2} = \frac{\pi(14)}{2} = 7\pi$. Therefore, the total perimeter is $54 + 7\pi$.

9. **The correct answer is (D).** The greatest common divisor must divide both terms and be the largest such divisor. Since there are only two terms, the greatest common divisor can be found by forming $x^a y^b$ where a is the smallest power of x from the two terms, and b is the smallest power of y from the two terms.

10. **The correct answer is (C).** $x - a$ is a factor of $f(x)$ if and only if $f(a) = 0$. Substitute $x = 2$ into $f(x) = 3x^3 - kx^2 + 5x + 2$, set the expression equal to zero, and solve for k.

11. **The correct answer is (A).** There are 16 marbles. Since the second draw is done without replacing the first marble, these two events are dependent events. The probability of choosing blue the first time and green the second is $\frac{7}{16} \times \frac{4}{15} = \frac{7}{60}$.

12. **The correct answer is (A).** The probability of any event is always between 0 and 1 inclusive. Also, one of either A or not A must occur. Thus, the probability of A and not A is 1.

13. **The correct answer is (D).** Set up a trigonometric equation to solve for x:

$$\cos(30°) = \frac{x}{12} \text{ or}$$

$$x = 12\cos(30°) = 12\frac{\sqrt{3}}{2} = 6\sqrt{3}.$$

14. **The correct answer is (B).** The amount by which the maximum is greater than the minimum is the absolute value of the difference of the two numbers, $|a - b|$.

Adding this to a and b produces twice the maximum, and dividing by 2 produces the maximum.

15. **The correct answer is (C).** Use a Venn diagram do organize the information. There are 9 students taking history and 5 taking both history and chemistry. Therefore, there must be 24 students taking only chemistry because a total of 29 students are taking chemistry. There are 2 students not taking chemistry or history.

16. **The correct answer is (A).** Reword the first premise to read, "If something is informative, then it is useful." This is equivalent to "If something is not useful, then it is not informative." Since the second premise says that some Web sites are not useful, we can deduce that "Some Web sites are not informative."

17. **The correct answer is (D).** The rate of change in the price per year is

$$\frac{28,000 - 40,000}{3} = -\$4000 / \text{year}.$$ The

starting price was $40,000 and the resulting linear equation is $V = 40,000 - 4000t$.

18. **The correct answer is (B).** Using the quadratic formula with $a = 1$, $b = -2$, and $c = 5$, we get the two roots:

$$\frac{-(-2) \pm \sqrt{(-2)^2 - 4(1)(5)}}{2(1)} = \frac{2 \pm 4i}{2} = 1 \pm 2i$$

19. **The correct answer is (A).** The mean is

$$\frac{15 + 21 + 32 + 15 + 27}{5} = 22, \text{ and the}$$

median is the middle number, 21, which is found after ordering the numbers. Their sum is $22 + 21 = 43$.

20. **The correct answer is (B).** The minimum value the function obtains is –6. The arrows indicate the graph continues to rise indefinitely, so there is no maximum value. Because there is no break in the graph, the function takes on all values from –6 inclusive to infinity.

POSTTEST ANSWER SHEET

1. Ⓐ Ⓑ Ⓒ Ⓓ	11. Ⓐ Ⓑ Ⓒ Ⓓ	21. Ⓐ Ⓑ Ⓒ Ⓓ	31. Ⓐ Ⓑ Ⓒ Ⓓ	41. Ⓐ Ⓑ Ⓒ Ⓓ
2. Ⓐ Ⓑ Ⓒ Ⓓ	12. Ⓐ Ⓑ Ⓒ Ⓓ	22. Ⓐ Ⓑ Ⓒ Ⓓ	32. Ⓐ Ⓑ Ⓒ Ⓓ	42. Ⓐ Ⓑ Ⓒ Ⓓ
3. Ⓐ Ⓑ Ⓒ Ⓓ	13. Ⓐ Ⓑ Ⓒ Ⓓ	23. Ⓐ Ⓑ Ⓒ Ⓓ	33. Ⓐ Ⓑ Ⓒ Ⓓ	43. Ⓐ Ⓑ Ⓒ Ⓓ
4. Ⓐ Ⓑ Ⓒ Ⓓ	14. Ⓐ Ⓑ Ⓒ Ⓓ	24. Ⓐ Ⓑ Ⓒ Ⓓ	34. Ⓐ Ⓑ Ⓒ Ⓓ	44. Ⓐ Ⓑ Ⓒ Ⓓ
5. Ⓐ Ⓑ Ⓒ Ⓓ	15. Ⓐ Ⓑ Ⓒ Ⓓ	25. Ⓐ Ⓑ Ⓒ Ⓓ	35. Ⓐ Ⓑ Ⓒ Ⓓ	45. Ⓐ Ⓑ Ⓒ Ⓓ
6. Ⓐ Ⓑ Ⓒ Ⓓ	16. Ⓐ Ⓑ Ⓒ Ⓓ	26. Ⓐ Ⓑ Ⓒ Ⓓ	36. Ⓐ Ⓑ Ⓒ Ⓓ	46. Ⓐ Ⓑ Ⓒ Ⓓ
7. Ⓐ Ⓑ Ⓒ Ⓓ	17. Ⓐ Ⓑ Ⓒ Ⓓ	27. Ⓐ Ⓑ Ⓒ Ⓓ	37. Ⓐ Ⓑ Ⓒ Ⓓ	47. Ⓐ Ⓑ Ⓒ Ⓓ
8. Ⓐ Ⓑ Ⓒ Ⓓ	18. Ⓐ Ⓑ Ⓒ Ⓓ	28. Ⓐ Ⓑ Ⓒ Ⓓ	38. Ⓐ Ⓑ Ⓒ Ⓓ	48. Ⓐ Ⓑ Ⓒ Ⓓ
9. Ⓐ Ⓑ Ⓒ Ⓓ	19. Ⓐ Ⓑ Ⓒ Ⓓ	29. Ⓐ Ⓑ Ⓒ Ⓓ	39. Ⓐ Ⓑ Ⓒ Ⓓ	49. Ⓐ Ⓑ Ⓒ Ⓓ
10. Ⓐ Ⓑ Ⓒ Ⓓ	20. Ⓐ Ⓑ Ⓒ Ⓓ	30. Ⓐ Ⓑ Ⓒ Ⓓ	40. Ⓐ Ⓑ Ⓒ Ⓓ	50. Ⓐ Ⓑ Ⓒ Ⓓ

answer sheet

Posttest

75 minutes • 50 questions

Directions: Each of the questions or incomplete statements below is followed by four suggested answers or completions. Select the one that is best in each case.

1. In the Venn diagram below, A and B represent sets. Which of the following represents the elements found in the union of Sets A and B?

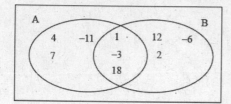

(A) $\{1, -3, 18\}$

(B) $\{4, -11, 7, 1, -3, 18\}$

(C) $\{4, -11, 7, 12, -6, 2\}$

(D) $\{4, -11, 7, 1, -3, 18, 12, -6, 2\}$

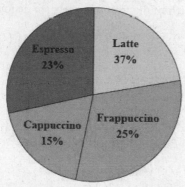

2. Two hundred college students are surveyed to determine their favorite coffee. The circle graph above shows the results of the survey. Which of the following is true?

(A) 20 more students chose Frappuccino® than Cappuccino.

(B) 27 fewer students chose Espresso than Latte.

(C) 14 fewer students chose Frappuccino than Latte

(D) 18 more students chose Espresso than Cappuccino.

3. The function $f(x) = x^2$ is translated 7 units to the left and 4 units down. Which of the following equations represents the translated function?

(A) $f(x) = (x - 7)^2 - 4$

(B) $f(x) = (x - 4)^2 + 7$

(C) $f(x) = (x + 7)^2 - 4$

(D) $f(x) = (x - 4)^2 - 7$

4. How many elements are found in the set of all even integers, such that $x > 8$ and $x \leq 24$?

5. Which of the following graphs represents the function $g(x) = (x - 3)^3 + 6$?

(A)

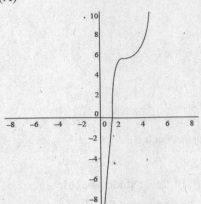

(B)

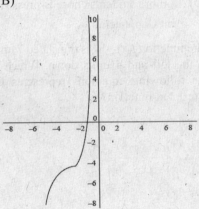

(C)

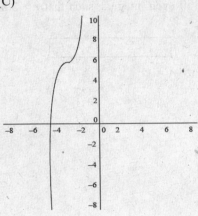

(D)

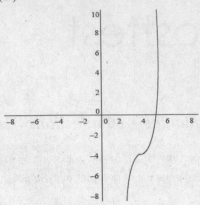

6. Mary draws a card from a deck, replaces the card, and then draws another card. What is the probability that she draws an ace and then a jack?

(A) $\dfrac{3}{13}$

(B) $\dfrac{1}{169}$

(C) $\dfrac{4}{13}$

(D) $\dfrac{4}{169}$

7. Which of the following sets are disjoint?

(A) $A = \{7, -9, 3, 4\}$ and
$B = \{2, -12, 8, 6\}$

(B) $A = \{-8, 10, -3\}$ and
$B = \{5, 10, -15\}$

(C) $A = \{13, 8, -9, 2, 6\}$ and
$B = \{-21, 18, 2, -4\}$

(D) $A = \{2, -9, 6, 3, 1\}$ and
$B = \{8, 9, -2, 1\}$

8. Which of the following is the correct simplification of $\log_6 1296^x$?

(A) $8x$

(B) $4x$

(C) $3x$

(D) $6x$

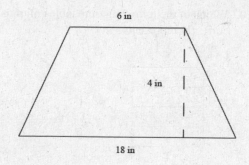

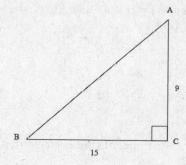

9. What is the area of the trapezoid above?

(A) 48 in.²

(B) 54 in.²

(C) 96 in.²

(D) 32 in.²

10. Which of the following equations is parallel to the line $y = -4x + 16$?

(A) $y = \frac{1}{4}x - 9$

(B) $y = -4x - 7$

(C) $y = -\frac{1}{4}x + 6$

(D) $y = 4x + 2$

If it is Monday, then Kim goes grocery shopping.

11. What is the converse of the statement above?

(A) If Kim does not go grocery shopping, then it is not Monday.

(B) If Kim goes grocery shopping, then it is Monday.

(C) If it is not Monday, then Kim goes grocery shopping.

(D) If it is not Monday, then Kim does not go grocery shopping.

12. Given the triangle above, which of the following best represents the measurement of angle B?

(A) 51.95°

(B) 47.43°

(C) 30.96°

(D) 53.13°

13. Anna surveyed candidates from different political parties as to which state they considered the most influential in an upcoming election. She recorded the results of her survey in the table below. What is the probability that a party candidate who chose Virginia is a Democrat?

Party Candidates	Iowa	Florida	Virginia	Arizona
Republicans	3	9	2	4
Democrats	2	8	12	9
Independents	14	7	6	3

(A) $\frac{3}{5}$

(B) $\frac{12}{31}$

(C) $\frac{6}{11}$

(D) $\frac{6}{7}$

14. Given $f(x) = (x + 4)^2$ and $g(x) = -4x$, what is $g(f(x))$?

(A) $16x^2 - 32x + 16$

(B) $-4x^2 - 64$

(C) $-4x^2 - 32x - 64$

(D) $16x^2 + 32x - 16$

15. What is the value of x in the equation $\log_7 343 = x$?

16. A cafeteria offers 4 different meats, 6 different vegetables, 3 different fruits, and 2 different breads. How many possible meal combinations are there?

17. Which of the following represents a subset of the set of all real numbers, such that $x \geq -2$ and $x < 8$?

(A) $\{9, -\sqrt{5}, 4.8, 7.2\}$

(B) $\left\{-1.5, \sqrt{2}, 6\frac{3}{4}, 0, -2\right\}$

(C) $\left\{-\frac{7}{8}, 4.9, 0, -\sqrt{3}, -\sqrt{9}\right\}$

(D) $\left\{-\frac{5}{2}, \frac{2}{3}, \sqrt{64}, 7\right\}$

18. Given Set A = {16, 12, −9, 2, 3} and Set B = {−2, 14, 2, 12}, how many elements are found in $A \cap B$?

(A) 2

(B) 3

(C) 4

(D) 5

19. Which of the following is listed in order from greatest to least?

(A) $|-5|, |14|, |18|, |-24|, |-40|$

(B) $|-4|, |8|, |-3|, |-10|, |19|$

(C) $|42|, |19|, |15|, |-24|, |-27|$

(D) $|-32|, |18|, |-7|, |-4|, |2|$

20. Which of the following truth table columns correctly represents $\sim p \vee \sim q$?

(A)

$\sim p \vee \sim q$
F
T
T
T

(B)

$\sim p \vee \sim q$
F
F
F
T

(C)

$\sim p \vee \sim q$
T
F
F
F

(D)

$\sim p \vee \sim q$
T
T
T
F

21. How many prime numbers are between 51 and 100?

(A) 9

(B) 10

(C) 11

(D) 12

22. How many composite numbers are greater than 14 and less than 31?

(A) 4

(B) 8

(C) 12

(D) 14

4, 3, 8, 6, 2, 1, 9, 7, 4, 6

23. The number of presentations made by a consultant per year over a period of 10 years is listed above. What is the mean number of presentations made by the consultant per year?

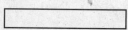

24. A bag contains 7 red marbles, 5 green marbles, 4 blue marbles, and 6 yellow marbles. Fred pulls out a marble, replaces it, and then pulls out another marble. What is the probability that he pulls out a red marble, followed by another red marble?

(A) $\frac{1}{11}$

(B) $\frac{49}{484}$

(C) $\frac{21}{242}$

(D) $\frac{7}{66}$

25. How many factors are there in the prime factorization of 1200?

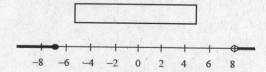

26. Which of the following inequalities is represented by the graph above?

(A) $-7 \le x \le 8$

(B) $x \le -7$ or $x > 8$

(C) $-7 \le x < 8$

(D) $x < -7$ or $x \ge 8$

27. Given that $A = \{9, 22, -4, 3, 2\}$ and $B = \{-1, 8, 6\}$, how many ordered pairs are in the cross-product from A to B?

(A) 12

(B) 14

(C) 15

(D) 16

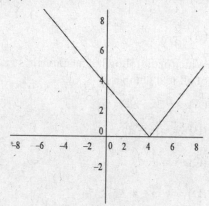

28. What is the domain of the function graphed above?

(A) All real numbers greater than or equal to 4

(B) All real numbers greater than or equal to 0

(C) All real numbers greater than or equal to -10 and less than or equal to 10

(D) All real numbers

29. Which of the following represents the reflection of the function $y = -12x + 2$ over the y-axis?

(A) $y = 12x + 2$

(B) $y = -12x - 2$

(C) $y = -\frac{1}{12}x + \frac{1}{6}$

(D) $y = 12x - 2$

30. Lynn flips a coin and rolls a 6-sided die. What is the probability that she gets heads and rolls a number greater than 2?

(A) $\frac{1}{3}$

(B) $\frac{1}{6}$

(C) $\frac{1}{4}$

(D) $\frac{2}{3}$

31. Which of the following functions has a range of all real numbers?

(A) $y = 3x - 9$

(B) $y = |x - 2|$

(C) $y = \frac{1}{x} + 6$

(D) $y = x^2 + 4$

32. A corporate office will give away airline tickets to 6 employees. If the office has 47 employees, how many ways can the group of 6 employees be chosen?

(A) 10,737,573

(B) 21,537,577

(C) 5,231,058,280

(D) 7,731,052,560

33. Which of the following represents the sum of $(-8 + 6i) + (4 - 12i)$?

(A) $-4 + 6i$

(B) $4 + 6i$

(C) $-4 - 6i$

(D) $4 - 6i$

34. A total of 35 college students enter a math competition. How many ways can the students place first, second, or third?

[　　　　　　　　]

35. Which of the following is an irrational number?

(A) $\frac{7}{8}$

(B) $\frac{7}{11}$

(C) $\frac{5}{9}$

(D) $\frac{6}{7}$

36. Given $f(x) = 12x - 8$ and $g(x) = \frac{x}{2}$, what is $f(g(x))$?

(A) $6x - 6$

(B) $6x - 4$

(C) $6x - 2$

(D) $6x - 8$

37. Which of the following divisibility rules are correct?

 I. A number is divisible by 4 if the last two digits are divisible by 4.
 II. A number is divisible by 5 if the last digit is a 0 or 5.
 III. A number is divisible by 6 if it is divisible by 2 or 3.
 IV. A number is divisible by 8 if the last two digits are divisible by 8.

(A) I and II

(B) I, II, and III

(C) I, II, and IV

(D) I, II, III, and IV

38. Which of the following graphs represents the solutions to the inequality $6x + 3 \le 9$?

(A)

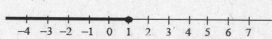

(B)

(C)

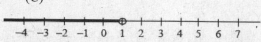

(D)

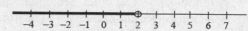

39. Which of the following graphs represents a one-to-one function?

(A)

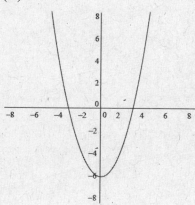

(B)

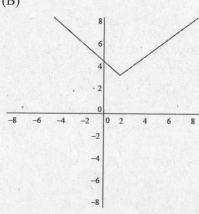

(C)

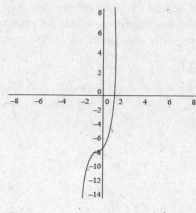

(D)

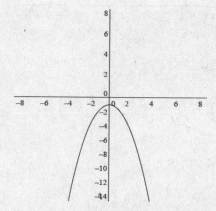

40. Which of the following statements are true?
  I. Real numbers are a subset of the set of rational numbers.
  II. Integers are a subset of the set of whole numbers.
  III. Natural numbers are a subset of the set of integers.
  IV. Irrational numbers are a subset of the set of rational numbers.

(A) I and II

(B) II and IV

(C) III only

(D) I, II, and III

41. Brian opens a savings account with $25 and deposits $20 per month. Which of the following graphs represents the amount of money in his savings account over *x* months?

(A)

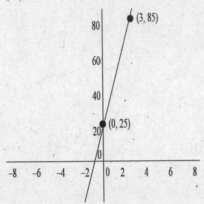

(B)

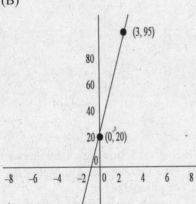

(C)

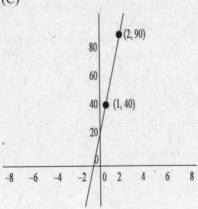

(D)

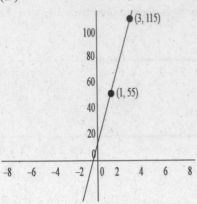

12, 18, 32, 19, 14, 38, 16, 22, 29, 37, 44, 11

42. The numbers above show how many swimming pools a hotel accreditation agency inspected during one year. Which of the following best represents the standard deviation of the number of pools inspected?

(A) 11.91

(B) 11.26

(C) 12.34

(D) 12.17

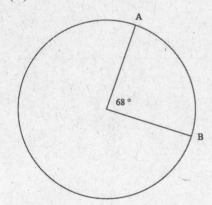

43. Given the circle above, what is the measure of $\overset{\frown}{AB}$?

(A) 34°

(B) 17°

(C) 68°

(D) 136°

44. Which of the following is the inverse of the function $y = 3x - 12$?

(A) $y = \frac{1}{3}x + 4$

(B) $y = 3x + 12$

(C) $y = \frac{1}{3}x - 4$

(D) $y = 3x - 4$

If Henry attends a math conference, then it is spring.

45. What is the inverse of the statement above?

(A) If it is spring, then Henry attends a math conference.

(B) If it is not spring, then Henry does not attend a math conference.

(C) If Henry attends a math conference, then it is not spring.

(D) If Henry does not attend a math conference, then it is not spring.

46. Which of the following truth table columns correctly represents $(p \vee \sim q) \wedge \sim p$?

(A)

$(p \vee \sim q) \wedge \sim p$
F
T
T
F

(B)

$(p \vee \sim q) \wedge \sim p$
F
F
F
T

(C)

$(p \vee \sim q) \wedge \sim p$
T
T
T
F

(D)

$(p \vee \sim q) \wedge \sim p$
T
T
T
T

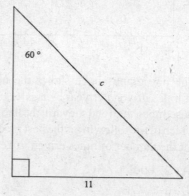

47. Which of the following best represents the length of side c in the triangle above?

(A) 11.2

(B) 11.7

(C) 12.7

(D) 13.9

48. Jacob draws a card from a deck, replaces it, and then draws another card. What is the probability that he draws a spade or an ace?

(A) $\frac{1}{52}$

(B) $\frac{4}{13}$

(C) $\frac{8}{13}$

(D) $\frac{17}{52}$

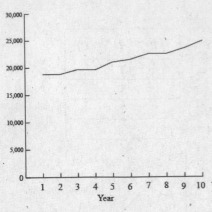

49. The line graph above shows the number of miles driven per year by a sales person. Based upon the trend shown in the line graph, which of the following is the best prediction for the number of miles driven in Year 14?

(A) 27,000

(B) 32,000

(C) 36,000

(D) 39,000

If a focus group has a conference call, then it is Wednesday.

50. Which of the following represents the negation of the statement above?

(A) A focus group does not have a conference call, and it is Wednesday.

(B) A focus group has a conference call, and it is not Wednesday.

(C) A focus group has a conference call, and it is not a weekday.

(D) A focus group does not have a conference call, and it is not Wednesday.

ANSWER KEY AND EXPLANATIONS

1. D	11. B	21. B	31. A	41. A
2. A	12. C	22. C	32. A	42. B
3. C	13. A	23. 5	33. C	43. C
4. 8	14. C	24. B	34. 39,270	44. A
5. A	15. 3	25. 7	35. D	45. D
6. B	16. 144	26. B	36. D	46. B
7. A	17. B	27. C	37. A	47. C
8. B	18. A	28. D	38. A	48. B
9. A	19. D	29. A	39. C	49. A
10. B	20. A	30. A	40. C	50. B

1. **The correct answer is (D).** The union of Sets A and B includes all elements in Set A or Set B. Therefore, the elements found in the union of Sets A and B can be written as $\{4, -11, 7, 1, -3, 18, 12, -6, 2\}$.

2. **The correct answer is (A).** You can find the number of students choosing each type of coffee by finding the product of each percentage and the total number of students surveyed, or 200. Thus, 46 students chose Espresso, 74 students chose Latte, 50 students chose Frappuccino®, and 30 students chose Cappuccino. Twenty more students chose Frappuccino than Cappuccino.

3. **The correct answer is (C).** A shift of 7 units to the left is indicated by an inclusion of +7, inside the parentheses. A shift of 4 units down is represented by a subtraction of 4 from the squared quantity. Therefore, a translation of the parent function $y = x^2$ by 7 units to the left and 4 units down is represented by the equation $y = (x + 7)^2 - 4$.

4. **The correct answer is (8).** The even integers greater than 8 and less than or equal to 24 are 10, 12, 14, 16, 18, 20, 22, and 24. Thus, 8 even integers are found within this interval.

5. **The correct answer is (A).** The function $g(x) = (x - 3)^3 + 6$ is a translation of the parent function $g(x) = x^3$, 3 units to the right and 6 units up. The graph for choice (A) reveals this translation.

6. **The correct answer is (B).** The probability of the events can be determined by using the formula $P(\text{A and B}) = P(A) \cdot P(B)$. Thus, the probability can be written as $P(\text{A and B}) = \frac{4}{52} \cdot \frac{4}{52}$, which equals $\frac{16}{2704}$, or $\frac{1}{169}$.

7. **The correct answer is (A).** Disjoint sets are sets that do not have any elements in common. This is true for the sets given for choice (A).

8. **The correct answer is (B).** The logarithmic equation can be rewritten as $\log_6(6^4)^x$, which can be rewritten as $\log_6 6^{4x}$, or $4x$.

9. **The correct answer is (A).** The area of a trapezoid can be found by using the formula $A = \frac{1}{2}(b_1 + b_2)h$, where b_1 and b_2 represent the length of the bases and h represents the height. Substituting the values shown on the figure allows you to write: $A = \frac{1}{2}(6 + 18)(4)$, which equals 48. Therefore, the trapezoid has an area of 48 square inches.

10. **The correct answer is (B).** Parallel lines have the same slope; thus, a line parallel to the given line must have a slope of -4. The line $y = -4x - 7$ has a slope of -4, so it is parallel to the given line.

11. **The correct answer is (B).** The converse of a statement is represented as $q \to p$, where q represents the conclusion and p represents the hypothesis. Thus, the converse can be written as "If Kim goes grocery shopping, then it is Monday."

12. **The correct answer is (C).** The measurement of angle B can be found by calculating the inverse tangent of angle B using this equation: $\tan^{-1} B° = \dfrac{9}{15}$. Thus, the measure of angle B is approximately $30.96°$.

13. **The correct answer is (A).** The value of the event in question is 12; twelve Democratic candidates chose Virginia as the most influential state. The total number of candidates who chose Virginia is 20. Therefore, the probability that a party candidate who chose Virginia as the most influential state is a Democrat is $\dfrac{12}{20}$, or $\dfrac{3}{5}$.

14. **The correct answer is (C).** The composition of the functions requires $f(x)$ to be evaluated within $g(x)$. Therefore, $(x + 4)^2$ must be substituted for x in the expression $-4x$. Doing so gives $-4(x+4)^2$, which can be simplified as $-4x^2 - 32x - 64$.

15. **The correct answer is (3).** The logarithmic equation is written in the form $\log_b a = x$, where b represents the base, a represents the answer or result, and x represents the exponent. The value of x is 3 because $7^3 = 343$.

16. **The correct answer is (144).** The problem is a counting problem. The number of different meal combinations can be found by calculating the product of the number of different meats, different vegetables, different fruits, and different breads; $4 \cdot 6 \cdot 3 \cdot 2 = 144$. Thus, there are 144 different meal combinations.

17. **The correct answer is (B).** The set given for choice (B) includes only elements that are greater than or equal to -2 and less than 8.

18. **The correct answer is (A).** The intersection of Sets A and B include all elements common to both sets. Thus, $A \cap B = \{2, 12\}$, showing two elements in the intersection.

19. **The correct answer is (D).** The sequence given for choice (D) is listed in order from greatest to least. Taking the absolute value of each integer allows you to write the sequence as 32, 18, 7, 4, 2, which is written in order from greatest to least.

20. **The correct answer is (A).** The disjunction of two sets includes all elements included in either set. Thus, the disjunction of $\sim p \vee \sim q$ implies a truth value of "true" whenever $\sim p$ or $\sim q$ is true. The truth table is shown below:

p	q	$\sim p$	$\sim q$	$\sim p \vee \sim q$
T	T	F	F	F
T	F	F	T	T
F	T	T	F	T
F	F	T	T	T

21. **The correct answer is (B).** The prime numbers found between 51 and 100 are 53, 59, 61, 67, 71, 73, 79, 83, 89, and 97. Thus, 10 prime numbers are found between 51 and 100.

22. **The correct answer is (C).** The composite numbers greater than 14 and less than 31 are as follows: 15, 16, 18, 20, 21, 22, 24, 25, 26, 27, 28, and 30. Thus, 12 composite numbers are in the given interval.

23. **The correct answer is (5).** The mean can be determined by summing the number of presentations given each year and dividing by the total number of years, or 10. The mean can thus be calculated by writing:
$$\frac{4 + 3 + 8 + 6 + 2 + 1 + 9 + 7 + 4 + 6}{10},$$
which equals $\dfrac{50}{10}$, or 5.

24. **The correct answer is (B).** The probability of the events can be determined by using the formula $P(A \text{ and } B) = P(A) \cdot P(B)$. Thus, the probability can be written as

P(A and B) $= \frac{7}{22} \cdot \frac{7}{22}$, which equals $\frac{49}{484}$.
Note that since the first marble is replaced, the sample size for the second draw does not change.

25. **The correct answer is (7).** The prime factorization of 1200 can be written as $2 \cdot 2 \cdot 2 \cdot 2 \cdot 3 \cdot 5 \cdot 5$. Thus, the prime factorization of 1200 has 7 factors.

26. **The correct answer is (B).** The graph represents all real numbers less than or equal to -7 or all real numbers greater than 8, which can be represented by the inequality $x \leq -7$ or $x > 8$.

27. **The correct answer is (C).** The cross-product from A to B can be represented as $A \times B = \{(9,-1),(9,8),(9,6),(22,-1),(22,8),(22,6),(-4,-1),(-4,8),(-4,6),(3,-1),(3,8),(3,6),(2,-1),(2,8),(2,6)\}$. The number of ordered pairs found in the cross-product is equal to the product of the number of elements in Set A and the number of elements in Set B. The number of ordered pairs in this cross-product is 15; notice $5 \cdot 3 = 15$.

28. **The correct answer is (D).** The domain of the given absolute value function is all real numbers; all real numbers are allowed as input or x-values.

29. **The correct answer is (A).** The reflection of a function over the y-axis can be achieved by making the x-value negative. Therefore, the given function $y = -12x + 2$ can be reflected over the y-axis by graphing the function $y = 12x + 2$.

30. **The correct answer is (A).** The probability of the events can be determined by using the formula P(A and B) $= P$(A) $\cdot P$(B). Thus, the probability can be written as P(A and B) $= \frac{1}{2} \cdot \frac{4}{6}$, which equals $\frac{4}{12}$, or $\frac{1}{3}$.

31. **The correct answer is (A).** The linear function has a range, or output values/y-values, of all real numbers. The range is not restricted, nor is the domain.

32. **The correct answer is (A).** The problem involves a combination whereby order does not matter. The combination can be determined by using the formula $\frac{n!}{r!(n-r)!}$, where n represents the number of subjects and r represents the number in the group. Substituting the given values allows you to write: $\frac{47!}{6!(47-6)!}$, or $\frac{47!}{6!41!}$, which equals 10,737,573.

33. **The correct answer is (C).** The given sum can be written as $-8 + 6i + 4 - 12i$. Note that imaginary numbers are added, just like other terms with the same variable. Therefore, the sum can be reduced to $-4 - 6i$.

34. **The correct answer is (39,270).** The problem involves a permutation because order matters. The permutation can be calculated using the formula $\frac{n!}{(n-r)!}$. Substituting the value of 35 for n and the value of 3 for r allows you to write: $\frac{35!}{(35-3)!}$, or $\frac{35!}{32!}$, which equals 39,270. Thus, there are 39,270 ways the 35 students can place first through third place.

35. **The correct answer is (D).** The fraction $\frac{6}{7}$ is non-terminating and non-repeating; therefore, it is irrational.

36. **The correct answer is (D).** The composition of the functions requires $g(x)$ to be evaluated within $f(x)$. Therefore, $\frac{x}{2}$ must be substituted for x in the expression $12x - 8$. Doing so gives $12\left(\frac{x}{2}\right) - 8$, which can be simplified as $\frac{12x}{2} - 8$, or $6x - 8$.

37. **The correct answer is (A).** The first and second divisibility rules are correct. The divisibility rule given for Statement III is incorrect because a number is divisible by 6 if it is divisible by both 2 and 3. The divisibility rule given for Statement IV is incorrect because the last three digits of a number must be divisible by 8, in order for the number to be divisible by 8.

38. The correct answer is (A). The inequality can be rewritten as $6x \leq 9 - 3$, where $x \leq 1$. The solutions to the inequality are all real numbers that are less than or equal to 1. The graph for choice (A) represents this solution.

39. The correct answer is (C). A one-to-one function also has an inverse function. The function will pass both the vertical and horizontal line tests, showing that no x-value is mapped to more than one y-value and no y-value is mapped to more than one x-value. The cubic function given for choice (C) is a one-to-one function.

40. The correct answer is (C). The only true statement is the statement that all natural numbers are a subset of the set of integers. Recall that the natural numbers are a subset of whole numbers, whole numbers are a subset of integers, integers are a subset of rational numbers, and rational numbers are a subset of the real number system, with irrational numbers serving as a separate subset within the real number system.

41. The correct answer is (A). The initial deposit serves as the y-intercept, while the constant deposit each month serves as the slope. Therefore, the equation of the line is $y = 20x + 25$. The graph for choice (A) reveals a y-intercept of \$25. The slope can be calculated by writing $\frac{85 - 25}{3 - 0}$, which equals $\frac{60}{3}$, or 20. Therefore, the slope and y-intercept for the graph shown for choice (A) is correct.

42. The correct answer is (B). The standard deviation can be calculated using the following formula: $s_x = \sqrt{\dfrac{\sum\left(x - \bar{x}\right)^2}{n - 1}}$, where x represents each score, $\bar{x}$ represents the mean, and n represents the number of scores. Substituting the approximate mean of 24.33, each score, and the sample size into the formula gives $s_x = \sqrt{\dfrac{1394.6668}{11}}$, which is approximately 11.26.

43. The correct answer is (C). The measure of the central angle is equal to the measure of the minor arc.

44. The correct answer is (A). The inverse of the function can be written by switching the x- and y-values and solving for y. The inverse of the function can be written as $x = 3y - 12$; solving for y gives: $y = \frac{1}{3}x + 4$.

45. The correct answer is (D). The inverse of a statement is represented by $\sim p \to \sim q$, where $\sim p$ represents the negation of p and $\sim q$ represents the negation of q. Thus, the inverse can be written as, "If Henry does not attend a math conference, then it is not spring."

46. The correct answer is (B). The conjunction of two sets includes elements common to both sets. The disjunction of two sets includes elements found in either set. A "true" truth value can be determined in a conjunction when a "true" value is found in both sets. A "true" truth value can be found in a disjunction when a "true" value is found in either set. The truth table is shown below:

p	q	$\sim p$	$\sim q$	$(p \vee \sim q)$	$(p \vee \sim q) \wedge \sim p$
T	T	F	F	T	F
T	F	F	T	T	F
F	T	T	F	F	F
F	F	T	T	T	T

47. The correct answer is (C). The length of side c can be determined by calculating the sine of $60°$. You can write $\sin 60° = \dfrac{11}{c}$ and solve for c by writing:

$$c \cdot \sin 60° = \frac{11}{c} \cdot c$$
$$c \cdot \sin 60° = 11$$
$$\frac{c \cdot \sin 60°}{\sin 60°} = \frac{11}{\sin 60°}$$
$$c \approx 12.7$$

48. The correct answer is (B). The probability of non-mutually exclusive events A or B can be determined using the formula $P(A \text{ or } B) = P(A) + P(B) - P(A \text{ and } B)$. Substituting the given probabilities allows you to write $\frac{13}{52} + \frac{4}{52} - \frac{1}{52}$, which simplifies to $\frac{16}{52}$, or $\frac{4}{13}$.

49. The correct answer is (A). The change in the number of miles driven from year to year is approximately 600 miles. Such an increase over a period of 4 years indicates a number of miles driven for Year 14 of $24{,}000 + 2{,}400$, or $26{,}400$; $27{,}000$ miles is closest to this value.

50. The correct answer is (B). The negation of a conditional statement can be represented as $\sim (p \rightarrow q)$, or $p \wedge \sim q$. The negation of the conclusion, or q, can be written as "It is not Wednesday." Therefore, the negation of the given statement is "A focus group has a conference call, and it is not Wednesday."

PART IV

HUMANITIES

PRETEST ANSWER SHEET

1. Ⓐ Ⓑ Ⓒ Ⓓ Ⓔ   11. Ⓐ Ⓑ Ⓒ Ⓓ Ⓔ   21. Ⓐ Ⓑ Ⓒ Ⓓ Ⓔ   31. Ⓐ Ⓑ Ⓒ Ⓓ Ⓔ   41. Ⓐ Ⓑ Ⓒ Ⓓ Ⓔ
2. Ⓐ Ⓑ Ⓒ Ⓓ Ⓔ   12. Ⓐ Ⓑ Ⓒ Ⓓ Ⓔ   22. Ⓐ Ⓑ Ⓒ Ⓓ Ⓔ   32. Ⓐ Ⓑ Ⓒ Ⓓ Ⓔ   42. Ⓐ Ⓑ Ⓒ Ⓓ Ⓔ
3. Ⓐ Ⓑ Ⓒ Ⓓ Ⓕ   13. Ⓐ Ⓑ Ⓒ Ⓓ Ⓔ   23. Ⓐ Ⓑ Ⓒ Ⓓ Ⓔ   33. Ⓐ Ⓑ Ⓒ Ⓓ Ⓔ   43. Ⓐ Ⓑ Ⓒ Ⓓ Ⓔ
4. Ⓐ Ⓑ Ⓒ Ⓓ Ⓔ   14. Ⓐ Ⓑ Ⓒ Ⓓ Ⓔ   24. Ⓐ Ⓑ Ⓒ Ⓓ Ⓔ   34. Ⓐ Ⓑ Ⓒ Ⓓ Ⓔ   44. Ⓐ Ⓑ Ⓒ Ⓓ Ⓔ
5. Ⓐ Ⓑ Ⓒ Ⓓ Ⓔ   15. Ⓐ Ⓑ Ⓒ Ⓓ Ⓔ   25. Ⓐ Ⓑ Ⓒ Ⓓ Ⓔ   35. Ⓐ Ⓑ Ⓒ Ⓓ Ⓔ   45. Ⓐ Ⓑ Ⓒ Ⓓ Ⓔ
6. Ⓐ Ⓑ Ⓒ Ⓓ Ⓔ   16. Ⓐ Ⓑ Ⓒ Ⓓ Ⓔ   26. Ⓐ Ⓑ Ⓒ Ⓓ Ⓔ   36. Ⓐ Ⓑ Ⓒ Ⓓ Ⓔ   46. Ⓐ Ⓑ Ⓒ Ⓓ Ⓔ
7. Ⓐ Ⓑ Ⓒ Ⓓ Ⓔ   17. Ⓐ Ⓑ Ⓒ Ⓓ Ⓔ   27. Ⓐ Ⓑ Ⓒ Ⓓ Ⓔ   37. Ⓐ Ⓑ Ⓒ Ⓓ Ⓔ   47. Ⓐ Ⓑ Ⓒ Ⓓ Ⓔ
8. Ⓐ Ⓑ Ⓒ Ⓓ Ⓔ   18. Ⓐ Ⓑ Ⓒ Ⓓ Ⓔ   28. Ⓐ Ⓑ Ⓒ Ⓓ Ⓔ   38. Ⓐ Ⓑ Ⓒ Ⓓ Ⓔ   48. Ⓐ Ⓑ Ⓒ Ⓓ Ⓔ
9. Ⓐ Ⓑ Ⓒ Ⓓ Ⓔ   19. Ⓐ Ⓑ Ⓒ Ⓓ Ⓔ   29. Ⓐ Ⓑ Ⓒ Ⓓ Ⓔ   39. Ⓐ Ⓑ Ⓒ Ⓓ Ⓔ   49. Ⓐ Ⓑ Ⓒ Ⓓ Ⓔ
10. Ⓐ Ⓑ Ⓒ Ⓓ Ⓔ   20. Ⓐ Ⓑ Ⓒ Ⓓ Ⓔ   30. Ⓐ Ⓑ Ⓒ Ⓓ Ⓔ   40. Ⓐ Ⓑ Ⓒ Ⓓ Ⓔ   50. Ⓐ Ⓑ Ⓒ Ⓓ Ⓔ

answer sheet

Pretest

35 minutes • 50 questions

Directions: Each of the questions or incomplete statements below is followed by five suggested answers or completions. Select the one that is best in each case.

Example: **SAMPLE ANSWER**

Claude Monet and August Renoir are most associated with which art movement?

(A) Romanticism

(B) Expressionism

(C) Realism

(D) Impressionism

(E) Surrealism

Monet and Renoir were both nineteenth-century French artists and leading figures in the Impressionist movement. **The correct answer is (D).**

1. An extremely prolific composer during the Classical period, he completed more than 600 works, among which are included *Eine kleine Nachtmusik, Don Giovanni,* and *The Abduction from the Seraglio.* The composer described is
   (A) Ludwig van Beethoven
   (B) Johann Sebastian Bach
   (C) Peter Ilyich Tchaikovsky
   (D) George Frideric Handel
   (E) Wolfgang Amadeus Mozart

2. Which of the following deals with a Norwegian housewife who realizes her own self-worth and abilities despite a demeaning relationship with her overbearing husband?
   (A) Tennessee Williams' *A Streetcar Named Desire*
   (B) Henrik Ibsen's *A Doll's House*
   (C) George Bernard Shaw's *Pygmalion*
   (D) Oscar Wilde's *A Woman of No Importance*
   (E) Arthur Miller's *The Crucible*

3. Which of the following correctly pairs an artist with the work he created?
   (A) *The Scream* … Pablo Picasso
   (B) *The Creation of Adam* … Leonardo da Vinci
   (C) *The Last Judgment* … Michelangelo Buonarroti
   (D) *American Gothic* … Henri Matisse
   (E) *Impression, Sunrise* … Vincent van Gogh

4. Which of the following has as its central theme a dystopian society in which critical thought is strongly discouraged and reading is strictly forbidden?
   (A) *Catch-22*
   (B) *The Grapes of Wrath*
   (C) *Anthem*
   (D) *Fahrenheit 451*
   (E) *1984*

Questions 5–7 refer to the following people.

   (A) Georgia O'Keeffe, Salvador Dali, Man Ray

   (B) Cecil B. DeMille, Akira Kurosawa, Francis Ford Coppola

   (C) Anton Chekov, Neil Simon, Noel Coward

   (D) Scott Joplin, John Philip Sousa, George Gershwin

   (E) Lewis Carroll, Emily Dickenson, Ralph Waldo Emerson

5. Which is a group of nineteenth-century poets?

6. Which is a group of playwrights?

7. Which is a group of surrealist painters?

8. Who wrote *Leviathan,* one of the most influential political philosophy books ever written?

   (A) Blaise Pascal

   (B) Thomas Hobbes

   (C) Gottfried Wilhelm von Leibniz

   (D) St. Thomas Aquinas

   (E) René Descartes

9. The terms "oculus," "minaret," "colonnade," "portico," and "nave" are primarily associated with

   (A) painting

   (B) film

   (C) architecture

   (D) ballet

   (E) opera

10. Tom Sawyer, Becky Thatcher, and Huckleberry Finn are characters created by

   (A) Herman Melville

   (B) Walt Whitman

   (C) Ernest Hemmingway

   (D) Nathaniel Hawthorne

   (E) Mark Twain

11. The *Iliad* was written by

   (A) Dante

   (B) Homer

   (C) Virgil

   (D) Ovid

   (E) Sophocles

12. Which of the following correctly pairs a composer with a work he created?

   (A) Richard Wagner … *The Flying Dutchman*

   (B) Claude Debussy … *Moonlight Sonata*

   (C) Peter Ilyich Tchaikovsky … *In the Hall of the Mountain King*

   (D) Johann Sebastian Bach … *Four Seasons*

   (E) Antonio Vivaldi … *Goldberg Variations*

13. The films *Vertigo, Rear Window,* and *North by Northwest* were directed by

   (A) Howard Hawks

   (B) Orson Welles

   (C) Ingmar Bergman

   (D) Alfred Hitchcock

   (E) Stanley Kubrick

Questions 14–16 refer to the following.

   (A) California during the Great Depression

   (B) Long Island, New York, during the Roaring Twenties

   (C) Georgia during the American Civil War and Reconstruction

   (D) Spain during the Spanish Civil War

   (E) Poland during the Holocaust

14. Which is the setting for most of the events of *For Whom the Bell Tolls*?

15. Which is the setting for most of *Of Mice and Men*?

16. Which is the setting for most of *The Great Gatsby*?

17. Bernini, Caravaggio, and Rembrandt are among the primary representatives of which art movement?

    (A) Baroque

    (B) Expressionism

    (C) Rococo

    (D) Neo-Classical

    (E) Fauvism

18. Which of the following terms describes a form of dramatic discourse in which a character directly addresses the audience without being heard by other characters?

    (A) Soliloquy

    (B) Denouement

    (C) Chorus

    (D) Monologue

    (E) Aside

Questions 19–21 refer to the following except from William Shakespeare's *Julius Caesar*.

> O, pardon me, thou bleeding piece of earth,
> That I am meek and gentle with these butchers!
> Thou art the ruins of the noblest man
> That ever lived in the tide of times.
> 5 Woe to the hand that shed this costly blood!
> Over thy wounds now do I prophesy
> (Which like dumb mouths do ope their ruby lips
> To beg the voice and utterance of my tongue)
> A curse shall light upon the limbs of men;
> 10 Domestic fury and fierce civil strife
> Shall cumber all the parts of Italy;
> Blood and destruction shall be so in use,
> And dreadful objects so familiar,
> That mothers shall but smile when they behold
> 15 Their infants quarter'd with the hands of war;
> All pity choked with custom of fell deeds,
> And Caesar's spirit ranging for revenge,
> With Ate by his side come hot from hell,
> Shall in these confines with a monarch's voice
> 20 Cry "Havoc!" and let slip the dogs of war,
> That this foul deed shall smell above the earth
> With carrion men, groaning for burial

19. Lines 6–8 use which of the following figures of speech?

    (A) Onomatopoeia

    (B) Assonance

    (C) Simile

    (D) Non sequitur

    (E) Hyperbole

20. These lines are spoken by which character?

    (A) Cicero

    (B) Brutus

    (C) Cassius

    (D) Octavius

    (E) Antony

21. These lines are addressed to

    (A) Antony

    (B) Caesar

    (C) Brutus

    (D) Cicero

    (E) Casca

22. Which of the following films was based on author Joseph Conrad's *Heart of Darkness*?

    (A) *From Here to Eternity*

    (B) *Out of Africa*

    (C) *Apocalypse Now*

    (D) *The Bridge on the River Kwai*

    (E) *Casablanca*

23. The work pictured above is

    (A) an oil painting

    (B) a fresco

    (C) an etching

    (D) a sculpture

    (E) a mobile

24. The painting shown above was created by

(A) Claude Monet

(B) Henri Matisse

(C) Georges Seurat

(D) Vincent Van Gogh

(E) Edgar Degas

25. The landmark political tome *The Communist Manifesto* was written by

(A) Alexis de Tocqueville

(B) Jean-Paul Sartre

(C) Immanuel Kant

(D) Karl Marx

(E) Jean-Jacques Rousseau

26. An actor who plays a clown in a comedy troupe finds himself in the middle of an emotionally charged love triangle and loses his grip on reality as the troupe perform an act that seemingly mirrors their ongoing drama.

The sentence above describes which opera?

(A) *Pagliacci*

(B) *The Marriage of Figaro*

(C) *Cavalleria Rusticana*

(D) *The Barber of Seville*

(E) *La Boheme*

27. Which of the following painters is recognized as one of the leading figures of the abstract expressionist movement?

(A) Andy Warhol

(B) Salvador Dali

(C) Pablo Picasso

(D) Edouard Manet

(E) Jackson Pollock

28. Who wrote *Common Sense*, an influential pamphlet that encouraged the American colonies to declare their independence from England?

(A) Benjamin Franklin

(B) John Adams

(C) Thomas Paine

(D) Patrick Henry

(E) Thomas Jefferson

29. Which of the following films was directed by Cecil B. DeMille?

(A) *Citizen Kane*

(B) *It's a Wonderful Life*

(C) *The Ten Commandments*

(D) *Lawrence of Arabia*

(E) *Modern Times*

30. The instrument above makes a plucking sound when a key is pressed. It is a/an

(A) guitar

(B) accordion

(C) harpsichord

(D) cello

(E) clarinet

31. He believed that all forms of knowledge could be gained solely through reason and without reliance on experience.

The philosopher and theory referred to in the sentence above are

(A) John Locke … empiricism

(B) Friedrich Nietzsche … existentialism

(C) René Descartes … rationalism

(D) David Hume … skepticism

(E) Immanuel Kant … idealism

32. The terms "fugue," "timbre," and "elegy" are primarily associated with

(A) theater

(B) music

(C) ballet

(D) painting

(E) film

33. Which nineteenth-century author wrote *Treasure Island* and *Strange Case of Dr. Jekyll and Mr. Hyde*?

(A) Charles Dickens

(B) Herman Melville

(C) Nathaniel Hawthorne

(D) Rudyard Kipling

(E) Robert Louis Stevenson

Questions 34–35 refer to the following poem.

THE CHARIOT

Because I could not stop for Death,
He kindly stopped for me;
The carriage held but just ourselves
And Immortality.

5 We slowly drove, he knew no haste,
And I had put away
My labor, and my leisure too,
For his civility.

We passed the school, where children strove
10 At recess, in the ring;
We passed the fields of gazing grain,
We passed the setting sun.

Or rather, he passed us;
The dews grew quivering and chill,
15 For only gossamer my gown,
My tippet only tulle.

We paused before a house that seemed
A swelling of the ground;
The roof was scarcely visible,
20 The cornice but a mound.

Since then 'tis centuries, and yet each
Feels shorter than the day
I first surmised the horses' heads
Were toward eternity.

34. The "house" described in lines 17–20 refers to
(A) the speaker's home
(B) a humble dwelling
(C) a nearby trench
(D) the speaker's grave
(E) an animal's makeshift shelter

35. Lines 12–13 serve as an example of which figure of speech?
(A) Personification
(B) Onomatopoeia
(C) Alliteration
(D) Synecdoche
(E) Metaphor

36. Artists associated with this nineteenth-century art movement favored creating images with small, thin brush strokes and emphasized the changing qualities of light and the inclusion of movement and unusual visual angles.

Which of the following movements is referred to above?
(A) Expressionism
(B) Cubism
(C) Romanticism
(D) Impressionism
(E) Realism

37. Which is a group of architects?

    (A) Geoffrey Chaucer, Allen Ginsberg, Ogden Nash

    (B) Henri Matisse, Francisco de Goya, Frida Kahlo

    (C) Aaron Copland, Hector Berlioz, Antonin Dvorak

    (D) Le Corbusier, I.M. Pei, Frank Lloyd Wright

    (E) Frank Capra, John Ford, Federico Fellini

38. A native of Boston, Massachusetts, her personal battles with emotional anguish and depression served as the catalyst for much of her landmark confessional poetry. Seemingly obsessed with death and self-destruction, she wrote feverishly, publishing numerous poems and a novel before taking her own life in her London apartment.

    The poet described is

    (A) Jane Austen

    (B) Sylvia Plath

    (C) Emily Dickinson

    (D) Anne Sexton

    (E) Phyllis Wheatley

39. What is the correct chronological order of the following painters?

    I. Auguste Rodin
    II. Rembrandt
    III. Sandro Botticelli

    (A) III, II, I

    (B) II, I, III

    (C) I, III, II

    (D) II, III, I

    (E) I, II, III

40. In which of William Shakespeare's plays does an aging monarch vow to divide his kingdom among his three daughters only on the condition that they are wed first?

    (A) *The Tempest*

    (B) *Richard III*

    (C) *Othello*

    (D) *King Lear*

    (E) *As You Like It*

41. Which of the following ballets is set to music composed by Peter Ilyich Tchaikovsky?

    (A) *Don Quixote*

    (B) *Le Corsaire*

    (C) *Romeo and Juliet*

    (D) *Cinderella*

    (E) *Swan Lake*

Questions 42–44 refer to the following lines.

    (A) "The man who makes an appearance in the business world, the man who creates personal interest, is the man who gets ahead. Be liked and you will never want."

    (B) "This above all: to thine own self be true, And it must follow, as the night the day, Thou canst not then be false to any man."

    (C) "The human animal is a beast that dies but the fact that he's dying don't give him pity for others, no sir."

    (D) "What's in a name? That which we call a rose by any other name would smell as sweet."

    (E) "My wit is more polished than your mustache. The truth which I speak strikes more sparks from men's hearts than your spurs do from the cobblestones."

42. Which line is from Shakespeare's *Hamlet*?

43. Which line is from Arthur Miller's *Death of a Salesman*?

44. Which line is from Shakespeare's *Romeo & Juliet*?

45. Which painting was created by Leonard da Vinci?

    (A) *The Birth of Adam*

    (B) *Storm on the Sea of Galilee*

    (C) *The Birth of Venus*

    (D) *The School of Athens*

    (E) *Virgin of the Rocks*

46. The source material for the 1964 film *My Fair Lady* was written by which playwright?

(A) Arthur Miller

(B) George Bernard Shaw

(C) Tennessee Williams

(D) Neil Simon

(E) David Mamet

47. The plot of which novel follows a young German soldier fighting in the midst of World War I?

(A) *All Quiet on the Western Front*

(B) *Catch-22*

(C) *The Sound and the Fury*

(D) *The Red Badge of Courage*

(E) *Cry, the Beloved Country*

48. All of the following artists are considered part of the surrealist movement EXCEPT

(A) Georgia O'Keeffe

(B) Max Ernst

(C) Andy Warhol

(D) MC Escher

(E) Marcel Duchamp

49. *The Prince*, a classic work of philosophy designed to serve as a guide to leadership, was written by

(A) Plato

(B) Thomas Moore

(C) Voltaire

(D) Niccolò Machiavelli

(E) Aristotle

50. Which of the following terms is used in sheet music to indicate that the tempo should be very fast?

(A) Legato

(B) Presto

(C) Grandioso

(D) Mezzo

(E) Allegro

ANSWER KEY AND EXPLANATIONS

1. E	11. B	21. B	31. C	41. E
2. B	12. A	22. C	32. B	42. B
3. C	13. D	23. B	33. E	43. A
4. D	14. D	24. C	34. D	44. D
5. E	15. A	25. D	35. A	45. E
6. C	16. B	26. A	36. D	46. B
7. A	17. A	27. E	37. D	47. A
8. B	18. E	28. C	38. B	48. C
9. C	19. C	29. C	39. A	49. D
10. E	20. E	30. C	40. D	50. B

1. **The correct answer is (E).** Wolfgang Amadeus Mozart was the Classical period composer responsible for *Eine kleine Nachtmusik, Don Giovanni,* and *The Abduction from the Seraglio.*

2. **The correct answer is (B).** The synopsis given in the question most accurately describes Henrik Ibsen's *A Doll's House.*

3. **The correct answer is (C).** *The Last Judgment* was painted by Michelangelo Buonarroti. Choice (A), *The Scream,* was painted by Edvard Munch. Choice (B), *The Creation of Adam,* was painted by Michelangelo Buonarroti. Choice (D), *American Gothic,* was painted by Grant Wood. Choice (E), *Impression, Sunrise,* was painted by Claude Monet.

4. **The correct answer is (D).** A dystopian society in which critical thought is strongly discouraged and reading is strictly forbidden is the central theme of *Fahrenheit 451.*

5. **The correct answer is (E).** Lewis Carroll, Emily Dickenson, and Ralph Waldo Emerson are a group of nineteenth-century poets.

6. **The correct answer is (C).** Anton Chekov, Neil Simon, and Noel Coward are a group of playwrights.

7. **The correct answer is (A).** Georgia O'Keeffe, Salvador Dali, and Man Ray are a group of surrealist painters.

8. **The correct answer is (B).** *Leviathan,* a highly influential political philosophy book and one of the earliest writings to describe social contract theory, was written by Thomas Hobbes.

9. **The correct answer is (C).** The terms are all primarily associated with architecture. An oculus is a circular window or opening. A minaret is typical feature of Islamic mosques. A colonnade is a continuous series of columns. A portico is a porch leading into a building. A nave is the central part of a church approaching the main altar.

10. **The correct answer is (E).** Famed American author Mark Twain created the characters Tom Sawyer, Becky Thatcher, and Huckleberry Finn in his novels *Tom Sawyer* and *Huckleberry Finn.*

11. **The correct answer is (B).** The *Iliad* was an epic poem written by Homer, the Ancient Greek poet who also authored the *Odyssey.*

12. **The correct answer is (A).** Choice (A) is correct because *The Flying Dutchman* was written by German composed Richard Wagner.

13. **The correct answer is (D).** *Vertigo, Rear Window*, and *North by Northwest* were all directed by renowned English director Alfred Hitchcock.

14. **The correct answer is (D).** Most of the events of author Ernest Hemingway's *For Whom the Bell Tolls* take place in Spain during the Spanish Civil War.

15. **The correct answer is (A).** Most of the events of author John Steinbeck's *Of Mice and Men* take place in California during the Great Depression.

16. **The correct answer is (B).** Most of the events of author F. Scott Fitzgerald's *The Great Gatsby* take place on Long Island, New York during the Roaring Twenties.

17. **The correct answer is (A).** Bernini, Caravaggio, and Rembrandt are three of the most representative artists of the Baroque art movement.

18. **The correct answer is (E).** An aside is a form of dramatic discourse in which a character directly addresses the audience without being heard by other characters.

19. **The correct answer is (C).** In lines 6–8, the speaker compares Caesar's wounds to mouths using the word "like." This is an example of simile, which is a comparison of two things through the use of the words "like" or "as."

20. **The correct answer is (E).** The lines are spoken by Antony immediately following the assassination of Caesar.

21. **The correct answer is (B).** Antony delivers his lines to the desecrated corpse of Caesar.

22. **The correct answer is (C).** Joseph Conrad's *Heart of Darkness* was the chief inspiration for Francis Ford Coppola's 1979 film *Apocalypse Now.*

23. **The correct answer is (B).** The painting shown is *The Last Supper*, a famous fresco by Leonardo da Vinci. A fresco is a watercolor painting created on wet plaster on a wall or ceiling.

24. **The correct answer is (C).** The painting shown is *Sunday Afternoon on the Island of La Grande Jatte* by Georges Seurat.

25. **The correct answer is (D).** *The Communist Manifesto*, which is held to be one of the most influential political philosophy books ever written, was published by Karl Marx in 1848.

26. **The correct answer is (A).** The sentence describes the plot of *Pagliacci*, a late nineteenth-century opera written by Ruggiero Leoncavallo.

27. **The correct answer is (E).** Jackson Pollock is generally regarded as one of the leading figures of the abstract expressionist movement.

28. **The correct answer is (C).** *Common Sense* was written by Thomas Paine, who also authored a number of other influential pamphlets during the Revolutionary War.

29. **The correct answer is (C).** Cecil B. DeMille directed the 1956 epic film *The Ten Commandments*.

30. **The correct answer is (C).** The instrument shown is the harpsichord, an early variation of the instrument we know today as the piano. When you press a key on a harpsichord, a string is plucked. The instrument was popular during the Renaissance.

31. **The correct answer is (C).** The sentence describes the thoughts expressed by René Descartes in his philosophical theory of rationalism.

32. **The correct answer is (B).** "Fugue," "timbre," and "elegy" are associated with music. A fugue is a musical composition specifically written for three to six voices. Timbre refers to tone color. An elegy is an instrumental piece intended to express praise for the deceased.

33. **The correct answer is (E).** *Treasure Island* and *Strange Case of Dr. Jekyll and Mr. Hyde* were written by Robert Louis Stevenson.

34. **The correct answer is (D).** The "house" referenced in the poem's fifth stanza is meant to represent the speaker's grave, her final destination on her journey with death.

35. **The correct answer is (A).** The lines "We passed the setting sun. / Or rather, he passed us;" are an example of personification, as the sun is referred to as though it is a person and is endowed with human qualities.

36. **The correct answer is (D).** Painters associated with the impressionism movement favored creating images with small, thin brush strokes and emphasized the changing qualities of light and the inclusion of movement and unusual visual angles.

37. **The correct answer is (D).** Le Corbusier, I.M. Pei, and Frank Lloyd Wright are all famous architects.

38. **The correct answer is (B).** The poet described is Sylvia Plath.

39. **The correct answer is (A).** The correct chronological order of the three painters is III, II, I. Botticelli was a renaissance painter, Rembrandt painted during the Baroque period, and Rodin was a postimpressionist.

40. **The correct answer is (D).** In *King Lear*, the title character decides that he wants to retire from the throne and promises to divide his lands among his three daughters once they are married.

41. **The correct answer is (E).** Tchaikovsky composed the accompanying music for *Swan Lake*.

42. **The correct answer is (B).** The line "This above all: to thine own self be true, And it must follow, as the night the day, Thou canst not then be false to any man," comes from Shakespeare's *Hamlet*.

43. **The correct answer is (A).** The line "The man who makes an appearance in the business world, the man who creates personal interest, is the man who gets ahead. Be liked and you will never want," comes from Arthur Miller's *Death of a Salesman*.

44. **The correct answer is (D).** The line "What's in a name? That which we call a rose by any other name would smell as sweet," comes from Shakespeare's *Romeo and Juliet*.

45. **The correct answer is (E).** *Virgin of the Rocks*, which depicts the moment when a young John the Baptist met the family of Jesus Christ as they were traveling to Egypt, was painted by Leonardo da Vinci.

46. **The correct answer is (B).** The source material for *My Fair Lady*, which was the stage play *Pygmalion*, was written by George Bernard Shaw.

47. **The correct answer is (A).** *All Quiet on the Western Front* follows a young German soldier who finds himself on the battlefields of World War I.

48. **The correct answer is (C).** Andy Warhol was one of the most influential artists in the pop art movement.

49. **The correct answer is (D).** *The Prince* was written by Niccolò Machiavelli, an Italian Renaissance philosopher.

50. **The correct answer is (B).** The term "presto" is used in sheet music to indicate that the tempo of the composition should be very fast.

OVERVIEW ANSWER SHEET

1. Ⓐ Ⓑ Ⓒ Ⓓ Ⓔ   3. Ⓐ Ⓑ Ⓒ Ⓓ Ⓔ   5. Ⓐ Ⓑ Ⓒ Ⓓ Ⓔ   7. Ⓐ Ⓑ Ⓒ Ⓓ Ⓔ   9. Ⓐ Ⓑ Ⓒ Ⓓ Ⓔ

2. Ⓐ Ⓑ Ⓒ Ⓓ Ⓔ   4. Ⓐ Ⓑ Ⓒ Ⓓ Ⓔ   6. Ⓐ Ⓑ Ⓒ Ⓓ Ⓔ   8. Ⓐ Ⓑ Ⓒ Ⓓ Ⓔ   10. Ⓐ Ⓑ Ⓒ Ⓓ Ⓔ

answer sheet

Overview

The CLEP Humanities test assesses your general knowledge of cultural topics such as literature, music, art, and architecture. Spanning all the historical eras of world culture, the test includes questions on everything from novels, prose, poetry, philosophy, and drama to art history, painting, sculpture, music, dance, theater, and film. While most of the questions on the CLEP Humanities test will be based on Western culture, you should also expect to find some questions (about 5–10 percent) that focus on various Asian, Latin American, or African cultures.

Preparing for the CLEP Humanities exam can be difficult. "Humanities" is a very broad subject that includes a great deal of information about a wide variety of subjects. In most cases, the best way to ensure that you are ready for the test is to review any available humanities textbooks. These textbooks will provide you with a comprehensive overview of the material on which the CLEP Humanities test is based.

The exam contains about 140 questions that you must answer in 90 minutes.

The questions on the CLEP Humanities test can be grouped into two basic categories:

1. Literature (50 percent of the questions on the test)
2. Fine Arts (50 percent of the questions on the test)

Questions on this CLEP test are about the following subjects:

Drama (10 percent or 14 questions)

- Plays
- Playwrights
- Shakespearean drama

Poetry (10–15 percent or 14–21 questions)

- Poems
- Poets
- Poetic forms
- Figures of speech

Fiction (15–20 percent or 21–28 questions)

- Novels
- Short stories
- Other fictional literature
- Novelists and other fiction writers

chapter 9

Nonfiction (10 percent or 14 questions)

- Historical literature
- Political literature
- Philosophy

Visual Arts (20 percent or 28 questions)

- Art history
- Art movements
- Artists
- Painting
- Sculpture
- Other art forms

Music (15 percent or 21 questions)

- Composers
- Compositions
- Music history

Performing arts (10 percent or 14 questions)

- Film
- Dance

Architecture (5 percent or 7 questions)

- Architectural history
- Architects
- Famous structures

Questions on the CLEP Humanities test are divided approximately evenly among the following historical eras:

- Classical
- Medieval
- Renaissance
- Seventeenth century
- Eighteenth century
- Nineteenth century
- Twentieth century

LITERATURE

Literary Terminology

Some literature questions on the CLEP Humanities test may require you to identify and/or define selected literary terms. Familiarizing yourself with some of these terms will help you better understand the questions you will encounter on the test and improve your overall performance. Following are some literary terms commonly seen on the CLEP Humanities test:

Term	Definition
Allegory	A form of narrative that doubles as an extended metaphor
Alliteration	The repetition of initial sounds in consecutive or nearby words
Anaphora	The intentional repetition of a word or phrase at the beginning of a number of consecutive verses, clauses, or paragraphs
Aside	A speech given by a character that is directed specifically to the audience or reader and not heard by other characters
Blank verse	A type of verse made up of unrhymed lines in the same meter, often iambic pentameter
Denouement	The final resolution of the conflict in a story
Didacticism	A form of artistic philosophy in which the instructional and informative qualities of literature and other art forms are emphasized
Elegy	A form of poetry that is written in elegiac couplets and intended to express sorrow for the dead
Epic	A long, loftily composed narrative poem that usually centers on a heroic main character and illustrates the history of a nation or a people
Free verse	A form of poetry made up of lines that do not follow a distinct meter pattern or rhyme
Foil	A secondary character whose attributes contrast with those of the primary character
Haiku	A traditional Japanese form of poetry that usually consists of three lines and seventeen syllables
Hyperbole	A figure of speech referring to exaggeration
Imagery	Use of language intended to evoke any or all of the senses
Irony	A literary device intended to illustrate that something is not as it may appear
Limerick	A form of humorous or nonsensical poetry
Lyric poetry	A type of song-like poetry intended to express the experience of emotions
Metaphor	A figure of speech in which two ordinarily unrelated things are compared to illustrate some similarity between them
Motif	The dominant or recurring theme of a work
Onomatopoeia	The use of a word that imitates the sound it is meant to represent

Personification	The act of endowing an inhuman creature or object with human qualities
Point of view	The vantage point from which a narrative is told
Poetry	Written language composed using rhythmic structure
Prose	Written language composed using normal grammatical structure and natural flow of speech
Rhyme	A pattern of words containing similar sounds
Rhymed verse	A form of poetry in which the ends of lines rhyme
Satire	A literary device used to make light of human weaknesses
Setting	The time and place in which a fictional work takes place
Simile	A figure of speech in which two unlike things are compared using the terms "like" or "as"
Soliloquy	A dramatic device in which a character expresses his thoughts or feelings to himself for the benefit of the audience without addressing any other characters
Sonnet	A style of poetry that uses a distinct metrical structure and often consists of fourteen lines composed with a specific rhyming scheme
Stanza	A grouping of lines in a poem
Symbolism	A figure of speech in which a word, object, or action is used to represent something other than its literal definition
Theme	The main idea or lesson that a writer attempts to express in a work
Tragedy	A work of literature that is based on human suffering
Verse	A line of poetry

Ancient Greek Literature

Ancient Greece is the source of some of the oldest and most influential literature ever written. The poetic, dramatic, and philosophical works produced by the Ancient Greeks had a profound effect that continues to be felt to this day. Ancient Greek literature is often seen as the foundation on which modern Western culture was built.

Greek Poetry

The roots of Ancient Greek literature lie in epic and lyrical poetry. The epic and lyrical poems of Ancient Greece reflect the civilization's history and culture. The earliest examples of Ancient Greek literature can be traced back as far as Mycenaean Greece (c. 1600 B.C.E. – c. 1100 B.C.E.) and the epic poems written by Homer. Though he himself largely remains shrouded in mystery, Homer's works are generally considered to be the greatest works of epic poetry ever written. Homer's two major works are

- *The Iliad:* Homer's great historical epic, *The Iliad,* recounts the events of the Trojan War through the mythological warrior Achilles. It takes place over the course of a few weeks during the last year of the decade-long war.

- *The Odyssey:* *The Odyssey* follows the Ancient Greek hero Odysseus (also known as Ulysses) as he undertakes a long and dangerous journey home after the fall of Troy. As Odysseus endures the ten-year journey back to Ithaca, his wife, Penelope, who believes he has died, is forced to cope with a line of prospective bridegrooms who vie for the right to marry her.

Believed to have lived around the same time as Homer, Hesiod is another influential Ancient Greek poet. Known for speaking of himself in his own works, Hesiod completed two major works that have been an important source of information on early Greek mythology, agriculture, economics, astronomy, and time keeping. His poems include:

- **Works and Days:** *Works and Days* provides a chronology of Greek history that is divided into five distinct stages: the Golden Age, the Silver Age, the Bronze Age, the Heroic Age, and the Iron Age. Hesiod also discusses pagan ethics and illustrates the virtue of hard work.

- **Theogony:** In *Theogony*, Hesiod presents one of the earliest and most significant explanations of Greek mythology and the pagan creation myth. One of the most important source documents for Greek mythology, it offers the pagan explanation for the world's creation at the hands of creatrix goddesses Chaos and Earth and introduces countless gods, goddesses, and other important figures.

Greek Drama

In addition to their poetic contributions, the Ancient Greeks also played an important role in the development of drama and theatre. Greek theatre, which thrived between approximately 550 and 220 B.C.E., was the birthplace of the modern stage play and remains one of Ancient Greece's most important contributions to Western civilization.

The two primary types of Ancient Greek drama are tragedy and comedy. Tragedies focus on a tragic hero who suffers some form of misfortune. Comedies are more lighthearted than tragedies and usually involve the misadventures of laughable characters, political satire, and other forms of humor. It is commonly divided into three periods: Old Comedy, Middle Comedy, and New Comedy.

Ancient Greek dramatists and actors frequently made use of masks designed to help convey emotions and other details. They also allowed a single actor to play multiple roles in the same play. The different appearance of each mask helped the audience distinguish between various characters and recognize their genders, ages, and social distinctions.

Ancient Greek dramas were typically performed in amphitheatres, which were special structures specifically designed for staging plays. These amphitheatres could hold thousands of people and served as incredible examples of early acoustic design.

Of the many great theatres built in Ancient Greece, none is more famous today than the Theatre of Dionysus. Located in Athens, the Theatre of Dionysus regularly played host to the City Dionysia festival, during which many classical dramatists completed against one another to determine who was the most skilled at their craft.

Following are some of the most significant Ancient Greek dramatists:

- **Aeschylus:** Often called the father of tragedy, he is well known for his trilogies. He is best known for *Oresteia*, a trilogy of tragedies that includes *Agamemnon*, *The Libation Pourers,* and *The Furies*. *Oresteia* details the end of a curse placed on the House of Atreus. In *Agamemnon*, the title character, the King of Argos and a general in the Trojan War, is forced to sacrifice his daughter to the goddess Diana so that he can conquer Troy. His wife mourns for their daughter and vows revenge for her death. When Agamemnon returns home, she kills him. In *The Libation Pourers*, Agamemnon's other children avenge his death and kill their mother. In *The Furies*, one of the dead king and queen's sons, Orestes, seeks atonement for the death of his parents and puts an end to his family's blood feud.

- **Sophocles:** Sophocles earned his reputation as a skilled dramatist after defeating Aeschylus at the City Dionysia festival. His works are known for illustrating the significance of human error, the wickedness of evil, and the suffering it causes. He is best known for *Ajax*, the tale of the Greek warrior Ajax and his humiliation and subsequent suicide at Troy; *Antigone*, in which corruption and a lack of reason leads to a triple suicide; *Electra*, the story of Electra, the daughter of Agamemnon and his wife Clytemnestra, and her plot to avenge her father's death; and *Oedipus the King*, about a young prince who is expelled from his family after an oracle predicts that he will murder his father and impregnate his mother and who still manages to inadvertently fulfill the horrifying prophecy.

- **Euripides:** A political dramatist, Euripides' plays centered on ethics, pacifism, and the problems that arise when political leaders try to be rational and understanding. He is best known for *Electra*, another version of the tale of Agamemnon's daughter; *Hecuba*, the story of a mythological queen who loses a daughter and seeks revenge for the murder of her son; *Hippolytus*, a tragedy about the son of the mythological founder of Athens, Theseus; *Iphigenia at Aulis*, another depiction of the Trojan War that includes both Agamemnon and Achilles; *Medea*, the tale of a woman who takes her revenge on an unfaithful husband; and *The Trojan Women*, which depicts the atrocities of war through the events of the Trojan War and the slaughter of all of the children of Troy to prevent Greece's enemy from ever becoming powerful again.

GRECO-ROMAN GODS AND GODDESSES

Greek Name	Domain	Roman Name
Zeus	king of the gods, rain, clouds, thunderbolts	Jupiter
Hera	queen of the gods, marriage, married women	Juno
Hades	the underworld, wealth	Pluto
Poseidon	the sea	Neptune
Aphrodite	beauty, love	Venus
Phoebus Apollo	sun, light, healing, truth	Apollo
Pallas Athena	wisdom	Minerva
Ares	war	Mars
Artemis	wildlife	Diana
Dionysus	theatre, wine	Bacchus
Hermes	commerce	Mercury

Ancient Latin Literature

As the dominance of Ancient Greece was replaced by that of Ancient Rome, the Romans, who were generally less culturally engaged than their Greek counterparts, began to integrate much of the Greek culture into their own. In time, Roman writers, artists, and architects began to develop their own unique style and the age of Latin literature began to emerge.

Undoubtedly, the most well known figure in all of Latin literature is Virgil, who famously wrote the epic poem *The Aeneid*. As Homer's epic poems did for Ancient Greece, *The Aeneid* describes the origins of Rome. In *The Aeneid*, a Trojan named Aeneas journeys to Italy and eventually becomes the ancestor of the Romans.

The Romans also adopted drama from the Greeks. Following are a number of notable Roman dramatists.

ROMAN DRAMATISTS

Dramatist	Form	Notable Works
Lucius Livius Andronicus	Tragedies	*Achilles, Aegisthus, Aiax Mastigophorus* (*Ajax with the Whip*), *Andromeda, Antiopa, Danae, Equus Troianus, Hermiona, Tereus*
Quintus Ennius	Tragedies	*Annales, Epicharmus, Euhemerus, Hedyphagetica, Saturae*
Marcus Pacuvius	Tragedies	*Antiope, Teucer, Armorum Judicium, Dulorestes, Chryses, Niptra*
Plautus	Comedies	*Amphitryon, Asinaria, Aulularia, Bacchides, Captivi, Casina*

Satire was another important component of Latin literature. Three major Latin satirists were Gaius Lucilius, Horace, and Juvenal. Gaius Lucilius is often considered the inventor of Latin poetical satire. Unfortunately, only about 1,300 lines of his work remain intact today. Horace, perhaps the best known Roman satirist, most notably wrote the *Satires,* a book of poems about the political policies of Octavian (later known as Augustus). His other poetic works include *Odes* and *Epistles*. Juvenal is best known for having written sixteen satirical poems concerned with the difficulties of Roman life under the reviled emperor Domitian and his immediate successors. A number of famous phrases and epigrams—for example, "bread and circuses" and "who will guard the guards themselves?"—can be attributed to Juvenal.

Medieval Literature

As the ancient world gave way to the Middle Ages, literature continued to evolve. Many of the works produced by European writers during this period are considered to be among the greatest ever created.

Everyman, written by an anonymous writer in the late fifteenth century, is an allegorical morality play that deals with the concept of salvation and what men are required to do to attain it. The Everyman, who is representative of the entire human race, attempts to procure help from other characters, each of whom represents an abstract theme (such as fellowship), to improve his chances for salvation.

As the story progresses, the struggle between good and evil manifests itself through the interactions of the various characters.

The epic poem *Beowulf*, also written by an unknown author and believed to have been composed sometime between the eighth and eleventh centuries, tells the tale of a Scandinavian hero named Beowulf. In the story, a fearsome creature named Grendel kills and eats the warriors of King Hroðgar, the leader of the Danes. Hroðgar summons Beowulf to deal with Grendel. The story is structured around Beowulf's battles with Grendel, Grendel's mother, and a dragon. After emerging victorious from his battles with Grendel and his mother, Beowulf returns home to Geatland and is crowned king. Fifty years later, he is forced to fight a dragon and is mortally wounded in battle.

Between 1308 and 1321, Dante Alighieri wrote *The Divine Comedy*, an epic poem that is often considered to be among the greatest contributions to Italian literature ever created. This allegorical masterpiece presents a look at the afterlife based on Christian theology and the teachings of the medieval Western church. In the poem, Dante himself travels through and explores the afterlife. Beginning from the depths of Hell, Dante ascends through the various levels of the inferno and into purgatory before finally reaching Heaven. Dante's personal journey is often viewed as an allegory for the soul's journey toward God and redemption.

In the early 1350s, Italian author Giovanni Boccaccio composed a collection of allegorical tales known as *The Decameron*. *The Decameron* features a wide variety of stories that touch on everything from wit to practical jokes. Among its best-known content is a series of love stories that range from eroticism to tragedy. *The Decameron,* perhaps most importantly, also serves as a key historical documentation of life in the Middle Ages.

Said to have been inspired by *The Decameron, The Canterbury Tales*, by Geoffrey Chaucer, is another collection of tales composed near the end of the fourteenth century. Each of the stories included in *The Canterbury Tales* is told by a member of a group of pilgrims traveling from Southwark to the St. Thomas Becket shrine at Canterbury Cathedral. Through the pilgrims' tales, Chaucer constructs a critical representation of fourteenth-century life in England and of the Church. Two of the best-known of Chaucer's tales include *The Wife of Bath's Tale*, which offers a look at the societal role of women at the time of its writing, and *The Merchant's Tale*, which is centered on the theme of the morality of women and often is remembered for its apparent anti-feminist commentary.

Sir Gawain and the Green Knight, an alliterative romantic poem written during the latter half of the fourteenth century by an unknown author, is also held among the great English works of the Middle Ages. In the story, Sir Gawain, a knight of King Arthur's Round Table and the king's nephew, accepts a challenge from a strange green warrior who says he will allow anyone to strike him with his axe if they will accept a return blow a year and a day later. Though the warrior is beheaded, the warrior survives and Gawain must fulfill his part of the agreement. As date of his return blow approaches, Gawain successfully resists the charms of a lord's beautiful wife but ultimately gives in to the temptation of invincibility.

Renaissance Literature

Without question, the greatest and most influential contributor to literature during the Renaissance was English playwright William Shakespeare. Shakespeare's tragedies and comedies alike are widely regarded as the greatest stage dramas ever written. The following are included in his great body of work:

Tragedies

- *Romeo and Juliet:* A pair of lovers from two feuding families struggle to maintain their relationship despite the bitter hatred between their opposing houses.

- *Hamlet:* A young prince desires to avenge his father's murder.

- *Macbeth:* A general murders his king so that he may fulfill a prophecy that he will ascend to the throne.

- *Othello:* A jealous king murders his wife over rumors of unfaithfulness that later prove to be untrue.

- *Julius Caesar:* The great Roman consul is betrayed and murdered on the Senate floor by a mob led by his friend Brutus.

- *King Lear:* An aging king attempts to divide his kingdom among his three daughters.

- *Anthony and Cleopatra:* A Roman consul and an Egyptian queen engage in a love affair.

- *Titus Andronicus*

- *Coriolanus*

- *Timon of Athens*

- *Troilus and Cressida*

Comedies

- *A Midsummer Night's Dream:* Mischievous fairies meddle in the lives of lovers and actors who spend a night in the forest.

- *The Merchant of Venice:* A merchant in desperate need of money puts up his own body as collateral but is spared from having to make good on his deal when his cargo ship sinks.

- *The Comedy of Errors:* Two sets of long lost brothers are reunited.

- *Much Ado About Nothing*

- *As You Like It*

- *The Taming of the Shrew*

- *Twelfth Night*

- *All's Well That Ends Well*

- *The Merry Wives of Windsor*

- *Measure for Measure*

- *Love's Labor's Lost*

Histories

- *Henry VI, Parts I, II, and III*

- *Richard II*

- *Richard III*

- *King John*

- *Henry V*
- *Henry VIII*

Romances
- *The Tempest*
- *The Winter's Tale*
- *Cymbeline*
- *Pericles*

Neoclassical Literature

The Renaissance came to a close around 1625, as the European political atmosphere grew increasingly conservative. In England, Puritan dictator Oliver Cromwell took a firm stance against the arts, shuttering theatres and condemning any "lavish" forms of art. With this, spirituality, rational thinking, and science regained their earlier prominence and the Neoclassical Period was born. Despite the repression of the arts, however, several important writers and significant works of literature emerged from this era.

Perhaps one of the best-known and influential works to come out of the Neoclassic Period was *Paradise Lost* by John Milton. A renowned epic poem, *Paradise Lost* recounts a celestial war in which God and Jesus fight against the angel Lucifer for control of the universe. In the story, God and Jesus emerge victorious and condemn Lucifer and his followers to eternity in Hell. Milton later wrote a follow-up to *Paradise Lost* called *Paradise Regained*.

Another key literary figure of the Neoclassical Period was Alexander Pope. Pope, a deformed but vastly intelligent writer, established himself as a cutting satirist through his philosophical poems, the most notable of which include *Essay on Man* and *Essay on Criticism*. Pope is recognized not only for satirizing the social and political landscape of his time, but also for satirizing his own literary contemporaries as he did in his most famous work, the epic poem *The Rape of the Lock*. *The Rape of the Lock* parodied the epic form, making light of the fact that it remained popular even though many of the epics written at the time were so poorly composed. Pope also famously translated *The Iliad* and *The Odyssey* into English using heroic couplet, a form for which Pope is still considered the undisputed master to this day.

Jonathan Swift was another neoclassical satirist known for his frequently bitter tone. Most notably, he once suggested, in a pamphlet called *A Modest Proposal*, that Irish children should be sold as food. Swift's best-known work was the novel *Gulliver's Travels*, in which a shipwrecked sailor awakes to find himself in Lilliput, a land populated by a race of miniature people. Though it is often read as a children's book, *Gulliver's Travels* is, in fact, a carefully constructed satire of both the human race and neoclassical English society.

One of the leading figures of the latter portion of the Neoclassical Period was Dr. Samuel Johnson, an accomplished English author, biographer, poet, and essayist. A prolific writer, Johnson wrote for a number of magazines and periodicals and completed a variety of works, including the poems *The Vanity of Human Wishes* and *London*, the biography *The Life of Richard Savage*, and the play *Irene*. Later in his career, Johnson spent nine years compiling the *Dictionary of the English Language*, the first great English dictionary. He also is remembered for *Lives of the Most Imminent English Poets*, a massive collection of biographies and critiques of seventeenth- and eighteenth-century English poets.

Outside England, the French author and philosopher Voltaire was a major neoclassical figure. Accomplished in nearly every literary form of his day, Voltaire wrote thousands of letters, books, and other works. His best-known and influential work was the satire *Candide*, in which he vigorously attacked Gottfried Leibniz and his philosophy of optimism for the passivity he believed it created. Other works by Voltaire include the poems *Henriade* and *The Maid of Orleans* and the critical work *Commentaire sur Corneille*.

Romantic Literature

By the last few decades of the eighteenth century, the values of neoclassicism were quickly giving way to those of romanticism. Literature based on reason and sprawling heroic epics were falling out of favor. In an era of revolutions and great political upheaval, the upper classes, which had previously been the subject of many of the world's great writings, were replaced by the common man. The use of language was changing as well. While many of the great neoclassical works had been written in formal language only the educated could understand, new works were written in the common language, making literature more understandable for the average person. The era of romanticism introduces a broad spectrum of literary contributors who are still recognized as some of history's greatest writers today. Following are some notable figures from the era of romanticism:

- **William Wordsworth** ("The Reverie of Poor Susan," "The Old Cumberland Beggar," "Lines Written in Early Spring," "Ode: Imitations of Immorality," "The Prelude"): One of the earliest romantic writers, Wordsworth was a naturalist who wrote about the truth inherent in nature and the evils of urban living. He argued that man, a naturally good creature, was easily corruptible in an urban atmosphere. He was known for his ability to use simple language to illicit deep emotional responses from his readers.

- **Samuel Taylor Coleridge** ("The Rime of the Ancient Mariner," "Christabel," "Kubla Khan"): Though he wrote far more Shakespearean criticism than poetry, Coleridge is best known for his poetic works. He is most remembered for "The Rime of the Ancient Mariner," a salvation-themed poem about a sailor who invites the wrath of God upon his boat and crew after killing an albatross. It was his only contribution to *Lyrical Ballads*, a collection of poetry he published jointly with William Wordsworth.

- **Lord Byron** ("Childe Harold's Pilgrimage," "Don Juan"): Like Wordsworth, Lord Byron often wrote of the natural wonders of nature, though he is particularly known for his descriptive abilities. His writings gave rise to the concept of the Byronic hero, a man of great physical beauty, powerful emotions, and a sense of vitality.

- **John Keats** ("Ode on a Grecian Urn," "Ode to a Nightingale," "Endymion"): Keats was another of the masters of descriptive verse. Unlike Byron, however, Keats's talents for description came from a sense of what he called "negative capability," a state that he described as "being in uncertainties, mysteries, doubts, without any irritable reaching after fact and reason."

- **Percy Bysshe Shelley** ("To a Skylark," "Ode to the Wind," *Adonais*): Shelley notably defended Keats in his poetic work *Adonais,* when Keats was assailed by literary critics. He shared many of the same views of nature as other romantics, but unlike many of his contemporaries, Shelley argued that physical beauty was an indication of the true inner beauty of the soul.

- **Ralph Waldo Emerson** (*Nature, Experience, The Poet*): An accomplished essayist and lecturer, Emerson, along with Henry David Thoreau, was among the earliest American romantics. He strongly advocated individualism and individual spirituality. His most well-known work is *Nature*, an essay in which he explained the philosophy of transcendentalism.

- **Henry David Thoreau** (*Walden, Civil Disobedience*): Like many of his romantic contemporaries, Thoreau strongly believed in the virtues of nature, so much so that he opted to spend two years living entirely independent from society in a forest near Walden Pond in Massachusetts. This experience led to his most significant work, a journal known as *Walden*. He was eventually arrested for failing to pay a tax to which he was fundamentally opposed. His imprisonment led him to write his other major work, *Civil Disobedience*, in which he defended the right of any citizen to reject any inherently evil laws.

- **Walt Whitman** (*Leaves of Grass*, "Song of Myself," "Crossing Brooklyn Ferry"): One of the most uninhibited writers of his time, Whitman's poetry is marked by frequent intentional misspellings and grammatical errors designed to further intensify the powerful emotion expressed in his works. His liberal approach to grammatical mechanics was often overshadowed by Whitman's graphic depictions of his characters' intimate relations, which were quite shocking to many readers in the conservative society of the time. His most substantial work, the poetry collection *Leaves of Grass*, is a classic example of romanticism in which he praises nature as man's mother and brother.

- **Emily Dickinson** ("Because I could not stop for death," "I heard a Fly buzz when I died," "There is a certain slant of light"): A woman who lived much of her life in solitude, Dickinson is known for her iconic poetry marked by precise attention to detail and carefully crafted grammatical structure. Her deliberate use of grammar, notably through punctuation such as dashes and commas, resulted in a poetic form filled with vivid imagery and intense emotion that allowed for clear, distinct communication between Dickinson and her readers. She is often regarded as the greatest of all female American poets.

- **Edgar Allen Poe** ("The Telltale Heart," "The Cask of Amontillado," "The Raven"): Among the most widely read American writers of his era, Poe is renowned for his chilling tales of mystery and terror. With works like "The Telltale Heart" and "The Cask of Amontillado," Poe mastered and legitimized the short story format and is still held as one of the true masters of that genre. Poe was also an adept poet, having composed a long list of great poetic works that includes "The Raven," "The Bells," and "A Dream Within a Dream."

- **Mark Twain** (*The Adventures of Tom Sawyer, Adventures of Huckleberry Finn, A Connecticut Yankee in King Arthur's Court*)" Of all American novelists, none is associated more with the American spirit and the idea of Americana than Samuel Clemens, better known as Mark Twain. His two classic novels, *The Adventures of Tom Sawyer* and *Adventures of Huckleberry Finn*, paint the definitive picture of American life during the antebellum period in which he lived. Twain's dramatic abilities and mastery of writing in dialects led him to become one of the most highly regarded authors in American history.

- **Nathaniel Hawthorne** (*The Scarlet Letter, The House of Seven Gables*): Hawthorne is best known for his Puritan drama *The Scarlet Letter*, in which a young Puritan woman becomes impregnated after an affair with a minister but refuses to divulge his identity even as she is forced to wear a large, red letter A on her clothing to denote her sin. Much of Hawthorne's work, which is steeped in the theme of man's inherent evil and sinfulness, is considered dark romanticism.

- **Herman Melville** (*Moby Dick*, *Billy Budd*): Melville's most renowned work, *Moby Dick*, is a classic American novel that follows the story of Ishmael, a wandering sailor who finds himself on a ship belonging to Captain Ahab, a whaler obsessed with capturing a specific whale named Moby Dick. Through Ishmael, Melville touches on a variety of themes, including the class system, good and evil, and religion. Along with the posthumously released *Billy Budd* and his other works, *Moby Dick* made Melville one of America's most influential native writers.

Modern Literature

Over the course of the nineteenth and twentieth centuries, a wide range of influential authors and novelists emerged. The following table lists some of these authors and a few of their most notable works.

ADDITIONAL NINETEENTH-CENTURY AND NOTABLE TWENTIETH-CENTURY AUTHORS

Author	Noted Works
Jane Austen	*Pride and Prejudice, Sense and Sensibility*
Mary Shelley	*Frankenstein*
Alexandre Dumas	*The Three Musketeers, The Count of Monte Cristo*
Charlotte Brontë	*Jane Eyre*
Emily Brontë	*Wuthering Heights*
Charles Dickens	*A Christmas Carol, A Tale of Two Cities, Great Expectations, The Adventures of Oliver Twist*
Victor Hugo	*Les Misérables, The Hunchback of Notre-Dame*
Louisa May Alcott	*Little Women*
Leo Tolstoy	*War and Peace, Anna Karenina*
Jules Verne	*20,000 Leagues Under the Sea, Around the World in Eighty Days, A Journey to the Center of the Earth*
Bram Stoker	*Dracula*
Robert Louis Stevenson	*Treasure Island, Strange Case of Dr. Jekyll and Mr. Hyde*
Rudyard Kipling	*The Jungle Book, The Man Who Would Be King*
Sir Arthur Conan Doyle	*The Adventures of Sherlock Holmes, The Hound of the Baskervilles, The Lost World*
Stephen Crane	*The Red Badge of Courage*
H.G. Wells	*The Time Machine, War of the Worlds, The Invisible Man*
Joseph Conrad	*Heart of Darkness, The Secret Agent*
Upton Sinclair	*The Jungle, King Coal, Oil!*
F. Scott Fitzgerald	*The Great Gatsby, This Side of Paradise*
Virginia Woolf	*A Room of One's Own, Mrs. Dalloway, The Waves*
William Faulkner	*The Sound and the Fury, As I Lay Dying*

Ernest Hemingway	*The Old Man and the Sea, For Whom the Bell Tolls, A Farewell to Arms*
John Steinbeck	*Of Mice and Men, The Grapes of Wrath, East of Eden*
James Joyce	*Finnegan's Wake, Ulysses*
George Orwell	*Nineteen Eighty-Four, Animal Farm*
Ray Bradbury	*Fahrenheit 451, The Illustrated Man*
J.D. Salinger	*Catcher in the Rye*
Jack Kerouac	*On the Road, Mexico City Blues*
Joseph Heller	*Catch-22*
Kurt Vonnegut	*Slaughterhouse Five, Cat's Cradle*

ARCHITECTURE

In addition to questions about the visual and performing arts, the CLEP Humanities test also contains questions related to the subject of architecture. Although these questions account for only a small percentage of the exam, it is important to be prepared to tackle them.

ARCHITECTURAL TERMINOLOGY

Term	Definition
Arch	A curved or pointed structural member supported at the sides or ends
Art deco style	A highly lavish, ornamental twentieth-century architectural style
Art nouveau style	A popular late-nineteenth and early-twentieth century architectural style marked by the frequent depiction of leaves and flowers arranged in flowing, sinuous lines
Buttress	A structure built against or projecting from a wall for the purpose of providing additional support for the wall
Byzantine style	A fifth-century C.E. architectural style developed in the Byzantine Empire and marked by massive domes, square bases, rounded arches, spires, and extensive use of glass
Column	A support pillar composed of a base, cylindrical shaft, and a capital
Corinthian column	The most ornate of the Greek-style columns, marked by their acanthus leaf decorated capitals
Doric column	The simplest Greek-style column, usually marked by fluted sides, a smooth, rounded capital, and no base
Gothic style	A prominent medieval European architectural style marked by pointed arches, ribbed vaults, and flying buttresses

Ionic column	A Greek-style column marked by a capital with scroll-like decorations and a rounded base
Minaret	A tall spire with an onion-shaped or conical crown commonly seen in Islamic architecture
Pyramid	Ancient Egyptian structure in which all outer surfaces are built in a triangular shape and designed to converge into a single point at the peak
Vault	An arched support structure of a ceiling or roof

Famous Structures

Some questions on the CLEP Humanities test may require you to identify a famous structure based on an image or other information. The following is a brief guide to some of the famous structures with which you may need to be familiar.

FAMOUS STRUCTURES

Structure	Image
The Acropolis (Athens, Greece)	
Pyramid (Egypt)	

The Parthenon (Athens, Greece)	
Notre Dame Cathedral (Paris, France)	
Hagia Sophia (Istanbul, Turkey)	

| The Pantheon (Rome, Italy) |  |
| Westminster Abbey (London, England) |  |

Florence Cathedral (Florence, Italy)	
Basilica di San Vitale (Rome, Italy)	
St. Peter's Basilica (Vatican City)	

Palace of Versailles (Versailles, France)	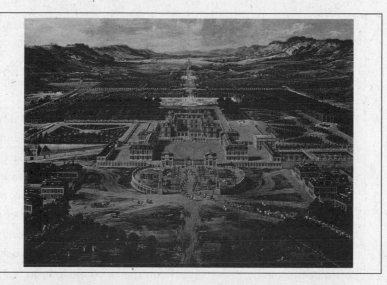

Additional Notable Structures

- St. Paul's Cathedral (London, England)
- St. Mark's Cathedral (Venice, Italy)
- The Alhambra (Grenada, Spain)
- The Tower of London (London, England)
- St. Martin-in-the-Fields (London, England)
- Basilica of Sant'Apollinare in Classe (Ravenna, Italy)
- The Taj Mahal (Agra, India)
- Palatine Chapel (Aachen, Germany)
- Dome of the Rock (Jerusalem, Israel)

PAINTING

The CLEP Humanities test includes a significant number of questions about the art of painting. To answer these questions, you will need to be familiar with a broad range of topics, including art history, famous artists and their works, the different forms of painting, and more. The following is a brief list of terms you should review before the test.

Term	Definition
Abstract expressionism	Mid-twentieth-century American art style popular during the World War II era and noted for the use of brushstrokes, texture, and oversized canvasses
Cubism	Early twentieth-century art style marked by its geometric forms, fragmentation of its object, and abstraction
Dada	Twentieth-century art movement that emerged as a disillusioned response to World War I; marked by absurdity, unpredictability, and a sense of revolt

Expressionism	Twentieth-century art style in which distortion and exaggeration are used to evoke an emotional response in the viewer
Fauvism	Similar to expressionism; noted for bold application of arbitrary color
Fresco	A type of painting applied directly to damp plaster; typically seen on walls and ceilings
Impressionism	Nineteenth-century art style aimed at depicting the general impression elicited from a particular scene and the technique of using unmixed primary colors and small brushstrokes to recreate the effect of reflected light
Modernism	A nineteenth- and twentieth-century art movement noted for its rejection of tradition and traditional forms of art
Post-modernism	A response to modernism that refers to the collision of various artistic and cultural styles that followed modernism; post-modernist works frequently have numerous meanings and possible interpretations
Still life	A type of painting in which everyday household items or foods are presented in a simple, straightforward manner
Surrealism	Twentieth-century art movement based on the concept of expressing human imagination as experienced in dreams
Tempera	A painting process in which a water-soluble material is used instead of paint
Rococo	Eighteenth-century art movement deeply influenced by feminine tastes; Rococo era works are noted for their depictions of frivolous subjects rendered through delicate colors and gentle forms
Romanticism	Nineteenth-century art movement known for its beautiful, individualistic, and deeply emotional style

Notable Works and Artists

Many painting-related questions on the CLEP Humanities test will present an image of a particular painting and ask you to identify the title of the piece, name the artist responsible for it, or recognize some other detail about the work. The following is a brief listing of some notable artists and paintings you can use to begin preparing for the painting questions you will encounter on the CLEP.

NOTABLE PAINTERS AND PAINTINGS

Painter	Work
Leonard da Vinci	*The Last Supper*
Leonard da Vinci	*Mona Lisa*

| Michelangelo | 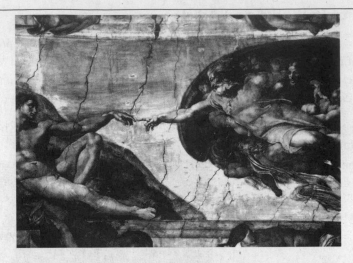 *The Creation of Adam* |
| Sandro Botticelli |  *The Birth of Venus* |

Vincent van Gogh	
	Starry Night
Georges Seurat	
	A Sunday Afternoon on the Island of La Grande Jatte

Rembrandt van Rijn	
	The Storm on the Sea of Galilee
Peter Paul Rubens	
	The Elevation of the Cross

Johannes Vermeer

Girl With a Pearl Earring

SCULPTURE

The visual arts portion of the CLEP Humanities test will include some questions related to the art of sculpture. Like many of the painting questions, sculpture questions on the exam may present you with an image of a particular sculpture and ask you for the title of the work, the name of the artist who created it, or other information related to the work. The following is a brief list of some famous sculptors and their most notable works, which you may encounter on the test.

Michelangelo

- *David*
- *Pieta*
- *Moses*
- *The Deposition*

Donatello

- *David*
- *Mary Magdalene*
- *Equestrian Statue of the Gattamelata*

Giovanni Bernini

- *The Ecstasy of Saint Teresa*
- *Apollo and Daphne*
- *Fountain of the Four Rivers*

Auguste Rodin

- *The Thinker*
- *The Kiss*

Alexandros of Antioch

- *Venus de Milo*

MUSIC, FILM, AND DANCE

As stated earlier, the fine arts questions on the CLEP Humanities test are divided into two main categories: visual arts and performing arts. The performing arts questions on the exam are designed to test your knowledge of various types of music, famous composers and compositions, forms of dance, and important films and directors.

Music questions on the CLEP Humanities test may require an understanding of some special terminology specific to that art form. The following list provides some musical terms with which you may want to familiarize yourself in preparation for the exam.

Term	Definition
A cappella	A vocal performance given without musical accompaniment
Adagio	A slow moving, restful tempo
Andante	A tempo said to be "at a walking pace"
Allegro	A musical direction meaning to play quickly and energetically
Aria	A duet or solo piece of music meant to express a singer's emotions or feelings
Cantata	A multiple-movement musical commentary performed by a soloist and a chorus accompanied by at least one instrument, frequently an organ
Concerto	A secular, three-movement form of instrumental music
Grave	A slow, solemn tempo
Key	A musical composition's central note
Libretto	The text of an opera or other musical work
Moderato	A moderately paced tempo
Presto	A very fast tempo
Opera	A text-based form of music
Oratorio	A choral work; can be of sacred or secular nature; solely a vocal performance; may include a narrator, chorus, soloists, or an orchestra
Toccata	A virtuoso piece specifically designed to demonstrate the abilities of both the instrument and the performer; frequently composed for the organ

The performing arts questions on the CLEP Humanities test cover a wide range of artistic forms and genres. The following is a brief list of significant contributors to the performing arts along with their primary genre and notable works.

KEY PERFORMING ARTS PERSONALITIES

Person	Genre	Notable Works
Johann Sebastian Bach	Music	*Brandenburg Concertos, Goldberg Variations, Toccata and Fugue in D minor*
Ludwig van Beethoven	Music	*Moonlight Sonata, Für Elise, Ninth Symphony*
Johannes Brahms	Music	*Brahms' Lullaby, A German Requiem, Violin Concerto in D Major*
Frédéric Chopin	Music	*Etude for piano No. 12 in C minor ("Revolutionary"), Nocturne for piano No. 2 in E flat major, Fantasy-Impromptu for piano in C sharp minor*
Aaron Copland	Music	*Appalachian Spring, Billy the Kid, Fanfare for the Common Man*
Claude Debussy	Music	*Clair de Lune, Golliwog's Cakewalk, Prelude to the Afternoon of a Faun*
Cecil B. DeMille	Film	*The Ten Commandments, The Greatest Show on Earth, The King of Kings*
Federico Fellini	Film	*La Dolce Vita, 8½, I Vitelloni*
Gilbert and Sullivan	Musical Theater	*H.M.S. Pinafore, The Pirates of Penzance, The Mikado*
Edvart Grieg	Music	*In the Hall of the Mountain King, Morning Mood, Lyric Pieces*
Georg Friederic Handel	Music	*Messiah, Water Music, Music for the Royal Fireworks*
Alfred Hitchcock	Film	*Vertigo, Psycho, North by Northwest*
Scott Joplin	Music	*The Entertainer, Maple Leaf Rag, The Ragtime Dance*
Akira Kurosawa	Film	*Rashomon, The Hidden Fortress, Seven Samurai*

Wolfgang Amadeus Mozart	Music	*Requiem Mass, Don Giovanni, Eine Kleine Nachtmusik*
Giacomo Puccini	Opera	*La Bohème, Tosca, Madame Butterfly*
Igor Stravinsky	Opera/Ballet	*The Firebird, The Rite of Spring, The Nightingale*
Pyotr Ilyich Tchaikovsky	Music/Ballet	*1812 Overture, Swan Lake, The Nutcracker*
Giuseppe Verdi	Opera	*Rigoletto, La Traviata, Aïda*
Antonio Vivaldi	Music	*The Four Seasons, Gloria, Concerto in A Minor*

Some music questions on the CLEP Humanities test may ask you for information about different types of musical instruments used today and in previous eras. The following is a brief list of musical instruments with which you may want to familiarize yourself before taking the exam.

MUSICAL INSTRUMENTS

Instrument	Type	Definition
Violin	String	The smallest, most common, and highest-pitched orchestral instrument
Viola	String	Similar to the violin, though slightly larger; has a "middle-register" pitch
Cello	String	Large, mellow sounding stringed instrument
Bass	String	Largest and deepest-pitched stringed instrument
Flute	Wind	Small, high-pitched wind instrument
Piccolo	Wind	Smaller version of a flute
Clarinet	Wind	Single reed instrument capable of a wide range of notes
Oboe	Wind	Double reed instrument similar to the clarinet
Saxophone	Wind	Single reed instrument commonly used for jazz compositions
Bassoon	Wind	Large, deep-pitched double reed instrument
French Horn	Brass	Brass instrument played with the right hand inside the bell; difficult to play

Trumpet	Brass	Plays high-pitched, brassy notes; can be played with a mute
Tuba	Brass	Large, low-pitched brass instrument
Trombone	Brass	Has a wide note range as result of its slide
Cymbals	Percussion	Metal percussive instruments used to make a "crashing" sound
Snare Drum	Percussion	In a classical setting, used for rolls or providing accents
Timpani	Percussion	Deeper drum that can produce notes or provide rolls
Bass Drum	Percussion	Used primarily for keeping a beat
Piano	Keyboard	Widely used instrument played through the use of a keyboard that causes hammers to strike steel strings
Harpsichord	Keyboard	Older, alternative version of a piano that produces a sound through plucking strings

HUMANITIES: REVIEW QUESTIONS

1. Which of the following artists is most closely associated with the Pop Art movement?

   (A) Jackson Pollack

   (B) Salvador Dali

   (C) Pablo Picasso

   (D) Georgia O'Keeffe

   (E) Andy Warhol

2. Living in a dystopian society known as Oceania, Winston Smith is a humble civil servant who is responsible for altering historical records in order to perpetuate the omniscience of Oceania's all-powerful political party, known simply as the Party. Over time, however, Winston grows increasingly disillusioned with his situation and begins to rebel against the Party.

   The novel described above is

   (A) *Fahrenheit 451*

   (B) *Animal Farm*

   (C) *A Clockwork Orange*

   (D) *1984*

   (E) *The Catcher in the Rye*

3. The songs "Alexander's Ragtime Band," "Puttin' on the Ritz," and "God Bless America" were all written by which composer?

   (A) Aaron Copeland

   (B) Irving Berlin

   (C) George Gershwin

   (D) Scott Joplin

   (E) Leonard Bernstein

Questions 4–6 refer to the following people.

   (A) Igor Stravinsky, Sergei Rachmaninoff, Felix Mendelssohn

   (B) Robert Frost, Elizabeth Barrett Browning, T.S. Eliot

   (C) Harper Lee, Jack Kerouac, Ray Bradbury

   (D) Francois Truffaut, Fritz Lang, Billy Wilder

   (E) Henrik Ibsen, Harold Pinter, Eugene Ionesco

4. Which is a group of novelists?

5. Which is a group of poets?

6. Which is a group of playwrights?

7. The Empire State Building in New York City, New York, is an example of which type of architecture?

   (A) Art Nouveau

   (B) Gothic

   (C) Modernism

   (D) Art Deco

   (E) Roman

8. Which of the following correctly pairs a poet with a work he or she created?

   (A) John Keats … "Ode to a Nightingale"

   (B) E.E. Cummings … "The Hallow Men"

   (C) Charlotte Brontë … "I'm Nobody! Who are you?"

   (D) Ralph Waldo Emerson … "Fire and Ice"

   (E) Edgar Allan Poe … "O Captain! My Captain!"

9. The *Aeneid* was written by

   (A) Homer

   (B) Ovid

   (C) Hesiod

   (D) Virgil

   (E) Lucan

10. Paul Cézanne is often referred to as the father of which late nineteenth- and early twentieth-century art movement?

   (A) Expressionism

   (B) Cubism

   (C) Modernism

   (D) Fauvism

   (E) Impressionism

ANSWER KEY AND EXPLANATIONS

1. A	3. B	5. B	7. D	9. D
2. D	4. C	6. E	8. A	10. C

1. **The correct answer is (A).** Andy Warhol, best known for works like *Campbell's Soup I*, is closely related to the Pop Art movement.

2. **The correct answer is (D).** The novel described is author George Orwell's *1984*.

3. **The correct answer is (B).** Twentieth-century composer Irving Berlin wrote the songs "Alexander's Ragtime Band," "Puttin' on the Ritz," and "God Bless America."

4. **The correct answer is (C).** Harper Lee, Jack Kerouac, and Ray Bradbury are all novelists.

5. **The correct answer is (B).** Robert Frost, Elizabeth Barrett Browning, and T.S. Eliot are all poets.

6. **The correct answer is (E).** Henrik Ibsen, Harold Pinter, and Eugene Ionesco are all playwrights.

7. **The correct answer is (D).** The Empire State Building is an example of Art Deco architecture.

8. **The correct answer is (A).** John Keats was the author of "Ode to a Nightingale."

9. **The correct answer is (D).** The *Aeneid* was written by classical Roman poet Virgil.

10. **The correct answer is (C).** Paul Cézanne is frequently referred to as the father of Modernism.

POSTTEST ANSWER SHEET

1. Ⓐ Ⓑ Ⓒ Ⓓ Ⓔ	11. Ⓐ Ⓑ Ⓒ Ⓓ Ⓔ	21. Ⓐ Ⓑ Ⓒ Ⓓ Ⓔ	31. Ⓐ Ⓑ Ⓒ Ⓓ Ⓔ	41. Ⓐ Ⓑ Ⓒ Ⓓ Ⓔ
2. Ⓐ Ⓑ Ⓒ Ⓓ Ⓔ	12. Ⓐ Ⓑ Ⓒ Ⓓ Ⓔ	22. Ⓐ Ⓑ Ⓒ Ⓓ Ⓔ	32. Ⓐ Ⓑ Ⓒ Ⓓ Ⓔ	42. Ⓐ Ⓑ Ⓒ Ⓓ Ⓔ
3. Ⓐ Ⓑ Ⓒ Ⓘ Ⓔ	13. Ⓐ Ⓑ Ⓒ Ⓓ Ⓔ	23. Ⓐ Ⓑ Ⓒ Ⓓ Ⓔ	33. Ⓐ Ⓑ Ⓒ Ⓓ Ⓔ	43. Ⓐ Ⓑ Ⓒ Ⓓ Ⓔ
4. Ⓐ Ⓑ Ⓒ Ⓓ Ⓔ	14. Ⓐ Ⓑ Ⓒ Ⓓ Ⓔ	24. Ⓐ Ⓑ Ⓒ Ⓓ Ⓔ	34. Ⓐ Ⓑ Ⓒ Ⓓ Ⓔ	44. Ⓐ Ⓑ Ⓒ Ⓓ Ⓔ
5. Ⓐ Ⓑ Ⓒ Ⓓ Ⓔ	15. Ⓐ Ⓑ Ⓒ Ⓓ Ⓔ	25. Ⓐ Ⓑ Ⓒ Ⓓ Ⓔ	35. Ⓐ Ⓑ Ⓒ Ⓓ Ⓔ	45. Ⓐ Ⓑ Ⓒ Ⓓ Ⓔ
6. Ⓐ Ⓑ Ⓒ Ⓓ Ⓔ	16. Ⓐ Ⓑ Ⓒ Ⓓ Ⓔ	26. Ⓐ Ⓑ Ⓒ Ⓓ Ⓔ	36. Ⓐ Ⓑ Ⓒ Ⓓ Ⓔ	46. Ⓐ Ⓑ Ⓒ Ⓓ Ⓔ
7. Ⓐ Ⓑ Ⓒ Ⓓ Ⓔ	17. Ⓐ Ⓑ Ⓒ Ⓓ Ⓔ	27. Ⓐ Ⓑ Ⓒ Ⓓ Ⓔ	37. Ⓐ Ⓑ Ⓒ Ⓓ Ⓔ	47. Ⓐ Ⓑ Ⓒ Ⓓ Ⓔ
8. Ⓐ Ⓑ Ⓒ Ⓓ Ⓔ	18. Ⓐ Ⓑ Ⓒ Ⓓ Ⓔ	28. Ⓐ Ⓑ Ⓒ Ⓓ Ⓔ	38. Ⓐ Ⓑ Ⓒ Ⓓ Ⓔ	48. Ⓐ Ⓑ Ⓒ Ⓓ Ⓔ
9. Ⓐ Ⓑ Ⓒ Ⓓ Ⓔ	19. Ⓐ Ⓑ Ⓒ Ⓓ Ⓔ	29. Ⓐ Ⓑ Ⓒ Ⓓ Ⓔ	39. Ⓐ Ⓑ Ⓒ Ⓓ Ⓔ	49. Ⓐ Ⓑ Ⓒ Ⓓ Ⓔ
10. Ⓐ Ⓑ Ⓒ Ⓓ Ⓔ	20. Ⓐ Ⓑ Ⓒ Ⓓ Ⓔ	30. Ⓐ Ⓑ Ⓒ Ⓓ Ⓔ	40. Ⓐ Ⓑ Ⓒ Ⓓ Ⓔ	50. Ⓐ Ⓑ Ⓒ Ⓓ Ⓔ

answer sheet

Posttest

35 minutes • 50 questions

Directions: Each of the questions or incomplete statements below is followed by five suggested answers or completions. Select the one that is best in each case.

Example: **SAMPLE ANSWER**

 Ⓐ ● Ⓒ Ⓓ Ⓔ

A solo operatic piece specifically intended to express the emotions of a main character is known as a/an

    (A) interlude

    (B) aria

    (C) cavatina

    (D) libretto

    (E) serenade

An aria, which is sung by a solo performer, is an operatic piece that is designed to showcase the emotions of one of the main characters. **The correct answer is (B).**

1. Matsuo Bashō is best known for his contributions to which form of poetry?

    (A) Limerick

    (B) Haiku

    (C) Sonnet

    (D) Ballad

    (E) Ode

2. Atticus Finch, Boo Radley, and Mayella Ewell are all characters featured in which novel?

    (A) John Steinbeck's *The Grapes of Wrath*

    (B) Emily Brontë's *Wuthering Heights*

    (C) Ernest Hemmingway's *For Whom the Bell Tolls*

    (D) Harper Lee's *To Kill a Mockingbird*

    (E) George Orwell's *Animal Farm*

3. This Romantic era composer completed a total of seven symphonies, eleven overtures, eleven operas, three ballets, and a wide range of other works. Some of his most famous works include the *1812 Overture*, *Swan Lake*, and *The Nutcracker*. The composer is

    (A) Franz Schubert

    (B) Richard Wagner

    (C) Pyotr Ilyich Tchaikovsky

    (D) Johann Strauss

    (E) Felix Mendelssohn

4. A strong believer in the American Dream and the promise of easily attainable success, this apprehensive, delusional traveling salesman becomes increasingly frustrated as he realizes neither he nor his sons have achieved his dream and, as a result, his mental state quickly begins to deteriorate.

The sentence above describes

    (A) Stanley Kowalski

    (B) Tom Wingfield

    (C) George Gibbs

    (D) John Proctor

    (E) Willy Loman

5. The artists who participated in this twentieth-century art movement created works specifically designed to express the imagery experienced in dreams and were heavily influenced by the Freudian concept of the unconscious.

Which of the following movements is referred to above?

(A) Dada

(B) Constructivism

(C) Expressionism

(D) Surrealism

(E) Fauvism

6. Which of the following is a group of Elizabethan poets?

(A) Edmund Spencer, Christopher Marlowe, Philip Sidney

(B) William Wordsworth, Lord Byron, John Keats

(C) Alexander Pope, Jonathan Swift, John Dryden

(D) John Donne, Richard Crashaw, John Milton

(E) Lord Tennyson, Robert Browning, Gerard Manley Hopkins

7. *On the Origin of Species*, a highly influential piece of scientific literature that served to lay the groundwork for the theory of evolution, was written by

(A) Isaac Newton

(B) Charles Darwin

(C) Galileo Galilei

(D) Max Planck

(E) René Descartes

Questions 8–10 refer to the following periods in art and music history.

(A) Renaissance

(B) Baroque

(C) Classical

(D) Romantic

(E) Modern

8. To which period do Liszt, Chopin, and Verdi belong?

9. To which period do Bernini, Rembrandt, and Caravaggio belong?

10. To what period do Debussy, Puccini, and Rachmaninoff belong?

11. The films *Sunset Boulevard*, *Double Indemnity*, and *Some Like It Hot* were directed by

(A) John Huston

(B) D.W. Griffith

(C) Cecil B. DeMille

(D) Frank Capra

(E) Billy Wilder

12. Which playwright wrote *Barefoot in the Park*, *The Odd Couple*, and *Biloxi Blues*?

(A) David Mamet

(B) Neil Simon

(C) Tennessee Williams

(D) Arthur Miller

(E) Terrence McNally

13. Written in 1787 by Wolfgang Amadeus Mozart, this opera follows the story of a young, ill-behaving nobleman who cruelly mistreats everyone in his life until his boorish ways lead him to a harrowing yet deserved fate.

The work described is

(A) *The Abduction from the Seraglio*

(B) *The Damnation of Faust*

(C) *Don Giovanni*

(D) *Pagliacci*

(E) *The Impresario*

14. Which composer is best known for *The Planets*, a seven-part orchestral piece that features a movement for each of the seven extraterrestrial planets known to exist at the time of its composition?

(A) Franz Liszt

(B) Hector Berlioz

(C) Carl Orff

(D) Gustav Holst

(E) Sergei Prokofiev

Questions 15–17 refer to the following people.

(A) Gianlorenzo Bernini, Sandro Botticelli, Auguste Rodin

(B) Jean-Luc Godard, Francois Truffaut, Federico Fellini

(C) Anton Chekhov, Harold Pinter, Noel Coward

(D) Maurice Ravel, George Gershwin, Irving Berlin

(E) Joseph Heller, Leo Tolstoy, Kurt Vonnegut

15. Which is a group of playwrights?

16. Which is a group of film directors?

17. Which is a group of novelists?

18. *In Praise of Folly*, a sixteenth-century essay that decried the ongoing corruption in the Roman Catholic Church, was written by

(A) Desiderius Erasmus

(B) Thomas More

(C) Martin Luther

(D) John Calvin

(E) Huldrych Zwingli

19. A row of columns that carries an entablature or arches is known as a

(A) pediment

(B) buttress

(C) vault

(D) colonnade

(E) parapet

20. Born in Spain in 1881, this famous modern-era artist cofounded the cubism movement and created countless influential paintings, some of which include *Garçon à la Pipe*, *Les Demoiselles d'Avignon*, and *Le guitariste*.

The sentence above describes

(A) Paul Cézanne

(B) Pablo Picasso

(C) Georges Braque

(D) Jackson Pollock

(E) Salvador Dalí

21. The work pictured above is a self-portrait by which artist?

(A) Edouard Manet

(B) Paul Gauguin

(C) Auguste Rodin

(D) Henri Matisse

(E) Vincent van Gogh

22. During the late-nineteenth and early-twentieth centuries, this English author penned four novels and fifty-six short stories starring fictional detective Sherlock Holmes, a character who has become synonymous with the detective fiction genre.

The sentence above refers to

(A) Thomas Hardy

(B) Robert Louis Stevenson

(C) Arthur Conan Doyle

(D) H.G. Wells

(E) John Buchan

23. A strange inventor creates a dancing, life-sized doll with which a young man, mistaking it for a real girl, falls in love, much to the dismay of his jilted fiancé, who later dresses up as the doll to win back his heart.

Which ballet does the sentence above describe?

(A) *Coppélia*

(B) *Giselle*

(C) *La Bayadère*

(D) *Paquita*

(E) *Le Corsaire*

Questions 24–26 refer to the following excerpt from a play.

> Is this a dagger which I see before me,
> The handle toward my hand? Come, let me clutch thee.
> I have thee not, and yet I see thee still.
> Art thou not, fatal vision, sensible
> 5 To feeling as to sight? Or art thou but
> A dagger of the mind, a false creation,
> Proceeding from the heat-oppressed brain?
> I see thee yet, in form as palpable
> As this which now I draw.
> 10 Thou marshal'st me the way that I was going,
> And such an instrument I was to use.
> Mine eyes are made the fools o' the other senses,
> Or else worth all the rest. I see thee still,
> And on thy blade and dudgeon gouts of blood,
> 15 Which was not so before. There's no such thing:
> It is the bloody business which informs
> Thus to mine eyes. Now o'er the one half-world
> Nature seems dead, and wicked dreams abuse
> The curtain'd sleep; witchcraft celebrates
> 20 Pale Hecate's offerings; and wither'd Murther,
> Alarum'd by his sentinel, the wolf,
> Whose howl's his watch, thus with his stealthy pace,
> With Tarquin's ravishing strides, towards his design
> Moves like a ghost. Thou sure and firm-set earth,
> 25 Hear not my steps, which way they walk, for fear
> Thy very stones prate of my whereabout,
> And take the present horror from the time,
> Which now suits with it. Whiles I threat, he lives;
> Words to the heat of deeds too cold breath gives.
> 30 I go, and it is done; the bell invites me.
> Hear it not, Duncan, for it is a knell
> That summons thee to heaven, or to hell.

24. Which figure of speech is utilized in line 26?

    (A) Onomatopoeia

    (B) Metaphor

    (C) Simile

    (D) Personification

    (E) Antithesis

25. The "bloody business" mentioned in line 16 refers to

    (A) witchcraft

    (B) murder

    (C) war

    (D) torture

    (E) genocide

26. The lines are spoken by

    (A) Mercutio in *Romeo and Juliet*

    (B) Hamlet in *Hamlet*

    (C) Edgar in *King Lear*

    (D) Brutus in *Julius Caesar*

    (E) Macbeth in *Macbeth*

27. Vincent van Gogh, Georges Seurat, and Auguste Rodin are most associated with which art movement?

    (A) Neo-classical

    (B) Romanticism

    (C) Fauvism

    (D) Post-impressionism

    (E) Rococo

28. A young girl who suffered through frequent abuse both as an orphan being raised by her aunt and as a student at a strict boarding school becomes a governess and falls in love with the master of the house, only to have her wedding plans interrupted by a stunning secret from his past.

    Which novel does the sentence above describe?

    (A) *Wuthering Heights*

    (B) *Jane Eyre*

    (C) *Pride and Prejudice*

    (D) *Emma*

    (E) *Little Women*

29. Which of the following composers was Johann Sebastian Bach's closest contemporary?

    (A) Edvard Grieg

    (B) Franz Joseph Haydn

    (C) Sergei Prokofiev

    (D) Ludwig van Beethoven

    (E) Antonio Vivaldi

30. *The Divine Comedy*, one of the best-known epics, was written by

    (A) John Milton

    (B) Giovanni Boccaccio

    (C) Dante Alighieri

    (D) Edmund Spenser

    (E) Geoffrey Chaucer

31. One of the most respected writers of the twentieth century, this author penned several novels that focused on the difficulties of war and man's struggles against nature, which often served as a reflection of his personal life experiences. Among his most famous works were *For Whom the Bell Tolls*, *The Old Man and the Sea*, and *A Farewell to Arms*.

    The author referred to above is

    (A) Ernest Hemingway

    (B) Herman Melville

    (C) John Steinbeck

    (D) George Orwell

    (E) Jack Kerouac

Questions 32–34 refer to the following image.

32. The work shown above was created by
    (A) Raphael
    (B) Sandro Botticelli
    (C) Michelangelo
    (D) Donatello
    (E) Leonardo da Vinci

33. The work can best be described as a/an
    (A) etching
    (B) oil painting
    (C) watercolor
    (D) fresco
    (E) illumination

34. The work can be found in
    (A) the Pantheon
    (B) Westminster Abbey
    (C) the Vatican
    (D) St. Mark's Cathedral
    (E) the Duomo of Florence

35. In the midst of World War II, a cynical nightclub owner is faced with the dilemma of choosing between being with the woman he loves or assisting her and her husband, a Czech Resistance leader, to safely escape from Nazi-occupied, Vichy-controlled North Africa.

This sentence describes which of the following films?
    (A) *From Here to Eternity*
    (B) *The African Queen*
    (C) *Lawrence of Arabia*
    (D) *Notorious*
    (E) *Casablanca*

36. *The Republic*, an Ancient Greek dialogue that describes justice and attempts to define the characteristics of a just city and a just man, was written by

    (A) Aristotle

    (B) Plato

    (C) Sophocles

    (D) Epicurus

    (E) Socrates

37. Notre Dame Cathedral in Paris, France, is an example of which type of architecture?

    (A) Romanesque

    (B) Medieval

    (C) Baroque

    (D) Victorian

    (E) Gothic

Questions 38–40 refer to the following lines from the plays of William Shakespeare.

    (A) "The play's the thing, wherein I'll catch the conscience of the king."

    (B) "Double, double toil and trouble; fire burn and cauldron bubble."

    (C) "I kissed thee ere I killed thee, no way but this, killing myself, to die upon a kiss."

    (D) "Good-night, good-night! Parting is such sweet sorrow that I shall say good-night till it be morrow."

    (E) "Cowards die many times before their deaths; the valiant never taste of death but once."

38. Which line is from *Othello?*

39. Which line is from *Macbeth?*

40. Which line is from *Julius Caesar?*

Questions 41–42 refer to the following poem.

Take this kiss upon the brow!
And, in parting from you now,
Thus much let me avow--
You are not wrong, who deem
5   That my days have been a dream;
Yet if hope has flown away
In a night, or in a day,
In a vision, or in none,
Is it therefore the less gone?
10   All that we see or seem
Is but a dream within a dream.
I stand amid the roar
Of a surf-tormented shore,
And I hold within my hand
15   Grains of the golden sand--
How few! yet how they creep
Through my fingers to the deep,
While I weep--while I weep!
O God! can I not grasp
20   Them with a tighter clasp?
O God! can I not save
One from the pitiless wave?
Is all that we see or seem
But a dream within a dream?

41. Which of the following contains an example of onomatopoeia?

(A) Line 3

(B) Line 7

(C) Line 13

(D) Line 19

(E) Line 23

42. Lines 19–22 contain an example of

(A) simile

(B) anaphora

(C) hyperbole

(D) synecdoche

(E) oxymoron

43. Which of the following plays was written by Thornton Wilder?

(A) *Easy Virtue*

(B) *The Seagull*

(C) *The Matchmaker*

(D) *Major Barbara*

(E) *The Glass Menagerie*

Questions 44–45 refer to the following image.

44. The sculpture pictured above is known as

(A) *The Thinker*

(C) *Pieta*

(C) *David*

(D) *The Dying Gaul*

(E) *Moses*

45. The sculpture was created by

(A) Michelangelo

(B) Bernini

(C) Donatello

(D) Modigliani

(E) Rodin

46. Which group of films was directed by Akira Kurosawa?

(A) *The Seventh Seal, Wild Strawberries, Through a Glass Darkly*

(B) *The Lady from Shanghai, Touch of Evil, The Magnificent Ambersons*

(C) *Metropolis, The Big Heat, M*

(D) *Rashomon, Throne of Blood, The Hidden Fortress*

(E) *Battleship Potemkin, October, Strike*

47. Often called the "Father of Modern Philosophy," his writings, particularly *Meditations on First Philosophy*, played a major role in the development of Western philosophy since the seventeenth century. He is also considered one of the major figures in the school of rationalism.

The philosopher described above is

(A) Immanuel Kant

(B) René Descartes

(C) John Locke

(D) Jean-Jacques Rousseau

(E) Thomas Hobbes

48. Which twentieth-century composer wrote *Rhapsody in Blue?*

(A) Aaron Copland

(B) Igor Stravinsky

(C) George Gershwin

(D) Scott Joplin

(E) Leonard Bernstein

Questions 49–50 refer to the following works by Charles Dickens.

(A) *David Copperfield*

(B) *Great Expectations*

(C) *A Tale of Two Cities*

(D) *The Life and Adventures of Nicholas Nickleby*

(E) *Oliver Twist*

49. Which takes place amongst the events that led to the French Revolution?

50. Which follows the story of a young orphan boy as he struggles to cope with his difficult existence?

ANSWER KEY AND EXPLANATIONS

1. B	11. E	21. E	31. A	41. C
2. D	12. B	22. C	32. A	42. B
3. C	13. C	23. A	33. D	43. C
4. E	14. D	24. D	34. C	44. A
5. D	15. C	25. B	35. E	45. E
6. A	16. B	26. E	36. B	46. D
7. B	17. E	27. D	37. E	47. B
8. D	18. A	28. B	38. C	48. C
9. A	19. D	29. E	39. B	49. C
10. E	20. B	30. C	40. E	50. E

1. **The correct answer is (B).** Matsuo Bashō, a seventeenth-century Japanese poet, is best known for his contributions to the haiku form of poetry.

2. **The correct answer is (D).** Atticus Finch, Boo Radley, and Mayella Ewell are among the main characters featured in Harper Lee's *To Kill a Mocking Bird*.

3. **The correct answer is (C).** The Romantic era composer responsible for the *1812 Overture*, *Swan Lake*, and *The Nutcracker*, among many other works, is Pyotr Ilyich Tchaikovsky.

4. **The correct answer is (E).** The sentence describes Willy Loman, the main character in playwright Arthur Miller's *Death of a Salesman*.

5. **The correct answer is (D).** Artists associated with the Surrealism movement created art based on the imagery of dreams and were influenced by Sigmund Freud's theories about the unconscious.

6. **The correct answer is (A).** Edmund Spencer, Christopher Marlowe, and Philip Sidney were all poets during the Elizabethan era.

7. **The correct answer is (B).** Charles Darwin, a noted nineteenth-century English naturalist, was the author of *On the Origin of Species*.

8. **The correct answer is (D).** Liszt, Chopin, and Verdi belong to the Romantic period.

9. **The correct answer is (A).** Bernini, Rembrandt, and Caravaggio belong to the Renaissance period.

10. **The correct answer is (E).** Debussy, Puccini, and Rachmaninoff belong to the Modern period.

11. **The correct answer is (E).** *Sunset Blvd.*, *Double Indemnity*, and *Some Like It Hot* were all directed by Billy Wilder.

12. **The correct answer is (B).** The plays *Barefoot in the Park*, *The Odd Couple*, and *Biloxi Blues* were written by Neil Simon.

13. **The correct answer is (C).** The sentence describes Mozart's famous opera *Don Giovanni*.

14. **The correct answer is (D).** Gustav Holst is best known as the composer responsible for *The Planets*.

15. **The correct answer is (C).** Anton Chekhov, Harold Pinter, and Noel Coward comprise a group of playwrights.

16. **The correct answer is (B).** Jean-Luc Godard, Francois Truffaut, and Federico Fellini comprise a group of film directors.

17. **The correct answer is (E).** Joseph Heller, Leo Tolstoy, and Kurt Vonnegut comprise a group of novelists.

18. **The correct answer is (A).** *In Praise of Folly* was written by Desiderius Erasmus in 1511.

19. **The correct answer is (D).** A colonnade is a series of columns that carries an entablature or arches.

20. **The correct answer is (B).** Pablo Picasso cofounded the cubism movement and painted *Garçon à la Pipe*, *Les Demoiselles d'Avignon*, and *Le guitariste*.

21. **The correct answer is (E).** Titled *Self-portrait*, this work was completed by Dutch post-Impressionist painter Vincent van Gogh in 1889.

22. **The correct answer is (C).** The character Sherlock Holmes and the many novels and short stories in which he appears were created by Arthur Conan Doyle.

23. **The correct answer is (A).** The ballet described is *Coppélia*, composed by Léo Delibes.

24. **The correct answer is (D).** In line 26, Shakespeare employs personification with the line "thy very stones prate of my whereabout." *Prate* means "to talk idly," something a stone could only do if imbued with human qualities.

25. **The correct answer is (B).** In line 16, the phrase "bloody business" refers to murder. Specifically, it refers to Macbeth's forth-coming murder of King Duncan.

26. **The correct answer is (E).** The lines are spoken by Macbeth, the title character of Shakespeare's *Macbeth,* just before he murders King Duncan.

27. **The correct answer is (D).** Vincent van Gogh, Georges Seurat, and Auguste Rodin are associated with the Post-impressionism movement of the late-nineteenth and early-twentieth centuries.

28. **The correct answer is (B).** The sentence describes the basic plot of *Jane Eyre*, an 1847 novel by English author Charlotte Brontë.

29. **The correct answer is (E).** Johann Sebastian Bach (1685–1750) was an active composer during the Baroque period between 1600 and 1750. As such, his closest contemporary would be his fellow Baroque composer Antonio Vivaldi (1678–1741).

30. **The correct answer is (C).** *The Divine Comedy*, a three-part epic that follows the author on his journey from the depths of Hell to the wonder of Heaven, was written by fourteenth-century Italian poet Dante Alighieri.

31. **The correct answer is (A).** The sentences describe American novelist Ernest Hemingway.

32. **The correct answer is (A).** The work depicted is *School of Athens* by Renaissance artist Raphael.

33. **The correct answer is (D).** *School of Athens* is best described as a fresco, which is a type of mural painting done on a wall or ceiling.

34. **The correct answer is (C).** *School of Athens* can be found in the Apostolic Palace at the Vatican.

35. **The correct answer is (E).** The sentence describes the 1942 film *Casablanca*.

36. **The correct answer is (B).** *The Republic* was written by Plato circa 380 B.C.E.

37. **The correct answer is (E).** With its pointed arches, ribbed vaults, and flying buttresses, Paris' Notre Dame Cathedral is a prime example of Gothic architecture.

38. **The correct answer is (C).** "I kissed thee ere I killed thee, no way but this, killing myself, to die upon a kiss" is from *Othello*. It is spoken by the title character in Act V.

39. **The correct answer is (B).** "Double, double toil and trouble; fire burn and cauldron bubble" is from *Macbeth*. It is spoken by the witches in Act IV.

40. **The correct answer is (E).** "Cowards die many times before their deaths; the valiant never taste of death but once" is from *Julius Caesar*. It is spoken by the title character in Act II.

41. **The correct answer is (C).** Line 13, "I stand amid the roar," contains an example of onomatopoeia, as the word "roar" serves to imitate the source of the sound it describes.

42. **The correct answer is (B).** The repetitious use of the phrase "O God! can I not…" in lines 19–22 is an example of anaphora.

43. **The correct answer is (C).** *The Matchmaker*, which was later turned into the musical *Hello, Dolly!* was written by American playwright Thornton Wilder.

44. **The correct answer is (A).** The title of the pictured sculpture is *Le Penseur*, or *The Thinker* in English.

45. **The correct answer is (E).** *The Thinker* was created by French sculptor Auguste Rodin in 1902.

46. **The correct answer is (D).** Japanese director Akira Kurosawa directed *Rashomon, Throne of Blood, The Hidden Fortress*, and many other films.

47. **The correct answer is (B).** René Descartes, who wrote *Meditations on First Philosophy* and was a major figure in the school of rationalism, was one of the most influential Western philosophers of all time.

48. **The correct answer is (C).** *Rhapsody in Blue* is widely considered to be one of the greatest works ever composed by George Gershwin.

49. **The correct answer is (C).** The events of *A Tale of Two Cities* take place in the years leading up to the French Revolution.

50. **The correct answer is (E).** The story of *Oliver Twist* follows the young title character as he suffers through life in an orphanage and other hardships.

PART V
SOCIAL SCIENCES AND HISTORY

PRETEST ANSWER SHEET

1. Ⓐ Ⓑ Ⓒ Ⓓ Ⓔ	11. Ⓐ Ⓑ Ⓒ Ⓓ Ⓔ	21. Ⓐ Ⓑ Ⓒ Ⓓ Ⓔ	31. Ⓐ Ⓑ Ⓒ Ⓓ Ⓔ	41. Ⓐ Ⓑ Ⓒ Ⓓ Ⓔ
2. Ⓐ Ⓑ Ⓒ Ⓓ Ⓔ	12. Ⓐ Ⓑ Ⓒ Ⓓ Ⓔ	22. Ⓐ Ⓑ Ⓒ Ⓓ Ⓔ	32. Ⓐ Ⓑ Ⓒ Ⓓ Ⓔ	42. Ⓐ Ⓑ Ⓒ Ⓓ Ⓔ
3. Ⓐ Ⓑ Ⓒ Ⓓ Ⓔ	13. Ⓐ Ⓑ Ⓒ Ⓓ Ⓔ	23. Ⓐ Ⓑ Ⓒ Ⓓ Ⓔ	33. Ⓐ Ⓑ Ⓒ Ⓓ Ⓔ	43. Ⓐ Ⓑ Ⓒ Ⓓ Ⓔ
4. Ⓐ Ⓑ Ⓒ Ⓓ Ⓔ	14. Ⓐ Ⓑ Ⓒ Ⓓ Ⓔ	24. Ⓐ Ⓑ Ⓒ Ⓓ Ⓔ	34. Ⓐ Ⓑ Ⓒ Ⓓ Ⓔ	44. Ⓐ Ⓑ Ⓒ Ⓓ Ⓔ
5. Ⓐ Ⓑ Ⓒ Ⓓ Ⓔ	15. Ⓐ Ⓑ Ⓒ Ⓓ Ⓔ	25. Ⓐ Ⓑ Ⓒ Ⓓ Ⓔ	35. Ⓐ Ⓑ Ⓒ Ⓓ Ⓔ	45. Ⓐ Ⓑ Ⓒ Ⓓ Ⓔ
6. Ⓐ Ⓑ Ⓒ Ⓓ Ⓔ	16. Ⓐ Ⓑ Ⓒ Ⓓ Ⓔ	26. Ⓐ Ⓑ Ⓒ Ⓓ Ⓔ	36. Ⓐ Ⓑ Ⓒ Ⓓ Ⓔ	46. Ⓐ Ⓑ Ⓒ Ⓓ Ⓔ
7. Ⓐ Ⓑ Ⓒ Ⓓ Ⓔ	17. Ⓐ Ⓑ Ⓒ Ⓓ Ⓔ	27. Ⓐ Ⓑ Ⓒ Ⓓ Ⓔ	37. Ⓐ Ⓑ Ⓒ Ⓓ Ⓔ	47. Ⓐ Ⓑ Ⓒ Ⓓ Ⓔ
8. Ⓐ Ⓑ Ⓒ Ⓓ Ⓔ	18. Ⓐ Ⓑ Ⓒ Ⓓ Ⓔ	28. Ⓐ Ⓑ Ⓒ Ⓓ Ⓔ	38. Ⓐ Ⓑ Ⓒ Ⓓ Ⓔ	48. Ⓐ Ⓑ Ⓒ Ⓓ Ⓔ
9. Ⓐ Ⓑ Ⓒ Ⓓ Ⓔ	19. Ⓐ Ⓑ Ⓒ Ⓓ Ⓔ	29. Ⓐ Ⓑ Ⓒ Ⓓ Ⓔ	39. Ⓐ Ⓑ Ⓒ Ⓓ Ⓔ	49. Ⓐ Ⓑ Ⓒ Ⓓ Ⓔ
10. Ⓐ Ⓑ Ⓒ Ⓓ Ⓔ	20. Ⓐ Ⓑ Ⓒ Ⓓ Ⓔ	30. Ⓐ Ⓑ Ⓒ Ⓓ Ⓔ	40. Ⓐ Ⓑ Ⓒ Ⓓ Ⓔ	50. Ⓐ Ⓑ Ⓒ Ⓓ Ⓔ

answer sheet

Pretest

40 minutes • 50 questions

Directions: Each of the questions or incomplete statements below is followed by five suggested answers or completions. Select the one that is best in each case.

1. One of the fundamental changes that took place from 1980–2010 was a gradual
   - (A) solidifying of male and female gender roles within the family structure
   - (B) expansion of the family to include two or three generations per home unit
   - (C) increase in the average number of children per family
   - (D) replacement of rigid gender roles with flexible definitions within the family structure
   - (E) loss of feminine economic independence

2. Which of the following cultures established a far-reaching political infrastructure, designed roads and pathways suitable for caravan transportation, and secured a transportation network from attack?
   - (A) Greek
   - (B) Trojan
   - (C) Gothic
   - (D) Roman
   - (E) Carolingian

3. Which of the following theorists was responsible for establishing sociology as an academic discipline, providing the first critical studies of suicide, and presenting one of the most well-regarded theories of religion?
   - (A) Karl Marx
   - (B) Emile Durkheim
   - (C) Frederick Engels
   - (D) Anthony Gramsci
   - (E) Anthony Giddens

"Take up the White Man's burden—/ Send forth the best ye breed—/ Go bind your sons to exile / To serve your captives' need"

4. The statement above is most characteristic of which of the following?
   - (A) Marcus Garvey
   - (B) Neville Chamberlain
   - (C) Lord Percy Shelley
   - (D) Rudyard Kipling
   - (E) William Blake

"Dignify and glorify common labor. It is at the bottom of life that we must begin, not at the top. "

5. The statement above is most characteristic of which of the following?
   - (A) W.E.B Du Bois
   - (B) Booker T. Washington
   - (C) Marcus Garvey
   - (D) Kwame Nkruma
   - (E) Malcolm X

Chapter 11

6. In sociology and anthropology, endogamy occurs when

   (A) marriage takes place outside a homogenous unit

   (B) the choice of marriage partners is not restricted in any way

   (C) marriage is celebrated as an end-of-life event

   (D) marriage takes place within a homogenous unit

   (E) marriages are arranged for social and economic reasons

7. A person who lived in Massachusetts during the seventeenth century and was deeply religious, believed in tightly knit communities, and advocated conservative social goals would most probably have been a

   (A) Puritan

   (B) Quaker

   (C) Calvinist

   (D) Pilgrim

   (E) Royalist

8. Which of the following is an example of Marxist historical materialism?

   (A) The study of population movements over a millennium

   (B) A detailed analysis of linguistic changes in the last century

   (C) A historical study of grain production and use

   (D) A critique of cultural forms of expression

   (E) A detailed analysis of religious observance over a year

9. In the early twentieth century, fascism had the LEAST influence in which of the following countries?

   (A) Italy

   (B) Spain

   (C) Germany

   (D) Romania

   (E) Estonia

10. After their defeat in the Second Boer War, Dutch settlers in South Africa often

    (A) emigrated to the United States

    (B) allied with local populations to maintain political security

    (C) remained in concentration camps with extremely poor conditions

    (D) accepted the Zulu right to the Dutch Congo

    (E) fled to Great Britain for political asylum

11. One of the fundamental changes that took place in the 1920s was a gradual

    (A) increase in the authority of the elderly as economic downturns spurred conservative social agendas

    (B) increase in the independence of the youth founded on the new freedom afforded by the automobile

    (C) decline in the power of socially progressive organizations

    (D) decline in consumerism due to stock-market fluctuations

    (E) decline in the authority of the federal government

12. For African Americans, abolition of slavery during the nineteenth century resulted in which of the following?

    (A) Government assistance to freed slaves in the form of cash and crop subsidies

    (B) The return to deplorable agricultural labor conditions under the sharecropping system

    (C) The right to vote in national elections

    (D) The mass exodus of freed slaves to Liberia as part of the back-to-Africa movement

    (E) Government endorsement of desegregating educational systems

13. Of the following, which group was the first to establish trade links with both China and the upper portions of the British Isles?
    - (A) Greeks
    - (B) Romans
    - (C) Arabs
    - (D) Mongols
    - (E) Byzantines

14. Of the following, which modern country is considered to be the earliest known area of occupation for early humans?
    - (A) Ethiopia
    - (B) Egypt
    - (C) Afghanistan
    - (D) Iraq
    - (E) Iran

15. The most immediate consequence of the expansion of Standard Oil Co. in the 1870s and 1880s was
    - (A) widespread support for trusts and monopolies
    - (B) federal regulation of oil and petroleum products
    - (C) better treatment of workers due to the expanding influence of labor unions
    - (D) greater interest in locally produced goods and services
    - (E) the development of trusts to skirt government regulations on monopolies

16. Which of the following prompted Caucasian Americans to move to the suburbs during the middle of the twentieth century?
    - I. Increasing racial tensions in major metropolitan cities
    - II. The ability to own more conspicuous wealth in non-urban areas
    - III. The impact of environment regulation and the expansion of the suburban park system
    - (A) II only
    - (B) I and III only
    - (C) II and III only
    - (D) I and II only
    - (E) I, II, and III

"...he intends only his own gain, and he is in this, as in many other cases, led by an invisible hand to promote an end which was no part of his intention. Nor is it always the worse for the society that it was not part of it. By pursuing his own interest he frequently promotes that of the society more effectually than when he really intends to promote it."

17. The quotation above best expresses the philosophy of
    - (A) Karl Marx
    - (B) Adam Smith
    - (C) Henry Kissinger
    - (D) Thomas Malthus
    - (E) John Keynes

18. Rachel Carson's novel *Silent Spring* depicts the movement in U.S. history known as
    - (A) conservatism
    - (B) environmentalism
    - (C) neo-liberalism
    - (D) anarchism
    - (E) feminism

19. To avoid facing social marginalization, members of a group will often
    - (A) assume alpha roles through divergent characteristics
    - (B) criticize those seen to be in superior positions
    - (C) associate with inferior members of the society
    - (D) separate themselves socially from the group
    - (E) conform to the attitudes and behaviors of the group

20. Byzantine culture and influences were most significant in shaping the institutions of which of the following countries?
    - (A) Pakistan, Sri Lanka, and Afghanistan
    - (B) Turkey, Bulgaria, and Russia
    - (C) Turkey, Cyprus, and Israel
    - (D) Egypt, Jordon, and Israel
    - (E) Syria, Iraq, and Turkey

21. Construction of the Suez Canal shortened the sailing time between France and
    (A) London
    (B) New York
    (C) India
    (D) Egypt
    (E) Germany

22. Which of the following is an example of turnout bias in voting behavior?
    (A) Mandatory full participation in Australian national elections
    (B) The high turnout of African American voters in the 2008 U.S. presidential election
    (C) The automatic voter registration of all French citizens
    (D) The decrease in Belgium voter turnout after voting was declared non-compulsory
    (E) The decrease in voter participation in Germany after joining the European Union

23. Which of the following is an example of an isopleth map?
    (A) Modern political borders in Western Europe
    (B) Elevation of the Himalayas Mountain Range and surrounding areas
    (C) The magnetic strength of areas surrounding Antarctica
    (D) Population density of suburban areas in the American Southwest
    (E) Geological stratification in the Grand Canyon

24. Homer's novel *The Odyssey* depicts the period of Greek history known as the
    (A) Trojan War
    (B) Persian War
    (C) Gilded Age
    (D) Carthaginian War
    (E) Alexandrian Age

25. A fundamental change that took place in the sixteenth and seventeenth centuries was a gradual
    (A) increase in religious conflict between Roman Catholic and Protestant faiths
    (B) decline in the power of the German princes
    (C) decrease in the pressure of international trade on Dutch trading ports
    (D) decline in British colonial authority
    (E) increase in nationalistic feeling among peoples of the Dutch Congo

26. The declaration of Panamanian Independence in 1903 resulted in
    (A) expanded export trade to Columbia
    (B) the predominance of U.S. economic interests in the Panama Canal construction
    (C) Columbia's acquisition of Panama
    (D) the effective blockading of Panamanian ports to foreign trade
    (E) a significant weakening of the Monroe Doctrine

27. Demographic surveys of entire populations commonly make use of
    (A) telephone surveys
    (B) indirect methods of collecting data
    (C) Rorschach tests
    (D) true-or-false questionnaires
    (E) collective interviews

28. Which of the following is an example of the Atlantic Triangular Trade?
    (A) The export of cotton through overland routes
    (B) The exchange of European trinkets for African slaves
    (C) The expansion of French colonial possessions in the New World
    (D) The loss of the straits of Gibraltar as a trading port
    (E) The introduction of a unified currency between the Caribbean and New England

29. As depicted above, Iceland could be described as which of the following?

(A) Fragmented state

(B) Protected state

(C) Nation-state

(D) Associated state

(E) Concessionary state

30. Which of the following was a result of the 1941 bombing of the U.S. naval base at Pearl Harbor?

(A) The native population of the Hawaiian Islands decreased dramatically.

(B) The attack galvanized the American government to join World War II.

(C) The United States decreased its presence at satellite naval stations.

(D) The United States shifted its primary means of defense from the navy to the air force.

(E) The population of the United States military dramatically declined due to widespread desertion.

31. The United States Immigration Act of 1924 was significant because it

(A) led to decreased immigration from Western Europe

(B) led to increased emigration of scientists and intellectuals

(C) led to decreased immigration from Asia

(D) prohibited immigration from the Axis Powers

(E) prohibited immigration of unmarried women

32. An individual who believes in a strong authoritarian government that rules through military control favors

(A) anarchy

(B) democracy

(C) oligarchy

(D) socialism

(E) fascism

33. Which of the following Eastern European countries was one of the original members of the Warsaw Treaty Organization of Friendship, Cooperation, and Mutual Assistance (Warsaw Pact)?

(A) Kosovo

(B) Croatia

(C) Belarus

(D) Greece

(E) Serbia

34. The area of the USSR at its height was approximately

(A) half the area of the African continent

(B) the same as the area of the communist-controlled territory in South America

(C) two times the area of the United States

(D) one-sixth of the earth's land area

(E) ten times the area of California

35. In the late nineteenth century, the ideas of Karl Marx had the LEAST influence in which of the following countries?

(A) Russia

(B) England

(C) Germany

(D) Spain

(E) France

36. Which of the following is the most significant importer of coffee beans?

    (A) Russia

    (B) France

    (C) United States

    (D) Columbia

    (E) Italy

37. The Supreme Court of the United States can overrule decisions made by the executive and legislative branches in order to

    (A) ensure that all laws agree with the U.S. Constitution

    (B) prevent unreasonable economic losses as a result of new laws

    (C) safeguard state sovereignty over federal law

    (D) deny unfair election practices

    (E) provide an opportunity for popular participation in the legislative process

38. A traveler going from point 1 to point 2 on the map above would cross which mountain range?

    (A) Alps

    (B) Himalayas

    (C) Atlas

    (D) Andes

    (E) Rockies

39. Which of the following reflects a state of full employment?

    (A) All citizens of a specific nation hold a wage-paying job.

    (B) All citizens who choose to work can gain employment.

    (C) A set percentage of workers are hired annually.

    (D) A set percentage of workers are let go annually.

    (E) No citizens may work at part-time levels.

40. Which of the following is NOT compatible with the traditional concept of socialism?

    (A) A single-party system

    (B) A strong military

    (C) A personality cult of the party leader

    (D) Elected officials

    (E) Government economic control

41. Which of the following economic policies is most likely to result in an equilibrium price?

    (A) An unexpected demand for rare products or services

    (B) A supply that outreaches the demand

    (C) A dramatic decrease in demand

    (D) A supply that exactly meets the demand

    (E) Unpredictable shifting of both supply and demand

"I went to the woods because I wished to live deliberately, to front only the essential facts of life, and see if I could not learn what it had to teach, and not, when I came to die, discover that I had not lived."

42. The statement above is most characteristic of which of the following?

    (A) Ansel Adams

    (B) Theodore Roosevelt

    (C) Henry David Thoreau

    (D) William Seward

    (E) Chief Powhatan

43. As a result of the Compromise of 1850, the status of a territory as either slave or free was determined by

    (A) congressional vote

    (B) grandfather clauses

    (C) executive privilege

    (D) popular sovereignty

    (E) economic necessity

44. Of the following, which reflects cost as the result of scarcity and choice?

(A) The development of new product when previous models prove insufficient

(B) The loss of leisure time when choosing to follow academics

(C) The artificial creation of scarcity to flood the market with goods

(D) The dependence on market fluctuations to dictate supply levels

(E) Choosing to create an overabundance of good to deny the possibility of scarcity

45. Israel became an independent state as a result of the

(A) Peace of Paris

(B) Camp David Accords

(C) Oslo Accords

(D) Israel-Jordan Treaty of Peace

(E) Partition Plan for Palestine

46. Which of the following areas of the brain is involved in the control of memory storage and formation?

(A) Amygdala

(B) Hippocampus

(C) Hypothalamus

(D) Parietal Lobe

(E) Cortex

47. Which of the following would increase the demand for agricultural workers in the short run?

(A) A decrease in crop yields

(B) An increase in the cost of supporting laborers

(C) A decrease in international demand

(D) An increase in crop productivity

(E) A decrease in mechanized labor

48. Which of the following theorists asserted that all human beings are governed by a combination of primal urges, rational thoughts, and self-awareness?

(A) Sigmund Freud

(B) Thomas Malthus

(C) Kurt Lewin

(D) William Schutz

(E) Gustave Le Bon

49. Which of the following is an example of anticipatory socialization?

(A) New students meeting each other on the first day of instruction

(B) Returning to civilian life after serving in the military

(C) Young children learning to share

(D) Young adults learning the social norms for dating and courtship

(E) Preparing for a job interview by rehearsing

50. Which of the following would challenge the reliability of variables in a psychological experiment?

(A) An unmolested control group

(B) A double blind testing

(C) A positive correlation between variables

(D) Professional subjectivity

(E) A causal relationship between variables

ANSWER KEY AND EXPLANATIONS

1. D	11. B	21. C	31. C	41. D
2. D	12. B	22. B	32. E	42. C
3. B	13. B	23. D	33. C	43. D
4. D	14. A	24. A	34. D	44. B
5. B	15. E	25. A	35. B	45. E
6. D	16. D	26. B	36. C	46. B
7. A	17. B	27. B	37. A	47. E
8. C	18. B	28. B	38. C	48. A
9. E	19. E	29. C	39. B	49. E
10. C	20. B	30. B	40. D	50. D

1. **The correct answer is (D).** During the period of 1980–2010, rigid gender roles within the home were gradually abandoned in favor of more fluid definitions.

2. **The correct answer is (D).** The Romans were responsible for establishing a vast political network that relied heavily on the construction and maintenance of safe transportation networks.

3. **The correct answer is (B).** Emile Durkheim was responsible for establishing sociology as an academic discipline, partially due to his pioneering work on religion and suicide.

4. **The correct answer is (D).** The statement above is drawn from Rudyard Kipling's poem "The White Man's Burden," which rationalized imperialism as a moral obligation.

5. **The correct answer is (B).** Booker T. Washington urged African Americans to exploit agricultural and industrial opportunities as a means of social advancement during Reconstruction.

6. **The correct answer is (D).** Endogamy occurs when the choice of marriage partners is restricted to the members within a homogenous group.

7. **The correct answer is (A).** The Puritans were the primary settlers of Massachusetts. This tight-knit religious group advocated strict adherence to a conservative moral code, strong community ties, and self-reliant economic development.

8. **The correct answer is (C).** Marxist historical materialism is the analysis of human production over time and how the production of material goods, in this case grain products, alters human relationships.

9. **The correct answer is (E).** During the early twentieth century, fascist political parties rose to power in Italy, Spain, Germany, and Romania. Estonia was not formed until the dissolution of the Soviet Union at the very end of the twentieth century.

10. **The correct answer is (C).** The Boer War is noted for the presence of extremely brutal British concentration camps that kept the Boer population in squalid conditions even after the war had ended.

11. **The correct answer is (B).** The 1920s are characterized by the increasing independence of the youth as "flappers" and "bootleggers." They publically rejected the conservative social standards of their parents' generation.

12. **The correct answer is (B).** For many African Americans in the nineteenth century, abolition meant a return to deplorable agricultural conditions under the share-cropping system due to the lack of government aid to freed slaves.

13. **The correct answer is (B).** The Romans maintained active trade routes from Italy to China, the "Silk Road," and to modern-day Scotland using an advanced system of road construction and maintenance.

14. **The correct answer is (A).** Paleoanthropologists located their oldest known skeleton to date, "Lucy," in modern-day Ethiopia.

15. **The correct answer is (E).** Standard Oil Co. formed trusts to successfully manipulate the market and put smaller companies out of business.

16. **The correct answer is (D).** The exodus of Caucasian Americans from major urban centers, sometimes referred to as "white flight," was prompted both by the fear of racial conflict in urban centers and the ability to participate more fully in 1950s consumerism.

17. **The correct answer is (B).** Adam Smith argued that the "invisible hand" governed the economic system and individuals, by working for their own self-interest, helped society as a whole.

18. **The correct answer is (B).** Rachel Carson's novel *Silent Spring* catalogs the negative environmental effects of pesticide use.

19. **The correct answer is (E).** Members of a group will often conform to predominant attitudes and behaviors within the group to avoid social marginalization.

20. **The correct answer is (B).** Byzantine culture was rooted in modern-day Turkey but spread significantly to both Bulgaria and Russia through economic trading and militaristic expansion.

21. **The correct answer is (C).** The Suez Canal, often called "The Highway to India," shortened the sailing time between major Western European countries, such as France and India.

22. **The correct answer is (B).** The unusually high turnout of African American voters in the 2008 U.S. presidential election reflects a turnout bias in voting behavior.

23. **The correct answer is (D).** An isopleth map reflects values that cannot be drawn from a single point, such as population density.

24. **The correct answer is (A).** *The Odyssey* recounts the adventures of Odysseus as he returns home after fighting in the Trojan War.

25. **The correct answer is (A).** The sixteenth and seventeenth centuries are characterized by repeated European wars of religion, most notably the Thirty Years War that elevated the power of German princes and the Schmalkaldic War in the Holy Roman Empire.

26. **The correct answer is (B).** The Panamanian Revolution, supported economically and militarily by the U.S. government, demonstrated the predominance of U.S. interest in the Panama Canal.

27. **The correct answer is (B).** In demographic surveys of entire populations, indirect methods of collecting data are often used to gather the largest amount of material regarding the population.

28. **The correct answer is (B).** The first leg of the Atlantic Triangular Trade included the exchange of European trinkets for West African slaves, who were then transferred to the Caribbean to work primarily on sugar plantations.

29. **The correct answer is (C).** Iceland, as denoted by its cultural and physical isolation, is a prime example of a modern nation-state.

30. **The correct answer is (B).** The United States became militarily involved in World War II after the bombing of Pearl Harbor revealed that the nation was at risk.

31. **The correct answer is (C).** The United States Immigration Act of 1924 instituted a quota system that targeted immigration levels from Asian countries.

32. **The correct answer is (E).** Fascism is denoted by a strong authoritarian government that uses its military to enforce single-party rule.

33. **The correct answer is (C).** Belarus had a Soviet-imposed Communist government in the second half of the twentieth century and thus was forced to be a member of the original Warsaw Pact formed by the Soviet Union.

34. **The correct answer is (D).** At the height of its power, the USSR covered one-sixth of the earth's total land area.

35. **The correct answer is (B).** The ideas of Karl Marx did not make a significant impact on England in the late nineteenth century.

36. **The correct answer is (C).** The United States is the most significant importer of coffee beans in the world.

37. **The correct answer is (A).** The Supreme Court can overrule a legislative or executive decision if it determines that the decision is not compatible with the U.S. Constitution.

38. **The correct answer is (C).** A traveler going from point 1 to point 2 on the map would cross through the Atlas Mountain Range.

39. **The correct answer is (B).** The state of full employment is defined as a market state that allows all citizens who want to work the opportunity to do so.

40. **The correct answer is (D).** Socialism does not traditionally feature elected officials.

41. **The correct answer is (D).** An equilibrium price is achieved when the supply exactly meets the demand.

42. **The correct answer is (C).** Henry David Thoreau was a major figure in the transcendentalist movement, a social and political movement that stressed an understanding of the natural world as a path to self-awareness.

43. **The correct answer is (D).** The Compromise of 1850 introduced the concept of popular sovereignty, giving the inhabitants of each territory the right to vote for or against the legalization of slavery in the territory.

44. **The correct answer is (B).** Loss of leisure time often reflects the intersection of choice, scarcity, and cost. In this scenario, the cost of choosing to pursue scarce knowledge is leisure time.

45. **The correct answer is (E).** Israel became an independent state due to the UN Partition Plan for Palestine, which divided Jewish and Muslim populations into what would become Israel and Palestine.

46. **The correct answer is (B).** The hippocampus is primarily responsible for the control of memory storage and formation.

47. **The correct answer is (E).** A decrease in mechanized labor would result in an increased demand for agricultural labor in the short run.

48. **The correct answer is (A).** Sigmund Freud argued that human beings are governed by a combination of primal urges, rational thoughts, and self-awareness.

49. **The correct answer is (E).** Preparing for a job interview by rehearsing is an example of an individual anticipating a specific social interchange. This is anticipatory socialization.

50. **The correct answer is (D).** Undue subjectivity on behalf of the scientist conducting the experiment could challenge the overall reliability of the data.

OVERVIEW ANSWER SHEET

1. Ⓐ Ⓑ Ⓒ Ⓓ Ⓔ 3. Ⓐ Ⓑ Ⓒ Ⓓ Ⓔ 5. Ⓐ Ⓑ Ⓒ Ⓓ Ⓔ 7. Ⓐ Ⓑ Ⓒ Ⓓ Ⓔ 9. Ⓐ Ⓑ Ⓒ Ⓓ Ⓔ
2. Ⓐ Ⓑ Ⓒ Ⓓ Ⓔ 4. Ⓐ Ⓑ Ⓒ Ⓓ Ⓔ 6. Ⓐ Ⓑ Ⓒ Ⓓ Ⓔ 8. Ⓐ Ⓑ Ⓒ Ⓓ Ⓔ 10. Ⓐ Ⓑ Ⓒ Ⓓ Ⓔ

answer sheet

Overview

The CLEP Social Sciences and History test assesses your general knowledge of a broad range of topics, including U.S. and world history, political science, geography, economics, psychology, sociology, anthropology, and more. The specific content of this exam is based on materials drawn from typical introductory level college courses related to these subjects. You will have 90 minutes to answer the approximately 120 questions that make up the test.

Preparing for the CLEP Social Sciences and History test can be difficult. Since the exam includes questions that are based on such a wide variety of subjects, you will have a considerable amount of material to review. While this chapter provides you with a basic overview of the topics covered on the exam, you will most likely want to take some time to review some history and social sciences textbooks for a more in-depth review.

Again, the test is comprised of approximately 120 questions. These questions are broken down into six main categories:

History (40 percent or 48 questions)
- United States History (17 percent)
- Western Civilization (15 percent)
- World History (8 percent)

Government/Political Science (13 percent or 16 questions)
- Comparative politics
- International relations
- Methods
- United States institutions
- Voting and political behavior

Geography (11 percent or 13 questions)
- Cartographic methods
- Cultural geography
- Physical geography
- Population
- Regional geography
- Spatial interaction

Economics (10 percent or 12 questions)
- Economic measurements
- International trade

- Major theorists and schools
- Monetary and fiscal policy
- Product markets and resource markets
- Scarcity, choice, and opportunity cost

Psychology (10 percent or 12 questions)

- Aggression
- Biopsychology
- Conformity
- Group process
- Major theorists and schools
- Methods
- Performance
- Personality
- Socialization

Sociology (10 percent or 12 questions)

- Demography
- Deviance
- Family
- Interaction
- Major theorists and schools
- Methods
- Social change
- Social organizations
- Social stratification
- Social theory

Anthropology (6 percent or 7 questions)

- Cultural anthropology
- Ethnography
- Major theorists and schools
- Methods
- Paleoanthropology

HISTORY

The subject of history accounts for the largest individual portion of the CLEP Social Sciences and History test. As indicated above, it includes questions related to three specific historical disciplines: U.S. history, Western civilization, and world history.

The following is a brief overview of some of the key history topics on which exam questions on the CLEP Social Sciences and History test are based. Keep in mind that this overview is only intended as a brief guide to the subject matter you will need to study further on your own.

U.S. History

The largest percentage of history questions on the CLEP Social Sciences and History test will be U.S. history questions. The following table will provide you with a brief guide to the topics you may want to review to prepare for these questions.

U.S. HISTORY TOPICS

Period	Dates	Notable Topics
Colonial Period	c. 1600–1776	European discovery, early colonization, indigenous societies, origins of slavery, early immigration, role of religion, colonial expansion and development, colonial relations with Great Britain
American Revolution and Early Republic	1776–1849	Declaration of Independence, Revolutionary War, founding fathers, The Constitution, establishment of the American government, development of democracy, formation and growth of political parties, Western exploration and expansion, economic growth and development
Civil War and Reconstruction	1849–1877	Slavery and the abolition movement, political and economic tensions between the North and South, Civil War, major political figures of the Civil War era, abolition of slavery, Reconstruction

Industrial Revolution, the Progressive Era, and World War I	1877–1919	The changing nature of occupational structure, work, and labor organization, urbanization and industrialization, economic growth, European immigration, progressive reform, American imperialism, American involvement in World War I
The 1920s, Great Depression, and World War II	1920–1945	The Roaring Twenties, 1929 stock market crash, the Great Depression, the New Deal, isolationism, American involvement in World War II, emergence as a superpower
Cold War, Cultural Revolutions, Social Change, Emergence of Modern America	1945–Present	Communism, nuclear arms build-up, the Space Race, civil rights movement, women's liberation, consumerism, recent history

Western Civilization

Approximately 15 percent of the history questions found on the CLEP Social Sciences and History test will be based on materials commonly covered in introductory level college courses on Western civilization. This is a very broad subject that covers an extremely long period of time, so you may want to use the following table as a brief guide to some of the specific topics you will need to review for these questions.

WESTERN CIVILIZATION TOPICS

Period	Dates	Notable Topics
Ancient Near East	c. 4th millennium B.C.E.–c. 6th to 4th century B.C.E.	Mesopotamia, Sumer, the Fertile Crescent, early development of law and politics, early religions, Ancient Egypt
Ancient Greece	Classical Antiquity–c. 146 B.C.E.	Political evolution, Ancient Greek culture, philosophy, Hellenistic religion, Greek mythology
Ancient Rome	753 B.C.E.–1453 C.E.	Roman kingdom, republic, and empire, Roman political structure, Roman culture and thought, early Christianity, Germanic invasions, the fall of Rome

Medieval Age	c. 476 C.E.–c. 1526 C.E.	Byzantium and the spread of Islam, the Crusades, medieval politics and culture, rise of the medieval Church, feudalism, medieval monarchies
Renaissance and Reformation	c. 1300s C.E.–c. 1600s C.E.	Renaissance culture and politics, the Plague, scientific revolution, the role and influence of the Catholic Church, the Protestant Reformation
Early Modern Period	c. 1500s C.E.–c. 1800s C.E.	European exploration, discovery of the Americas, the Commercial Revolution, early modern political development, colonialism and imperialism, the Age of Revolution
Late Modern/Contemporary Period	c. 1800s C.E.–Present	The Industrial Revolution, political and economic progress and thought, technological developments, imperialism in Africa and Asia, World War I, the interwar period, World War II, the Cold War, recent history

World History

Finally, the history portion of the CLEP Social Sciences and History test will include some questions that pertain to general world history. These questions will cover the history of Asia, Africa, Australia, the Americas, and Europe from prehistory to the modern era. Many of these questions will be based on global themes and interactions. In preparing for world history questions, you may want to review any topics not specifically covered in the U.S. history or western civilization sections.

GOVERNMENT/POLITICAL SCIENCE

Approximately 13 percent of the questions on the CLEP Social Sciences and History test will pertain to government or political science. These questions are designed to test your understanding of basic political science and the American government system.

The following is a brief overview of some of the key government and political science topics on which exam questions on the CLEP Social Sciences and History test are based. Keep in mind that this overview is only intended as a brief guide to the subject matter you will need to study further on your own.

Comparative Politics

Comparative politics is an approach to studying the world's various political systems that is intended and specifically designed to allow us to better understand such systems through comparison. In this way, comparative politics can be used to highlight the differences and similarities between the many different political systems in existence both contemporarily and historically. The practitioners of comparative politics usually look for political trends and attempt to develop theories or hypotheses to explain these trends. Since this field does not have a single definitive focus, the focus and scope of a particular comparative politics study can vary significantly.

International Relations

The terms "international relations" refers to the study of the relationships shared between various countries. This includes direct relationships between various states, indirect relationships that take place through various inter-governmental organizations, and international non-governmental organizations, as well as non-governmental organizations and multinational corporations. Questions related to this field are likely to involve topics such as foreign affairs, foreign policy, diplomacy, and more.

Methods

In the course of their studies, political scientists will make use of a wide variety of methodologies to gather data and draw conclusions. As with other social sciences, the methods used in political science vary depending on the specific type of information the researcher is attempting to attain. Political scientists often make use of primary sources like historical documents and official records, as well as secondary sources like scholarly journal articles or other reports. Researchers also often engage in data gathering through survey research, case studies, statistical analysis, and model building. For the CLEP Social Sciences and History test, you will need to develop a basic knowledge of these methods and an understanding of how to interpret the data attained through such methods.

U.S. Institutions

The government and political science portion of the CLEP Social Sciences and History test will also include questions about the structure and functions of the United States government. You will need to have a basic understanding of the branches of government (executive, legislative, judicial) and their specific roles and responsibilities. You may also want to familiarize yourself with the roles of major government agencies.

Voting and Political Behavior

Finally, the government and political science portion of the exam will also include questions related to voting and political behavior. Some topics to review for these questions may include elections, voting history, the Electoral College, the political party system, the major political parties, factors that influence party affiliation and voting, common political trends, and more.

GEOGRAPHY

Some questions on the CLEP Social Sciences and History test will be focused on the subject of geography. These questions are designed to test your understanding of the basic fundamentals of geographic study. To prepare for these questions, you will need to become familiar with basic geography terminology, some of the various branches of geography, the methods of cartography, and more.

The following is a brief overview of some of the key geography topics on which exam questions on the CLEP Social Sciences and History test are based. Keep in mind that this overview is only intended as a brief guide to the subject matter you will need to study further on your own.

Cartographic Methods

Cartography is the science of making maps. For the CLEP Social Sciences and History test, you will need to be able to demonstrate a basic understanding of cartography and the methods of mapmaking. In modern cartography, there are a wide variety of maps used for many unique purposes. In addition to maps that simply illustrate a geographic appearance of an area of land, we also have maps that highlight specific details about the land, such as its elevation, vegetation, or population. Some of the most common types of maps include physical maps, road maps, climate maps, economic/resource maps, political maps, and topographic maps. To prepare yourself for any questions on the exam that might deal with cartography, you should take time to review the basic principles of cartography and the common types of maps.

Cultural Geography

The CLEP Social Sciences and History test is likely to include some questions related to cultural geography, which is the study of cultural norms and products and how they vary and relate among different areas and places. Cultural geographers study how cultural phenomena, such as language, spirituality, and economy, vary or remain consistent between different areas. Some specific topics you might encounter in questions related to cultural geography include globalization, westernization, cultural assimilation, cultural hegemony, imperialism, colonialism, internationalism, immigration, emigration, and more.

Physical Geography

Another realm of geography included on the CLEP Social Sciences and History test is physical geography, which refers to the study of Earth's natural features and phenomena from a spatial perspective. This field is comprised of a number of subdisciplines, including the following:

- **Meteorology/Climatology:** The study of the Earth's atmosphere and weather
- **Biogeography:** The geographic study of plant and animal life

- **Geomorphology:** The study of Earth's physical landscape
- **Pedology:** The study of soils
- **Hydrology:** The study of waters

Physical geography questions on the exam may be related to any of these subdisciplines.

Population

One of the major themes of the geography questions found on the CLEP Social Sciences and History test is population. In geographic terms, population refers to the total number of a given species living in a particular area at a particular time. Many aspects of cultural, regional, and physical geography are based on plant and/or animal populations. Beyond the simple number of a species living in a certain area, populations are also studied for the genetic variations found within.

Regional Geography

Other geography questions on the CLEP Social Sciences and History test may be related to regional geography. Regional geography is a specific subdiscipline of geography devoted to the study of world regions. Specifically, regional geography is concerned with the distinct characteristics of a given region. These characteristics might include a region's physical geographic features, plant and animal life, human elements, and more.

Spatial Interaction

Finally, the geography portion of the CLEP Social Sciences and History test will likely also feature some questions related to spatial interaction. Closely tied to economics, spatial interaction is a geographic concept that refers to the flow of people, products, services, or information between various places according to the ebb and flow of localized supply and demand.

ECONOMICS

Another major subject covered on the CLEP Social Sciences and History test is economics. Economics is the science of the production, distribution, and consumption of goods and services. It can be viewed and interpreted from any number of scales ranging from global to local.

The following is a brief overview of some of the key economics topics on which exam questions on the CLEP Social Sciences and History test are based. Keep in mind that this overview is only intended as a brief guide to the subject matter you will need to study further on your own.

Economic Measurements

The term "economic measurements" refers to the methods we use to gauge the general health of the economy. These methods of measurement allow us to analyze the state of the economy at a given moment and determine what actions might help induce positive change. Although there are many different types of economic measurements, three of the most widely used and relied upon include the following.

Gross Domestic Product

The Gross Domestic Product (GDP) is an economic measurement that indicates the market value of all of the final goods and services produced within the economy in one year. The GDP is often seen as a major indication of a country's standard of living.

Gross National Product

The Gross National Product (GNP) is essentially another version of the GDP. Where the GDP is based on the market value of all of the final goods and services produced within the economy in one year, the GNP adds to that the gain on overseas investments and subtracts the capital gains of foreign nationals or companies operating domestically. GDP, however, is the more commonly used measurement today.

Gross National Income

The Gross National Income (GNI) is another economic measurement of the total value of the goods and services generated in a country within one year. The GNI is arrived at by adding a country's net income from other countries to its GDP.

International Trade

Some of the economics questions on the CLEP Social Sciences and History test will be based on the concept of international trade. International trade is the act of exchanging capital, goods, and services across international borders. This exchange plays a pivotal role in the health of national economies and the global economy. To prepare for questions that deal with international trade, you will need to become familiar with some specific terminology. A brief guide to some of these important terms appears below.

INTERNATIONAL TRADE TERMINOLOGY

Term	Definition
Appreciation	The increase in the purchasing power of a given currency in comparison to that of other currencies
Balance of Payments	Monetary payments made by a particular country to other countries and payments made by other countries to that particular country
Balance of Payments Deficit	A deficit in the balance of payments that occurs when a country does not receive an adequate level of foreign currency to pay for its imports
Balance of Trade	The sum total value of all exports and imports of physical merchandise
Depreciation	A decline in the purchasing power of a given currency in comparison to that of other currencies
Devaluation	An official governmental act to intentionally depreciate the state currency so as to increase foreign interest

Favorable Balance of Trade	Occurs when more physical merchandise is exported than imported
Floating/Flexible Exchange Rate	A type of exchange rate wherein supply and demand determine the value of foreign currency
Foreign Exchange Rate	The value of foreign currency
Free Trade	International trading that is not subject to tariff or non-tariff restrictions
General Agreement on Tariffs and Trade (GATT)	A global organization designed to promote free trade; enforced the GATT agreement until 1995
Invisible Items	Physically intangible merchandise (e.g., securities or loans)
North American Free Trade Agreement (NAFTA)	Instituted a common market amongst the North American countries of the United States, Canada, and Mexico
Protectionism	A tactic used by a nation to restrict the influx of imports with the intention of reducing their ability to compete with similar domestic products by imposing tariffs or non-tariff barriers
Visible Items	Physically tangible merchandise
World Trade Organization (WTO)	Organization that took over enforcement of the GATT agreement in 1995

Major Theorists and Schools

Many of the economics questions on the CLEP Social Sciences and History test will likely ask you for information pertaining to specific schools of economic thought and prominent economic theorists. The following table will provide you with a brief guide to the major schools of economic thought and some of the key theorists associated with each.

ECONOMIC SCHOOLS OF THOUGHT

School	Theory	Prominent Proponents
Mercantilism	The prosperity and security of a country can only be ensured by strong governmental control of foreign trade	Thomas Mun, Jean Bodin, Jean Baptiste Colbert, John Locke
Physiocracy	National wealth is derived only from the value of "land agri- culture" or "land development"	Anne Robert Jacques Turgot, François Quesnay, John Law, Pierre le Pesant de Boisguilbert

Classical	The best possible economy is a self-regulating market system that is specifically designed to meet the economic needs of the people	Adam Smith, David Hume, Thomas Malthus, David Ricardo, John Stuart Mill
Marxism	A commodity's value is directly related to the labor required to produce it; the value of a commodity rightfully belongs to the workforce that produces the commodity	Karl Marx, Friedrich Engels
Keynesian	During a market economy recession, government intervention is needed to increase spending	John Maynard Keynes
Monetarism	The supply of money is the primary determinant of economic viability; minimal government intervention	Milton Friedman

Monetary and Fiscal Policy

Another topic that is often touched upon within the economics portion of the CLEP Social Sciences and History test is monetary and fiscal policy. Government economic regulation in the form of monetary and fiscal policy plays a pivotal role in our ability to maintain economic stability. Monetary and fiscal policy affords the government a means by which to ensure the stability and ongoing viability of the U.S. economy while still allowing the open market system to operate relatively independent of government influence.

Fiscal policy refers to the government's ability to tax and spend in order to ensure economic stability. Aimed at achieving full employment with price stability, fiscal policy includes such actions as taxation, the borrowing of public monies through the sale of bonds, and governmental expenditures on various goods and services.

FISCAL POLICY MEASURES AND GOALS

Measure	Goal
Increase in government expenditures	Lower unemployment
Lower taxes	Lower unemployment
Increase governmental borrowing	Lower unemployment
Decrease in government expenditures	Reduce inflation
Raise taxes	Reduce inflation
Decrease governmental borrowing	Reduce inflation

Monetary policy is concerned with the supply of money in circulation at any given time. Like fiscal policy, monetary policy is also aimed at achieving full employment with price stability. To meet this goal, the government must enact policies that will ensure that there is an appropriate amount of money in circulation based on present economic conditions. Regulation of the monetary supply is the responsibility of the Federal Reserve Bank, a semi-independent federal institution. Their control of the money supply is exercised primarily through their influence over commercial banks' ability to lend funds. This control is based on three main monetary policy measures: open market operations, the discount rate, and reserve requirements.

Used more often than any other form of monetary policy, open market operations refer to the Federal Reserve Bank's ability to buy or sell securities. If the current economic situation dictates that more money and credit should be made available, the Federal Reserve Bank will buy securities from the open market. The sale of these securities generates additional money for commercial banks to lend to consumers, which, in turn, may lead to lower interest rates and increased consumer and business spending. Conversely, if the economic situation requires that less money and credit should be available, the Federal Reserve Bank will sell securities. This reduces the amount of money commercial banks have to lend and leads to a higher interest rate and less consumer and business spending.

The Federal Reserve Bank can also control the money supply through manipulation of the discount rate, which is the interest rate that the Federal Reserve Bank charges other banks to borrow funds. By raising or lowering the discount rate, the Federal Reserve Bank can influence open market interest rate or indicate a potential change in the future of monetary policy.

Though not often used as a monetary policy tool, the Federal Reserve Bank can also influence the money supply through alterations to its reserve requirements. The Federal Reserve Bank's reserve requirements require all financial institutions to set aside a certain portion of their own reserves to be held at a Reserve bank. Altering these requirements allows for a more predicable demand for bank reserves, which, in turn, increases the Federal Reserve Bank's influence over interest rate changes.

Product Markets and Resource Markets

There are two major types of macroeconomic markets: product markets and resource markets. The economic portion of the CLEP Social Sciences and History test often includes questions pertaining to these markets.

In product markets, final goods and services (i.e., all of the production output that makes up the Gross Domestic Product) are exchanged. Within a product market, these final goods and services are sold mainly by the business sector to consumers in the four macroeconomic sectors (household, business, government, and foreign). Product markets are often the primary factor in economic analysis, as they provide a clear indication of the GDP and offer insight into the rates of inflation and unemployment.

In resource markets, the four factors of production (labor, capital, land, and entrepreneurship) are exchanged, rather than final goods and services. Within a resource market, the four factors of production are sold by the household sector to the business sector. Though generally viewed as secondary in importance to product markets, resource markets have a direct relationship with product markets. When product market activity increases, more productive resources will be hired through the resource market. If product market activity decreases, a surplus of unemployed resources will develop in the resource market.

Scarcity, Choice, and Opportunity Cost

Scarcity, choice, and opportunity cost are three of the basic fundamental elements of economics. Resources are naturally scarce in the world. Since we have a limited supply of resources with which to produce the goods and services the public demands, we must carefully choose how to allocate these resources. Every time we make such a choice as to how we use our limited resources, we encounter opportunity cost, which refers to the cost of using whatever limited resources we must allocate in order to be able to produce the goods and services of our choosing. At its very core, economics is an exercise of rational choice, which means choosing options that offer us the maximum value for our scarce resources at the lowest cost.

PSYCHOLOGY

As part of its focus on the social sciences, the CLEP Social Sciences and History test includes some questions related to the science of psychology. One of the major sciences of human behavior, psychology is aimed at understanding how the human mind works. Since its inception as a distinct science in 1879, psychology has emerged as one of the most important tools for understanding and treating mental health issues.

The following is a brief overview of some of the key psychology topics on which exam questions on the CLEP Social Sciences and History test are based. Keep in mind that this overview is only intended as a brief guide to the subject matter you will need to study further on your own.

Aggression

Many psychology questions on the CLEP Social Sciences and History test will involve the common terminology of the field. Aggression is one such term. It refers to a type of behavior that is meant to cause some form of pain, humiliation, or other harm. Aggression can manifest itself in many different forms and may be verbal, physical, or mental. There are two primary types of aggression: affective and predatory. Affective aggression is a hostile, retaliatory form of aggression that is often impulsive. Predatory aggression, on the other hand, is often premeditated and goal-oriented.

Biopsychology

Some psychology questions on the CLEP Social Science and History test may concern the field of biopsychology, which is also known as behavioral neuroscience or psychobiology. This unique field of psychology, which combines elements of basic psychology and neuroscience, is based on the analysis of how our behaviors, thoughts, and emotions are influenced by the brain and neurotransmitters. Many biopsychology experiments are conducted on non-human animal subjects that can offer insight into human pathology.

Conformity

Another psychology term commonly seen on the CLEP Social Sciences and History test, conformity refers to the act of aligning one's beliefs, attitudes, and behaviors with that which is perceived as normal within a group or the larger society. Conformity often results from either unconscious influences or direct social pressure and will frequently manifest itself in a subject regardless of whether the subject is with a group of other people or alone. Conformity is also influenced by the desire for security, as non-conformity to social norms often results in social rejection.

Group Process

One of the specific fields of psychology often referenced in questions on the CLEP Social Sciences and History test is that of the group process. The study of group processes, which is often known as group dynamics, is, specifically, the study of the behaviors exhibited by a group and the individuals within the group. The individuals within a group, which is defined as two or more people who share some form of social relationship, tend to develop observable dynamic processes unique to the group and not seen among random individuals outside the group. The processes that are commonly seen to emerge in groups include the establishment of norms, the formation of roles and relations within the group, increased social influence and a desire to belong, as well as a wide range of other behavioral effects.

Major Theorists and Schools

The CLEP Social Sciences and History test also features questions pertaining to the major schools of thought in psychology and the important theorists behind them. The following table will provide you with a brief guide to the major schools of psychological thought and some of the key theorists associated with each.

MAJOR SCHOOLS OF THOUGHT IN PSYCHOLOGY AND PROMINENT PROPONENTS

School	Theory	Prominent Proponents
Structuralism	Based on analyzing and reducing mental processes into their fundamental components	Wilhelm Wundt, Edward Titchener
Functionalism	Focused on the roles that mental processes play; a response to structuralism	William James, John Dewey, Harvey Carr
Behaviorism	All behaviors can be explained by environmental causes, as opposed to internal forces; based on observable behavior	John B. Watson, Ivan Pavlov, B. F. Skinner
Psychoanalysis	Emphasized the unconscious mind's influence on behavior	Sigmund Freud, Carl Jung, Erik Erikson
Humanistic Psychology	Centered on the concepts of individual free will, personal growth, and self-actualization; a response to psychoanalysis and behaviorism	Abraham Maslow, Carl Rogers

Gestalt Psychology	People experience things as unified wholes, so it is necessary to examine the whole of an experience, rather than its individual parts; a response to structuralism	Christian von Ehrenfels, Edmund Husserl, Max Wertheimer
Cognitive Psychology	Focused on the mental processes that determine how people think, perceive, remember, and learn	Ulric Neisser, Noam Chomsky, Donald Broadbent

Methods

The CLEP Social Sciences and History test often includes questions related to the research methods commonly used by psychologists to collect scientific data. In the course of collecting such data, psychologists regularly utilize information from other scientific fields in order to arrive at a more complete and precise understanding and explanation of the psychological phenomena they are investigating. Some of the many research methods used by psychologists include:

- Survey questionnaires
- Ratings
- Self-reports
- Case studies
- Personality tests
- Attitude tests
- Intelligence tests
- Structured interviews
- Journal records
- Direct observation
- Behavior sampling

Performance

Another branch of psychology often featured on the CLEP Social Sciences and History test is performance psychology. Performance psychology is based on the various factors that allow people (whether individually, in a group, or on a team) to achieve the maximum level of success (whether in sports, business, or other aspects of life). Performance psychologists study these factors and analyze how they contribute to performance. With the ever-increasing competitiveness in the sports world and in business, performance psychology has grown significantly in popularity in recent years.

Personality

You may also encounter some questions on the CLEP Social Sciences and History test that deal with a branch of psychology known as personality psychology. A personality is the culmination of all of the unique patterns of thought, emotions, and behaviors present in a particular individual.

Personality psychology is the study of this phenomenon and has three main focuses: developing a complete analysis of a subject and his or her key psychological processes, investigating individual differences, and investigating human nature. There exists a wide array of theoretical explanations as to how and why different types of personalities develop, including humoral theories, morphological theories, psychoanalytic theories, trait theories, and more.

Socialization

Socialization is yet another term you will likely see on the CLEP Social Sciences and History test. Socialization refers to the process by which an individual person is integrated into a group or society and learns to behave in the manner subscribed to by that group or society. The process of socialization is studied extensively in psychology and other social sciences. This process is influenced by three key factors:

1. **Culture:** The behavior pattern shared between individuals within a society; passed from generation to generation through language, religion, philosophy, and the arts and sciences

2. **Subculture:** Refers to a distinct group within a larger culture; often characterized by social class, social role, or ethnic identity; within these groups, certain behaviors not common to the larger society are retained as a result of the differences between the members of the subculture and the general members of the culture-at-large

3. **Social Dyad:** A simple personal interaction between two people in which a reciprocal learning process occurs; the primary example of a social dyad is the relationship shared between a parent and child

SOCIOLOGY

Along with psychology, the CLEP Social Sciences and History test will also include questions on sociology, which is the systematic study of societies, social institutions, and social relationships. Much like their counterparts in psychology, sociologists study groups, their development and structure, and the function of human social behavior within. The goal of a sociologist is to build a mass of interrelated sociological knowledge that can be used to generalize, explain, or even predict patterns of behavior.

The following is a brief overview of some of the key sociology topics on which exam questions on the CLEP Social Sciences and History test are based. Keep in mind that this overview is only intended as a brief guide to the subject matter you will need to study further on your own.

Demography

One particular branch of sociology often featured on the CLEP Social Sciences and History test is demography. Demography is the study of human population. A typical demographic study examines the size, structure, and distribution of a given population and the changes that occur within it as a result of natural phenomena such as birth, aging, death, and migration. Such studies may be focused on a whole society or on subcultures that are defined by particular characteristics such as nationality/ethnicity, religious beliefs, educational background, or economic class.

Deviance

As with the psychology portion of the CLEP Social Sciences and History test, there are a number of important sociological terms you will need to be familiar with. One such term is deviance, which refers to any action or behavior that violates the cultural norms or rules of a given society. What exactly qualifies as deviant behavior can vary from society to society, meaning a particular behavior that is considered to be deviant in one society may be viewed as perfectly normal and acceptable in another. The study of deviance is closely related to the study of the emergence, evolution, and enforcement of the societal norms that dictate what behaviors are defined as deviant in a society. While the purpose and reason for some societal norms is fairly obvious (e.g., the idea that killing others is wrong), other norms can often be seen as somewhat arbitrary, having no clear moral or logical foundation (e.g., table manners). Regardless of the background of the norms of a society, any behavior that is seen as being a violation of those norms is generally considered deviant.

Family

Of the many groups sociologists study, there is perhaps none more important to human social development than the family. The family is the most basic, fundamental social institution to which most individuals are exposed from an early age. For this reason, sociologists often study the family for the critical role it plays in the process of socialization. In addition to its role as a social institution, the family is also sociologically significant because it is, in and of itself, a unique social group with its own boundaries, roles, norms, values, and statuses. To some sociologists, the family is a microcosm of the society-at-large.

Sociological studies of the family can focus on a broad range of topics, a few of which include:

- Family demography
- How social change effects the family
- Familial interactions with other social groups
- Contemporary diversity of the family form
- Relationships between family members
- Issues related to parenthood and/or childhood

Interaction

Another key piece of sociological terminology that often appears on the CLEP Social Sciences and History test is interaction (also known social interaction or social relation). In a sociological context, interaction refers to a relationship shared between two or more people. These interactions lie at the very foundation of the social structure. As such, interactions are one of the most important and most studied aspects of sociology. Common social interactions can be grouped into one of four categories: accidental, repeated, regular, or regulated. Many of the sociology questions on the exam are likely to be related in some way with social interactions of some manner.

Major Theorists and Schools

Since the primary emergence of sociology in the nineteenth century, there have been countless notable social scientists and philosophers who have made many significant contributions to the development of the field. Through these pioneers, numerous sociological schools of thought that continue to have a major influence on modern sociology have been established. The following is a brief guide to some of the key contributors to the development of sociology and the various schools of thought with which they are associated.

MAJOR SOCIOLOGICAL THEORISTS AND SCHOOLS OF THOUGHT

Theorist	School of Thought	Major Tenets
Auguste Comte	Positivism	Social evolution occurs in three phases: theological, metaphysical, positive; in the positive stage, scientific explanation is based on observation, experiment, and comparison; positive explanations are justified by the scientific method
Herbert Spencer	Social Darwinism	The fittest, most capable members of society should be allowed to thrive, while the weaker and less capable members of society should be allowed to die off; an elitist theory based on Darwin's theory of evolution
Emile Durkheim	Social Integration	People have a level of attachment to their social groups; abnormally high or low levels of attachment to these groups may increase the likelihood of suicide
Karl Marx	Conflict Theory	Ideological perspectives which focus on the social, political, or material inequality of a particular social group; often emphasize power struggles (e.g., class conflict); usually in stark contrast to more dominant theories

Max Weber	Bureaucracy	Advocated bureaucracies that could provide an effective means of decision-making, controlling resources, protecting workers and accomplishing organizational goals
George Herbert Mead	Symbolic Interaction	Individuals act towards things on the basis of the meanings they have applied to those things; such meanings are based on social interaction and altered through interpretation
Charles Horton Cooley	The Looking-Glass Self	A person's concept of self is borne out of society's interpersonal interactions and the perceptions of others
C. Wright Mills	The Power Elite	The ordinary citizen is largely a powerless subject of manipulation by the interwoven interests of political, military, and corporate leaders

Methods

Some sociology questions on the CLEP Social Sciences and History test are related to the research methods commonly employed by modern sociologists. All sociological studies begin with the selection of the unit of analysis, which is the social entity to be studied. Once a unit of analysis has been chosen, the researcher must decide what type of research method to use. In contemporary sociology, researchers use a variety of unique data-gathering methods, some of which include:

- **Surveys:** Respondents are asked to answer a series of questions presented either verbally or on a written questionnaire

- **In-depth interview:** A subject is asked to respond at-length to a set of questions; may include open-ended conversation

- **Field research:** A researcher observes and, to some extent, interacts with individuals in their natural environment

- **Document study:** A researcher gathers data from source documents like newspapers, official records, etc.

- **Experiment:** A researcher tests a specific hypothesis about a causal relationship

In addition, sociological researchers also have the option of doing a cross-sectional or longitudinal study. A cross-sectional study is based on data from a single point in time, whereas a longitudinal study is based on data collected at several different points in time or over an extended period of time.

Social Change

The CLEP Social Sciences and History test also often features questions related to the concept of social change. Social change is described as any modification of a society's social order. The term "social change" is often used in reference to social progress or sociocultural evolution. It can also be used in reference to sociopolitical revolutions or social movements.

There are numerous theories concerning social change. While it is generally agreed that some form of social change is constantly occurring, there are many divergent hypotheses in regards to the nature of that change. Some of the theories about the nature of social change include:

- the concept of social change as an overall decline or degeneration from a greater previous state.

- the concept of a cyclical pattern of social change that includes recurrent, alternating phases of growth and decline.

- the concept of social change as an ongoing process of continuous social progress.

- the concept of social change as a evolution from one social form to another.

Social Organizations

The CLEP Social Sciences and History test often contains questions that deal with social organizations. The term social organization (or institution) refers to a structure of social order that dictates the expected behavior of a particular set of individuals within a larger society. Social organizations are designed to meet specific needs of the society and each serves a specific social purpose. As a whole, these organizations are used to maintain specific standards, perpetuate necessary daily functions, and provide a framework for socially acceptable behavior. Some of the many common contemporary social organizations include:

- The family
- Marriage
- Religion
- Educational institutions
- Medical institutions
- Legal institutions
- Police and military institutions
- Corporate institutions
- Mass media
- Civil institutions

Social Stratification

Another sociology concept that frequently appears on the CLEP Social Sciences and History test is social stratification. Social stratification refers to a social framework that divides the world's inhabitants on the basis of three critical social factors: class, status, and power.

1. **Class:** Refers to an individual's economic place in a society; class is primarily determined by material wealth

2. **Status:** Refers to an individual's social standing within a society; status is based on the public perception of an individual and is often, though not always, influenced by the individual's class and power

3. **Power:** Refers to an individual's ability to influence others in spite of resistance

In many contemporary Western societies, social stratification has led to the development of distinct class systems. Most of these systems organize members of the society into one of three classifications: upper class, middle class, and lower class. In more diverse societies, these classes may be further subdivided.

Two main theorists are associated with social stratification: Karl Marx and Max Weber. Marx, who was opposed to capitalism, argued that social stratification would inevitably lead to class exploitation on the part of the upper class, or the bourgeoisie, who owned the means of production. He believed that, driven by the desire for profit, the bourgeoisie would exploit the working class, or the proletariat, by forcing them to work under poor conditions to make as much money as possible. He also believed that a revolt by the proletariat would be inevitable.

Max Weber, on the other hand, argued that the class system was, in fact, more complicated than Marx supposed. He introduced the three-component theory of stratification discussed above and suggested that there were actually four primary classes: the upper class, the white collar workers, the petite bourgeoisie, and the manual working class. He also argued that material wealth was not the overwhelmingly influential factor in social stratification that Marx claimed it was.

Social Theory

Lastly, the sociology portion of the CLEP Social Sciences and History test also includes questions related to social theory. Social theory is the process through which social scientists use abstract and/ or complicated theoretical models to describe, analyze, and explain the social environment. Social theories provide us with insight into the social forces that shape our world and inform our lives. Moreover, these theories allow us to understand that the intricacies of our social existence are not merely random, but actually distinct, patterned behaviors that can be studied and understood. There are many different social theories, both historical and modern. Many of these theories have already been discussed. As you prepare for the sociology portion of the Social Sciences and History test, it is recommended that you spend some time studying the wide array of social theories that have emerged over the course of human history.

ANTHROPOLOGY

The final subject included on the CLEP Social Sciences and History test is anthropology. Anthropology is the study of *Homo sapiens*, the only species of the genus "man" still in existence today. It is primarily concerned with the role of male and female humans in the origins of the species, the historical classification of and the relationship between the various races of the species, the specific physical and environmental characteristics of humans, and the social and cultural relationships shared between male and female humans as they evolved.

The following is a brief overview of some of the key anthropology topics on which exam questions on the CLEP Social Sciences and History test are based. Keep in mind that this overview is only intended as a brief guide to the subject matter you will need to study further on your own.

Cultural Anthropology

Some of the anthropology questions on the CLEP Social Sciences and History test will be related to cultural anthropology. This unique branch of anthropology focuses on the study of human culture. More specifically, cultural anthropology includes the study of topics like religion and mythology, art and music, political systems, social hierarchies, family dynamics, social customs and traditions, economics, food, and more. Through the study of these factors, cultural anthropologists seek to construct a better understanding of the overall human experience and to narrow the cultural divides that separate us. While most cultural anthropology studies are concerned with primitive societies that still exist within the modern world, many are also conducted with subcultures within larger, modern societies.

Ethnography

The CLEP Social Sciences and History test also frequently contains some questions that pertain to the field of ethnography. Based on cultural anthropology, ethnography is a descriptive study of a selected society in which the researcher completely immerses himself or herself in the culture of the group he or she is studying as a means of collecting data. This method, known as fieldwork, though it can be quite fruitful, is often difficult to carry out objectively, as it is dependent on the ethnographer's ability to consciously avoid any self-centered thinking. A well-executed ethnography, however, can provide us with a valuable understanding of foreign cultures that may ultimately serve to bring all world cultures closer together.

Major Theorists and Schools

The CLEP Social Sciences and History test is likely to feature questions concerned with the major schools of thought in anthropology and the important theorists associated with them. The following table will provide you with a brief guide to the major schools of anthropological thought and some of the important theorists who contributed to each.

MAJOR SCHOOLS OF THOUGHT IN ANTHROPOLOGY AND PROMINENT PROPONENTS

School	Theory	Prominent Proponents
American Materialism	Based on the belief that the framework of a society is primarily built on economic and technological factors	Karl Marx , Frederick Engels, Leslie White, Julian Steward, Marvin Harris
Cognitive Anthropology	Based on the relationship shared between human culture and human cognitive thought	Ward Goodenough, Charles Frake, Harold Conklin

Cross-Cultural Analysis	Holds that statistical cross-cultural comparisons are possible because people of different cultures naturally share some common behavioral traits as a result of the need to perpetuate the species	Sir Edward Burnett Tylor, William Graham Sumner, George P. Murdock, Alfred Louis Kroeber, Harold E. Driver, Clellan Ford, David Levinson
Culture and Personality School	Aimed at discovering national character, model personality types, and configurations of personality through the study of individual characteristics and personalities	Sigmund Freud, Erik Erikson, Edward Sapir, Benjamin Lee Whorf, Ruth Benedict, Margaret Mead, Abram Kardiner, Ralph Linton, Cora Dubois, Clyde Kluckhohn
Diffusionism and Acculturation	Aimed at explaining culture on the basis of the development and spread of cultural traits between societies	Franz Boas, Leo Frobenius, Fritz Graebner, A. C. Haddon, Thor Heyerdahl, A. L. Kroeber, Freidrich Ratzel, W. H. R. Rivers, Father Pater Wilhelm Schmidt, G. Elliot Smith, Clark Wissler
Ecological Anthropology	Based on the complicated relationships shared between people and the environment in which they live	Thomas R. Malthus, Julian Steward, Leslie White, Marvin Harris, Roy A. Rappaport, Harold Conklin
Feminist Anthropology	Focuses on the role of gender in anthropology	Margaret Mead, Sherry Ortner, Michelle Rosaldo, Ruth Benedict
Functionalism	Based on explaining how the various parts of society work together by way of an organic analogy that compares the parts of a society to the parts of a living organism	E.E. Evans-Pritchard, Sir Raymond Firth, Meyer Fortes, Sir Edmund Leach, Lucy Mair, Bronislaw Malinowski, Robert K. Merton, Talcott Parsons, A.R. Radcliffe-Brown, Audrey Richards
Historicism	Merged the theory of diffusionism with the notion that societies would eventually adapt to changing circumstances	Grafton Elliot Smith, R. Fritz Graebner, Franz Boas, Alfred Louis Kroeber, Ruth Benedict, Robert H. Lowie, Edward Sapir, Paul Radin, Clark Wissler
Marxist Anthropology	A school of anthropology based on the themes of Marxism	Karl Marx, Frederich Engels, Maurice Bloch, Eric Wolf, Antonio Gramsci, Louis Althusser, Maurice Godelier

Postmodernist Anthropology	A school of anthropological thought that is, itself, a criticism of anthropology	Michael Agar, Jean Baudrillard, Jacques Derrida, Michel Foucault, Clifford Geertz, Ian Hodder, Jean-Francois Lyotard, Nancy Scheper-Hughes
Social Evolutionism	Based on the idea that all cultures naturally evolve from simple groups to complex societies	Johann Jacob Bachofen, Sir James George Frazer, Sir John Lubbock, Sir Henry James Sumner Maine, John F. McLellan, Lewis Henry Morgan, Sir Edward Burnett Tylor
Structuralism	A theory of linguistics that suggests that we all speak the same language but are unable to fully understand the unique grammatical rules that determine the specific manner in which we arrange words	Claude Lévi-Strauss, Ferdinand de Saussure, Roman Jakobson, Marcel Mauss, Jacques Derrida, Michel Foucault
Symbolic and Interpretive Anthropology	Based on the examination of cultural symbols and how such symbols might be interpreted so as to expand our understanding of a given society	Clifford Geertz, Victor Witter Turner, David Schneider, Mary Douglas

Methods

As with the other social sciences on the CLEP Social Sciences and History test, you can expect to encounter some questions related to the research methods commonly used by anthropologists. These methods include:

- **Participant Observation:** An anthropologist spends an extended period of time directly interacting with (and possibly living within) the society he or she is studying

- **Interviews:** An anthropologist conducts interviews with the inhabitants of a society so as to learn about their own views on their society

- **Cross-Cultural Comparison:** An anthropologist compares the culture he or she is studying to other cultures

- **Historical Analysis:** An anthropologist studies a culture's historical documents to learn about their past

- **Survey Research:** An anthropologist composes and distributes questionnaires designed to gather information and opinions from the members of a culture

- **Archival/Media Research:** An anthropologist uses archival or media-related sources to further his or her understanding of the culture being studied

Paleoanthropology

The anthropology portion of the CLEP Social Sciences and History test may also include some questions related to the field of paleoanthropology. Naturally, the sciences of anthropology and paleontology, which is the study of prehistoric life, are closely related. The field of paleoanthropology includes elements of both sciences. Specifically, paleoanthropology is concerned with study of the origins of humankind through the hominid evidence found in fossilized records. In the course of their studies, paleoanthropologists assess such fossils through the use of various techniques related to physical anthropology, comparative anatomy, and the theory of evolution. Interest in the field of paleoanthropology first emerged in the nineteenth century, when the earliest evidence of human evolution first emerged.

SOCIAL SCIENCES AND HISTORY: REVIEW QUESTIONS

1. The belief that government intervention is necessary to increase spending during a recession in a market economy would most likely be associated with which economic theory?
   - (A) Classical
   - (B) Physiocracy
   - (C) Keynesian
   - (D) Marxism
   - (E) Monetarism

2. World War I was officially ended with the signing of which treaty?
   - (A) Treaty of Paris
   - (B) Potsdam Treaty
   - (C) Treaty of Ghent
   - (D) Jay's Treaty
   - (E) Treaty of Versailles

3. A scientist who studies soil would likely be considered an expert in which field of physical geography?
   - (A) Biogeography
   - (B) Pedology
   - (C) Geomorphology
   - (D) Hydrology
   - (E) Meteorology

4. Sociologist Herbert Spencer is most often associated with which sociological school of thought?
   - (A) Social Darwinism
   - (B) Positivism
   - (C) Conflict Theory
   - (D) Bureaucracy
   - (E) Social Integration

5. The publication of *The Ninety-Five Theses* marked one of the most significant events of the Protestant Reformation. This landmark work was written by
   - (A) John Calvin
   - (B) Desiderius Erasmus
   - (C) John Knox
   - (D) Martin Luther
   - (E) Ulrich Zwingli

6. All societies follow the same pattern of development, naturally progressing from a simple group to a complex society with a vast system of interconnected subcultures.

   An anthropologist who adheres to which school of thought would be most likely to agree with the above statement?
   - (A) Functionalism
   - (B) Social Evolutionism
   - (C) Diffusionism and Acculturation
   - (D) Structuralism
   - (E) Postmodernist Anthropology

7. In a resource market, the four factors of production are primarily sold by which sector?
   - (A) Business
   - (B) Government
   - (C) Household
   - (D) Foreign
   - (E) Financial

8. The annexation of Hawaii into a U.S. territory was completed with the passage of the
   - (A) Treaty of Greenville
   - (B) Adams-Onis Treaty
   - (C) Hay-Bunau-Varilla
   - (D) Newlands Resolution
   - (E) Platt Amendment

9. Affective aggression would best be described as
   - (A) retaliatory
   - (B) premeditated
   - (C) goal-oriented
   - (D) passive-aggressive

10. Which of the following psychology theorists suggests that the human psyche was divided into three separate parts known as the id, ego, and super-ego?
    - (A) Ivan Pavlov
    - (B) Sigmund Freud
    - (C) Noam Chomsky
    - (D) Carl Jung
    - (E) Wilhelm Wundt

ANSWER KEY AND EXPLANATIONS

1. C	3. B	5. D	7. C	9. A
2. E	4. A	6. B	8. D	10. B

1. **The correct answer is (C).** Keynesian economic theory states that government intervention is necessary to increase spending during a recession in a market economy.

2. **The correct answer is (E).** World War I was officially brought to a close with the signing of the Treaty of Versailles.

3. **The correct answer is (B).** A subfield of physical geography, pedology is the study of soils.

4. **The correct answer is (A).** Having coined the phrase "survival of the fittest," Herbert Spencer is closely associated with the Social Darwinism school of thought.

5. **The correct answer is (D).** *The Ninety-Five Theses* were written by Martin Luther, a German priest who is credited as the initiator of the Protestant Reformation.

6. **The correct answer is (B).** An anthropologist who adheres to Social Evolutionism would be most likely to agree with the statement because the Social Evolutionist view holds that all cultures naturally evolve from simple groups to complex societies.

7. **The correct answer is (C).** In resource markets, the four factors of production are normally sold by the household sector to the business sector.

8. **The correct answer is (D).** Hawaii was officially annexed to the United States as a territory by the Newlands Resolution, which was signed into law by the U.S. Congress in 1898.

9. **The correct answer is (A).** Affective aggression is typically characterized as retaliatory, hostile, or impulsive.

10. **The correct answer is (B).** Famed psychoanalyst Sigmund Freud asserted that the human psyche consisted of three separate parts known as the id, ego, and super-ego.

POSTTEST ANSWER SHEET

1. Ⓐ Ⓑ Ⓒ Ⓓ Ⓔ   11. Ⓐ Ⓑ Ⓒ Ⓓ Ⓔ   21. Ⓐ Ⓑ Ⓒ Ⓓ Ⓔ   31. Ⓐ Ⓑ Ⓒ Ⓓ Ⓔ   41. Ⓐ Ⓑ Ⓒ Ⓓ Ⓔ
2. Ⓐ Ⓑ Ⓒ Ⓓ Ⓔ   12. Ⓐ Ⓑ Ⓒ Ⓓ Ⓔ   22. Ⓐ Ⓑ Ⓒ Ⓓ Ⓔ   32. Ⓐ Ⓑ Ⓒ Ⓓ Ⓔ   42. Ⓐ Ⓑ Ⓒ Ⓓ Ⓔ
3. Ⓐ Ⓑ Ⓒ Ⓓ Ⓔ   13. Ⓐ Ⓑ Ⓒ Ⓓ Ⓔ   23. Ⓐ Ⓑ Ⓒ Ⓓ Ⓔ   33. Ⓐ Ⓑ Ⓒ Ⓓ Ⓔ   43. Ⓐ Ⓑ Ⓒ Ⓓ Ⓔ
4. Ⓐ Ⓑ Ⓒ Ⓓ Ⓔ   14. Ⓐ Ⓑ Ⓒ Ⓓ Ⓔ   24. Ⓐ Ⓑ Ⓒ Ⓓ Ⓔ   34. Ⓐ Ⓑ Ⓒ Ⓓ Ⓔ   44. Ⓐ Ⓑ Ⓒ Ⓓ Ⓔ
5. Ⓐ Ⓑ Ⓒ Ⓓ Ⓔ   15. Ⓐ Ⓑ Ⓒ Ⓓ Ⓔ   25. Ⓐ Ⓑ Ⓒ Ⓓ Ⓔ   35. Ⓐ Ⓑ Ⓒ Ⓓ Ⓔ   45. Ⓐ Ⓑ Ⓒ Ⓓ Ⓔ
6. Ⓐ Ⓑ Ⓒ Ⓓ Ⓔ   16. Ⓐ Ⓑ Ⓒ Ⓓ Ⓔ   26. Ⓐ Ⓑ Ⓒ Ⓓ Ⓔ   36. Ⓐ Ⓑ Ⓒ Ⓓ Ⓔ   46. Ⓐ Ⓑ Ⓒ Ⓓ Ⓔ
7. Ⓐ Ⓑ Ⓒ Ⓓ Ⓔ   17. Ⓐ Ⓑ Ⓒ Ⓓ Ⓔ   27. Ⓐ Ⓑ Ⓒ Ⓓ Ⓔ   37. Ⓐ Ⓑ Ⓒ Ⓓ Ⓔ   47. Ⓐ Ⓑ Ⓒ Ⓓ Ⓔ
8. Ⓐ Ⓑ Ⓒ Ⓓ Ⓔ   18. Ⓐ Ⓑ Ⓒ Ⓓ Ⓔ   28. Ⓐ Ⓑ Ⓒ Ⓓ Ⓔ   38. Ⓐ Ⓑ Ⓒ Ⓓ Ⓔ   48. Ⓐ Ⓑ Ⓒ Ⓓ Ⓔ
9. Ⓐ Ⓑ Ⓒ Ⓓ Ⓔ   19. Ⓐ Ⓑ Ⓒ Ⓓ Ⓔ   29. Ⓐ Ⓑ Ⓒ Ⓓ Ⓔ   39. Ⓐ Ⓑ Ⓒ Ⓓ Ⓔ   49. Ⓐ Ⓑ Ⓒ Ⓓ Ⓔ
10. Ⓐ Ⓑ Ⓒ Ⓓ Ⓔ   20. Ⓐ Ⓑ Ⓒ Ⓓ Ⓔ   30. Ⓐ Ⓑ Ⓒ Ⓓ Ⓔ   40. Ⓐ Ⓑ Ⓒ Ⓓ Ⓔ   50. Ⓐ Ⓑ Ⓒ Ⓓ Ⓔ

answer sheet

Posttest

40 minutes • 50 questions

Directions: Each of the questions or incomplete statements below is followed by five suggested answers or completions. Select the one that is best in each case.

1. A contour interval delineates regions of varying
   (A) political alliance
   (B) temperature
   (C) elevation
   (D) water depth
   (E) religious affiliation

"Do not put such unlimited power into the hands of the Husbands. Remember all Men would be tyrants if they could. If particular care and attention is not paid to the Ladies we are determined to foment a Rebellion, and will not hold ourselves bound by any Laws in which we have no voice, or Representation."

2. The statement above is most characteristic of which of the following?
   (A) Carrie A. Nation
   (B) Abigail Adams
   (C) Martha Washington
   (D) Ann Hutchinson
   (E) Mary Todd Lincoln

3. Which of the following best describes the methodology of the Marshall Plan as a component of U.S. foreign policy during the Cold War?
   (A) The Marshall Plan provided aid to organizations that sought out and "blacklisted" domestic communists.
   (B) The Marshall Plan was created by Senator McCarthy to eliminate all perceived communists from the U.S. military.
   (C) The Marshall Plan was intended to open diplomatic conversations between communist and non-communist countries.
   (D) The Marshall Plan was a formal declaration of war against communism that outlined the U.S. policy of "containment."
   (E) The Marshall Plan provided aid to countries resisting communism in the belief that economic prosperity would hinder the advance of the "Red Menace."

"I expect to see the State, which is in a position to calculate the marginal efficiency of capital goods on long views and on the basis of the general social advantage, taking an ever greater responsibility for directly organizing investment."

4. The quotation above best expresses the philosophy of
   (A) John Maynard Keynes
   (B) Adam Smith
   (C) David Hume
   (D) William Stanley Jevons
   (E) Fengbo Zhang

"We cannot shut out of view the fact, within the knowledge of all, that the public health, the public morals, and the public safety, may be endangered by the general use of intoxicating drinks; nor the fact established by statistics accessible to every one, that the idleness, disorder, pauperism and crime existing in the country, are, in some degree... traceable to this evil."

5. The statement above is most characteristic of which of the following?
(A) Upton Sinclair
(B) Reverend Increase Mathers
(C) Pauline Sabin
(D) Franklin Roosevelt
(E) Carrie Nation

6. In anthropology, the cultural relativism approach seeks to explain behavior in terms of
(A) hereditary factors
(B) cross-cultural comparisons
(C) the context of an individual culture
(D) global standards
(E) the relative distance from the culture of the observer

7. The most immediate consequence of the Gulf of Tonkin Resolution was
(A) a formal declaration of war by Congress
(B) the removal of U.S. military troops from Vietnam
(C) the expansion of U.S. military action into Cambodia and Laos
(D) the authorization for President Johnson to use military force in Vietnam
(E) widespread student protests at universities as part of the free speech movement

8. Which of the following is the most lucrative oil-producing state in the United States?
(A) California
(B) Texas
(C) South Carolina
(D) Hawaii
(E) Alaska

9. A person who lived in the 1830s in the United States and believed in universal suffrage, a strong executive branch, the election of judicial figures, and geographic expansion most probably would have been a/an
(A) Jeffersonian
(B) Federalist
(C) Jacksonian
(D) Anti-Federalist
(E) Whig

10. Gross national product (GNP) calculations commonly make use of
(A) the market value of all products and services produced annually
(B) the taxation percentages for domestic products
(C) international tariffs and free-trade restrictions
(D) currency-rate conversions
(E) standard of living variances

11. Which of the following is a physical marker of Homo sapiens?
(A) A prominent brow ridge
(B) A low, slanted forehead
(C) Occipital buns
(D) Disproportionally short arms
(E) A pronounced chin

12. The most immediate consequence of the Wall Street Crash of 1929 was
(A) the widespread expansion of credit systems and speculation
(B) the expansion of federal powers to include social-relief programs
(C) better treatment of non-union laborers
(D) greater sympathy for the plight of immigrant workers
(E) decreased federal power to regulate the market

13. Which of the following prompted the United States to boycott the 1980 Summer Olympics in Moscow?

   I. Soviet occupation of Afghanistan
   II. War crimes committed under Stalin
   III. The building of the Berlin Wall

  (A) I only
  (B) II only
  (C) III only
  (D) I and III only
  (E) II and III only

14. Margaret Mitchell's novel *Gone with the Wind* primarily depicts the period of U.S. history known as the

  (A) Great Depression
  (B) Early Republic
  (C) Lost Generation
  (D) Era of Good Feelings
  (E) Reconstruction

15. As depicted above, the Basques could be described as which of the following?
  (A) Unitary state
  (B) Stateless nation
  (C) Transnational state
  (D) Nation-state
  (E) Multi-ethnic empire

16. Which of the following is true of the Camp David Accords of 1978?
  (A) It established Israeli control of the Gaza strip.
  (B) It created the United Nations.
  (C) It formed an alliance between Libya and Egypt.
  (D) It established diplomatic negotiations between Egypt and Israel.
  (E) It guaranteed Egyptian citizens the right to a democratic government.

"By three methods we may learn wisdom: First, by reflection, which is noblest; Second, by imitation, which is easiest; and third by experience, which is the bitterest."

17. The quotation above best expresses the philosophy of
  (A) Gandhi
  (B) Muhammad
  (C) Confucius
  (D) Thomas Locke
  (E) Sir Thomas Moore

18. In the late twentieth century, the fall of the Soviet Union had the LEAST influence in which of the following countries?
  (A) Estonia
  (B) Latvia
  (C) Ukraine
  (D) Poland
  (E) Bulgaria

19. One of the fundamental changes that took place during the first and second centuries was a gradual
  (A) increase in local autonomy and independent community spirit
  (B) decline in agricultural production
  (C) decrease in the pressure of international trade on trans-Saharan caravan routes
  (D) decline in religious conflict
  (E) increase in centralized political and economic authority

20. Prior to the sinking of the *Lusitania,* the official stance of the United States toward the Great War in Europe was that of

(A) isolation

(B) active involvement

(C) indifference

(D) economic boycott

(E) warmongering

21. In the period between 1580 and 1680, witchcraft trials had the LEAST influence in which of the following countries?

(A) Scotland

(B) North America

(C) Germany

(D) Spain

(E) Sweden

22. Which of the following statements about the concept of retaliatory aggression is correct?

(A) It is possible only in the presence of a perceived injury.

(B) It involves an act of aggression that is accomplished without premeditation.

(C) It rests on the need for written justice systems.

(D) It is a socially constructed aggressive behavior.

(E) It is a prerequisite for predatory aggression.

23. Which of the following is true of the Treaty of Maastricht?

(A) It established the European Coal and Steel Coalition.

(B) It created the European Union.

(C) It established a universal currency for England, France, Italy, and Spain.

(D) It formed the United Nations.

(E) It guaranteed the continuity of local import and export tariffs.

"Chronic wrongdoing, or an impotence which results in a general loosening of the ties of civilized society, may in America, as elsewhere, ultimately require intervention by some civilized nation, and in the Western Hemisphere the adherence of the United States to the Monroe Doctrine may force the United States, however reluctantly, in flagrant cases of such wrongdoing or impotence, to the exercise of an international police power."

24. The statement above is most characteristic of which of the following?

(A) Theodore Roosevelt

(B) James Monroe

(C) William Jennings Bryan

(D) Thomas Jefferson

(E) Henry David Thoreau

25. Of the following, which group was the first to establish trade links with both India and the Arabian Peninsula?

(A) The Romans

(B) The French

(C) The Portuguese

(D) The Greeks

(E) The Byzantines

26. European imperialism in Australia in the late eighteenth century differed from European imperialism of Australia in later periods in which of the following ways?

(A) It consisted primarily of forced penal relocation programs.

(B) It discouraged the integration of indigenous populations.

(C) It combined geographic exploration with commerce.

(D) It met with resistance from indigenous populations.

(E) It represented an unprecedented geographic claim to new territory.

27. One of the fundamental changes that took place in the middle of the twentieth century was a gradual

(A) increase in the population of urban centers

(B) increase in the population of suburban developments

(C) decrease in pressure of the aging population on economic resources

(D) decrease in life expectancy

(E) decline in population movement and immigration

28. In sociology and anthropology, gentrification occurs when

(A) upper-class sections of society are replaced by lower-class sections

(B) social stratification divides the gentry from the upper class on hereditary grounds

(C) upper-class sections of society argue for additional civic rights

(D) social stratification is accomplished using gentle, non-violent methods

(E) lower-class sections of society are replaced by upper-class sections

29. Which of the following was formed by the American Colonization Society as a settlement for freed slaves?

(A) Liberia

(B) Algeria

(C) Ghana

(D) Nigeria

(E) Togo

30. Alaska became part of the territorial holdings of the United States as a result of

(A) the Gadsden Purchase

(B) the Adam-Onis Treaty

(C) Seward's Folly

(D) the Peace of Paris

(E) the Soviet Non-Aggression Pact

31. Which of the following designed methods for making paper and gunpowder, provided a valuable eastward trade route for Western Europe, and became major international spice merchants?

(A) The Romans

(B) The Chinese

(C) The Japanese

(D) The Greeks

(E) The Merovingians

32. Which of the following is the most significant effect of the Internet and social media on national elections in the United States?

(A) Centralizing political information and party platforms in a single-digital location

(B) Improving the ability of everyday citizens to be involved in the political process

(C) Defining elections as non-modern phenomena

(D) Reducing citizen involvement at the grassroots level

(E) Decreasing the total number of political parties

33. Which of the following is NOT compatible with the traditional conception of a meritocracy?

(A) Civil-service entrance exams

(B) Competitive academic environments

(C) Political clientelism

(D) Local and national elections

(E) Income variance among citizens

34. Which of the following theorists asserted that all human beings progress through nine stages of development and that the ego served as the governing factor for human progress?

(A) Kurt Lewin

(B) Erik Erikson

(C) Alfred Adler

(D) Mary Ainsworth

(E) Mary Whiton Calkins

35. Self-actualization refers to the quality of being

(A) selfish and self-seeking

(B) desirous of professional psychological assistance

(C) aware of one's full potential

(D) unable to situate one's own needs in relation to others'

(E) able to govern the id and ego using the superego

36. The Electoral College of the United States denies some power to both the people and the legislative branch in order to

    (A) prevent citizen participation in national elections

    (B) allow the president and vice president to be elected by popular vote

    (C) safeguard checks and balances in the election process

    (D) deny candidates the ability to use media opportunities

    (E) provide protection of executive privilege

37. Which of the following is true of the Fourth Amendment to the U.S. Constitution?

    (A) It established freedom of religion.

    (B) It created the Electoral College.

    (C) It declared slavery null and void.

    (D) It prevented against unreasonable search and seizure.

    (E) It guaranteed citizens the right to peaceably assemble.

38. The classification of acts as deviant increases in groups that are

    (A) heterogeneous

    (B) self-actualized

    (C) homogeneous

    (D) fragmented

    (E) poorly defined

39. A traveler going from point 1 to point 2 on the map above would cross which mountain range?

    (A) Himalayas

    (B) Sierra Nevada

    (C) Alps

    (D) Andes

    (E) Atlas

40. The area of the United States is approximately

    (A) half the area of China

    (B) three times larger than Brazil

    (C) half the size of Russia

    (D) equal to the area of Western Europe

    (E) six times the area of India

41. For native Hawaiians, the overthrow of Queen Liliuokalani in 1893 resulted in which of the following?

    (A) Continuation of autonomous local leadership

    (B) The enthusiastic adoption of U.S. rule

    (C) The loss of political and cultural sovereignty

    (D) The establishment of a displaced monarchy the mainland

    (E) The immediate establishment of Hawaii as a U.S. state

42. To stabilize international exchange rates, the International Monetary Fund (IMF) would most likely

    (A) require reparations payments from wealthier countries

    (B) encourage member banks to withdraw their savings in uncertain economic times

    (C) offer conditional loans to poorer countries

    (D) decrease interest rates on European-based currencies

    (E) raise restrictions against the import and export of goods

43. Which of the following economic policies is likely to result in the greatest increase in marginal utility?

    (A) Oversaturation of the market

    (B) Keeping production in line with the needs of the demand

    (C) Allowing the demand for a good or service to remain unmet

    (D) Failing to acquire additional goods or services

    (E) Allowing the supply of a good to dictate the market value

44. Which of the following statements regarding the process of population definition is true?

    (A) Cultural factors, such as education, religion, and nationality, can define societies.

    (B) Populations are defined only through political boundaries.

    (C) Population density is not determined by socio-economic factors.

    (D) The population of the nation-state must be formed before cultural societies can develop.

    (E) Defining a population is a simple sociological task.

45. Which of the following has been a sacred site for both Jews and Muslims?

    (A) Hagia Sophia in Istanbul

    (B) Angor Wat in Cambodia

    (C) The Holy Temple in Jerusalem

    (D) Church of the Holy Sepulchre in Jerusalem

    (E) Cumorah, New York

46. Which of the following areas of the brain is involved in control of reasoning and problem solving?

    (A) Hypothalamus

    (B) Thalamus

    (C) Frontal lobe

    (D) Pons

    (E) Medulla oblongata

47. Which of the following is NOT compatible with the traditional understanding of group dynamics?

    (A) Group therapy session

    (B) Online virtual communities

    (C) Small educational learning environments

    (D) Independent study

    (E) Youth groups and organizations

48. Which of the following is NOT compatible with the traditional conception of representative democracy?

    (A) The Electoral College

    (B) The Senate

    (C) The Executive Branch

    (D) The Judicial Branch

    (E) The House of Representatives

49. Of the following, which best represents affectional action?

    (A) Revenge

    (B) Conversation

    (C) Habit

    (D) Self-reflection

    (E) Custom

50. The most immediate consequence of the Balfour Declaration of 1917 was

(A) British support for a Jewish national homeland

(B) The creation of Israel

(C) The Seven Days War

(D) An armistice between Israel and Palestine

(E) British support for the Suez Canal

ANSWER KEY AND EXPLANATIONS

1. C	11. E	21. D	31. B	41. C
2. B	12. B	22. A	32. B	42. C
3. E	13. A	23. B	33. C	43. B
4. A	14. E	24. A	34. B	44. A
5. E	15. B	25. D	35. C	45. C
6. C	16. D	26. A	36. C	46. C
7. D	17. C	27. B	37. D	47. D
8. E	18. E	28. E	38. C	48. D
9. C	19. E	29. A	39. C	49. A
10. A	20. A	30. C	40. C	50. A

1. **The correct answer is (C).** A contour interval delineates land regions of varying elevation.

2. **The correct answer is (B).** Abigail Adams was an early proponent of women's rights who encouraged her husband, John Adams, to "remember the women" during the Continental Congress.

3. **The correct answer is (E).** The Marshall Plan provided economic aid to Greece and Turkey during the Cold War to bolster the national economy, thus making it better able to resist communism.

4. **The correct answer is (A).** The quotation reflects the economic and political views of John Maynard Keynes.

5. **The correct answer is (E).** Carrie Nation was a strong advocate of prohibition who advocated the use of violence to draw attention to the movement.

6. **The correct answer is (C).** The cultural relativism approach seeks to explain behavior and social customs within the context of an individual culture.

7. **The correct answer is (D).** The Gulf of Tonkin Resolution allowed President Johnson to use "conventional" levels of military force in Vietnam without a formal declaration of war.

8. **The correct answer is (E).** Alaska produces approximately 14 percent of the oil drilled domestically within the United States.

9. **The correct answer is (C).** Andrew Jackson is credited with starting a movement to lessen the power of Congress by expanding male suffrage and pushing for elections, not appointments, of judicial figures.

10. **The correct answer is (A).** The gross national product (GNP) is calculated using the market value of all goods and services produced within a country within a year.

11. **The correct answer is (E).** Homo sapiens feature a pronounced chin, a physical marker that has not been found on earlier forms of humans.

12. **The correct answer is (B).** As a result of the Wall Street Crash of 1929, the power of the federal government grew to encompass domestic relief programs, such as Medicare and Social Security.

13. **The correct answer is (A).** President Jimmy Carter led the United States in a boycott of the 1980 Olympics to protest the Soviet occupation of Afghanistan.

14. **The correct answer is (E).** Margaret Mitchell's novel *Gone with the Wind* is primarily set in the period immediately following the Civil War, which is known as Reconstruction.

15. **The correct answer is (B).** The Basques are a stateless nation, which is defined as a distinct cultural group without clearly defined political borders.

16. **The correct answer is (D).** The Camp David Accords established peaceful negotiations between Egypt and Israel to end the armed conflict between the two nations.

17. **The correct answer is (C).** The quotation reflects the philosophical outlook of Confucius.

18. **The correct answer is (E).** Bulgaria is the only country listed that did not experience a military revolution as a direct result of the fall of the Soviet Union in the late twentieth century.

19. **The correct answer is (E).** During the first and second century, the Roman Empire consolidated political and economic authority, thus uniting a vast geographic range under a single bureaucratic system.

20. **The correct answer is (A).** The United States maintained an official policy of isolation from the beginning of the Great War in 1914 until the sinking of the *Lusitania* provided a cause for U.S. entry in 1917.

21. **The correct answer is (D).** During the time period from 1580 to 1680, major public witchcraft trials were held in Scotland, North America, Germany, and Sweden.

22. **The correct answer is (A).** The concept of retaliatory aggression requires a perceived injury in order to take place.

23. **The correct answer is (B).** The Treaty of Maastricht finalized the European Union, a collective political decision-making body that guarantees free trade among its participants. While the Maastricht treaty also formalized the Euro, the United Kingdom chose not to participate in the universal currency.

24. **The correct answer is (A).** The statement is drawn from the Roosevelt Corollary, an addition to the Monroe Doctrine that allowed the United States to intervene in the political, economic, and social affairs of South American countries.

25. **The correct answer is (D).** Under the leadership of Alexander the Great, the Greek empire expanded to include parts of the Arabian Peninsula, Egypt, Macedonia, Anatolia, Judea, Gaza, and Punjab, India.

26. **The correct answer is (A).** The earliest form of imperialism in Australia was the forced relocation of convicts. Throughout the entire imperialistic history of Australia, conflicts ensued between settlers and indigenous populations, geographic exploration took place, and the scope of the territory marked was unprecedented.

27. **The correct answer is (B).** One of the fundamental changes that took place in the middle of the twentieth century was the gradual growth of suburban developments.

28. **The correct answer is (E).** Gentrification occurs when upper-class sections of the social stratification gradually replace lower-class sections.

29. **The correct answer is (A).** The back-to-Africa movement from the middle of the nineteenth century was organized by the American Colonization Society. This movement urged freed slaves to make their homes in Liberia.

30. **The correct answer is (C).** Alaska became part of the territorial holdings of the United States through "Seward's Folly," officially known as the Alaska Purchase.

31. **The correct answer is (B).** The Chinese participated in trade with Western Europe along the Silk Road, a connection that was also responsible for bringing paper and gunpowder to Europe.

32. **The correct answer is (B).** The rise of the Internet and social media sites has expanded the opportunity for everyday citizens to be involved in the political process.

33. **The correct answer is (C).** Political clientelism is not compatible with the traditional conception of a meritocracy because it rewards political alliances instead of personal merits.

34. **The correct answer is (B).** Erik Erikson was a neo-Freudian who argued that humans pass through nine stages of development and that their ultimate success in life was a result of the ego as a governing factor.

35. **The correct answer is (C).** The quality self-actualization refers to a state of mind wherein an individual is aware of his or her own potential and actively takes steps to reach that potential.

36. **The correct answer is (C).** The Electoral College of the United States checks and balances the election process to ensure that the final decision is fair, well balanced, and reflective of the desires of all people.

37. **The correct answer is (D).** The Fourth Amendment of the U.S. Constitution outlaws unreasonable search and seizure.

38. **The correct answer is (C).** Deviance is more actively defined, rooted out, and punished in homogeneous groups.

39. **The correct answer is (C).** A traveler going from point 1 to point 2 on the map would cross through the Alps.

40. **The correct answer is (C).** The area of the United States is approximately equal to half the size of Russia.

41. **The correct answer is (C).** The overthrow of Queen Liliuokalani in 1893 resulted in a loss of political and cultural sovereignty for the Hawaiian people due to increasing U.S. involvement in the area.

42. **The correct answer is (C).** The International Monetary Fund attempts to stabilize international exchange rates by offering conditional loans to poorer countries.

43. **The correct answer is (B).** The marginal utility of a good or service can be increased by allocation of the production schedule so that the supply keeps pace with the demand.

44. **The correct answer is (A).** Cultural factors, such as education, religion, and nationality, exercise a strong influence on the ways in which populations are formed and defined.

45. **The correct answer is (C).** The Holy Temple in Jerusalem has been a site of both a Jewish temple and a Muslim mosque.

46. **The correct answer is (C).** The frontal lobe is primarily responsible for the control of reasoning and problem solving.

47. **The correct answer is (D).** Individual study is not compatible with the traditional understanding of group dynamics because it does not rely on interaction with others for personal growth.

48. **The correct answer is (D).** The judicial branch is not compatible with the traditional conception of representative democracy because it features members who are appointed and not elected by the people.

49. **The correct answer is (A).** Affectional actions, such as revenge, are the result of unchecked emotions.

50. **The correct answer is (A).** The Balfour Declaration was a British proclamation promising government support for a Jewish national homeland.

PART VI

NATURAL SCIENCES

PRETEST ANSWER SHEET

1. Ⓐ Ⓑ Ⓒ Ⓓ Ⓔ	11. Ⓐ Ⓑ Ⓒ Ⓓ Ⓔ	21. Ⓐ Ⓑ Ⓒ Ⓓ Ⓔ	31. Ⓐ Ⓑ Ⓒ Ⓓ Ⓔ	41. Ⓐ Ⓑ Ⓒ Ⓓ Ⓔ
2. Ⓐ Ⓑ Ⓒ Ⓓ Ⓔ	12. Ⓐ Ⓑ Ⓒ Ⓓ Ⓔ	22. Ⓐ Ⓑ Ⓒ Ⓓ Ⓔ	32. Ⓐ Ⓑ Ⓒ Ⓓ Ⓔ	42. Ⓐ Ⓑ Ⓒ Ⓓ Ⓔ
3. Ⓐ Ⓑ Ⓒ Ⓓ Ⓔ	13. Ⓐ Ⓑ Ⓒ Ⓓ Ⓔ	23. Ⓐ Ⓑ Ⓒ Ⓓ Ⓔ	33. Ⓐ Ⓑ Ⓒ Ⓓ Ⓔ	43. Ⓐ Ⓑ Ⓒ Ⓓ Ⓕ
4. Ⓐ Ⓑ Ⓒ Ⓓ Ⓔ	14. Ⓐ Ⓑ Ⓒ Ⓓ Ⓔ	24. Ⓐ Ⓑ Ⓒ Ⓓ Ⓔ	34. Ⓐ Ⓑ Ⓒ Ⓓ Ⓔ	44. Ⓐ Ⓑ Ⓒ Ⓓ Ⓔ
5. Ⓐ Ⓑ Ⓒ Ⓓ Ⓔ	15. Ⓐ Ⓑ Ⓒ Ⓓ Ⓔ	25. Ⓐ Ⓑ Ⓒ Ⓓ Ⓔ	35. Ⓐ Ⓑ Ⓒ Ⓓ Ⓔ	45. Ⓐ Ⓑ Ⓒ Ⓓ Ⓔ
6. Ⓐ Ⓑ Ⓒ Ⓓ Ⓔ	16. Ⓐ Ⓑ Ⓒ Ⓓ Ⓔ	26. Ⓐ Ⓑ Ⓒ Ⓓ Ⓔ	36. Ⓐ Ⓑ Ⓒ Ⓓ Ⓔ	46. Ⓐ Ⓑ Ⓒ Ⓓ Ⓔ
7. Ⓐ Ⓑ Ⓒ Ⓓ Ⓔ	17. Ⓐ Ⓑ Ⓒ Ⓓ Ⓔ	27. Ⓐ Ⓑ Ⓒ Ⓓ Ⓔ	37. Ⓐ Ⓑ Ⓒ Ⓓ Ⓔ	47. Ⓐ Ⓑ Ⓒ Ⓓ Ⓔ
8. Ⓐ Ⓑ Ⓒ Ⓓ Ⓔ	18. Ⓐ Ⓑ Ⓒ Ⓓ Ⓔ	28. Ⓐ Ⓑ Ⓒ Ⓓ Ⓔ	38. Ⓐ Ⓑ Ⓒ Ⓓ Ⓔ	48. Ⓐ Ⓑ Ⓒ Ⓓ Ⓔ
9. Ⓐ Ⓑ Ⓒ Ⓓ Ⓔ	19. Ⓐ Ⓑ Ⓒ Ⓓ Ⓔ	29. Ⓐ Ⓑ Ⓒ Ⓓ Ⓔ	39. Ⓐ Ⓑ Ⓒ Ⓓ Ⓔ	49. Ⓐ Ⓑ Ⓒ Ⓓ Ⓔ
10. Ⓐ Ⓑ Ⓒ Ⓓ Ⓔ	20. Ⓐ Ⓑ Ⓒ Ⓓ Ⓔ	30. Ⓐ Ⓑ Ⓒ Ⓓ Ⓔ	40. Ⓐ Ⓑ Ⓒ Ⓓ Ⓔ	50. Ⓐ Ⓑ Ⓒ Ⓓ Ⓔ

answer sheet

Pretest

40 minutes • 50 questions

Directions: Each of the questions or incomplete statements below is followed by five suggested answers or completions. Select the one that is best in each case.

1. All of the following organs are part of the digestive system EXCEPT the
   (A) mouth
   (B) stomach
   (C) liver
   (D) intestines
   (E) kidneys

2. Which of the following are characteristics of eukaryotic cells?
   I. They typically produce through simple fission.
   II. They are usually between 1 and 2 micrometers in size.
   III. Genetic material is contained in a nucleus.
   (A) I only
   (B) II only
   (C) III only
   (D) I and II only
   (E) II and III only

3. During prenatal development in mammals, which of the following forms immediately after the morula?
   (A) Zygote
   (B) Blastocyst
   (C) Embryo
   (D) Fetus
   (E) Neonate

4. Which of the following is true of the theory of evolution known as punctuated equilibrium?
   I. It theorizes that organisms are constantly, slowly evolving.
   II. It posits that changes are caused by gene mutations.
   III. It may explain new structures that appear suddenly.
   (A) I only
   (B) II only
   (C) III only
   (D) I and II only
   (E) II and III only

5. A person driving in a car travels at a speed of 45 km/hour for 4 hours. The person then turns the car around and drives in the opposite direction at a speed of 55 km/hour for 1.5 hours. What is the car's total displacement in kilometers?
   (A) 5.5
   (B) 47.7
   (C) 97.5
   (D) 195.0
   (E) 262.5

6. Which of the following is the geological time period during which life forms first appeared and oxygen became part of Earth's atmosphere?
   (A) Precambrian
   (B) Quaternary
   (C) Devonian
   (D) Triassic
   (E) Tertiary

7. The name of the cell organelle that carries out protein synthesis is
   (A) chloroplast
   (B) mitochondria
   (C) ribosome
   (D) lysosome
   (E) cytoskeleton

8. If a man with a recessive X-linked trait and a female carrier reproduce, which of the following statements is true?
   (A) All male offspring will be carriers of the recessive gene.
   (B) All male offspring will be homozygous for the recessive gene.
   (C) There is a 50 percent chance that male offspring will exhibit the trait.
   (D) There is no chance that female offspring will exhibit the trait.
   (E) There is a 50 percent chance that female offspring will be homozygous dominant.

9. The sun in our solar system is a
   (A) blue dwarf star
   (B) brown dwarf star
   (C) white dwarf star
   (D) red dwarf star
   (E) yellow dwarf star

10. Two species of cacti in the same desert are similar in appearance. If these plant species are unrelated, the theory that BEST explains why they are similar is
   (A) gradualism
   (B) divergent evolution
   (C) speciation
   (D) convergent evolution
   (E) punctuated equilibrium

11. Which of the following is true of electrons?
   I. They have a negative charge.
   II. They are found in the nucleus.
   III. They are heavier than protons.
   (A) I only
   (B) II only
   (C) III only
   (D) I and II only
   (E) II and III only

12. Which of the following components of the immune system produces antibodies?
   (A) Thymus
   (B) White blood cells
   (C) Spleen
   (D) Red blood cells
   (E) Bone marrow

13. A population of deer inhabits a forest in a temperate region of the United States. The maximum number of deer the forest can support with its resources is known as the
   (A) limiting factor
   (B) carrying capacity
   (C) population density
   (D) density-dependent capacity
   (E) density-independent factor

14. Which of the following layers of Earth's atmosphere is where the coldest spot on Earth can be found?
   (A) Exosphere
   (B) Thermosphere
   (C) Mesosphere
   (D) Stratosphere
   (E) Troposphere

15. If a trait is recessive, a parent that is heterozygous and one that is homozygous for the recessive gene could produce offspring with which of the following genotypes?
   I. Homozygous recessive
   II. Heterozygous
   III. Homozygous dominant
   (A) I only
   (B) II only
   (C) III only
   (D) I and II only
   (E) II and III only

16. The sun's energy is produced mainly through a nuclear fusion reaction in which hydrogen is converted to
   (A) sodium
   (B) carbon
   (C) nitrogen
   (D) oxygen
   (E) helium

17. All of the following are true of organisms that belong to the kingdom Protista EXCEPT

    (A) most are multicellular

    (B) some are autotrophs

    (C) they are eukaryotic

    (D) some are fungi

    (E) they are found mainly on land

18. Which of the following is true of the elementary particles known as quarks?
    I. They are also known as hadrons.
    II. The different types are called flavors.
    III. They are positively charged.

    (A) I only

    (B) II only

    (C) III only

    (D) I and II only

    (E) II and III only

19. Which of the following biological classifications is more general than order and more specific than kingdom?

    (A) Domain

    (B) Family

    (C) Genus

    (D) Phylum

    (E) Species

20. Which of the following is true of the nucleus of an atom?
    I. It has a neutral charge.
    II. It is surrounded by an electron cloud.
    III. It represents about one-tenth of the atom's total size.

    (A) I only

    (B) II only

    (C) III only

    (D) I and II only

    (E) II and III only

21. Which of the following terms describes the chemical reaction shown below?

    $P_2O_5 + 3H_2O \rightarrow 2H_3PO_4$

    (A) Synthesis

    (B) Single displacement

    (C) Decomposition

    (D) Double displacement

    (E) Acid-base

22. Which of the following would be the complementary DNA strand for the following DNA sequence: ACG?

    (A) GCA

    (B) TGC

    (C) UGC

    (D) TCG

    (E) UCG

23. A rocket ship is traveling through space at a speed of 5000 miles/hour. Someone inside a second rocket ship traveling toward the first ship at a speed of 3000 miles/hour turns on a flashlight. According to the theory of special relativity, what would be the measured speed of the flashlight beam if the measurement was taken by the observers in the first ship? (The speed of light is 669,600,000 miles/hour.)

    (A) 669,595,000 miles per hour

    (B) 669,597,000 miles per hour

    (C) 669,600,000 miles per hour

    (D) 669,603,000 miles per hour

    (E) 669,605,000 miles per hour

24. All of the following are examples of density-independent factors that could limit the growth of a population of squirrels EXCEPT

    (A) a water shortage due to drought

    (B) a flood or hurricane

    (C) humans cutting down trees

    (D) increased competition for food

    (E) a food shortage due to snow

25. The general form of a double displacement reaction is

    (A) $A + B \rightarrow AB$

    (B) $AB \rightarrow A + B$

    (C) $A + BC \rightarrow AC + B$

    (D) $AB + CD \rightarrow AC + BD$

    (E) $HA + BOH \rightarrow H_2O + BA$

26. When biologists study populations, they typically classify organisms as *r* strategists or *K* strategists. Which of the following is true of *r* strategists?

  I. They have long life spans.

  II. They have low rates of infant mortality.

  III. They can reproduce rapidly.

(A) I only

(B) II only

(C) III only

(D) I and II only

(E) II and III only

27. All of the following statements are true of metamorphic rocks EXCEPT

(A) marble and slate are types of metamorphic rock

(B) they are exposed to high temperatures as they develop

(C) tectonic movement can lead to their creation

(D) they are formed from other types of rocks, such as igneous

(E) the minerals they contain are arranged in crystal form

28. Starfish belong to the phylum

(A) Echinodermata

(B) Arthropoda

(C) Chordata

(D) Porifera

(E) Platyhelminthes

29. A blue flower with the genotype BB and a red flower with the genotype RR are cross-pollinated during an experiment. If the type of inheritance is incomplete dominance, which color(s) could the offspring be?

  I. Purple

  II. Blue

  III. Blue with red tips

(A) I only

(B) II only

(C) III only

(D) I and II only

(E) II and III only

30. A scientist is studying an unknown chemical compound. The scientist observes that the compound has a high melting point and dissolves in water. This compound is most likely held together by which of the following types of bonds?

(A) Multi-metallic

(B) Polar covalent

(C) Metallic

(D) Covalent

(E) Ionic

31. All of the following are true of liquids EXCEPT

(A) their shape can be altered

(B) the particles they contain touch

(C) they are denser than gases

(D) they exhibit surface tension

(E) their volume is changeable

32. Which of the following properties of sound is determined in part by the frequency of a sound wave?

(A) Wavelength

(B) Amplitude

(C) Tone

(D) Volume

(E) Pitch

33. The deepest layer of the epidermis where new skin cells are produced is the

(A) stratum corneum

(B) stratum germinativum

(C) stratum granulosum

(D) stratum lucidum

(E) stratum spinosum

34. Carbon has a number of isotopes, including C-14 and C-19. How many protons are in an atom of C-14?

(A) 6

(B) 8

(C) 14

(D) 19

(E) 20

35. Yeast is placed in a container, and culture is added. If the population size is recorded over time and the data is plotted on a graph, the curve will likely be

    (A) parabolic
    (B) exponential
    (C) linear
    (D) sinusoidal
    (E) sigmoid

36. A snowball is thrown straight up in the air at a speed of 1.8 meters/second. How long will it take for the snowball to fall back to the ground?

    (A) 0.18 seconds
    (B) 0.36 seconds
    (C) 0.90 seconds
    (D) 1.8 seconds
    (E) 5.4 seconds

37. According to the Ideal Gas Law, how many moles of gas would be in a 100-liter container if the pressure was 2375 kPa and the temperature was 42 °C? (R = 8.314 J K^{-1} mol^{-1})

    (A) 0.63
    (B) 1.59
    (C) 17.9
    (D) 42.0
    (E) 90.7

38. Which of the following describes the main difference between meiosis and mitosis?

    (A) Meiosis produces somatic cells.
    (B) Mitosis is composed of more phases.
    (C) Meiosis produces fewer daughter cells.
    (D) Mitosis results in daughter cells that are haploid.
    (E) Meiosis results in daughter cells that are haploid.

39. Which of the following moon phases immediately follows a first quarter moon?

    (A) Waxing crescent
    (B) New
    (C) Waning crescent
    (D) Full
    (E) Waxing gibbous

40. Which of the following land features is a narrow section of land that joins two larger land forms?

    (A) Cove
    (B) Headland
    (C) Fjord
    (D) Isthmus
    (E) Peninsula

41. Heterotrophs obtain the energy needed by the cells to produce ATP by

    (A) ingesting organic compounds
    (B) oxidizing minerals
    (C) fixing nitrogen
    (D) converting light energy
    (E) breaking down fats

42. Which of the following hormones released by the hypothalamus gland triggers the onset of puberty in females?

    (A) GnRH
    (B) LH
    (C) FSH
    (D) HCG
    (E) DHEA

43. Which of the following statements are true of oceanic trenches found on the seafloor?

    I. They are submarine volcanoes.
    II. They are the result of tectonic subduction zones.
    III. They are the deepest parts of the ocean.

    (A) I only
    (B) II only
    (C) III only
    (D) I and II only
    (E) II and III only

44. If a large population of plants decreased in size due to weather conditions, populations belonging to which of the following categories would be affected first?

    (A) Producers
    (B) Decomposers
    (C) Primary consumers
    (D) Secondary consumers
    (E) Tertiary consumers

45. Which of the following planets has an atmosphere composed of hydrogen, helium, and methane; has a rotation time of 16 hours; and has 13 known moons?

    (A) Neptune

    (B) Uranus

    (C) Saturn

    (D) Jupiter

    (E) Mercury

46. The specific heat capacity of a metal is 2.3 Joules/g°C. If 349 Joules of heat are added to the system and the temperature of the metal increases from 19°C to 57°C, what is the mass of the metal sample?

    (A) 2.66 grams

    (B) 3.99 grams

    (C) 5.44 grams

    (D) 7.99 grams

    (E) 9.22 grams

47. In humans, the portion of the sperm cell that has digestive enzymes that aid in penetration of the ovum is the

    (A) plasma membrane

    (B) acrosome

    (C) nucleus

    (D) mitochondria

    (E) flagellum

48. What is the balanced equation for the chemical reaction shown below?

    $$C_6H_5COOH + O_2 \rightarrow CO_2 + H_2O$$

    (A) $2\ C_6H_5COOH + O_2 \rightarrow CO_2 + H_2O$

    (B) $2\ C_6H_5COOH + O_2 \rightarrow 14\ CO_2 + H_2O$

    (C) $2\ C_6H_5COOH + 15\ O_2 \rightarrow 14\ CO_2 + 6\ H_2O$

    (D) $2\ C_6H_5COOH + 14\ O_2 \rightarrow 15\ CO_2 + 6\ H_2O$

    (E) $2\ C_6H_5COOH + 6\ O_2 \rightarrow 14\ CO_2 + 3\ H_2O$

49. The unit used to measure electricity that is defined as the electrical current due to electrons with a certain charge moving past a given point in 1 second is

    (A) wattage

    (B) volt

    (C) electromotive force

    (D) coulomb

    (E) ampere

50. In humans, which of the following changes have occurred by four weeks after fertilization?

    I. The lymph glands have developed.

    II. The sex can be determined.

    III. The neural tube has begun to form.

    (A) I only

    (B) II only

    (C) III only

    (D) I and II only

    (E) II and III only

ANSWER KEY AND EXPLANATIONS

1. E	11. A	21. A	31. E	41. A
2. C	12. B	22. B	32. E	42. A
3. B	13. B	23. C	33. B	43. E
4. E	14. C	24. D	34. A	44. C
5. C	15. D	25. D	35. E	45. A
6. A	16. E	26. C	36. B	46. B
7. C	17. D	27. E	37. E	47. B
8. C	18. B	28. A	38. E	48. C
9. E	19. D	29. A	39. A	49. E
10. D	20. B	30. E	40. D	50. C

1. **The correct answer is (E).** The organs of the digestive system secrete enzymes to break down nutrients in food into forms that can be used by the body. This system includes the mouth, esophagus, stomach, large intestine, small intestine, and liver; the kidneys are part of the excretory system.

2. **The correct answer is (C).** Eukaryotic cells contain a nucleus, a structure that is absent in prokaryotic cells. The other two statements are true of prokaryotic cells; eukaryotic cells reproduce through mitosis or meiosis and are usually between 5 and 100 micrometers in size.

3. **The correct answer is (B).** After fertilization, the early stages of prenatal development occur in the following order: zygote, morula, blastocyst, and embryo. The fetal stage occurs after the embryonic stage, and a neonate is a newborn.

4. **The correct answer is (E).** The two major theories of how evolution occurs are punctuated equilibrium and gradualism. Punctuated equilibrium is the theory that change (which may include the emergence of new structures) occurs rapidly due to gene mutations; gradualism is the theory that organisms are constantly evolving at a slow rate.

5. **The correct answer is (C).** The car traveled 180 kilometers (45 km/hour × 4 hours = 180 km) in one direction and 82.5 kilometers (55 km/hour × 1.5 hours = 82.5 km) in the opposite direction, so the total displacement (the distance from the starting point) is the difference between the two distances (180 kilometers – 82.5 kilometers = 97.5 km).

6. **The correct answer is (A).** The Precambrian period ended approximately 544 million years ago and is the period when the moon formed, the Earth cooled, and prokaryotes and then eukaryotes appeared. The Quaternary period is the one we are in now, the Devonian period is when ferns appeared and amphibians evolved, the Triassic period marked the first appearance of dinosaurs, and the Tertiary period was when the earliest primates appeared.

7. **The correct answer is (C).** A single cell contains thousands of ribosomes that manufacture proteins. A chloroplast is an organelle in plant cells that aids in photosynthesis, the mitochondria are involved in energy production, the lysosomes assist with digestion and waste removal, and the cytoskeleton helps support the cell.

8. **The correct answer is (C).** If a man with a recessive X-linked trait (XtY) and a female carrier (XtXT) reproduce, their offspring would have the following genotypes: XTXt, XtXt, XTY, and XtY. There is a 50 percent

chance that male offspring will inherit the trait; these offspring will also exhibit the trait since there is no gene on the Y chromosome.

9. **The correct answer is (E).** The sun is a yellow dwarf, which is a young, main sequence star that is relatively small. Red dwarfs have relatively cool surface temperatures, white and brown dwarf stars are quite faint, and there are no blue dwarf stars (only blue giants).

10. **The correct answer is (D).** Convergent evolution is the theory that unrelated species become more similar over time if they inhabit the same type of environment, while divergent evolution suggests that related species become more dissimilar over time if they inhabit different environments. Gradualism and punctuated equilibrium are theories of how evolution occurs, and speciation refers to the emergence of new species.

11. **The correct answer is (A).** Electrons have a negative charge, protons have a positive charge, and neutrons do not carry a charge. Electrons are much smaller and lighter than protons, and they orbit the nucleus of an atom.

12. **The correct answer is (B).** Antibodies produced by white blood cells have a Y shape and bind to pathogens such as bacteria and viruses to aid in their destruction and removal. Red and white blood cells are produced by bone marrow, the thymus produces T cells, and the spleen's role is blood filtration.

13. **The correct answer is (B).** An environment's carrying capacity is the maximum number of individuals that that environment can support. A limiting factor is what stops a population from continuing to grow, population density is a measure of the number of individuals in a given area, and both density-dependent and density-independent factors limit the growth of populations.

14. **The correct answer is (C).** The mesosphere is the middle layer of Earth's atmosphere and extends to between 80 and 85 kilometers above Earth's surface. At the very top of this layer—a region known as the mesopause—is the coldest place on Earth (temperatures can plummet below –90°C).

15. **The correct answer is (D).** Using a Punnett square, it can be determined that a homozygous recessive parent (gg) and a heterozygous parent (Gg) would produce offspring with the following genotypes: Gg, Gg, gg, and gg. There is no chance that any of the offspring would inherit two copies of the dominant gene (G).

16. **The correct answer is (E).** In the nuclear fusion reaction in the sun that produces the vast majority (85 percent) of the sun's energy, two hydrogen atoms combine to produce helium. The hydrogen atoms weigh more than the helium produced, so the mass not consumed in the reaction is released as energy.

17. **The correct answer is (D).** The kingdom Protista consists of organisms that cannot be placed in the other kingdoms; there are no fungi, plants, or animals in this group. Protists are typically unicellular, are heterotrophs or autotrophs, are all eukaryotic, and are typically found in water.

18. **The correct answer is (B).** Hadrons, which include protons and neutrons, are composed of quarks. Quarks can have a charge of $-\frac{1}{3}$ or $+\frac{2}{3}$, and there are six different flavors: up, down, top, bottom, charm, and strange.

19. **The correct answer is (D).** The biological classifications, from most general to most specific, are as follows: life, domain, kingdom, phylum, class, order, family, genus, and species. Phylum and class are the only classifications that meet the criteria presented in the question, and only phylum is one of the answer choices.

20. **The correct answer is (B).** The nucleus represents less than one ten-thousandth of the atom's total size and is positively charged, since it is composed of protons and neutrons. The nucleus of an atom is surrounded by a dispersed electron cloud.

21. **The correct answer is (A).** A synthesis reaction is when a single, more complex

compound is formed from two (or more) simpler ones. Single and double displacement reactions are characterized by elements or ions that change positions during the reaction; a decomposition reaction involves a single, complex compound breaking down into simpler compounds or elements; and acid-base reactions produce water and ionic salts.

22. **The correct answer is (B).** In DNA, the nucleotide thymine always bonds to adenine, while cytosine always bonds to guanine. RNA contains uracil instead of thymine and always bonds to adenine.

23. **The correct answer is (C).** The theory of special relativity states that the speed of light is constant and absolute, and the measurement of this value is not influenced by an observer's frame of reference. Therefore, neither the speed of the first rocket ship nor the one approaching it will affect the measurement taken by the observers in the first ship.

24. **The correct answer is (D).** Density-independent factors can limit population growth but do not depend on the size of a population (examples are human activities, weather, and natural disasters). Density-dependent factors are influenced by population size; in this example more squirrels means increased competition for food, which will likely limit population growth.

25. **The correct answer is (D).** In a double replacement reaction, two new compounds are formed when ions are exchanged between the two reactants (an example is the reaction $AgNO_3$ + HCl → AgCl + HNO_3). Choice (A) is the general formula for a synthesis reaction, choice (B) is the formula for a decomposition reaction, choice (C) is the formula for a single displacement reaction, and choice (E) is the formula for an acid-base reaction.

26. **The correct answer is (C).** The approach of *r* strategists is to maximize their rate of growth; common traits are short gestation periods yielding large numbers of offspring, short life spans, and high rates of infant mortality. *K* strategists maintain stable population numbers over time so that they do not exceed the carrying capacity (*K*) of the environments in which they live.

27. **The correct answer is (E).** Metamorphic rocks (including marble and slate) are rocks that have had their structure and composition altered through intense heat and pressure, which can be the result of tectonic processes or their location far beneath Earth's surface. Igneous rocks are composed of minerals that are in the form of small or large crystals.

28. **The correct answer is (A).** Members of this kingdom are found exclusively in saltwater habitats and include starfish, sea urchins, and sea cucumbers. The phylum Arthropoda includes insects and spiders, Chordata includes mammals, Porifera includes sponges, and Platyhelminthes includes flatworms.

29. **The correct answer is (A).** Incomplete dominance is a type of inheritance in which the phenotype of offspring is a blend, or combination, of the phenotypes of the parents (red and blue combine to create purple in this example). If the resultant offspring were blue flowers with red tips, this would be an example of codominance.

30. **The correct answer is (E).** Ionic bonds develop between metals and nonmetals and involve the transfer of electrons. Compounds with ionic bonds have high melting points, usually dissolve in water, are brittle, and are good conductors of electricity.

31. **The correct answer is (E).** Liquids can change their shape and conform to that of a container, have particles that touch, have higher densities than gases since particles are packed closer together, and form a thin film on their surface that is known as surface tension. Although liquids can change their shape, their volume is constant.

32. **The correct answer is (E).** Sound waves with high frequencies are perceived as higher-pitched sounds (if they are within the range detectable by the human ear). Wavelength and amplitude are properties of sound waves as opposed to perceived sounds, and volume is determined by the amplitude of a wave.

33. **The correct answer is (B).** The five layers of the epidermis from the most superficial to the deepest are stratum corneum, stratum lucidum, stratum granulosum, stratum spinosum, and stratum germinativum (also known as stratum basale). New cells are produced in the deepest region through mitosis and gradually move toward the surface of the skin as they mature.

34. **The correct answer is (A).** The atomic number indicates the number of protons in an atom; according to the periodic table, carbon has 6. Isotopes are different forms of elements that contain varying numbers of neutrons; the number of protons remains the same.

35. **The correct answer is (E).** The population of yeast will increase quickly at first, but the growth rate will decrease and reach zero as the food source (the culture) is consumed. Therefore, the curve will have a sigmoid, or S, shape.

36. **The correct answer is (B).** The formula $V_f = V_i + at$ can be used to calculate the correct answer. The initial velocity is known, the acceleration of gravity (a) is a constant (-9.8 m/s^2), and the velocity of the snowball at its highest point is 0 m/s.

$$V_f = V_i + at$$

$$0 = 1.8 \text{ m/s} + (-9.8 \text{ m/s}^2 t)$$

$$-1.8 \text{ m/s} = -9.8 \text{ m/s}^2 t$$

$$0.18 \text{ s} = t$$

This is the time it takes for the snowball to reach its highest point; multiply the value by 2 to calculate the time it takes to return to its original position (0.18 s $\times$ 2 = 0.36 s).

37. **The correct answer is (E).** The Ideal Gas Law is represented by the equation $PV = nRT$; isolate n (number of moles) to make it easier to solve $\left(\frac{PV}{RT} = n\right)$. Convert the temperature to Kelvin ($42 + 273 = 315$ Kelvin) and plug in the known values to solve for n:

$$n = \left(\frac{2375 \text{ kPa} \times 100 \text{ L}}{8.314 \text{ J K}^{-1} \text{ mL}^{-1} \times 315 \text{ K}}\right)$$

$$n = 90.7 \text{ moles}$$

38. **The correct answer is (E).** Meiosis produces four haploid daughter cells, which means they contain one set of chromosomes. Mitosis produces diploid cells, meiosis results in more daughter cells than mitosis, meiosis has more phases, and meiosis is the process that produces gametes.

39. **The correct answer is (A).** In order, the phases of the moon following the first quarter phase are waxing crescent, new, waning crescent, third quarter, waning gibbous, full, and waxing gibbous. The completion of all of these phases takes about 30 days.

40. **The correct answer is (D).** An example of an isthmus is the Isthmus of Panama, which connects the Americas; both sides of these land strips are typically surrounded by water. A cove is a small bay, a headland is a piece of land that is typically high and ends abruptly, a fjord is an inlet surrounded by cliffs, and a peninsula is a section of land that is surrounded by water but connected to a larger piece of land.

41. **The correct answer is (A).** Humans are heterotrophs and must obtain energy for cells by consuming carbon-based food sources that contain protein, fat, and carbohydrates. Lithotrophs can convert nitrates and sulphur into usable energy, and autotrophs such as trees can create their own energy through photosynthesis and other chemical reactions.

42. **The correct answer is (A).** GnRH released by the hypothalamus stimulates the release of LH and FSH from the pituitary, which bring about the developmental changes associated with puberty, including the start of menstruation. HCG is released during pregnancy; DHEA is a steroid hormone but is not responsible for the onset of puberty.

43. **The correct answer is (E).** The deepest oceanic trenches are approximately 10 kilometers below sea level and are created when tectonic plates meet and subduction (one plate slides under the other) occurs as a result. Submarine volcanoes are known as guyots and seamounts.

44. **The correct answer is (C).** While secondary and tertiary consumers would eventually be affected, primary consumers (the organisms that rely on plants for food) would be affected first. Plants are producers, and decomposers such as bacteria break down dead plant and animal matter.

45. **The correct answer is (A).** Other characteristics of this eighth planet from the sun include the following: its average temperature is colder than −200°C, it is blue in color, it has five thin rings, and it takes about 165 years to revolve around the sun once.

46. **The correct answer is (B).** To get the correct answer, use the formula $Q = mc\Delta t$ and insert the provided values:

$$Q = mc\Delta t$$

$$349 \text{ Joules} = m(2.3 \text{ Joules/g}^\circ\text{C} \times 38^\circ\text{C})$$

$$\frac{349 \text{ Joules}}{(2.3 \text{ Joules/g}^\circ\text{C} \times 38^\circ\text{C})} = m$$

$$3.99 \text{ grams} = m$$

If you used 19°C as the value for Δt, you would have gotten choice (D), 7.99 grams. If you used 57°C as the value for Δt, you would have arrived at choice (A), 2.66 grams.

47. **The correct answer is (B).** The head of a sperm cell is composed of the plasma membrane, nucleus, and acrosome, the latter of which aids in fertilization by secreting enzymes that help penetrate the ovum. The midpiece is where spiral-shaped mitochondria are found, and the flagellum is a long tail responsible for sperm cell movement.

48. **The correct answer is (C).** A balanced equation has an equal number of atoms of each element on both sides. In answer choice (C), the number of atoms of each element on the right side and the left side of the equation are the same (14 carbon, 12 hydrogen, and 34 oxygen).

49. **The correct answer is (E).** An ampere is the unit used to measure current, and 1 amp is the electrical current generated by a group of electrons with a 1-coulomb charge as they move past a fixed point. Wattage is a measure of power, and volts are used to measure electromotive force.

50. **The correct answer is (C).** Just some of the changes that have occurred four weeks after fertilization include the start of neural tube formation, the formation of the neural plate and notochord, and the appearance of the liver bud. The lymph glands develop and the sex of the fetus can be determined by about three months after fertilization.

OVERVIEW ANSWER SHEET

1. Ⓐ Ⓑ Ⓒ Ⓓ Ⓔ   5. Ⓐ Ⓑ Ⓒ Ⓓ Ⓔ   9. Ⓐ Ⓑ Ⓒ Ⓓ Ⓔ   13. Ⓐ Ⓑ Ⓒ Ⓓ Ⓔ   17. Ⓐ Ⓑ Ⓒ Ⓓ Ⓔ

2. Ⓐ Ⓑ Ⓒ Ⓓ Ⓔ   6. Ⓐ Ⓑ Ⓒ Ⓓ Ⓔ   10. Ⓐ Ⓑ Ⓒ Ⓓ Ⓔ   14. Ⓐ Ⓑ Ⓒ Ⓓ Ⓕ   18. Ⓐ Ⓑ Ⓒ Ⓓ Ⓔ

3. Ⓐ Ⓑ Ⓒ Ⓓ Ⓔ   7. Ⓐ Ⓑ Ⓒ Ⓓ Ⓔ   11. Ⓐ Ⓑ Ⓒ Ⓓ Ⓔ   15. Ⓐ Ⓑ Ⓒ Ⓓ Ⓔ   19. Ⓐ Ⓑ Ⓒ Ⓓ Ⓔ

4. Ⓐ Ⓑ Ⓒ Ⓓ Ⓔ   8. Ⓐ Ⓑ Ⓒ Ⓓ Ⓔ   12. Ⓐ Ⓑ Ⓒ Ⓓ Ⓔ   16. Ⓐ Ⓑ Ⓒ Ⓓ Ⓔ   20. Ⓐ Ⓑ Ⓒ Ⓓ Ⓔ

answer sheet

Overview

The CLEP Natural Sciences test assesses your ability to understand and apply the scientific concepts you would encounter in introductory-level college science courses for non-science majors. You don't need knowledge of advanced scientific concepts to score well on this test.

The specific content of this exam is based on materials drawn from typical introductory-level college courses related to these subjects. You will have 90 minutes to answer the approximately 120 questions of the test.

The problems on the CLEP Natural Sciences test can be grouped into two basic categories:

1. Biological Sciences (50 percent of the questions on the test)
2. Physical Sciences (50 percent of the questions on the test)

Preparing for the CLEP Natural Sciences test can be difficult. Since the exam includes topics in both biological and physical sciences, you will have a considerable amount of material to review. While this book will provide you with a basic overview of the topics covered on the exam, you will most likely want to take some time to review some biology, chemistry, and physics textbooks for a more in-depth review.

Again, the test is comprised of approximately 120 questions. Questions are broken down into the following categories:

Evolution and Classification (10 percent or 12 questions)

- The origin of life
- Taxonomy and classification
- Geologic ages
- Evolution

Cellular and Molecular Biology (10 percent or 12 questions)

- Cell structure
- Protein synthesis
- Biochemical reactions
- Respiration
- Photosynthesis
- Cell cycle

Organisms and Heredity (20 percent or 24 questions)

- Digestion
- Respiration and Circulation
- Nervous and Endocrine

- Muscle and Skeletal
- Reproductive system
- Meiosis
- Heredity and traits

Ecology and Population Biology (10 percent or 12 questions)

- Ecosystems
- Biomes
- Population structure

The Atom (7 percent or 8 questions)

- Atomic and nuclear structure and properties
- Elementary particles
- Nuclear reactions

Elements and Reactions (10 percent or 12 questions)

- Chemical elements
- Compounds and reactions
- Molecular structure and bonding

Thermodynamics, Mechanics, and Relativity (12 percent or 14 questions)

- Heat, thermodynamics, and states of matter
- Classical mechanics
- Relativity

Electromagnetism and Wave Phenomena (4 percent or 5 questions)

- Electricity and magnetism
- Waves, light, and sound

The Structure of the Universe (7 percent or 8 questions)

- Galaxies
- Stars
- The solar system

Earth's History and Systems (10 percent or 12 questions)

- Atmosphere
- Hydrosphere
- Structure features
- Geologic processes
- History

BIOLOGICAL SCIENCES

Origin, Evolution, and Classification of Life

About 12 questions on the CLEP Natural Sciences test will be about the origin, evolution, and classification of living organisms.

Earth is approximately 4.6 billion years old, and life has existed on it for 3.5 billion years. Life arose in conditions very different from today—a reducing atmosphere and oceans filled with organic molecules. These organic compounds, precursors of life, are thought to have formed from simpler molecules. Scientists Miller and Urey tested this hypothesis by setting up a closed flask containing the gases and compounds thought to have been present on the early Earth. Simulating lightning in this closed system produced amino acids and hydrocarbons—building blocks of more-complex organic molecules.

GEOLOGIC TIMELINE

Eon (Millions of Years Ago)	Era (Millions of Years Ago)	Key Events
Phanerozoic 543–present	Cenozoic 65.5–present	Genus *Homo* appears Mammals, birds, and pollinating insects, and angiosperms diversify
	Mesozoic 251–65.5	Major extinction event (dinosaurs) Angiosperms (flowering seed plants) appear Earliest mammal-like creatures appear Dinosaurs and gymnosperms diversify
	Paleozoic 543–251	Major extinction event Reptiles and insects diversify Gymnosperms (seed plants) appear Vascular plants cover land Tetrapods and insects appear Bony fishes diversify Vascular plants diversify Plants and arthropods colonize land Cambrian "explosion" of animal phyla
Proterozoic 2500–543		Fossils of soft-bodied animals and algae (600) Oldest eukaryotic fossils (2200)
Archean 4600–2500		Atmospheric oxygen increases (2700) Oldest prokaryotic fossils (3500) Oldest rocks (3800)

Classification

All living things are divided into three broad domains, corresponding to structural and functional cell differences. These divisions arose early in Earth's history.

- **Eubacteria:** These "true" bacteria are simple cells that contain circular chromosomes floating free in the cytoplasm, surrounded by a cell membrane and a cell wall.

- **Archaea:** While archeans were previously grouped with bacteria, more recent findings suggest that they are very different and share certain features with eukaryotes. Many Archeans are extremeophiles, thriving in conditions of extreme temperature, salinity, pH, or pressure.

- **Eukarya:** Much larger than prokaryotes, eukaryotic cells have membrane-bound organelles, linear DNA coiled around histone proteins and contained in a nucleus, and introns.

Though it is currently subject to debate and modification as new evidence is discovered, the five-kingdom system is still widely used.

- **Prokarya:** Archaea and eubacteria

- **Protista:** This is a catch-all category for eukaryotes that fail to qualify for any of the kingdoms below, and the relationships among different groups of protists is not well known; both single-celled and multicellular algae are classified as protists rather than plants.

- **Fungi:** This kingdom includes both single-celled and multicellular eukaryotes: the yeasts used in baking and brewing and the macroscopic mushrooms found in the supermarket are all fungi. Fungi digest their food outside the cell, and many species are saprophytes or decomposers.

- **Plantae:** Multicellular, complex photosynthetic organisms, plants range from mosses to redwoods; all plant cells contain chloroplasts and are capable of photosynthesis.

- **Animalae:** Multicellular, complex heterotrophs, animals include a diversity of body plans.

Every organism has a unique scientific name consisting of a genus and a species (e.g., *Homo sapiens*). A genus may contain more than one species.

Just as a species belongs to a larger category called a genus, each genus belongs to an even larger category called a family, which in turn belongs to an order, and so on, in a hierarchy of *taxa* (*s.* taxon). From smallest to largest, the taxa are: *Species, Genus, Family, Order, Class, Phylum,* and *Kingdom.*

However, because nature cannot guarantee that each species will fit tidily into six higher-level taxa, intermediate categories are denoted by the prefixes *infra-, super-,* and *sub-* (e.g., *sub-class* or *super-order*). Some scientists use generic taxa in place of fixed category names.

CLASSIFICATION IN ACTION:

PLACENTAL MAMMALS BELONG TO *ALL* OF THE TAXA IN THE TABLE BELOW.

	Lancelets	Lampreys	Ray-finned fishes	Lobe-finned fishes	Amphibians	Reptiles, birds	Marsupials	Placental mammals
Chordata (notochord)	X	X	X	X	X	X	X	X
Vertebrata (vertebra)		X	X	X	X	X	X	X
Gnathostoma (jaws)			X	X	X	X	X	X
Sarcopterygii (lobed fins)				X	X	X	X	X
Tetrapoda (four limbs)					X	X	X	X
Amniota (land-adapted egg)						X	X	X
Mammalia (milk, hair)							X	X
Theria (placenta)								X

Evolution

Living things ranging from *E. coli* to elephants all descended from a common ancestor; that is the great premise of evolution, or descent with modification. Evolution explains the great diversity of life on Earth, while at the same time accounting for similarities at the cellular and molecular level. For example, nearly all organisms translate the DNA "alphabet" into the same genetic code.

Homologous features arise through evolutionary changes to the same set of tissues and organs (e.g., a dog's paw and a bat's wing). *Analogous features* result from similar adaptations to different tissues and organs (e.g., the wings of butterflies and bats).

Speciation is the formation of new species. Evolutionary theory explains speciation as a result of the separation of one species population from another, followed by the accumulation of differences that keep members of the two populations from interbreeding.

Natural selection, the mechanism for evolution proposed by Darwin, consists of the following key points:

- **Variation:** Individuals in a population differ, and some of these differences are heritable.
- **Overproduction:** Members of a population produce more offspring than the environment can support.
- **Competition:** Individual organisms must compete for resources.
- **Fitness Advantage:** Some individuals will be better able to attain resources and survive than others; these individuals will reproduce and leave more offspring.

- **Adaptation:** Over time, the genes for traits that enhance survival of offspring will increase in the population.

Note that natural selection is not the only mechanism for evolution. Sexual selection and neutral selection also drive changes in populations. The *founder effect* is one example of neutral selection.

The *endosymbiotic theory of eukaryotic organelles* suggests that many of the structures of eukaryotic cells arose from symbiotic relationships between a eukaryote and a prokaryote. For instance, the chloroplasts of plant cells are thought to have derived from a cyanobacterium that was engulfed by a larger eukaryote but not digested. The cyanobacterium would have been able to continue photo-synthesizing food, benefitting the eukaryote, which in turn provided protection.

What is a theory? The scientific definition of theory *differs* from its everyday use. A theory is a robust explanation for a large set of phenomena that is supported by multiple lines of evidence. A theory becomes accepted by the scientific community only after it has withstood rigorous scrutiny and testing.

Cellular and Molecular Biology

About 12 questions on the CLEP Natural Sciences test will be about the structure, function, and behavior of cells. Cells are composed of distinct organelles and structures, many of which are made up of structural proteins. In addition, proteins are essential to the continued existence of a cell, as they help to carry out the basic biochemical reactions that keep a cell alive. Finally, cells must divide to create new cells; for eukaryotic cells, this process involves *mitosis,* the replication of the nucleus.

The Structure of the Cell

In its simplest form a cell has an inside (the cytoplasm), a boundary separating the inside from the outside (the plasma membrane), and instructions that allow the cell to create the proteins it needs to survive (DNA). This adequately describes a *prokaryotic* cell, which contains a simple, circular chromosome in its cytoplasm. While prokaryotic cells are small and lack membrane-bound organelles, *eukaryotic* cells are characterized by their larger sizes and complex internal structures. The table below describes the structures found in eukaryotic cells.

PARTS OF THE EUKARYOTIC CELL

Structure	Description	Notes
Plasma membrane	Surrounding a cell's cytoplasm, this structure determines which molecules may enter the cell. Protein channels floating in the phospholipid bilayer allow ions and larger molecules to pass.	Phospholipids have a hydrophilic (polar) outer portion and a hydrophobic inner portion.
Cytoplasm	The cytoplasm contains membrane-bound organelles and ribosomes. A cytoskeleton provides structure and support.	
Centrosome	Organizing center of microtubules.	Centrioles present in animal cells
Nucleus	The control center of the cell, the nucleus contains the chromosomes, which consist of long DNA strands coiled around histone proteins.	The nucleolus is the site of ribosome assembly.
Ribosomes	Composed of both RNA and proteins, these small structures synthesize proteins from mRNA that exits the nucleus. Ribosomes may be free or bound to the ER.	Ribosomes are not membrane-bound and are often described as particles rather than organelles.
Endoplasmic reticulum (ER)	A complex network of membrane folds and sacs, the smooth ER is where the synthesis and metabolism of organic molecules takes place. Rough ER contains bound ribosomes, which produce the proteins secreted by the cell as well as new cell membrane.	The nuclear envelope is continuous with the ER. Along with the Golgi apparatus, they form the endomembrane system.
Golgi apparatus	The membrane sacs of the Golgi receive, modify, and secrete proteins made in the ER. Small sacs bud off the Golgi membrane to form vesicles, which transport proteins to other sites.	
Lysosomes	These small membrane sacs contain enzymes that digest macromolecules, key in phagocytosis.	Absent in plant cells
Vacuole	Plant cells contain a large, central vacuole that stores water, among other functions.	Plant cells only

Mitochondria	Sites of cellular respiration, mitochondria have two membranes; the inner membrane is intricately folded.	Both plant and animal cells contain mitochondria.
Chloroplasts	Sites of photosynthesis, chloroplasts contain connected stacks of thylakoids in a fluid called stroma. The thylakoids contain chlorophyll.	Only plants and photosynthetic protists (algae) contain chloroplasts.
Cell wall	Cell walls provide structure and rigidity. Plant cell walls are composed of cellulose, while the cell walls of fungi are made up of chitin.	Animal cells lack cell walls.

The diffusion of molecules and ions across the cell membrane, and its regulation, is essential to maintaining the osmotic balance of the cell. The cell membrane is *selectively permeable*. The processes described below may be carried out by the membrane.

- **Passive Transport:** No energy is required to move solutes across the cell membrane. Diffusion and facilitated diffusion are forms of active transport.

- **Diffusion:** This describes the movement of particles down a concentration gradient. Diffusion occurs until equilibrium is reached, at which point there is no net movement of particles.

- **Facilitated Diffusion:** Charged ions and polar molecules (such as water) cannot diffuse across the lipid bilayer, but can cross via transport proteins.

- **Active Transport:** Energy is used to move solutes against a concentration gradient. Active transport of ions creates electrical potential differences across the cell membrane.

The Cell Cycle

Eukaryotic cells undergo distinct stages in which they grow, replicate their DNA, duplicate the nucleus (mitosis), and divide. Cells spend most of their time (~90%) in *interphase*, during which they grow and synthesize a copy of their DNA. *M phase*, which includes both mitosis and cytokinesis, makes up a much smaller portion of the cell cycle (~10%). The stages of the cell cycle are described below. Disruptions of the cell cycle lead to cancer in multicellular organisms. (Note that prokaryotic cells divide through the simpler, analogous process of *binary fission*.)

THE EUKARYOTIC CELL CYCLE

Phase	Description	Notes
Interphase	G1 (gap 1): The cell grows, producing proteins and organelles. DNA is not yet replicated.	
	S (synthesis): Cell growth continues as DNA is replicated.	Chromosome number does not double, as the replicated strands are still attached.
	G2 (gap 2): Cell growth continues as the cell prepares to enter M phase.	
M Phase (mitosis and cytokineses)	Prophase: DNA, already replicated in S phase, condenses into visible chromosomes. The nuclear envelope begins to dissolve and the centrosomes move apart.	Although mitosis is divided into phases, it is actually a continuous process. In animal cells, each centrosome features a pair of centrioles. Though most plant cells lack centrioles, the formation of spindle fibers from the centrosome occurs as in animal cells.
	Metaphase: Chromosomes, consisting of sister chromatids joined at the centromere, align along the metaphase plate. Spindle fibers extend from each centriole to the centromeres.	
	Anaphase: Sister chromatids break apart at the centromere and are pulled to opposite centrioles by the shortening spindle fibers.	
	Telophase: Two nuclear envelopes reform around each set of chromosomes.	
	Cytokinesis: The division of one cell into two, cytokinesis may begin as early as telophase.	Cytokinesis in animal cells occurs by *cleavage*. In plants cells, a *cell plate* forms between the nuclei.

DNA, RNA, and Protein: The Central Dogma

Proteins are essential to the structure and function of the cell. Whatever a cell does is due to the proteins it contains. Proteins break down large molecules into building blocks (e.g., amino acids, nucleotide bases), convert nutrients into forms that can be used by the cell, create hormones and other biologically active compounds, control what enters and exits the cell (membrane protein channels), and make up much of the structure of the cell (e.g., the cytoskeleton, cilia). Enzymes, responsible for the chemical reactions that occur in living things, are proteins.

Proteins are large polypeptides made up of long sequences of amino acids joined together, like the beads on a necklace. Once assembled by the ribosome, a protein folds into a three-dimensional configuration, which allows it to function. For example, the three-dimensional structure of an enzyme creates its active site, the area that fits a substrate molecule and chemically changes it to a different product.

Mendel discovered genes long before scientists knew what they were made of or how they functioned. Genes could be studied as observable traits—a green pea or purple petals. But how do these traits come about? In the twentieth century, experiments by Hershey and Chase and by Chargaff determined that genes were composed of deoxyribonucleic acid, or DNA. Wilkins, Franklin, Watson, and Crick determined the structure of DNA: a long, unbranched polymer that forms hydrogen bonds with its complementary strand, which together wind into a double helix.

The long strands of DNA that make up the chromosomes consist of the nucleotide bases adenine, cytosine, guanine, and thymine—commonly abbreviated as A, C, G, and T. Because DNA is an unbranched polymer, the nucleotides occur in a sequence, just like the letters that make up this paragraph. Similarly, three consecutive nucleotides make up a *codon*, the word of the DNA language. (Note that only a small portion of the DNA in eukaryotes codes for genetic information.)

Similar to DNA, RNA is a string of nucleotide bases usually found as a single strand. Instead of thymine (T), RNA uses the base uracil (U). RNA can form complementary base pairs with DNA.

Because chromosomes cannot leave the nucleus, the information in DNA is *transcribed* or copied as a messenger RNA (mRNA) molecule. The mRNA travels out of the nucleus, where it is *translated* by a ribosome into a polypeptide—each codon specifying a particular amino acid. The correspondence of codons to amino acids is known as the *genetic code* and is the same for nearly all organisms. This transfer of information—genes to mRNA to proteins (polypeptides)—is known as the *central dogma* of molecular biology.

DNA polymerases replicate the entire genome in S phase. The DNA double strand is "unzipped" and complementary bases are paired to each strand, forming two new double strands. For this reason, DNA replication is termed "semi-conservative."

Biochemical Reactions

Within a single cell, thousands of chemical reactions occur every second, maintaining the cell's function and keeping it alive. These biochemical reactions comprise a cell's metabolism.

Enzymes are proteins that are able to catalyze biochemical reactions. Enzymes are not chemically altered or used up in the reactions they catalyze. Rather, by lowering the activation energy required, enzymes force the reactions to occur much more quickly than they otherwise would.

Enzymes have substrate specificity; the active site fits only one or a few molecules. Enzymes function within a narrow range of temperature, pH, and other conditions and may become denatured by heating.

Cellular respiration breaks down the six-carbon sugar glucose in a series of chemical reactions, each of which extracts an extra bit of chemical energy from the molecule. The chemical equation below shows that oxygen gas is required in the breakdown of a glucose molecule, and that water and carbon dioxide are produced in the process. However, this is a net equation, the chemical sum of a sequence of reactions.

$$C_6H_{12}O_6 + 6O_2 \rightarrow 6CO_2 + 6H_2O$$

Cellular respiration produces the molecule adenosine tri-phosphate, known as the "energy currency" of the cell because nearly all biochemical reactions require energy in the form of ATP. Joining a phosphate molecule to the precursor adenosine diphosphate (ADP) creates a portable source of chemical energy.

$ADP + P(i) \rightarrow ATP$

Cellular respiration proceeds in three stages:

1. **Gycolysis:** The splitting of glucose into a three-carbon compound occurs in the cytosol.
2. **Citric Acid Cycle:** This series of reactions occurs in the mitochondria and produces electrons.
3. **Oxidative Phosphorylation:** This process forms the majority of ATP. The electrons from the previous stage are transported to one side of the internal membrane of the mitochondrion, setting up a chemical gradient. The diffusion of electrons across this gradient generates ATP.

Aerobic respiration, described above, can produce 38 molecules of ATP for every molecule of glucose. Organisms such as bacteria and yeasts can carry out *anaerobic respiration,* also called fermentation, which does not require oxygen. This less-efficient process produces only two molecules of ATP.

Photosynthesis uses the energy obtained from sunlight to convert carbon dioxide and water molecules to glucose and oxygen. The net chemical equation for photosynthesis is shown, though, as for respiration, the equation is actually the net result of a complicated sequence of reactions.

$6CO_2 + 6H_2O \rightarrow C_6H_{12}O_6 + 6O_2$

Photosynthesis takes place in the chloroplast, where the thylakoid grana are rich in chlorophyll. Chlorophyll is the pigment that gives plants their green color and allows light energy to be harnessed. A chlorophyll molecule absorbs light energy, which raises one of its electrons to an "excited" state. This begins a sequence of reactions that end with synthesis of glucose and oxygen.

Structure, Function, Development, and Heredity

About 24 questions on the CLEP Natural Sciences test will assess knowledge of the *structure, function, development,* and *patterns of heredity* of organisms. This includes an understanding of plant structure and functions and the human body, as well as the process of meiosis and the inheritance of traits.

Plant Structure and Function

Plants are *autotrophs:* they produce their own food via photosynthesis. While all plants are photosynthetic, not all photosynthetic organisms are plants. Some bacteria, such as cyanobacteria, are capable of photosynthesis. Algae, photosynthesis eukaryotes with both single-celled and multicellular species, are classified as protists. Unlike algae, a true plant has both a shoot and a root: specialized tissues allowing terrestrial plants to attain light and carbon dioxide in the air, as well as water and nutrients from the soil.

The following categories help to elucidate the evolution of land plants. Consider how each adaptation allows plants to become less dependent on an aquatic environment.

- **Nonvascular seedless plants:** This group includes liverworts, hornworts, and true mosses. Because these simple plants lack a complex vascular system or true roots, they cannot grow very tall or large. The gametophyte (haploid) generation is the dominant form.

- **Vascular seedless plants:** This groups includes ferns and horsetails. These plants have complex vascular systems and true roots and leaves, allowing them to grow taller. The small gametophyte produces eggs and flagellated sperm, which join to form the dominant sporophyte (diploid).

- **Seed plants:** This group includes most familiar plants (e.g., conifers, grasses, and flowering plants). The gametophyte remains dependent on and protected by the dominant sporophyte. Seed plants produce pollen grains instead of flagellated sperm.

  o Gymnosperms: The naked-seed plants, which include conifers and ginkgos, produce exposed seeds, such as the pine nuts found between the tough scales of pine cones.

  o Angiosperms: The covered-seed plants include all flowering plants and others, such as grasses and cereals. The evolution of the seed allowed these plants to disperse farther, protected by the tough outer coating of the seed and nourished by the food stored within. Nearly all plants human beings rely on for food are angiosperms. A major division within this group separates the monocots from dicots.

The important structural adaptations of derived plants are described here.

- **Apical Meristem:** These regions of cell division, located at the tips of shoots and roots, allow a plant to grow both up, toward light and carbon dioxide, and down, toward water and minerals.

- **Vascular System:** Vascular plants have a complex system of transport vessels that carry water and minerals from the roots to the leaves and sugars from the leaves to the roots.

  o Xylem: The rigid walls of dead cells that make up xylem vessels conduct water and minerals and provide support for the plant.

  o Phloem: Phloem is made up of living cells that transport sugars and other organic compounds to all the tissues of the plant

- **Leaves:** These organs are essential for gas exchange and photosynthesis.

  o Mesophyl: This is the spongy tissue inside the leaf in which photosynthesis occurs.

  o Stomata: Stomata are pores on the surface of a plants' leaves, which allow the intake of air and the loss of water vapor.

  o Transpiration: Transpiration is the loss of water from the surface of a plant's leaves due to the continuous movement of water upwards through the xylem.

Animal Structure and Function

Animals are *heterotrophs,* relying on external sources for energy. All animals, no matter how simple or complex, have the same needs: to take in oxygen and nutrients, to eliminate carbon dioxide and other metabolic wastes, and to maintain the correct balance of water and salts. Sponges, the simplest animals, simply allow these substances to diffuse into and out of their tissues. More complex organisms, such as vertebrates, have specialized body systems.

The body's cells require glucose and other nutrients. To provide these, we must first break down ingested food until it is small enough to pass through the cell membranes of the digestive tract and be transported through the bloodstream to all the cells of the body. Food is broken down both mechanically and chemically as it passes through the digestive tract, until it consists of small molecules.

THE DIGESTIVE SYSTEM

Organ	Function	Notes
Mouth, tongue, teeth, salivary glands	Mechanical tearing and crushing of food, along with some chemical digestion, occurs.	Digestion of carbohydrates begins by salivary amylase.
Esophagus	Peristalsis moves food down this passageway from mouth to stomach.	The epiglottis closes over the trachea when swallowing.
Stomach	Digests food in highly acidic environment to produce chime.	Digestion of proteins by pepsin begins.
Liver and gall bladder	The liver produces bile, which mixes with chyme in the small intestine and emulsifies fats.	Bile is temporarily stored in the gall bladder so that it may be released in larger quantity.
Pancreas	Releases digestive enzymes into the top of the small intestine.	The pancreas, liver, and gall bladder are accessory organs food does not pass through.
Small intestine (upper)	Bile, pancreatic enzymes, and enzymes produced by the intestinal wall complete chemical digestion.	Digestion of nucleic acids and fats begins.
Small intestine (lower)	Villi and microvilli increase the surface area over which nutrients are absorbed.	Digested nutrients are absorbed and passed into the bloodstream.
Large intestine	Absorbs the water used in digestion back into the bloodstream; bacteria in the large intestine break down undigested nutrients and produce vitamins.	Failure to reabsorb this water can result in dehydration. The appendix occurs at the beginning of the large intestine.
Rectum and anus	Feces is temporarily stored in the rectum until it can be expelled through the anus.	

The respiratory and circulatory systems are essential for providing the body's cells with oxygen and ridding them of carbon dioxide. Because the circulatory system transports the oxygen that the respiratory system takes in, they are treated together here.

- **Air Intake:** Air taken in through the nasal activity or mouth enters the trachea, the cartilage-line tube in the center of the chest. The trachea splits into two smaller bronchi, which enter each lung and branch into a series of smaller bronchioles. The cells lining this tract are covered in cilia, microscopic "hairs" that help move bacteria and small particles out of the lungs.

- **Gas Exchange:** The bronchioles transport air to the alveoli of the lungs   the sac-like clusters where gases are exchanged. Oxygen in the air dissolves into the liquid lining the alveoli and passes across a thin membrane into the dense network of capillaries beneath. Hemoglobin, a complex, iron-containing protein in the blood, binds to the oxygen molecules. Carbon dioxide moves in the opposite direction, entering the air of the bronchioles. Countercurrent exchange occurs at the alveoli.

- **Breathing:** The intake and exhalation of air from the lungs is due to the action of the diaphragm, the sheet of muscle beneath the lungs, and the muscles of the ribs. When it contracts, the diaphragm moves down and the rib cage expands, increasing the volume of the chest cavity. This creates a negative pressure in the lungs, forcing them to expand and take air in. On exhalation, the relaxed diaphragm moves upward and the ribs cage gets smaller, constricting the chest cavity and pushing air out of the lungs.

If the task of the respiratory system is to take oxygen into the body, then the task of the circulatory system is to transport that oxygen to all of the body's cells.

- **Lungs to Heart:** Capillaries from the lungs merge to form the capillary veins, which transport blood to the left atrium of the heart. From there, the blood enters the left ventricle, where it is pumped through the aorta to all the tissues of the body.

- **Heart to Tissues:** The aorta branches to form smaller arteries, which in turn branch into ever smaller vessels and capillaries. Oxygen passes through the capillary walls into the cells, and carbon dioxide (and other wastes) pass in the opposite direction, to be transported back to the heart and lungs.

- **Tissues to Heart:** Capillaries merge to form larger and larger vessels as they leave the tissues, until they form the large veins that enter the right atrium of the heart.

- **Heart to Lungs:** From there, oxygen-poor blood passes into the right ventricle and is pumped through the pulmonary arteries to the lungs.

The blood continuously cycles through the body in this sequence: lungs, left atrium, left ventricle, body tissues, right atrium, right ventricle, lungs.

The *muscular system* and the *skeletal system* work together to allow movement. These systems play other important roles in vertebrates.

- **Muscle types:** The three types of muscle are smooth, skeletal (striated), and cardiac (heart). Only skeletal muscle, which attaches to the bones of the skeleton, can move voluntarily. Smooth muscle lines hollow organs, such as those of the digestive tract.

- **Opposing pairs:** Because muscle can only be stimulated to contract and cannot expand, skeletal muscles are arranged in opposing pairs: the contraction of one muscle relaxes the opposite muscle, and vice versa. (For example, the muscle used to bend your arm at the elbow is opposed to the muscle that straightens your arm.)

- **Muscle contraction:** Muscles are made up of bundles of muscle fibers—very long, multi-nucleated cells with protein filaments running through them that are capable of expanding and contracting. These filaments do not change in length; rather, they are composed of long protein chains that slide past each other. The binding of calcium ions to the filaments causes them to overlap; thus the muscle fibers shorten and the muscle contracts.

- **Bone:** Bone is a living tissue composed of cells in a matrix of hard minerals and collagen protein, which keeps bones from being brittle. Blood vessels and nerves connect to bones. The marrow inside the long bones also produces immune cells.

- **Cartilage:** This strong, flexible connective tissue lines the joints, connects the ribs to the vertebra, and forms parts of the nose and ears.

The vertebrate *nervous system* consists of the brain and spinal cord (the central nervous system, CNS) and all of the peripheral nerves traveling to and from the CNS, which make up the peripheral nervous system (PNS). The PNS is divided into the (largely) voluntary somatic nervous system, or the involuntary autonomic nervous system.

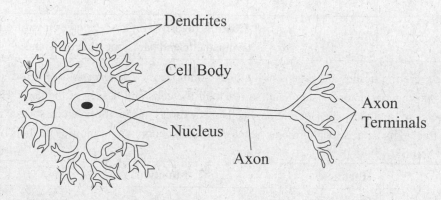

- **Neurons:** The human brain contains billions of neurons that form complex interconnections. Clusters of neurons are called ganglia.

  o *Sensory neurons* respond to stimuli from outside the CNS and carry a signal to the CNS.

  o *Motor neurons* travel from the CNS to other parts of the body, where they produce a response.

  o *Interneurons* of the CNS integrate and process the information from sensory neurons and produce signals in motor neurons. In a reflex reaction, such as a knee-jerk, this integration and processing occurs in the spinal cord.

- **Nerve:** A nerve is a long bundle of axons lined with protective sheath cells.

- **Action potentials:** All neurons communicate via electrical discharges that travel down the length of the axon, causing the intake of ions through membrane channels and temporarily changing the electrical potential of the cell.

- **Synapse:** Axons end in synaptic terminals which lie close to, but do not contact, the dendrites of downstream neurons. This gap is called the synapse.

- **Neurotransmitters:** These are released from the synaptic terminals and enter the gap, where they bind with membrane channels of the downstream neuron. This temporarily opens the channels, allowing ions to enter the cell and altering its electrical potential. Multiple signals can create or inhibit an action potential in the downstream neuron. (A neurotransmitter in the synapse is quickly taken up by the terminal or destroyed.) Different neurons in different parts of the nervous system release different neurotransmitters, such as serotonin, dopamine, acetylcholine, epinephrine, norepinephrine, or certain amino acids. A given neurotransmitter can be inhibitory, excitatory, or both.

THE PERIPHERAL NERVOUS SYSTEM (PNS)

Somatic Nervous System (voluntary)	Responds to external stimuli Carries signals to and from skeletal muscle Voluntary control and reflexes	
Autonomic Nervous System (involuntary)	Sympathetic	Arousal, "fight-or-flight" response
	Parasympathetic	Calming; opposes effects of sympathetic nervous system
	Enteric	Controls digestive organs. Receives input from sympathetic and parasympathetic systems.

Hormone-secreting tissues and organs in the body comprise the *endocrine system*. Hormones are secreted into the circulatory system, and so reach all the cells and tissues of the body. However, their effects are limited by the fact that only cells that express the appropriate cell surface receptor may be affected by a particular hormone. Some of the most common hormones and their functions are listed below.

Organ	Hormone	Function
Adrenal glands	Epinephrine Norepineprhine	Regulate blood glucose, metabolism, and blood vessel constriction
Ovaries*	Estrogens Progesterone	Promote growth of uterine lining and secondary sex characteristics
Pancreas	Insulin	Lowers blood glucose
	Glucagon	Raises blood glucose
Parathyroid glands	Parathyroid Hormone	Raises blood calcium
Pituitary gland	Anti-Diuretic Hormone	Promotes water retention
	Human Growth Hormone	Promotes growth and metabolism
	Follicle-Stimulating Hormone (FSH)	Promotes production of eggs and sperm
	Luteinizing Hormone (LH)	Stimulates gonads
	Thyroid-Stimulating Hormone	Stimulates thyroid gland
Testes*	Androgens	Promote sperm formation and secondary sex characteristics
Thyroid gland	Thyroid hormones	Regulate metabolism
	Calcitonin	Lowers blood calcium

*Both male and female gonads produce all of the sex hormones, though in differing proportions.

The kidneys filter metabolic wastes and help maintain osmotic balance. Tubules within the kidneys filter water and solutes from the blood. However, much of this filtrate is needed by the body. The kidney then reabsorbs almost all of the water, glucose molecules, ions, and other solutes in the filtrate, leaving a smaller quantity of fluid containing waste compounds—the urine. Mammalian urine is *hyperosmotic* to the fluids of the body, allowing water to be conserved.

The *reproductive systems* consist of the organs that produce gametes, as well as sex-specific organs.

- **Female Reproductive System:** A spike in LH and FSH causes an egg to mature and be released from the ovary. It moves through the Fallopian tubes and reaches the uterus, where fertilization may occur. The ovarian cells surrounding the released egg from the *corpus luteum*, which secretes estrogens and progesterone to maintain the endometrium of the uterus. If fertilization does not occur, the corpus luteum degenerates and menstrual flow ensues. The menstrual cycle then repeats itself.

- **Male Reproductive System:** Sperm are formed from cells in the semeniferous tubules of the testes. They then enter and pass through the epididymis, a series of coils, until they mix with seminal fluid and enter the urethra.

The gametes formed by the testes and ovaries are haploid and form via the special cell division process called *meiosis*. Meiosis proceeds in two stages, each of which repeats each phase of normal cell division, *mitosis*. Meiosis results in four daughter cells, each with a haploid set of chromosomes.

- **Crossing Over:** In prophase I of meiosis, sister chromatids pair with their homologues and exchange segments of DNA. Crossing over occurs and produces new combinations of alleles (haplotypes), increasing the genetic variation in offspring.

MEIOSIS (DIFFERENCES FROM MITOSIS ARE NOTED)

Meiosis I	Prophase I: Homologous pairs of sister chromatids exchange segments of DNA. This holds the pairs together until anaphase.
	Metaphase I: Homologous pairs of sister chromatids align along the metaphase plate.
	Anaphase I: Pairs of sister chromatids separate. Sister chromatids are no longer identical.
	Telophase I and Cytokinesis: Haploid cells, with duplicated DNA, form.
Meiosis II	Prophase II (as in mitosis)
	Metaphase II (as in mitosis)
	Anaphase II: Sister chromatids are not identical, and so each cell formed is unique.
	Telophase II and Cytokinesis: Two haploid cells form.

The Inheritance of Traits

Gregor Mendel discovered patterns in the inheritance of traits and called the units of inheritance *genes*. For the CLEP Natural Sciences test, understand how to analyze both monohybrid and dihybrid crosses using a Punnett square. Mendel derived his laws using monohybrid and dihybrid crosses of true-breeding pea plants.

- **Law of Segregation:** When Mendel crossed purple-flowered pea plants with white-flowered plants, all of the F1 generation plants were purple-flowered. When he crossed two of these offspring, the white-flower trait reappeared. This monohybrid cross showed that the genes for a trait segregate as *dominant* and *recessive* alleles.

- **Law of Independent Assortment:** Mendel crossed plants that produced round, yellow peas with plants that produced wrinkled, green peas. The F1 generation plants all produced round, yellow peas. When two of these plants were crossed, some of the F2 plants produced wrinkled, green peas, as expected. However, other F2 plants produced wrinkled, yellow and smooth, green peas as well—combinations of traits not seen in the previous generations. This dihybrid cross showed that traits assort independently of each other.

In mammals, sex is determined by the sex chromosomes, X and Y. Generally, females are XX, while males are XY. (Non-sex chromosomes are called *autosomes*.)

If a gene is located on an X chromosome, the recessive phenotype will appear more frequently in men than in women. Hemophilia and red-green color blindness are sex-linked traits.

Though *single-gene traits* are easiest to study, most characteristics are determined by the combined action of many genes. These are called *quantitative traits*.

Disorders caused by a single gene include: Tay-Sachs disease, cystic fibrosis, Huntington's disease, sickle-cell disease, and phenylketonuria.

Abnormalities in chromosome number are usually lethal. Some conditions, such as Down syndrome and sex chromosome differences, are a result of aneuploidy.

Fertilization of an egg cell by a sperm cell results in a zygote. This single cell then undergoes mitosis to produce all the cells, tissues, and organs of the developing embryo and fetus.

The human zygote undergoes *cleavage*, forming a solid ball of cells (the morula) which then becomes a hollow sphere with an inner cell mass (the blastocyst). The blastocyst then forms the gastrula, with distinct germ layers.

Three distinct cell populations of the gastrula go on to form specific organs and tissues in the embryo and fetus.

- **Endoderm:** Lining of digestive system and other internal organs; liver, pancreas, thymus, thyroid, and parathyroid glands

- **Mesoderm:** Muscular, skeletal, circulatory, excretory, lymphatic, and reproductive systems; muscular layer of digestive system; dermis

- **Ectoderm:** Nervous system, epidermis, enamel of teeth

- **Neural Tube:** This hollow tube forms from the ectoderm layer and becomes the central nervous system.

The formation of distinct tissues and organs is a result of cells differentiating and taking on specialized structures and functions. Since all embryonic cells contain the same DNA, differentiation is the result of differences in gene expression.

Stem cells can continue to divide to give rise to more-specialized cells and tissues.

Ecology and Population Biology

About 12 questions on the CLEP Natural Sciences test will be about ecology and population biology.

Ecosystems

An ecosystem includes all of the biotic and abiotic factors that influence it. Biotic factors include the *populations* of different species that make up the *community*. Abiotic factors include the chemical and physical characteristics of the environment.

The populations in an ecosystem are classified according to how they obtain energy. The energy in an ecosystem decreases at higher *trophic levels*. Typically, about 10 percent of the energy from one trophic level is transferred to the next higher level.

- **Producers:** Plants, algae, and cyanobacteria harness the energy of the Sun to produce food, making this energy available to consumers. Producers usually make up the bulk of an ecosystem.

- **Primary Consumers:** These heterotrophs consume producers directly and rely on the energy stored in producers for subsistence.

- **Secondary Consumers:** Because secondary consumers feed on primary consumers, the energy available to them is much less than the energy available to primary consumers, and their populations are accordingly smaller.

- **Tertiary Consumers:** Feeding on the much smaller energy reserve of secondary consumer populations, tertiary consumer populations are the smallest.

- **Decomposers:** Fungi, bacteria, earthworms, and insects break down dead organisms, returning the nutrients stored in the bodies to the soil, water, or air.

Oxygen, water, carbon, and nitrogen are exchanged among the biotic and abiotic components of an ecosystem.

- **Carbon Cycle:** Photosynthesis converts carbon in the atmosphere to glucose and its storage form, starch. Cellular respiration returns this carbon to the atmosphere. Non-biological processes, such as volcanic eruptions and combustion of fossil fuels, also produce carbon dioxide.

- **Nitrogen Cycle:** Atmospheric nitrogen must be fixed by bacteria and decomposers before it may be used by plants and animals. Soil bacteria also return nitrogen to the air. The creation of artificial fertilizers moves nitrogen from the air to the soil and water, where it may act as a pollutant.

- **Water Cycle:** Evaporation, transpiration, condensation, and surface and groundwater flow drive this cycle.

Terrestrial and aquatic *biomes* vary in abiotic factors (e.g., sunlight, temperature, precipitation, seasonal variation), but the general trend is that tropical biomes support a greater diversity of species than biomes closer to the poles.

Biodiversity consists of the number of different species along with the amount of genetic variation present within each species. Biodiversity is of concern to conservation ecologists because it is often essential to the continued survival of ecosystems.

Every species in an ecosystem has a *niche,* or method of survival. Ecosystems with a greater number of niches can support a larger number of species.

Population Biology

A population consists of individuals of the same species in an area, while population density is the number of individuals per unit area. Population ecology considers how populations are structured and how they may change over time.

The *dispersion,* or spacing, of a population may be uniform across an area, clumped as density is concentrated in only certain areas, or randomly distributed.

The size of a population is determined by factors such as the number of individuals migrating in and emigrating out.

Birth and death rates also influence the size and growth of a population. When the birth rate and death rate are equal, zero population growth occurs.

Demography is the study of vital statistics, their change over time, and their effects on population size and structure.

A graph that represents the proportions of individuals in a *cohort* still alive at subsequent ages is called a survivorship curve. Survivorship curves are classified as:

- **Type I:** Low death rates early in the cohort's life span with a pronounced drop later in life. K-selected species exhibit this curve.

- **Type II:** Death rate is constant over a cohort's life span.

- **Type III:** Death rate is highest early in the life-span, then flattens as the death rate of the few surviving individuals declines. R-selected species exhibit this curve.

There are several population growth models:

- **Exponential Growth:** Populations that are not constrained by limited resources may undergo exponential growth. The graph of an exponentially growing population shows a J-shaped curve, indicating that the rate of increase is itself increasing with time.

- **Logistic Growth:** An alternative to the exponential growth model is logistic growth, which assumes that a population will be limited at a certain size by the lack of resources in the environment. The graph of logistic population growth rises quickly, but then levels off. The point at which population growth ceases and the population size remains constant is termed the *carrying capacity* (K) of the environment (for that population).

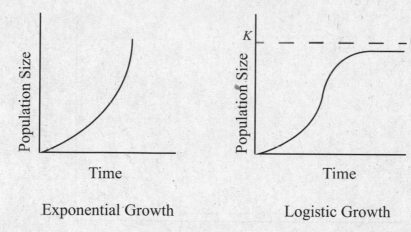

Exponential Growth   Logistic Growth

- **Population Cycles:** Some populations fluctuate between low and high densities. These patterns are usually linked to predator-prey relationships, with the populations of predators changing in sync and lagging behind changes in prey populations.

An organism may produce all of its offspring and die in a single year, or it may produce fewer offspring over a longer lifetime. These different life history strategies are influenced by both natural selection and population density.

- ***K*-selection:** When a population is at or near high densities (approaching K), natural selection will favor traits that allow survival in limited-resource conditions. *K*-selection favors density-dependent traits.

- ***r*-selection:** In contrast, when a population has abundant resources and is far from reaching K, then natural selection will favor traits that maximize the rate of reproduction. *r*-selected traits increase the rate of population growth.

A graph of the global human population from thousands of years ago to the present would show exponential growth. The human population steadily grew to about 0.5 billion in 1650, and then added another 6 billion in the next 350 years. However, the population growth rate has decreased in the past half century, and growth patterns vary from region to region.

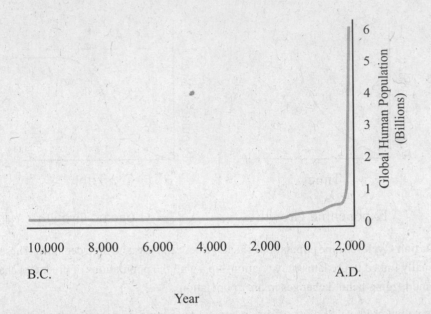

Year

- **Demographic Transition:** A given growth rate may be achieved with high birth and death rates, or low birth and death rates. A society with a high birth rate, along with high infant mortality and lethal infectious disease, may gain access to family planning services, vaccinations, clean water, and improved nutrition. This *demographic transition* results in a lower birth rate along with a lower death rate.

- **Age Structure:** A population may consist of roughly even numbers of children and young and middle-aged adults, or it may include a greater proportion of children, adolescents, and young adults. The proportion of members at various ages describes the *age structure* of a population. An uneven age structure that is skewed toward the young may predict future population growth as the young members go on to have children of their own.

- **Ecological Footprint:** Whether the global human population has a carrying capacity is a question asked by scientists, and their estimates vary widely. A more tractable question is that of the ecological footprint—the amount of land, water, and other resources used to support a population.

PHYSICAL SCIENCES

Physical science is the study of the physical world around us. It encompasses the field of physics, chemistry, geology, and astronomy. The physical science portion of the CLEP Natural Science exam assesses your knowledge of basic facts and concepts, your ability to interpret and understand information presented in a variety of formats, and how well you can apply the fundamental principles of physical science.

The physical science portion of the test consists of about 60 questions.

The Atom

About 7 percent of the test, or 3 to 4 questions, will address the structure of atoms, the structure of the atomic nucleus, the properties of elementary particles, and nuclear reactions. Atoms are the basic units of matter composed of the elementary particles protons, neutrons, and electrons. The first two are found in the atomic nucleus, while electrons are dispersed in the relatively expansive area around it. Nuclear reactions result in the formation of new elements due to changes in the number of an atom's protons and neutrons.

Atomic and Nuclear Structure and Properties

Objects are composed of tiny particles called atoms. All of the currently known atoms are represented in the periodic table of elements. Some of the most common atoms are oxygen, nitrogen, hydrogen, and carbon. Atoms are extremely tiny. To understand just how minute they are, consider that a single liter of air contains 1×10^{22} atoms!

Composed of electrons, protons, and neutrons, atoms contain a compact center called a nucleus. The nucleus contains the atom's protons and neutrons and is extremely dense. Although it makes up just a tiny portion of the volume of an atom, the nucleus accounts for most of its mass. The area surrounding the nucleus contains an extremely diffuse electron cloud—the vast majority of an atom is simply empty space. The figure below shows the general structure of an atom:

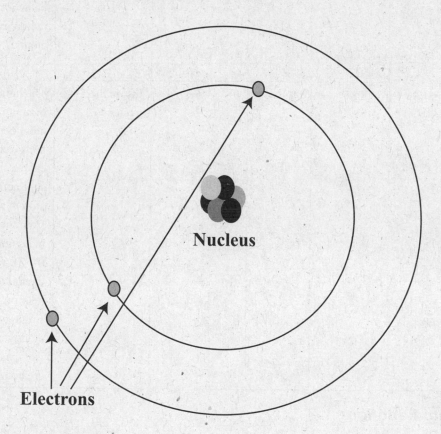

Nucleus

Electrons

Elementary Particles

The extremely tiny atoms that are the basic units of matter are composed of even smaller, more basic components known as elementary or fundamental particles. These include protons, electrons, and neutrons.

Elementary Particle	Mass in Atomic Mass Units	Relative Charge	Actual Charge	Location	Notes
Proton	1.0073	+1	$+1.602 \times 10^{-19}$	Inside the nucleus	The number of protons in an atom is equal to its atomic number (Z).
Electron	0.00055	−1	-1.602×10^{-19}	Surrounding the nucleus	Electrons determine the chemical behavior and reactivity of atoms.
Neutron	1.0087	0	0	Inside the nucleus	The number of neutrons an atom contains can be calculated by subtracting the atomic number from the mass number (A–Z). When the number of neutrons in a single type of atom varies, isotopes are created.

Nuclear Reactions

In a chemical reaction such as $2Na + Cl_2 \rightarrow 2NaCl$, the atoms on both sides of the equation are the same. They are merely combined or rearranged to form different products. This is not the case with nuclear reactions. When these occur, the number of protons and electrons is changed and entirely new elements are formed.

Elements that undergo nuclear reactions on their own because their nuclei are unstable are said to be radioactive. These elements emit radiation in the form of alpha, beta, and gamma rays as a result of these reactions. One example of a naturally radioactive isotope is $^{238}_{92}U$. It proceeds through a series of nuclear reactions to form $^{206}_{82}Pb$. The first two reactions in this series are $^{238}_{92}U \rightarrow ^{234}_{90}Th + ^{4}_{2}He$ and $^{234}_{90}Th \rightarrow ^{234}_{91}Pa + ^{0}_{-1}e$.

The two main kinds of nuclear reactions are nuclear fusion and nuclear fission. In nuclear fission reactions, the nucleus is split. Nuclear fission reactions release massive amounts of energy. In nuclear fusion reactions, two or more nuclei join together (fuse) to form a single nucleus. There is a resulting decrease in mass and an emission of energy. The Sun is powered by nuclear fusion reactions.

To balance equations for nuclear reactions, ensure the nucleon numbers and the proton numbers are equal on both sides. In the isotope $^{16}_{8}O$ 16 is the nucleon number and 8 is the proton number. The following is an example of a balanced nuclear equation: $^{16}_{7}N \rightarrow ^{16}_{8}O + ^{0}_{-1}e$.

Elements and Reactions

About 10 percent of the test, or 6 questions, will address chemical elements and compounds, reactions, and molecular structure and bonding. The elements are listed in the periodic table. Compounds consist of two or more elements and are typically formed through chemical reactions. There are six types of chemical reactions. Molecules are formed when two or more atoms are joined by covalent bonds, and their structure is influenced by the number of bonded and lone electron pairs they contain.

Chemical Elements and Compounds

All matter is comprised of the natural and manmade elements found in the periodic table. Some elements are hydrogen, lithium, oxygen, and carbon. Most periodic tables include the symbol for each element (C is the symbol for carbon, for instance), atomic number (this is the number of protons an element contains; carbon has 6), and atomic mass (this is equal to the sum of the element's protons and neutrons; carbon has an atomic mass of 12). All of the elements in the periodic table can be categorized as metals, non-metals, and metalloids. The following figure shows the location of these categories in the periodic table.

1 H																		2 He
3 Li	4 Be												5 B	6 C	7 N	8 O	9 F	10 Ne
11 Na	12 Mg												13 Al	14 Si	15 P	16 S	17 Cl	18 Ar
19 K	20 Ca	21 Sc	22 Ti	23 V	24 Cr	25 Mn	26 Fe	27 Co	28 Ni	29 Cu	30 Zn	31 Ga	32 Ge	33 As	34 Se	35 Br	36 Kr
37 Rb	38 Sr	39 Y	40 Zr	41 Nb	42 Mo	43 Tc	44 Ru	45 Rh	46 Pd	47 Ag	48 Cd	49 In	50 Sn	51 Sb	52 Te	53 I	54 Xe
55 Cs	56 Ba	57 *La	72 Hf	73 Ta	74 W	75 Re	76 Os	77 Ir	78 Pt	79 Au	80 Hg	81 Ti	82 Pb	83 Bi	84 Po	85 At	86 Rn
87 Fr	88 Ra	89 +Ac	104 Rf	105 Ha	106 Sg	107 Ns	108 Hs	109 Mt	110 110	111 111	112 112	113 113					

58 Ce	59 Pr	60 Nd	61 Pm	62 Sm	63 Eu	64 Gd	65 Tb	66 Dy	67 Ho	68 Er	69 Tm	70 Yb	71 Lu
90 Th	91 Pa	92 U	93 Np	94 Pu	95 Am	96 Cm	97 Bk	98 Cf	99 Es	100 Fm	101 Md	102 No	103 Lr

There are several periodic table patterns or trends:

- The vertical columns of the periodic table (called groups) contain elements with similar properties.

- Atomic radius decreases from left to right.

- Ionization energy increases from left to right.

- Electronegativity increases from left to right.

- Atomic radius increases from top to bottom.

- Ionization energy decreases from top to bottom.

- Electronegativity decreases from top to bottom.

When two or more elements combine with each other, they form chemical compounds. Compounds are represented using the symbols of the atoms they contain; this is known as a chemical formula. The compound sodium chloride, for example, is represented using the chemical formula NaCl.

The two main types of compounds are ionic and molecular.

Type of Compound	Description	Examples	Properties
Ionic	Created when a metal and a non-metal react	Ca_3N_2 NaCl KF	High melting points High boiling points Can conduct electricity in liquid form Brittle Often soluble in water
Molecular	Consist of two or more non-metals	H_2O HCl NH_3	Low melting points Low boiling points Do not conduct electricity Some can dissolve in water

Chemical Reactions

A chemical reaction occurs when two or more atoms react to form new compounds. Chemical reactions are represented using equations—the reactants are on the left side and the products are on the right side. For instance, the formation of carbon dioxide through the reaction of carbon and oxygen is represented with the following chemical equation: $C + O_2 \rightarrow CO_2$. The equations for all chemical reactions should be balanced. This means that the number of atoms of each element is the same on both sides of the equation. If there are unequal numbers of atoms, coefficients must be added. Consider the following equation:

$$NO \rightarrow N_2O + NO_2$$

The number of nitrogen atoms on the left side of the equation is 1. There is also 1 oxygen atom. On the right side, there are 3 atoms of nitrogen and 3 of oxygen. To balance this equation, add a 3 in front of the NO:

$$3\,NO \rightarrow N_2O + NO_2$$

The number of nitrogen and oxygen atoms is now the same on both sides.

There are six types of chemical reactions.

Type of Reaction	General Equation	Example	Description
Synthesis	$A + B \rightarrow AB$	$C + O_2 \rightarrow CO_2$	Two or more elements form a single compound.
Decomposition	$AB \rightarrow A + B$	$H_2SO_4 \rightarrow H_2O + SO_3$	One compound breaks down into simpler compounds.
Single Displacement	$A + BC \rightarrow AC + B$	$Fe + CuSO_4 \rightarrow FeSO_4 + Cu$	One atom switches places with another.
Double Displacement	$AB + CD \rightarrow AD + BC$	$Pb(NO_3)_2 + 2 KI \rightarrow PbI_2 + 2KNO_3$	Two new products are formed when the atoms in both reactants switch places.
Acid-Base	$HA + BOH \rightarrow H_2O + BA$	$HBr + KOH \rightarrow H_2O + KBr$	An acid containing an H^+ ion and a base containing an OH^- ion react to form water and a salt.
Combustion	$A + O_2 \rightarrow CO_2 + H_2O$	$C_3H_8 + 5O_2 \rightarrow 3CO_2 + 4H_2O$	Oxygen and another compound react to form carbon dioxide and water.

Molecular Structure and Bonding

Molecules are compounds that are formed when two or more atoms are joined by covalent bonds. These differ from ionic bonds in that free electrons in outer shells are shared rather than transferred. An example of a molecule that is formed by covalent bonds is water (H_2O). Oxygen can accept two additional electrons to fill its outer shell; each atom of hydrogen can accept one. Therefore, two atoms of hydrogen can bond with an oxygen atom to form a stable molecule of H_2O.

The figure below shows the shape of the water molecule and the shared electrons.

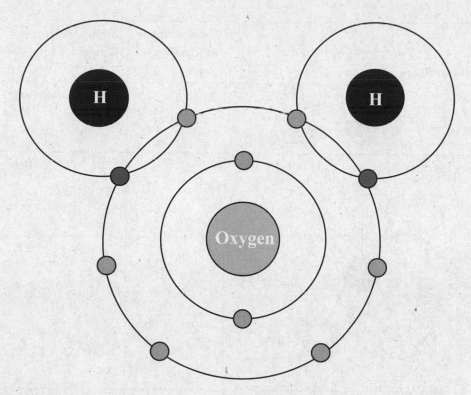

Water is held together with single covalent bonds, but multiple bonds are also possible, depending on the number of electrons an atom can accept. Nitrogen atoms, for instance, can accept three atoms, so the molecule N_2 is held together by a triple covalent bond.

Molecules have a three-dimensional structure. It's believed that their geometric shape is determined by the number of electron pairs they contain. Electrons repel each other, and the atoms in a molecule arrange themselves in such a way that these repulsions are minimized. Some of the more common molecular structures are presented in the following table:

Molecular Shape	Total Number of Electron Pairs	Angles Between Bonds	Example
Linear 	2	180°	$BeCL_2$
Trigonal Planar 	3	120°	BF_3
Tetrahedral 	4	109.5°	CH_4
Trigonal Pyramidal 	4 (1 lone electron pair)	Slightly less than 109.5°	NH_3

Bent	4 (2 lone electron pairs)	Slightly less than 109.5°	H_2O
Trigonal Bipyramidal	5	90° and 120°	PCL_5
Octahedral	6	90°	SF_6

Thermodynamics, Mechanics, and Relativity

About 12 percent of the test, or around 7 questions, will be related to heat, thermodynamics, states of matter, classical mechanics, and relativity. The study of heat involves looking at how thermal energy is transferred in systems governed by the laws of thermodynamics. Liquids, gases, and solids are the three states of matter, and each has distinct characteristics. Classical mechanics is the study of motion, which always occurs relative to a point of reference.

Heat

Heat is simply the transfer of thermal energy from one part of a system to another portion of the same system or a different system. Heat can be transferred in three main ways:

- **Conduction:** Electrons vibrate in their fixed positions when one part of an object is heated. Electrons collide with ones found in the nearby atoms, and thermal energy is transferred throughout the object being heated. An example is holding the tip of a metal knife over a flame; the entire knife will get hot due to conduction.

- **Convection:** Heated molecules become less dense and rise as a result. The denser, colder fluid then moves to the bottom, where it is heated and eventually rises too. Boiling water is an example of heating through convection.

- **Radiation:** Thermal energy is transmitted through electromagnetic waves such as ultraviolet waves and X-rays. Thermal energy from the Sun reaches Earth through the process of radiation.

One of the most important equations for studying thermal systems is $Q = mc\Delta t$. In this equation:

- **Q** represents the amount of heat energy the system lost or gained

- **m** stands for the mass of the substance

- **c** represents the specific heat capacity, the thermal energy required to increase the temperature of one gram of a substance by one degree Celsius

- **Δt** is the change in the temperature of the system

Using this equation, it is easy to calculate, for example, the energy needed to increase the temperature of 10 grams of water by 10 degrees Celsius. ($Q = mc\Delta t$; $Q = 10$ grams $\times 4.18$ Joules/gram°C $\times 10°C$; $Q = 418$ Joules)

If there is a phase change this also needs to be included in the calculation. For water, the *heat of fusion* is 334.8 Joules per gram. This is the energy needed to melt ice. The *heat of vaporization* is 2260 Joules per gram. This is the energy needed to change liquid water into steam.

Thermodynamics

Thermodynamics is the study of how thermal energy (heat) is changed into mechanical energy. There are three laws of thermodynamics (and a more recently developed "zeroth" law):

- The *First Law of Thermodynamics* states that energy in a thermodynamic system is always conserved—it cannot be created or destroyed. As it applies to thermodynamics, this law means that the amount of heat lost or gained by a system is equal to the amount of heat transferred by the system that gave or received the energy. The heat added to a system is always equal to the sum of the work performed by the system and the amount by which its thermal energy increased.

- The *Second Law of Thermodynamics* encompasses three important principles. First, it states that thermal energy flows from warmer areas or bodies to cooler ones. Second, it states that a heat engine cannot be 100 percent efficient; that is, all the thermal energy cannot be used to do mechanical work. Finally, the level of entropy (or disorder) in an isolated system will increase over time.

- The *Third Law of Thermodynamics* states that a system at absolute zero (0°Kelvin or −273.15°Celsius) would have zero entropy. No real thermodynamic system, however, can actually reach absolute zero.

- The *Zeroth Law of Thermodynamics* states that two systems in equilibrium with a third system are automatically also in equilibrium with each other.

States of Matter

The three most common states, or phases, of matter are liquids, solids, and gases. A fourth phase is plasma, an ionized form of gas found in outer space (although if fire is hot enough to ionize the gaseous components it can become plasma). Elements and compounds can change from solid, to liquid, to gas form; these transformations are typically physical changes.

STATE OF MATTER	DESCRIPTION
Solid	Particles are tightly packed together and typically arranged in a specific pattern; particles cannot move from their fixed positions; there is a definite shape and volume; solids cannot flow; they cannot be compressed easily; their volume does not change significantly with heating; solids become liquids when they melt and turn into gases through sublimation.
Liquid	Particles are close to each other but do not have a fixed arrangement; particles can move and change positions; liquids conform to the shapes of their containers; the volume is definite; liquids can flow; they cannot be compressed easily; there is a small change in volume with heating; liquids become solids when they freeze and turn into gases through vaporization.
Gas	Particles are far apart and do not have a fixed arrangement; particles can move freely; the volume and shape of gases are indefinite—gases will expand to fill their containers and take on their shapes; gases can flow; they are easily compressed; there is a substantial change in volume with heating; gases become liquids through condensation.

Classical Mechanics

Classical mechanics is the science of bodies in motion. Some of the concepts and formulas that are crucial to this field of study include:

- **Speed:** This is the distance an object moves during a specific period of time. The formula used to calculate speed is: $speed = \dfrac{distance}{time}$. Speed can be further classified as *instantaneous speed* and *average speed.* Instantaneous speed is the speed of an object at a specific moment in time. Average speed is calculated by dividing the total distance traveled by the time interval.

- **Velocity (v):** Speed indicates only how fast an object is traveling; velocity also indicates direction. If the speed of a car is 100 km/hour, its velocity could be 100 km/hour to the north, 100 km/hour to the east, 100 km/hour in a southeast direction, and so on.

- **Distance:** This is the total length of a trip. For example, a car that drove 100 kilometers one way and then turned around and drove 100 kilometers the other way traveled a distance of 200 kilometers.

- **Displacement (d):** This is the measure of how far a body traveled from its starting point. In the previous example, the displacement of the car would be zero kilometers since the starting and end points of the trip are the same.

- **Acceleration (a):** This indicates the rate at which an object's velocity is changing. The formula used to calculate acceleration is $acceleration = \dfrac{change\ in\ velocity}{time}$. If an object is in free fall, its acceleration is a constant: 9.8 m/s².

Four equations frequently used to study the motion of objects are:

1. $d = v_i t + \dfrac{1}{2}a + 2$

2. $v_f^2 = v_i^2 + 2ad$

3. $v_f = v_i + at$

4. $d = \left(\dfrac{v_i + v_f}{2}\right)t$

Newton's laws are also an important part of classical mechanics:

- Newton's *First Law of Motion* is also known as the law of inertia. It states that in the absence of outside forces, bodies at rest tend to stay at rest and bodies in motion tend to stay in motion.

- Newton's *Second Law of Motion* states that an object's acceleration is inversely related to its mass and directly related to the force applied to the object. This relationship is represented using the equation $F = ma$.

- Newton's *Third Law of Motion* states that for every action there is an equal and opposite reaction. If someone pushes on a wall, for example, the wall exerts a force in the opposite direction that is equal in magnitude.

Relativity

In the study of motion, speed and velocity are always relative. Consider the following statement: a car is traveling at a speed of 50 km/hour. This statement really means that the car and the passengers inside are traveling at a speed of 50 km/hour relative to the road. If other frames of reference were used to measure the car's speed, it would be different. For example, the driver's speed relative to the individual in the passenger's seat would be 0 km/hour, since neither person is traveling faster than the other. The car's speed could also be expressed relative to other cars on the road, a person walking along the shoulder, or even the orbit of the Earth. Similarly, an airplane's speed and/or velocity could be expressed relative to the ground, the clouds, or other objects in the sky. The most important thing to remember about measures of motion is that they are never absolute; speed and velocity are always expressed *relative to* something else, even if the frame of reference is not explicitly indicated.

Electromagnetism and Wave Phenomena

About 4 percent of the test, or 2 questions, will assess your knowledge of electricity and magnetism and light and sound waves. Charged particles called ions are responsible for electricity. These particles also create magnetic fields. Electric current can be used to create magnets, and magnets can be used to generate electric current. Light and sound exist in the form of waves. These waves have distinct properties and also have several in common, including wavelength, amplitude, and frequency.

Electricity and Magnetism

Electricity is the result of charged particles known as ions. Atoms can become positively or negatively charged when they gain or lose electrons. Electricity is what causes lightning, and it's also the reason why a balloon will stick to a wall if someone rubs it on his or her hair. Some of the formulas and terms related to the study of electricity are presented below:

- *Coulomb's law* describes the relationship between electric force and the distance between two charged particles. The equation to calculate electric force is $F = k \dfrac{q_1 q_2}{d^2}$ where F is equal to electric force, k is a constant ($9 \times 10^9 \, \text{N} \times \text{m}^2/\text{C}^2$), q_1 is the charge on one particle, q_2 is the charge on the other particle, and d is the distance between the two particles.

- *Electric potential energy* is the potential energy contained in a collection of charges. Electric potential is calculated using the equation: electric potential = electric potential energy ÷ amount of charge. The unit used to measure electric potential is volt. One volt is equal to 1 Joule/coulomb.

- *Electric current* is the term used to describe the flow of charged particles. The unit used to measure the rate of flow is ampere. One ampere is equal to one coulomb of charge flowing past a fixed point every second. Electric current can be described as direct current (the flow of particles is in one direction) or alternating current (particles flow in one direction, then the other).

- *Electrical resistance* is the extent to which the material particles are passing through resists the movement of those particles. The unit used to measure electrical resistance is the ohm (Ω).

- *Ohm's law* describes the relationship between current, voltage, and resistance. The formula is current = voltage ÷ resistance, or amperes = volts ÷ ohms.

- *Electric power* is the amount of work done by a system. It is calculated using the formula power = current × voltage.

Magnetism is closely related to electricity. When a charged particle moves, it produces its own magnetic field. Some of the basic principles of magnetism are outlined below:

- All magnets contain two poles known as the north and south poles.

- When two magnets are brought close to each other, north poles will repel north poles, south poles will repel south poles, and south poles will attract north poles.

- Magnets, like electrically charged particles, are surrounded by a characteristic field. This field is strongest at the poles.

- When substances such as iron are magnetized by placing them inside a coil of wire with current, it is due to the orderly alignment of the atoms they contain. These magnetized pieces of iron are called *electromagnets*.

- Magnets placed within a coil of wire can produce an electric current. This is called *electromagnetic induction*. Pushing a magnet into a coil and pulling it back out repeatedly creates alternating current.

Waves, Light, and Sound

Some of the general properties of waves:

- **Amplitude:** This is the maximum displacement of a wave. It is calculated by measuring the distance between the middle of a wave and its highest or lowest point (crest and trough, respectively).

- **Wavelength:** This is the distance between a certain portion of one wave and the corresponding portion of the wave next to it (the distance between wave crests, for example).

- **Frequency:** This is the number of complete waves per a unit of time. Frequency is often expressed as the number of waves per second. Frequency is measured in hertz (Hz).

- **Period:** This is the time it takes for a wave to complete one vibration.

- **Speed:** The speed of a wave is calculated using the equation: wave speed = wavelength × frequency.

- **Interference:** Waves can interact with each other and produce resultant waves. If the waves are in sync, the amplitude will increase. This is known as constructive interference. If the waves are out of sync, the amplitude will decrease. This is known as destructive interference.

We perceive sound because of waves (vibrations) that travel through mediums such as air, liquids, and solids. Waves are often represented using sine curves. Some of the important facts about and properties of sound waves include:

- **Reflection:** When sound waves are reflected, an echo is produced. Smooth, hard surfaces reflect sound best. The angle at which the sound wave bounces off a surface is equal to the angle at which it struck the surface.

- **Refraction:** Sound waves can become bent as they travel. This usually happens when the air through which waves are traveling has varying speeds and/or temperatures.

- **Doppler Effect:** An example of this is that a person standing still will perceive a train whistle as being higher-pitched as it approaches. When the source of sound moves toward an observer, each successive wave crest is emitted from a position closer to the observer than the previous wave. So, each wave takes less time to reach the observer, and the arrival of successive wave crests at the observer is reduced. This causes an increase in frequency. More waves are reaching the listener's ear in a given period of time, so the pitch sounds higher.

Unlike sound waves, light waves do not require a medium to propagate. The light from the Sun, for instance, can travel through the vacuum of space to reach Earth. Some important properties of light waves include:

- The frequency of light waves is what accounts for the perceived colors of objects. The reflected colors are the ones that are observed.

- *Diffraction* is the term used to describe the bending of light waves.

- While sound waves are longitudinal, light waves are transverse. In a transverse wave, the change in energy is perpendicular to the direction of propagation of the wave.

The Structure of the Universe

About 7 percent of the test, or 4 questions, will test your knowledge of galaxies, stars, and our solar system, all of which are components of the universe. Galaxies are massive systems bound by a gravitational field. The main types of galaxies are irregular, spiral, and elliptical. Stars are composed of mainly helium and hydrogen gas and have a well-defined life cycle. Our solar system includes Earth and the other planets and celestial bodies that orbit our Sun.

Galaxies

A galaxy is a huge system comprised of objects that are held in place by gravity. Typical components of galaxies include:

- Stars (these can number in the millions or trillions)
- Bodies orbiting stars (such as planets)
- Asteroids and other celestial bodies
- Black holes
- Dark matter
- Interstellar medium

There are three main types of galaxies:

Galaxy Type	Characteristics
Spiral (the Milky Way Galaxy is this type)	Have a shape that resembles a disk Centers contain luminous bulges Are likely composed of older stars Extremely bright Thought to represent only about 20 percent of the galaxies in the universe
Elliptical	Have a defined elliptical shape Are brightest at the center and grow fainter as the distance from the center increases Have a reddish color Are very old Frequently found in clusters Are the largest galaxies in the universe Can contain more than a trillion stars
Irregular	Shape is undefined Arrangement of stars, gas, and dust is random Contain relatively few stars Are the smallest galaxies Many orbit the Milky Way

Stars

Stars are massive bodies composed of gases—typically hydrogen and helium—that emit light. The brightness and luminosity of a star is determined by its distance away from the observer and its size. Stars that are closer, more massive, and/or larger are more luminous. The color of a star is determined by its temperature. The main star colors are:

- Blue-violet (~30,000 K)
- Blue-white (~20,000 K)
- White (~10,000 K)
- Yellow-white (~8,000 K)
- Yellow (~6,000 K)
- Orange (~4,000 K)
- Red orange (~3,000 K)

Stars have a defined life cycle that consists of the following stages:

Birth:

- Dust and gas accumulate into small clumps.
- The collection of matter becomes compressed due to gravity; its temperature increases.
- The collection of matter begins to rotate.
- More matter is drawn in and the temperature continues to rise.
- A small, central core that is extremely hot is formed; this is called a protostar.
- More gas and dust are drawn into the core.
- Nuclear fusion reactions begin and energy is released.
- Once a specific temperature and mass are reached, a massive release of gas removes the matter from the area surrounding the protostar.
- At this point, the protostar becomes a stable young star with a core, a radiative zone, and a convective zone.

Hydrogen Burning Stage (Main Sequence):

- Nuclear fusion reactions continue until all of the star's hydrogen is used up. Stars may remain in their main sequence for billions of years.

Death:

- The star runs out of the hydrogen needed for nuclear fusion.
- In stars similar to the Sun, gravity causes the core to become denser. Its temperature increases. The star becomes a red giant due to the expansion of its outer layers. At a certain temperature, helium is transformed into carbon. The star cools, eventually becoming a white and then a black dwarf.
- In stars that have masses larger than the Sun, helium is transformed into carbon, and then into other elements such as oxygen, magnesium, and iron. Eventually, an iron core will be created. It heats up and becomes extremely compact. This ultimately causes a huge explosion called a supernova. A neutron star or a black hole may be formed from the remnants of the star's core.

The Solar System

Our solar system is comprised of the planets, our Sun, and other celestial bodies. At the center of the universe is the Sun. Without this central star, all life on Earth as we know it would cease to exist. The Sun's energy is produced through nuclear fusion reactions in which hydrogen is converted to helium. The surface of the sun is composed of plasma approaching temperatures of 6,000 Kelvins.

The Sun is orbited by eight planets; Pluto is no longer classified as a planet. From the closest to the Sun to the farthest away, the four inner planets (sometimes also known as terrestrial planets) are Mercury, Venus, Earth, and Mars. These four planets are fairly close together and share several characteristics. They are small and dense, have thin atmospheres, and have solid crusts that contain minerals. From the closest to the sun to the farthest away, the outer planets are Jupiter, Saturn, Uranus, and Neptune. These planets also share several characteristics. They are much larger than the inner planets and have ring systems. Gas accounts for a significant portion of these low density planets.

The following figure shows the relative positions of the Sun and the planets of our solar system:

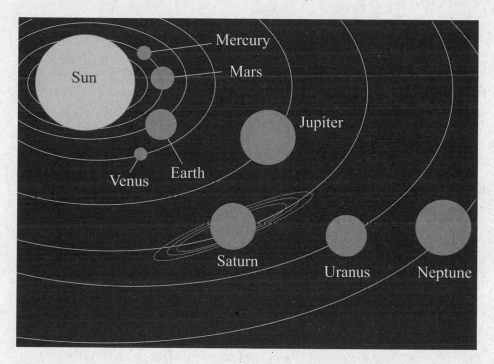

Finally, our solar system contains celestial bodies such as asteroids, meteoroids, and comets. The asteroid belt between Mars and Jupiter contains literally tens of thousands of asteroids. These small bodies resemble rocks and can have spherical or irregular shapes. They can have diameters of several hundred kilometers. The term used to describe relatively small asteroids is meteoroid. Finally, comets are bodies composed of dust or ice. They become luminous when they travel close to the Sun, and the ice they contain is partially vaporized.

Earth's History and Systems

About 10 percent of the test, or 6 questions, will test your knowledge of Earth's atmosphere, hydrosphere, structure features, geologic processes, and history. The atmosphere is the mixture of gases located above the Earth's surface, while the hydrosphere is comprised of all of our planet's water. The interior structure of Earth is comprised of the crust, the mantle, and the core. Geologic processes are responsible for the glaciers, mountains, volcanoes, and other features formed during the Earth's 4600-million-year history.

Atmosphere

The atmosphere is the mixture of gases that extends from just above Earth's surface to approximately 500 kilometers above ground level. Nitrogen and oxygen account for approximately 99 percent of the volume of Earth's atmosphere. Other elements found in trace amounts in the atmosphere are argon, neon, helium, methane, and hydrogen.

The atmosphere consists of four layers that have distinct properties:

The Troposphere:

- It extends to between 8 kilometers (near the poles) and 16 kilometers (over the equator) above ground level.

- Weather occurs in this layer.

- It is the thinnest layer.

- It accounts for most of the atmosphere's mass (roughly 90 percent).

- It is where most of the atmosphere's water vapor and clouds are found.

- Temperatures at the top are around −50°C.

The Stratosphere:

- It extends from the troposphere to about 50 kilometers above ground level.

- It is the location of the ozone layer.

- The average temperature at the top of the stratosphere is 0°C.

The Mesosphere:

- It extends from the stratosphere to about 80 kilometers above ground level.

- It does not absorb much radiation from the sun.

- Temperatures at the top are about −90°C.

The Thermosphere:

- It extends from the mesosphere to about 500 kilometers above ground level.

- This layer does not contain much air.

- The density of the air in the thermosphere is very low.

- It absorbs massive amounts of radiation.

- Temperatures can reach 2000°C.

Hydrosphere

Hydrosphere is the term used to describe Earth's water supply. It includes the water found in:

- Air

- Glaciers

- Rivers
- Lakes
- Streams
- Oceans
- Groundwater
- Soil

Water doesn't simply remain in one form and in the same location indefinitely. Instead, it is constantly moving because of the solar energy from the Sun, weather patterns, and simple gravity. This pattern of movement is known as the hydrologic, or water, cycle. In simple terms, it involves the evaporation of water from the ocean, which is then stored in the atmosphere and transported by winds. This moisture is eventually released in the form of precipitation, which re-enters the oceans once it reaches Earth.

As the following figure illustrates, the hydrologic cycle is, in reality, somewhat more complex.

THE WATER CYCLE

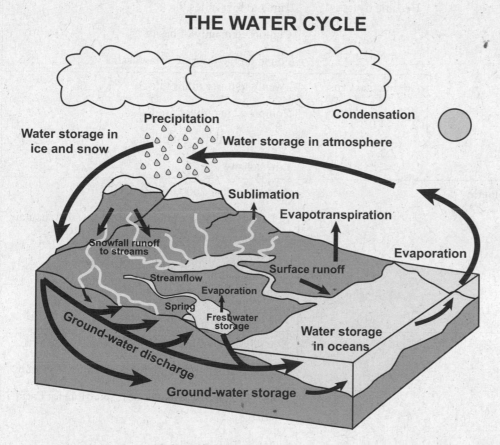

Processes involved in the hydrologic cycle include not only evaporation, the movement of moisture within the atmosphere, and precipitation, but also:

- **Snow and glacial melting:** When temperatures increase, the water stored in snow and glaciers is released, which produces runoff.

- **Runoff:** Not all precipitation falls directly back into the ocean. Water can also flow along the surface of the ground or be transported by moving rivers and streams. It might be absorbed by soil, evaporate, or enter water bodies such as lakes before once again reaching the ocean.

- **Infiltration:** This is the process by which water on the ground's surface is absorbed. It can be used to provide moisture to soil or as groundwater.

- **Underground water flow:** There is a huge amount of water beneath the ground's surface, and precipitation can enter the ground to become part of the store of underground water. This water may naturally enter the oceans over time or reemerge in areas with lower elevations due to gravity. Springs are supplied by underground water.

Structure Features

Earth's structure is composed of three distinct layers: the crust, the mantle, and the core. Each has unique structural features.

Layer		Description/Properties
Crust	Oceanic Crust	Three to four miles thick
		Composed mainly of basalt
		Found on the floor of ocean basins
	Continental Crust	Twenty to thirty miles thick
		Composed mainly of granite
		Found beneath the continents
		Low density
Mantle		Approximately 2000 miles thick
		Believed to consist mainly of rocks that contain abundant amounts of olivine
		Temperatures vary according to depth
		Upper portion is cool and brittle
		Lower portion is warm and soft
Core		Roughly 2000 miles thick
		Believed to consist mainly of nickel alloy and iron
		Contains radioactive materials responsible for Earth's internal heat
		Outer portion is liquid
		Inner portion is solid because of extreme pressure

The following image shows the various layers that comprise Earth's interior.

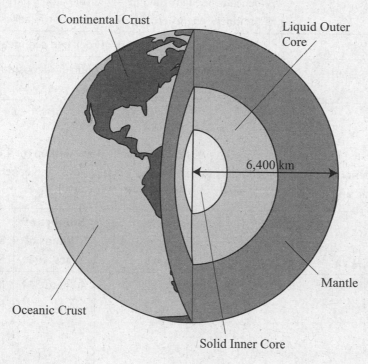

Geologic Processes

The structural features of Earth are created, altered, and destroyed through many different geologic processes.

Name of Geologic Process	Description
Desertification	The gradual conversion of fertile land into desert; can occur due to climate change or human activity.
Erosion	The removal of materials such as soil or rock from Earth's surface usually caused by water, wind, ice, or human activity; materials are typically transported and deposited in another location.
Folding	The bending of rocks or sediment that results in their deformation; can produce small ripples in a material or large mountains.
Glaciation	The formation and recession of glaciers; glaciers are large bodies of ice formed through the accumulation of snow.
Seafloor Spreading	The expansion of the ocean floor that results when two tectonic plates move away from each other.
Metamorphism	The change in the composition, consistency, or internal nature of existing rock caused by exposure to high temperatures, extreme pressure, and other chemical compounds.

Subduction	The process in which the edge of one tectonic plate gets pushed beneath the edge of another; when the subducted plate is released, the kinetic energy produced can cause earthquakes and tsunamis.
Stratification	The accumulation of layers of rock and sediment.
Alluvion	The building up of new land through the deposition of sediment; often occurs in areas surrounding rivers.

History

Scientists interested in Earth's history believe it is approximately 4600 million (or 4.6 billion) years old. This time period is often divided into supereons, eons, eras, periods, and epochs based on the evolution of plant and animal life.

Supereon and Eons	Era	Period	Epoch	Number of Millions of Years Ago	Significant Developments
Precambrian supereon: covers many eons, eras, periods, and epochs				4600 to 544	Microscopic life appears for the first time—these organisms are marine invertebrates without shells and simple marine algae.

Cambrian supereon and Phanerozoic eon	Paleozoic	Cambrian		544 to 505	Additional marine organisms emerge, including ones with protective outer shells.
		Ordovician		505 to 438	Marine life becomes more diverse and the first vertebrates appear.
		Silurian		438 to 408	The first terrestrial plants and the first land insects appear.
		Devonian		408 to 360	Primitive forests appear, marine life continues to diversify, and the first amphibians begin living on land.
		Carboniferous	Mississippian	360 to 320	Terrestrial plant life is well-established by this time, and the ocean contains numerous sharks.
			Pennsylvanian	320 to 286	There are many swamps.
		Permian		286 to 245	The first reptiles appear.

Cambrian supereon and Phanerozoic eon	Mesozoic (also known as the age of reptiles)	Triassic		245 to 208	This period marks the emergence of both dinosaurs and mammals.
		Jurassic		208 to 144	Dinosaurs become abundant and the first birds appear.
		Cretaceous		144 to 66	Dinosaurs become extinct.
	Cenozoic (also known as the age of mammals)	Paleogene	Paleocene	66 to 58	Primates appear.
			Eocene	58 to 37	Horses appear.
			Oligocene	37 to 24	Apes appear.
		Neogene	Miocene	24 to 5	Grazing mammals flourish.
			Pliocene	5 to 1.8	Grazing mammals become abundant.
		Quaternary	Pleistocene	1.8 to 0.01	Humans appear.
			Holocene	0.01 to present	Humans establish civilizations.

NATURAL SCIENCES: REVIEW QUESTIONS

1. All of the following taxa contain the species *Pycnopodia helianthoides*, the sunflower sea star. Which taxon contains the largest number of species?

   (A) Class Asteroidea

   (B) Family Asteriidae

   (C) Genus Pycnopodia

   (D) Order Forcipulatida

   (E) Phylum Echinodermata

2. Which of the following is a balanced equation for the nuclear reaction in which nitrogen is converted into oxygen?

   (A) $N_2 \rightarrow O_2$

   (B) $N_2 \rightarrow O_2 + {}^{0}_{-1}e$

   (C) $^{16}_{7}N \rightarrow {}^{16}_{8}O$

   (D) $^{16}_{7}N \rightarrow {}^{16}_{6}O + {}^{0}_{-1}e$

   (E) $^{16}_{7}N \rightarrow {}^{16}_{8}O + {}^{0}_{-1}e$

3. Which describes a correct sequence of events in Earth's history?

   I. First eukaryotes appear

   II. Atmospheric oxygen levels increase

   III. First tetrapods appear

   IV. Plants colonize land

   (A) I, IV, II, III

   (B) I, II, III, IV

   (C) II, I, IV, III

   (D) II, I, IV, III

   (E) II, IV, I, IV

4. Which of the following elements would have the smallest atomic radius?

   (A) Se

   (B) Ca

   (C) Ti

   (D) Co

   (E) Zn

5. A population is at the point shown on the graph below.

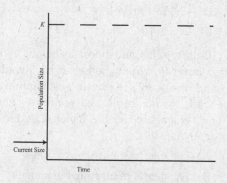

   This population will be under

   (A) *K*-selection, favoring traits that increase reproduction

   (B) *K*-selection, favoring traits that increase survival

   (C) *r*-selection, favoring traits that increase reproduction

   (D) *r*-selection, favoring traits that increase survival

   (E) neutral selection

6. A scientist is trying to determine whether a compound is ionic or molecular. Which of the following would be LEAST helpful in terms of making this determination?

   (A) Determining the melting point of the compound

   (B) Determining the boiling point of the compound

   (C) Determining whether the compound can conduct electricity

   (D) Determining whether the compound is soluble in water

   (E) Determining whether the compound contains a metal

7. The hormone that suppresses the growth of a plant's side shoots is produced in the

   (A) apical meristem

   (B) lateral meristem

   (C) mesophyll layer

   (D) root cortex

   (E) xylem

8. How much energy is needed to convert 5 grams of water at 35°C into steam?

   (A) 1358 Joules

   (B) 3032 Joules

   (C) 9273 Joules

   (D) 12,658 Joules

   (E) 1.53×10^7 Joules

9. Birds, reptiles, and dinosaurs belong to the same taxon, while mammals do not. Reptiles and dinosaurs have three-chambered hearts, while birds and mammals have four-chambered hearts. Which features are analogous?

   (A) The hearts of birds and reptiles

   (B) The hearts of birds and mammals

   (C) The hearts of birds and dinosaurs

   (D) The hearts of dinosaurs and reptiles

   (E) The hearts of mammals and dinosaurs

10. According to the *Second Law of Thermodynamics*, which of the following will occur if a person holds a piece of ice in their hand?

    (A) The thermal energy in both systems will be in equilibrium.

    (B) Thermal energy will flow from the person's hand to the ice.

    (C) The transfer of thermal energy will be 100 percent efficient.

    (D) Thermal energy will flow from the ice to the person's hand.

    (E) The two bodies will create a system with reduced entropy.

11. A man's hand touches a hot object, and he pulls it away quickly. Which sequence correctly describes the passage of the action potentials related to this event?

    (A) sensory neuron → brain → motor neuron

    (B) sensory neuron → spinal cord → motor neuron

    (C) sensory neuron → motor neuron → spinal cord → brain

    (D) sensory neuron → brain → spinal cord → motor neuron

    (E) sensory neuron → spinal cord → brain → motor neuron

12. Which of the following equations would be the BEST one to use to calculate the distance an object traveled if it was dropped and took 10 seconds to reach the ground?

    (A) $d = v_i t + \frac{1}{2}at^2$

    (B) $v_f^2 = v_i^2 + 2ad$

    (C) $v_f = v_i + at$

    (D) $d = \left(\frac{v_i + v_f}{2}\right)t$

    (E) $v = \frac{d}{t}$

13. Which best describes the chromosomes in metaphase of meiosis I?

    (A) Identical sister chromatids

    (B) Non-identical sister chromatids

    (C) Homologous pairs of single chromosomes

    (D) Single chromosomes, before crossing over

    (E) Single chromosomes, after crossing over

14. An electrical system has 23 amperes of current and 5 ohms of resistance. Which of the following expressions can be used to correctly calculate its voltage?

    (A) 23×5

    (B) $23 \div 5$

    (C) $23 + 5$

    (D) $23 - 5$

    (E) $(23 + 5)^2$

15. Which organelle is found in both plant and animal cells?

    (A) A large, central vacuole

    (B) A cell wall

    (C) Ribosomes

    (D) Centrioles

    (E) Mitochondria

16. Which of the following statements are true of elliptical galaxies?
    I. They contain relatively few stars.
    II. They account for about 20 percent of the Universe's galaxies.
    III. They are reddish in color.

    (A) I only
    (B) II only
    (C) III only
    (D) I and II only
    (E) II and III only

17. Which hormone decreases bone density?

    (A) Calcitonin
    (B) Parathyroid hormone
    (C) Testosterone
    (D) Thyroid hormone
    (E) Thyroid-stimulating hormone

18. An archaeologist discovers a fossil of a marine organism with a protective outer shell. The oldest this fossil could possibly be is

    (A) 286 million years old
    (B) 360 million years old
    (C) 408 million years old
    (D) 438 million years old
    (E) 544 million years old

19. Two fruit flies, each heterozygous for two genes, are crossed. What proportion of the offspring is expected to have one dominant and one recessive trait?

    (A) 1 of 16
    (B) 3 of 16
    (C) 6 of 16
    (D) 8 of 16
    (D) 12 of 16

20. Arranged in order from the closest to the ground to the farthest away, the layers of the atmosphere are

    (A) stratosphere, troposphere, mesosphere, thermosphere
    (B) mesosphere, stratosphere, troposphere, thermosphere
    (C) troposphere, stratosphere, mesosphere, thermosphere
    (D) thermosphere, troposphere, mesosphere, stratosphere
    (E) stratosphere, troposphere, mesosphere, thermosphere

ANSWER KEY AND EXPLANATIONS

1. A	5. C	9. B	13. B	17. B
2. E	6. D	10. B	14. A	18. E
3. C	7. A	11. B	15. E	19. C
4. A	8. D	12. A	16. C	20. C

1. **The correct answer is (A).** A class is a larger taxonomic category than an order, family, or genus. Therefore, class Asteroidea contains more species than any of the subordinate categories.

2. **The correct answer is (E).** Equations for nuclear reactions indicate the nucleon number and the proton number, which eliminates choices (A) and (B). These numbers must be equal on both sides of the equation. In choice (E), the number of nucleons on the left side of the equation is 16 and the number of protons is 7. On the right side of the equation, the number of nucleons is 16 (16 + 0) and the number of protons is 7 (8 + −1).

3. **The correct answer is (C).** Atmospheric oxygen levels rose early in Earth's history due to photosynthesis carried out by cyanobacteria. Eukaryotic cells came about before plants, and tetrapods (amphibians, birds, and mammals) arose last.

4. **The correct answer is (A).** The atomic radii of the elements in the periodic table decreases from left to right and increases from top to bottom. All of the elements in the answer choices are found in the same row (period), so the one found farthest to the right (Se) would have the smallest radius.

5. **The correct answer is (C).** Since the population is currently far from its carrying capacity, it will be under r-selection, for traits that increase reproduction.

6. **The correct answer is (D).** Boiling and melting points are high for ionic compounds and low for molecular ones. Ionic compounds in their liquid form can conduct electricity; molecular compounds cannot. Ionic compounds contain metals, while molecular compounds are comprised of non-metals. Many ionic compounds and some molecular compounds are soluble in water. Therefore, determining solubility in water would not allow a scientist to identify a compound as ionic or molecular with a high degree of certainty.

7. **The correct answer is (A).** Hormones produced in the apical meristem suppress the growth of lateral buds.

8. **The correct answer is (D).** First, calculate the energy needed to heat 5 grams of water to 100°C: $Q = mc\Delta t$; Q = 5 grams × 4.18 Joules/gram °C × 65 °C; Q = 1358.5 Joules. Then, calculate the energy needed to convert 5 grams of water at 100°C into steam: energy needed = mass × heat of vaporization; 5 grams × 2260 Joules per gram = 11,300 Joules. Finally, add these two values to calculate the total energy needed: 1358.5 Joules + 11,300 Joules = 12,658 Joules.

9. **The correct answer is (B).** The four-chambered hearts of birds and mammals are analogous features, meaning that they came about due to similar selective pressures.

10. **The correct answer is (B).** The *Second Law of Thermodynamics* encompasses three principles. Two are that heat engines can never be 100 percent efficient and that entropy in a system increases over time. It also states that thermal energy flows from warm to cool bodies or areas. In this case, energy will flow from the warmer hand to the ice.

11. **The correct answer is (B).** A reflex arc travels from the point of sensation to the spinal cord to motor neurons, which is why reflex actions occur before they can be stopped or modified by the brain.

12. **The correct answer is (A).** Choices (A) through (D) are known as the kinematic equations, while choice (E) is used to calculate velocity. In the scenario, the time is provided and v_i (initial velocity) can be assumed to be zero. The acceleration of gravity (a) is a constant. Choice (A) is the best equation since it is the only one that does not require the final velocity to be known and does not need to be rearranged to isolate the variable being focused on (displacement, d).

13. **The correct answer is (B).** Because crossing over, the exchange of DNA segments between homologous chromosomes, occurs in anaphase of meiosis I, metaphase features non-identical sister chromatids.

14. **The correct answer is (A).** Ohm's law is represented by the equation: current = voltage ÷ resistance. The values for current and resistance are given in the question: 23 amperes = voltage ÷ 5 ohms. To solve for voltage multiply both sides by 5 ohms: 23 amperes × 5 ohms = voltage ÷ 5 ohms × 5 ohms.

15. **The correct answer is (E).** Mitochondria are found in both plant and animal cells and in nearly all eukaryotic cells.

16. **The correct answer is (C).** Irregular galaxies contain relatively few stars, and spiral galaxies are thought to account for about 20 percent of the Universe's galaxies. Elliptical galaxies are reddish in color, have bright centers, and can contain more than a trillion stars.

17. **The correct answer is (B).** The parathyroid hormone raises the level of calcium in the blood, decreasing the amount of calcium stored in bone.

18. **The correct answer is (E).** The first marine organisms with protective shells emerged during the Cambrian age. This took place 544 to 505 million years ago. Therefore, the fossil could not be more than 544 million years old.

19. **The correct answer is (C).** A dihybrid cross results in offspring with a 9:3:3:1 ratio of phenotypes. Nine of sixteen will be dominant for both traits, and one of sixteen will be recessive for both traits. The rest will be dominant for either trait, but not for both.

20. **The correct answer is (C).** Earth's atmosphere extends to approximately 500 km above ground level and consists of the troposphere (extends to between 8 and 16 kilometers above ground level), the stratosphere (ends about 50 km above ground level), the mesosphere (ends about 80 km above ground level), and the thermosphere (ends about 500 km above ground level).

POSTTEST ANSWER SHEET

1. Ⓐ Ⓑ Ⓒ Ⓓ Ⓔ   11. Ⓐ Ⓑ Ⓒ Ⓓ Ⓔ   21. Ⓐ Ⓑ Ⓒ Ⓓ Ⓔ   31. Ⓐ Ⓑ Ⓒ Ⓓ Ⓔ   41. Ⓐ Ⓑ Ⓒ Ⓓ Ⓔ

2. Ⓐ Ⓑ Ⓒ Ⓓ Ⓔ   12. Ⓐ Ⓑ Ⓒ Ⓓ Ⓔ   22. Ⓐ Ⓑ Ⓒ Ⓓ Ⓔ   32. Ⓐ Ⓑ Ⓒ Ⓓ Ⓔ   42. Ⓐ Ⓑ Ⓒ Ⓓ Ⓔ

3. Ⓐ Ⓑ Ⓒ Ⓓ Ⓔ   13. Ⓐ Ⓑ Ⓒ Ⓓ Ⓔ   23. Ⓐ Ⓑ Ⓒ Ⓓ Ⓔ   33. Ⓐ Ⓑ Ⓒ Ⓓ Ⓔ   43. Ⓐ Ⓑ Ⓒ Ⓓ Ⓔ

4. Ⓐ Ⓑ Ⓒ Ⓓ Ⓔ   14. Ⓐ Ⓑ Ⓒ Ⓓ Ⓔ   24. Ⓐ Ⓑ Ⓒ Ⓓ Ⓔ   34. Ⓐ Ⓑ Ⓒ Ⓓ Ⓔ   44. Ⓐ Ⓑ Ⓒ Ⓓ Ⓔ

5. Ⓐ Ⓑ Ⓒ Ⓓ Ⓔ   15. Ⓐ Ⓑ Ⓒ Ⓓ Ⓔ   25. Ⓐ Ⓑ Ⓒ Ⓓ Ⓔ   35. Ⓐ Ⓑ Ⓒ Ⓓ Ⓔ   45. Ⓐ Ⓑ Ⓒ Ⓓ Ⓔ

6. Ⓐ Ⓑ Ⓒ Ⓓ Ⓔ   16. Ⓐ Ⓑ Ⓒ Ⓓ Ⓔ   26. Ⓐ Ⓑ Ⓒ Ⓓ Ⓔ   36. Ⓐ Ⓑ Ⓒ Ⓓ Ⓔ   46. Ⓐ Ⓑ Ⓒ Ⓓ Ⓔ

7. Ⓐ Ⓑ Ⓒ Ⓓ Ⓔ   17. Ⓐ Ⓑ Ⓒ Ⓓ Ⓔ   27. Ⓐ Ⓑ Ⓒ Ⓓ Ⓔ   37. Ⓐ Ⓑ Ⓒ Ⓓ Ⓔ   47. Ⓐ Ⓑ Ⓒ Ⓓ Ⓔ

8. Ⓐ Ⓑ Ⓒ Ⓓ Ⓔ   18. Ⓐ Ⓑ Ⓒ Ⓓ Ⓔ   28. Ⓐ Ⓑ Ⓒ Ⓓ Ⓔ   38. Ⓐ Ⓑ Ⓒ Ⓓ Ⓔ   48. Ⓐ Ⓑ Ⓒ Ⓓ Ⓔ

9. Ⓐ Ⓑ Ⓒ Ⓓ Ⓔ   19. Ⓐ Ⓑ Ⓒ Ⓓ Ⓔ   29. Ⓐ Ⓑ Ⓒ Ⓓ Ⓔ   39. Ⓐ Ⓑ Ⓒ Ⓓ Ⓔ   49. Ⓐ Ⓑ Ⓒ Ⓓ Ⓔ

10. Ⓐ Ⓑ Ⓒ Ⓓ Ⓔ   20. Ⓐ Ⓑ Ⓒ Ⓓ Ⓔ   30. Ⓐ Ⓑ Ⓒ Ⓓ Ⓔ   40. Ⓐ Ⓑ Ⓒ Ⓓ Ⓔ   50. Ⓐ Ⓑ Ⓒ Ⓓ Ⓔ

answer sheet

Posttest

40 minutes • 50 questions

Directions: Each of the questions or incomplete statements below is followed by five suggested answers or completions. Select the one that is best in each case.

1. If an atom could be viewed with a microscope, an observer would note that the atom is mainly
   (A) protons
   (B) elementary particles
   (C) neutrons
   (D) empty space
   (E) electrons

2. Which of the following is part of the rock cycle?
   (A) Sediment becomes compacted to form igneous rock.
   (B) Metamorphic rock cools to form igneous rock.
   (C) Sediment is heated to form sedimentary rock.
   (D) Metamorphic rock melts to form magma.
   (E) Igneous rock cools to form sediment.

3. Which of the following is a property of solids?
   (A) Their particles can change positions.
   (B) They can be compressed with little effort.
   (C) Their particles vibrate when heat is applied.
   (D) They can flow and exhibit surface tension.
   (E) Their particles are randomly arranged.

4. Which of the following events occurs during mitotic prophase?
   (A) The spindle forms.
   (B) The sister chromatids separate.
   (C) The nuclear envelope reforms.
   (D) The cell plate forms.
   (E) The chromatids move to the poles.

5. In a breed of dog, the dominant B gene corresponds to black fur, while the recessive b gene corresponds to brown. What proportion of offspring would be heterozygous in a cross between a parent with a BB genotype and one with a Bb genotype?
   (A) 0%
   (B) 25%
   (C) 50%
   (D) 75%
   (E) 100%

6. A small-engine plane is flying at a velocity of 160 km/hour in a southerly direction relative to the ground. If it is blown off course by a westerly wind that has a velocity of 70 km/hour, what will the resultant velocity of the plane be relative to the ground?
   (A) 70 km/hour
   (B) 90 km/hour
   (C) 160 km/hour
   (D) 175 km/hour
   (E) 230 km/hour

7. Which of the following statements are true of lunar eclipses?

    I. They occur during a new moon.
    II. They occur when the Moon casts a shadow on Earth.
    III. They occur when Earth, Moon, and Sun align.

(A) I only

(B) II only

(C) III only

(D) I and II only

(E) II and III only

8. In the human circulatory system, blood from the upper part of the body flows into the heart via the

(A) right atrium

(B) superior vena cava

(C) pulmonary valve

(D) inferior vena cava

(E) pulmonary artery

9. During which of the following eras did the first fish, amphibians, and reptiles appear?

(A) Triassic

(B) Mesozoic

(C) Paleozoic

(D) Cenozoic

(E) Jurassic

10. A genetic counsellor creates a pedigree analysis for a couple to determine the couple's chances of giving birth to a child with cystic fibrosis (CF), which is a recessive disorder. If the counsellor finds that neither the woman's grandmother nor her grandfather had the disorder but one of their children did, which of the following conclusions can the counsellor make?

(A) The grandparents were both carriers of the CF gene.

(B) The grandmother only was a carrier of the CF gene.

(C) The woman has two copies of the CF gene.

(D) The grandfather only was a carrier of the CF gene.

(E) The woman's child will be a carrier of the CF gene.

11. Which of the following statements are true of elements that are classified as metals?

    I. They are typically solid at room temperature.
    II. They are often transparent or translucent.
    III. They are found on the right side of the periodic table.

(A) I only

(B) II only

(C) III only

(D) I and II only

(E) II and III only

12. It is generally accepted that organisms evolve through natural selection. Which of the following is the best definition of natural selection?

(A) Organisms with the best genetic makeup are able to reproduce.

(B) Organisms with the best genetic makeup live the longest.

(C) Organisms with the best genetic makeup seek out the best mates.

(D) Organisms with the best genetic makeup dominate their social groups.

(E) Organisms with the best genetic makeup exhibit the most common traits.

13. Which of the following statements are true of the Rayleigh waves produced during an earthquake?

    I. They exhibit whip-like motion.
    II. They travel faster than P waves.
    III. They are surface waves.

(A) I only

(B) II only

(C) III only

(D) I and II only

(E) II and III only

14. Two separate populations of robins reside in the same forest. Occasionally, two members from the different populations will mate and produce offspring. In population biology, the concept used to describe this is

    (A) coevolution

    (B) genetic drift

    (C) inbreeding

    (D) founder effect

    (E) dispersal

15. Protons and neutrons are composed of quarks. Which of the following quark combinations would be found in a neutron?

    (A) *up down down*

    (B) *up down top*

    (C) *up down up*

    (D) *up up bottom*

    (E) *up up up*

16. Biologists typically classify the distribution of populations as uniform, random, or clumped. Which of the following would most likely have a random distribution?

    (A) Ants living in nests made in rotting tree stumps

    (B) Trees located in a forest that is sparsely populated

    (C) Coyotes living in packs in a forest and close to food sources

    (D) Trees located in a forest where there is little space for roots

    (E) Coyotes that have a five-mile territory living separately in a forest

17. One person applies 20N of force to a block resting on a table. Another person applies 8N of force to the block in the opposite direction. According to Newton's second law of motion, what will the acceleration be if the block has a mass of 0.54 kg?

    (A) 6.48 m/s2

    (B) 14.8 m/s2

    (C) 22.2 m/s2

    (D) 37.0 m/s2

    (E) 51.8 m/s2

18. Which of the following statements are true of smooth muscle?

    I. It is found in the bladder.
    II. It is capable of stretching.
    III. It is under voluntary control.

    (A) I only

    (B) II only

    (C) III only

    (D) I and II only

    (E) II and III only

19. Which of the following elements is a noble gas?

    (A) Rb

    (B) Ca

    (C) Mo

    (D) Kr

    (E) O

20. All of the following statements are true of the inner planets EXCEPT

    (A) they include Mercury and Mars

    (B) they are relatively small in size

    (C) they are also known as terrestrial

    (D) they have many large satellites

    (E) they have solid crusts with minerals

21. A system does 72 Joules of external work, and its thermal energy increases by 54 Joules. According to the first law of thermodynamics, which of the following expressions could be used to calculate the amount of heat added to the system?

    (A) 72 Joules ÷ 54 Joules

    (B) 2 (72 Joules + 54 Joules)

    (C) 72 Joules × 54 Joules

    (D) $\frac{(72 \text{ Joules} - 54 \text{ Joules})}{2}$

    (E) 72 Joules + 54 Joules

22. The classification system developed by Robert Whitaker was the

    (A) two kingdom system

    (B) three kingdom system

    (C) four kingdom system

    (D) five kingdom system

    (E) six kingdom system

23. Simple diffusion is one of the three main mechanisms that control the movement of ions and molecules in and out of cells. One of the characteristics of simple diffusion is that

    (A) substances that are transported across the membrane are bound

    (B) the energy required for the process is produced through ATP hydrolysis

    (C) carrier proteins are needed to transport substances across the membrane

    (D) molecules move from an area of low concentration to one of high concentration

    (E) it occurs when there are different concentration gradients inside and outside the cell

24. The kingdom Animalia consists of both protostomes and deuterostomes. Which of the following statements are true of protostomes?

    I. They have bilateral symmetry.
    II. During embryonic development, the opening that develops first is the mouth.
    III. They comprise the phylum Echinodermata.

    (A) I only
    (B) II only
    (C) III only
    (D) I and II only
    (E) II and III only

25. When a brown rabbit is crossed with a white rabbit, some of the offspring have fur that is brown at the bottom and white at the tips. The pattern of heredity that most likely accounts for this phenotype is

    (A) codominance
    (B) incomplete dominance
    (C) multidominance
    (D) partial dominance
    (E) full dominance

26. The principle of relative dating used by Earth scientists that states that higher layers of sedimentary rock are younger than lower ones is known as

    (A) original horizontality
    (B) superposition
    (C) cross-cutting
    (D) inclusion
    (E) faunal succession

27. Which of the following occurs when a sodium (Na) atom and a chlorine (Cl) atom react?

    (A) Cl loses an electron.
    (B) Na loses an electron.
    (C) Cl loses a proton.
    (D) Na loses a proton.
    (E) Na and Cl share an electron.

28. The asteroid belt in our solar system is located between

    (A) Mercury and Venus
    (B) Venus and Earth
    (C) Earth and Mars
    (D) Mars and Jupiter
    (E) Jupiter and Saturn

29. Which of the following statements are true of the developmental process known as incomplete metamorphosis?

    I. It is how butterflies develop.
    II. It includes a nymph stage.
    III. It includes a pupa stage.

    (A) I only
    (B) II only
    (C) III only
    (D) I and II only
    (E) II and III only

30. An example of the method of heat transfer known as conduction is

    (A) an infrared heating system making a living area warmer

    (B) water boiling when a pot is placed on a stove burner

    (C) an entire nail getting hot when its tip is placed in a fire

(D) warmer, less dense air expanding and traveling upwards

(E) a light bulb warming a small area when a lamp is turned on

31. When studying the distributions of populations, scientists often consider not only crude density but also ecological density. Which of the following statements is correct regarding the relationship between crude and ecological density?

(A) Crude density is equal to ecological density.

(B) Crude density is usually greater than ecological density.

(C) Crude density is inversely related to ecological density.

(D) Crude density is usually less than ecological density.

(E) Crude density is double the value of ecological density.

32. Which of the following statements are true of the membranes that surround the cells of most organisms?

I. Membranes contain lipids with hydrophilic tails.
II. Membranes prevent any molecules from entering the cell.
III. Membranes are composed of two layers.

(A) I only

(B) II only

(C) III only

(D) I and II only

(E) II and III only

33. The possible blood types in humans are A, B, AB, or O. A and B are dominant. In a cross between someone with blood type AB and someone who is heterozygous for blood type A, what will be the ratio of offspring with blood type AB to offspring with blood type B?

(A) 3 : 1

(B) 2 : 1

(C) 1 : 1

(D) 1 : 2

(E) 1 : 3

34. When a single population is separated, two new, distinct populations may be established. These geographically isolated populations will develop slightly different genotypes over time. This type of speciation is known as

(A) allopatric

(B) polymorphic

(C) sympatric

(D) isolationist

(E) parapatric

35. Based on the bond energy values provided below, what amount of energy is required to break the chemical bonds in the reaction $3H_2 + N_2 \rightarrow 2NH_3$?

Bond	Bond Energy (kJ/mole)
H—H	436
N—N	159

(A) 754 kJ/mole

(B) 1308 kJ/mole

(C) 1467 kJ/mole

(D) 2934 kJ/mole

(E) 4401 kJ/mole

36. Which of the following statements are true of quasars?

I. They are fainter than galaxies.
II. They emit radio waves.
III. They are young elliptical galaxies.

(A) I only

(B) II only

(C) III only

(D) I and II only

(E) II and III only

37. Radioactive atoms emit *alpha*, *beta*, and *gamma* rays. All of the following are properties of *alpha* rays EXCEPT they

(A) contain two neutrons

(B) have a positive charge

(C) are fairly large in size

(D) often become helium

(E) can penetrate clothing

38. According to Ohm's law, what is the voltage of a toaster if the circuit has 39 Ω of resistance and 11 amperes of current?

(A) 0.28 volts

(B) 3.54 volts

(C) 50 volts

(D) 121 volts

(E) 429 volts

39. The bone of the human arm that extends from the elbow to the side of the wrist closest to the thumb is the

(A) radius

(B) ulna

(C) humerus

(D) patella

(E) tibia

40. The process of photosynthesis carried out within cells is often divided into light and dark reactions. Which of the following occurs during the dark reactions of photosynthesis?

(A) CO_2 is converted to organic molecules.

(B) H+ moves across the cell membrane.

(C) ATP and ADP are synthesized.

(D) The O_2 contained in H_2O is released.

(E) Light energy is used to produce NADPH.

41. The stage of mitotic cell division during which the DNA of the cell is replicated is

(A) interphase

(B) prophase

(C) metaphase

(D) anaphase

(E) telophase

42. When studying populations, scientists often calculate the effective population size using the following equation: $N_e = \frac{4 N_m N_f}{N_m + N_f}$. N_m is the number of breeding males and N_f is the number of breeding females. Which of the following would have the greatest effective population size?

(A) A population with 15 mature males and 15 mature females

(B) A population with 10 immature males, 10 mature males, and 10 mature females

(C) A population with 27 mature males and 3 mature females

(D) A population with 2 immature females, 13 mature males, and 15 mature females

(E) A population with 13 mature males and 17 mature females

43. Which of the following is an example of an acid-base reaction?

(A) $HBr + NaOH \rightarrow NaBr + H_2O$

(B) $C10H8 + 12\,O_2 \rightarrow 10\,CO_2 + 4\,H_2O$

(C) $2HNO_3 + H_2S \rightarrow 2\,H_2O + 2NO_2 + S$

(D) $NaCl + AgNO_3 \rightarrow NaNO_3 + AgCl$

(E) $2KClO3 \rightarrow 2KCl + 3O2$

44. In neurons, the branched extensions at the end that receive and carry information from other nerve cells are known as

(A) myelin sheaths

(B) Schwann cells

(C) somas

(D) dendrites

(E) cell bodies

45. Which of the following is the best definition of a syncline?

    (A) A fold in which the two sides are unequal

    (B) A fold in which the sides slope upward

    (C) A fold in which a tectonic plate is subducted

    (D) A fold in which the sides slope downward

    (E) A fold in which a tectonic plate is broken

46. All of the following are phyla that are part of the Animalia kingdom EXCEPT

    (A) Chordata

    (B) Echinodermata

    (C) Arthropoda

    (D) Annelida

    (E) Ascomycota

47. According to the theory of special relativity, one change observed in objects as they approach the speed of light is that objects traveling in a

    (A) horizontal direction will contract horizontally

    (B) vertical direction will expand vertically

    (C) horizontal direction will contract vertically

    (D) vertical direction will contract horizontally

    (E) horizontal direction will expand vertically

48. In humans, the kidney is composed of many basic units that filter blood and produce urine known as

    (A) renal pyramids

    (B) ureters

    (C) renal capsules

    (D) nephrons

    (E) renal papillae

49. Wave interference occurs when two waves meet. If those two waves are identical and in phase, the resultant wave will double in

    (A) frequency

    (B) amplitude

    (C) wavelength

    (D) period

    (E) speed

50. Which of the following eras of Earth's history is also known as the "age of the mammals"?

    (A) Oligocene

    (B) Eocene

    (C) Mesozoic

    (D) Cenozoic

    (E) Holocene

ANSWER KEY AND EXPLANATIONS

1. D	11. A	21. E	31. D	41. A
2. D	12. A	22. D	32. C	42. A
3. C	13. C	23. E	33. C	43. A
4. A	14. E	24. D	34. A	44. D
5. C	15. A	25. A	35. C	45. D
6. D	16. B	26. B	36. B	46. E
7. C	17. C	27. B	37. E	47. A
8. B	18. D	28. D	38. E	48. D
9. C	19. D	29. B	39. A	49. B
10. A	20. D	30. C	40. A	50. D

1. **The correct answer is (D).** Most of an atom's mass is contained in the nucleus; its diameter is about 10 thousand times smaller than that of the entire atom. The electrons surrounding the nucleus are extremely dispersed, so most of an atom consists of empty space.

2. **The correct answer is (D).** The rock cycle is often represented as a circle showing the processes that form sediment, magma, and the main types of rock. Magma cools to form igneous rock; the weathering and transportation of igneous rock results in sediment; sediment becomes compacted and forms sedimentary rock; sedimentary rock is transformed into metamorphic rock through extreme heat and pressure; and metamorphic rock melts to form magma.

3. **The correct answer is (C).** The particles of solids are arranged in a rigid, three-dimensional shape; solids cannot flow like liquids can and they are not easily compressed since particles are already touching and tightly packed together. Although the particles of a solid cannot change positions, they can vibrate when heat is applied, which eventually causes the solid to turn into a liquid.

4. **The correct answer is (A).** Mitosis is usually broken down into four stages: prophase, metaphase, anaphase, and telophase. During the first stage (prophase), the chromatin fibers condense into chromosomes, the nucleolus and nuclear envelope break down, and the spindle that will pull the chromatids to the poles develops.

5. **The correct answer is (C).** Use a Punnett square to determine the genotypes of the offspring: BB, BB, Bb, and Bb. Heterozygous offspring have a copy of both the recessive and dominant gene; in this example, two of the four offspring (50%) are heterozygous.

6. **The correct answer is (D).** The plane's velocity can be represented using a downward arrow ($\downarrow$) and the wind velocity can be represented using an arrow pointing left ($\leftarrow$). Put these arrows together to form two sides of a right triangle and then use the Pythagorean theorem to find the value of the unknown side—the resultant velocity relative to the ground.

$$c^2 = a^2 + b^2$$
$$c^2 = 160^2 + 70^2$$
$$c^2 = 25,600 + 4900$$
$$c^2 = 30,500$$
$$c = 175$$

7. **The correct answer is (C).** During a lunar eclipse, Earth's position is such that it is between the Sun and the Moon. Earth casts a shadow on the Moon during a lunar eclipse,

and these events always occur during a full moon.

8. **The correct answer is (B).** Blood from the upper part of the body enters the heart through the superior vena cava, while blood from the lower body enters through the inferior vena cava. From here, it travels the following path to reach the lungs: right atrium, tricuspid valve, right ventricle, pulmonary valve, and pulmonary artery.

9. **The correct answer is (C).** All of the following evolved during the Paleozoic Era, which lasted from about 590 million years ago until approximately 248 million years ago: fish, amphibians, reptiles, insects, land plants, and coal forests. The Mesozoic Era (which included the Triassic and Jurassic periods) was when dinosaurs appeared, and Cenozoic is the present era.

10. **The correct answer is (A).** The woman's grandparents had a child with CF, so both individuals must have been carriers of the CF gene (heterozygous) since the disease is recessive and neither had the disease. There is no indication that the woman has CF, and there is no way to conclude whether the woman is a carrier who will pass on the gene to a child based on the information provided.

11. **The correct answer is (A).** Metals such as sodium and potassium are typically solids at room temperature, are shiny and opaque, readily conduct heat and electricity, and can be bent or shaped into different forms. Most elements are metals; there are a comparatively small number of nonmetals, and these are found on the right of the periodic table.

12. **The correct answer is (A).** Organisms with desirable genetic makeups that aid in their survival live long enough to reproduce and pass those genes on to their offspring. Conversely, organisms that are not "genetically fit" or well-adapted to their environments are more likely to die off without producing any offspring.

13. **The correct answer is (C).** The two broad categories of waves produced during an earthquake are body waves and surface

waves. Rayleigh waves are one of two types of surface waves (love waves are the other type); they travel in an up-and-down motion and are slower than both P and S waves (both of these are body waves).

14. **The correct answer is (E).** Dispersal occurs when individuals that do not belong to a specific subpopulation breed with one or more members of that subpopulation. This is a common occurrence, except in populations that are geographically isolated, and helps maintain genetic diversity.

15. **The correct answer is (A).** *Up* quarks have a charge of $+\frac{2}{3}$ and *down* quarks have a charge of $-\frac{1}{3}$. Neutrons have no charge, and the quark combination *up down down* would result in a net charge of zero: $(+\frac{2}{3} + \frac{-1}{3} + \frac{-1}{3} = 0)$.

16. **The correct answer is (B).** Trees growing in a forest (unless there is extreme competition for soil and light) will usually have a random distribution, as will some invertebrates such as spiders. A uniform distribution would be found when animals have a defined territory and are competing with other members of their species or when the root and crown space for trees is very limited, and a clumped distribution is found in areas that contain scattered groups.

17. **The correct answer is (C).** According to Newton's second law of motion, the net force applied to an object is equal to its mass multiplied by its acceleration $\left(F_{net} = ma \text{ or } a = \frac{F_{net}}{m} \right)$. In this problem, the net force is the difference between the two forces, since they are applied in opposite directions (20 N − 8 N = 12 N) and the acceleration is 22.2 m/s² $\left(\begin{array}{l} a = \frac{F_{net}}{m} \\ a = \frac{12 \text{ N}}{0.54 \text{ kg}} \\ a \approx 22.2 \text{ m/s}^2 \end{array} \right)$.

18. **The correct answer is (D).** Smooth muscle is capable of stretching and is found in structures such as the digestive system,

uterus, and bladder. Smooth muscle contractions are involuntary.

19. **The correct answer is (D).** The vertical columns of the periodic table are known as groups. Group 18—the row at the far right of the periodic table—consists of the noble gases: He, Ne, Ar, Kr, Xe, and Rn.

20. **The correct answer is (D).** The inner planets, also known as the terrestrial planets, are Mercury, Venus, Earth, and Mars. They are small and dense, and have solid crusts that contain minerals. The only ones with natural satellites are Earth and Mars.

21. **The correct answer is (E).** The first law of thermodynamics relates to the idea that energy cannot be created or destroyed; therefore, when heat enters or exits a system, the amount of thermal energy gained or lost by the system and the heat transferred is the same. Mathematically, this can be represented using the following equation: Amount of heat entering a system = thermal energy gained + work done (heat transferred).

22. **The correct answer is (D).** Scientists have classified life using all of the systems mentioned, but the one developed by Robert Whitaker was the five kingdom classification system. The kingdoms in this system are Monera, Protista, Plantae, Fungi, and Animalia.

23. **The correct answer is (E).** Simple diffusion is the movement of molecules and ions across a cell membrane; these substances move from areas of high to low concentration. In facilitated diffusion, substances are bound and carrier proteins are involved, and active transport requires energy and involves the movement of substances from an area of low concentration to an area of high concentration.

24. **The correct answer is (D).** The protostomes are the members of the Annelida, Arthropoda, and Mollusca phyla. Characteristics of protostomes include the following: the first opening in the embryo is the mouth, they have bilateral symmetry and three germ layers, they have organs, and they have a true coelom.

25. **The correct answer is (A).** In the pattern of heredity known as codominance, the traits of both parents are expressed in offspring; in this example the offspring have fur that is both brown and white. In incomplete dominance, also known as partial dominance, the phenotypes of offspring represent a blend between the two parents; in this example the offspring might have light brown or tan fur.

26. **The correct answer is (B).** In any given sedimentary rock layer, the oldest rocks will be found near the bottom. Other principles used include original horizontality (sediment layers are even and layered almost directly on top of older sediment), cross-cutting (faults or intrusions are younger than the pre-existing rock in which they are found), inclusion (a rock piece found inside another type of rock is older than the containing rock), and faunal succession (fossils provide a record of how life evolved and can be used to estimate the age of rock samples regardless of where they are found).

27. **The correct answer is (B).** Reactions between atoms that result in the formation of compounds involve the loss, gain, and sharing of electrons. In the case of Na and Cl, Na (a metal) loses an electron and Cl (a nonmetal) gains an electron to form Na^+Cl^-.

28. **The correct answer is (D).** The asteroid belt in our solar system is composed of thousands of small bodies; some have irregular shapes and others resemble spheres. It is located in the relatively vast space between Mars and Jupiter.

29. **The correct answer is (B).** Incomplete metamorphosis consists of an egg stage, a nymph stage (nymphs are essentially wingless, smaller versions of adult insects), and an adult stage. Complete metamorphosis is the developmental process found in butterflies and consists of four stages: egg, larvae, pupa, and adult.

30. **The correct answer is (C).** Conduction is a type of heat transfer that occurs when heated electrons are able to move and come into contact with nearby electrons, a process that eventually transmits heat throughout the entire object. Choices (A) and (E) are

examples of radiation, while choices (B) and (D) are examples of convection.

31. **The correct answer is (D).** Crude density is the number of population members in a unit of space (120 robins/square mile, for example). Ecological density is the number of population members in an area that is suitable for and available as living space. This area will often be relatively small, so ecological density is typically greater than crude density.

32. **The correct answer is (C).** The membrane of most cells is a bilayer composed of lipids with hydrophobic tails and hydrophilic heads. Membranes are semipermeable, which means they prevent some (but not all) molecules from entering the cell.

33. **The correct answer is (C).** A cross between someone with blood type AB and someone with blood type AO would result in the following offspring: AA, AO, AB, BO. One quarter of the offspring have blood type AB and one quarter have blood type B, so the ratio is 1:1.

34. **The correct answer is (A).** Allopatric, or geographic, speciation is one of the three main mechanisms of speciation in which isolated populations develop different genotypes, phenotypes, and behaviors over time. Parapatric speciation occurs when populations are not geographically isolated, and sympatric speciation occurs within a population.

35. **The correct answer is (C).** To find the amount of energy required to break the chemical bonds in this reaction, first identify all of the bonds: H—H, H—H, H—H, and N—N. Then, use the values from the table to calculate the energy required to break all of the bonds: 436 kJ/mole + 436 kJ/mole + 436 kJ/mole + 159 kJ/mole = 1467 kJ/mole.

36. **The correct answer is (B).** Quasars are brighter than everything else that exists in the universe, including galaxies. These objects emit huge amounts of energy in the form of radio waves, and astronomers believe they are active spiral galaxies that are very young.

37. **The correct answer is (E).** Alpha particles are composed of two protons and two neutrons and, therefore, have a charge of +2. They can pick up electrons fairly easily and change into helium, are relatively large, and usually can't penetrate materials such as paper or clothing (beta and gamma rays can).

38. **The correct answer is (E).** Ohm's law states that current = voltage ÷ resistance. Use the values provided in the question to calculate the correct answer (11 amperes = voltage ÷ 39 Ω; 11 amperes × 39 Ω = voltage; 429 volts = voltage).

39. **The correct answer is (A).** The radius and ulna are the two long bones of the forearm; the end point of the first is closer to the thumb and the end point of the second is closer to the pinky finger. The humerus is the long bone of the upper arm, and the patella and tibia are bones of the leg.

40. **The correct answer is (A).** Photosynthesis is a chemical reaction during which sunlight is transformed into organic molecules through a series of reactions. The dark reactions of photosynthesis involve the conversion of CO_2 into organic molecules; energy for these reactions is provided by NADPH and ATP as opposed to light energy directly from the sun.

41. **The correct answer is (A).** The events of prophase are divided into the following phases: G1, synthesis, and G2. During G1, cellular molecules and proteins are synthesized; DNA is synthesized during the S phase; and G2 is a second, shorter period of growth that occurs before prophase.

42. **The correct answer is (A).** Even though all of the populations consist of 30 members, their effective population sizes vary. Use the equation to calculate the effective population size for each choice: [choice (A) is 30; choice (B) is 20; choice (C) is 11; choice (D) is 28; and choice (E) is 29]. The immature males and females are not included in the calculation.

43. **The correct answer is (A).** An acid-base reaction can be identified by looking for an H^+ ion (H^+Br^-) and an OH^- ion (Na^+OH^-)

on the reactant side and water and an ionic salt (Na^+Br^-) on the product side. In this example, HBr acts as the acid and NaOH acts as the base.

44. **The correct answer is (D).** Dendrites are short, highly branched structures that transmit information to the cell body of the neuron. The axon carries information away from the cell body and is often covered in a myelin sheath, Schwann cells are found along the axon, and the soma is the point where all of the signals carried by the dendrites converge before being transported along the axon.

45. **The correct answer is (D).** Rock layers that are subjected to compressive forces and stress may change their shape and develop folds. The two types of folds are syncline (which have a curved U shape in which the center is lower than the sides) and anticline (which have a curved shape in which the sides are lower than the center).

46. **The correct answer is (E).** Ascomycota is a phylum within the kingdom Fungi that includes truffle mushrooms and other species that use structures called asci to produce pods. Phyla within the kingdom Animalia include not only the ones mentioned in the answer choices, but also Mollusca, Nematoda, Platyhelminthes, Cnidaria, and Porifera.

47. **The correct answer is (A).** The idea of length contraction was theorized by George F. FitzGerald and represented with a mathematical formula by Hendrick A. Lorentz. Length contraction states that the length of objects decreases as their relative speeds increase; one important point is that the type of contraction (horizontal or vertical) will be the same as the type of motion.

48. **The correct answer is (D).** Although all of the answer choices are structures found in the kidney, the nephron is the basic unit of this excretory system organ. In humans, each kidney contains about a million nephrons.

49. **The correct answer is (B).** If two waves are identical and in phase, the property that will be altered when they meet is amplitude, which will be doubled in the resultant wave. The frequency, wavelength (less commonly known as period), and speed will not change.

50. **The correct answer is (D).** The Cenozoic Era began approximately 66 million years ago, is the present era, and is the time period during which mammals and humans emerged. Eocene, Oligocene, and Holocene are all epochs that are part of the Cenozoic Era, and the Mesozoic Era is the one that came between the Paleozoic and Cenozoic Eras.

APPENDIX

The CLEP Subject Exams

The CLEP Subject Exams

As mentioned in Chapter 1, the CLEP is a collection of thirty-three exams sponsored by the College Board. This book focuses on the five main CLEP exams: College Composition, College Mathematics, Humanities, Social Sciences and History, and Natural Sciences. These five tests cover a broad range of information spanning a number of subject areas. Some students, however, may opt to take any of the other twenty-eight CLEP exams, known as the CLEP Subject Exams.

The CLEP Subject Exams are developed by college faculty from across the country. Unlike the general exams, however, they are designed to indicate college-level mastery of course content in a specific subject area. Each college's CLEP policy is different, but across the nation, approximately 2,900 colleges and universities grant credit for certain CLEP exams. Those who earn a qualifying score on these exams have the opportunity to earn college credits or test out of certain college classes, thereby allowing them to advance to higher levels of academic study at a faster rate and earn their degrees in less time. Many students find that taking the CLEP Subject Exams helps them in the long run, by shortening the length of time it takes them to earn a degree and reducing the overall cost of their college education.

Most of the tests are composed mainly of multiple-choice questions and last about 90 minutes. A few exams include other question types or optional essays. The tests are computerized, but those who are unable to take the computerized exam can ask to take a paper-and-pencil exam. Only certain tests are available in this format, however. A few of the math and business tests allow for the use of a non-graphing, non-programmable calculator.

The CLEP Subject Exams fall into five general content categories:

1. Composition and Literature
2. World Languages
3. History and Social Sciences
4. Science and Math
5. Business

The following is a brief overview of what you can expect to see on each CLEP Subject Exam. For more specific information about each exam, visit the CLEP Web site at http://clep.collegeboard.org.

A TEST-BY-TEST BREAKDOWN

Composition and Literature

American Literature

OVERVIEW

- 90 minutes
- 100 multiple-choice questions
- Optional essay section (includes two essays to be answered in an additional 90-minute period; required by some institutions)

The American Literature exam focuses on literature created in the United States from colonial times to the present. The test focuses primarily on fiction and poetry, though students may encounter questions about drama and nonfiction (essay, autobiography) on the exam as well. About 45 to 60 questions on the exam require knowledge of specific literary works. The rest of the exam focuses on analyzing and interpreting literary works (25 to 40 questions); knowledge of literary terms, forms, and devices (5 to 10 questions); and understanding the historical, social, and literary background of specific works (10 to 15 questions). The following explains how the questions are divided among the various periods in American history:

- The Colonial and Early National Period, beginnings–1830 (15 questions)
- The Romantic Period, 1830–1870 (25 questions)
- The Period of Realism and Naturalism, 1870–1910 (20 questions)
- The Modernist Period, 1910–1945 (25 questions)
- The Contemporary Period, 1945–present (15 questions)

Analyzing and Interpreting Literature

OVERVIEW

- 90 minutes
- 80 multiple-choice questions
- Optional essay section (includes two essays to be answered in an additional 90-minute period; required by some institutions)

The Analyzing and Interpreting Literature exam focuses mainly on British (40–52 questions) and American (24–36 questions) literature, with a small percentage of works in translation from other cultures (4–12 questions). During the test, students must read passages and answer questions about them. While it is helpful to have a good understanding of a wide array of poetry, drama, fiction, and nonfiction, prior knowledge of the works included on the test is not required. The following is a breakdown of the Analyzing and Interpreting Literature exam according to genre and period:

Genre

- Poetry (28–36 questions)
- Prose (28–36 questions)
- Drama (12–24 questions)

Period

- Classical and Pre-Renaissance (2–6 questions)
- Renaissance and Seventeenth Century (16–24 questions)
- Eighteenth and Nineteenth Centuries (28–36 questions)
- Twentieth and Twenty-First Centuries (20–28 questions)

College Composition Modular

OVERVIEW

- 90 minutes
- 90 multiple-choice questions
- Optional essay section (may be provided by the college or by the CLEP; the CLEP essay section includes two essays to be answered in an additional 70-minute period; required by some institutions)

The College Composition Modular has replaced two former tests: English Composition (not to be confused with English Composition with Essay) and Freshman College Composition. The College Composition Modular requires knowledge of the basic rules of Standard Written English, rhetoric, and writing. The following is a breakdown of the approximate number of each type of question test-takers can expect to see on the multiple-choice portion of the exam:

- Revision Skills (36 questions)
- Using Source Materials (22–23 questions)
- Rhetorical Analysis (22–23 questions)
- Conventions of Standard Written English (9 questions)
- The essay portion of the exam is designed to assess students in the same areas.

English Literature

OVERVIEW

- 90 minutes
- 95 multiple-choice questions
- Optional essay section (includes three essays of which two must be answered in an additional 90-minute period; required by some institutions)

The English Literature exam focuses mainly on major authors and literary works throughout history. The multiple-choice portion of the test breaks down into the following two general categories:

1. Ability (57–62 questions)
2. Knowledge (33–38 questions)

The essay section includes three essays, the first of which is a persuasive analysis of a poem. For the second essay, students choose between one of two topics, both of which require students to write about a particular observation, position, or theme.

World Languages

French Language (Levels 1 and 2)

OVERVIEW

- 90 minutes (divided into three sections)
- 121 multiple-choice questions

The French Language exam is divided into three individually timed sections. Two sections focus on listening and a third focuses on reading. About 48–49 questions on the exam require responses to spoken selections. The other 72–73 questions are reading-based and include a combination of sentences, short passages, and long reading comprehension passages.

German Language (Levels 1 and 2)

OVERVIEW

- 90 minutes (divided into three sections)
- 120 multiple-choice questions

The German Language exam is divided into three individually timed sections. Two sections focus on listening and a third focuses on reading. About 48 questions on the exam require responses to spoken selections. The other 72 questions are reading-based and include a combination of sentences, short passages, and long reading comprehension passages.

Spanish Language (Levels 1 and 2)

OVERVIEW

- 90 minutes (divided into three sections)
- 120 multiple-choice questions

The Spanish Language exam is divided into three individually timed sections. Two sections focus on listening and a third focuses on reading. About 48 questions on the exam require responses to spoken selections. The other 72 questions are reading-based and include a combination of sentences, short passages, and long reading comprehension passages.

History and Social Sciences

American Government

OVERVIEW

- 90 minutes
- 90 multiple-choice questions

Students who take the American Government exam can expect to see questions about U.S. government and politics. The exam covers information typically taught in a one-semester, college-level American government course. Slightly more than half the exam tests students' knowledge of U.S. government and politics. The rest of the questions on the exam cover political processes, principles of government structures and procedures, and analysis and interpretation of government- and politics-related data. Following is a breakdown of the subject matter covered on the exam:

- Institutions and Policy Processes: Presidency, Bureaucracy, and Congress (27–32 questions)
- Federal Courts, Civil Liberties, and Civil Rights (13–18 questions)
- Political Parties and Interest Groups (13–18 questions)
- Constitutional Underpinnings of American Democracy (13–18 questions)
- Political Beliefs and Behavior (9–14 questions)

Human Growth and Development

OVERVIEW

- 90 minutes
- 90 multiple-choice questions

Students who take the Human Growth and Development exam can expect to encounter questions about all stages of human development—infancy, childhood, adolescence, adulthood, and aging. The test covers information that students would receive during a one-semester introductory course in human growth and development or developmental psychology. The following is a breakdown of the subject matter students may encounter on the Human Growth and Development exam:

- Cognitive Development (10–11 questions)
- Biological Development (9 questions)
- Theoretical Perspectives (9 questions)
- Social Development (9 questions)
- Family, Home, and Society (7 questions)
- Personality and Emotion (7 questions)
- Learning (7 questions)
- Language Development (7 questions)
- Perceptual Development (6 questions)
- Research Strategies and Methodology (4–5 questions)
- Schooling, Work, and Interventions (4–5 questions)
- Atypical Development (4–5 questions)
- Intelligence (3–4 questions)

Introduction to Educational Psychology

OVERVIEW

- 90 minutes
- 100 multiple-choice questions

Students who take the Introduction to Educational Psychology exam can expect to find questions based on information normally covered in a one-semester, college-level course in educational psychology. Students may see questions about learning, teaching methods, classroom management, child development, and other related topics. Following is a breakdown of the subject matter covered on the exam:

- Individual Differences (17 questions)
- Cognitive Perspective (15 questions)
- Development (15 questions)
- Testing (12 questions)
- Behavioral Perspective (11 questions)
- Motivation (10 questions)
- Pedagogy (10 questions)
- Research Design and Analysis (5 questions)
- Educational Aims and Philosophies (5 questions)

Introduction to Psychology

OVERVIEW

- 90 minutes
- 95 multiple-choice questions

The Introduction to Psychology exam tests students on knowledge typically acquired during an introductory, college-level psychology course. Students who take the exam can expect to see questions about basic psychological facts, concepts, and principles. Following are the topics covered on the Introduction to Psychology exam:

- Learning (9–11 questions)
- History, Approaches, and Methods (7–9 questions)
- Biological Bases of Behavior (7–9 questions)
- Developmental Psychology (7–9 questions)
- Psychological Disorders and Health (7–9 questions)
- Cognition (7–9 questions)
- Sensation and Perception (6–8 questions)
- Motivation and Emotion (6–8 questions)
- Treatment of Psychological Disorders (6–8 questions)
- Social Psychology (6–8 questions)
- States of Consciousness (4–6 questions)
- Statistics, Tests, and Measurement (2–4 questions)

Introduction to Sociology

OVERVIEW

- 90 minutes
- 100 multiple-choice questions

The Introduction to Sociology exam tests students on knowledge typically acquired during an introductory, college-level sociology course. Students who take the exam can expect to see questions about basic facts and concepts, as well as various theoretical approaches to sociology. Following are the topics covered on the Introduction to Sociology exam:

- Social Stratification (30 questions)
- Institutions (20 questions)
- Social Processes (20 questions)
- Social Patterns (15 questions)
- Sociological Perspective (15 questions)

Principles of Macroeconomics

OVERVIEW

- 90 minutes
- 80 multiple-choice questions

Students who take the Principles of Macroeconomics exam can expect to find questions based on information normally covered in a one-semester, college-level course in macroeconomics. Students may see questions about supply and demand, economic principles, economic growth, monetary and fiscal policies, the Federal Reserve Bank, and other related topics. Following is a subject-specific breakdown of the material covered on the exam:

- Inflation, Unemployment, and Stabilization Policies (16–24 questions)
- Financial Sector (12–16 questions)
- Measurement of Economic Performance (9–13 questions)
- National Income and Price Determination (8–12 questions)
- International Trade and Finance (8–12 questions)
- Basic Economic Concepts (6–10 questions)
- Economic Growth and Productivity (5–8 questions)

Principles of Microeconomics

OVERVIEW

- 90 minutes
- 80 multiple-choice questions

Students who take the Principles of Microeconomics exam can expect to find questions based on information normally covered in a one-semester, college-level course in microeconomics. Students may see questions about real-world situations, individual consumers and businesses, free markets, private markets, government intervention, and other related topics. Following is a subject-specific breakdown of the material covered on the exam:

- Firm Behavior and Market Structure (20–28 questions)
- Supply and Demand (12–16 questions)
- Production and Costs (8–12 questions)
- Theory of Consumer Choice (4–8 questions)
- Market Failure and the Role of Government (9–15 questions)

- Factor Markets (8–15 questions)

- Basic Economic Concepts (6–11 questions)

History of the United States I: Early Colonization to 1877

OVERVIEW

- 90 minutes

- 120 multiple-choice questions

Students who take the History of the United States I: Early Colonization to 1877 exam can expect to see questions about topics typically covered in the first semester of a two-semester survey in U.S. history. About 84 of the 120 questions focus on the period 1790–1877. The remaining 36 questions cover the period 1500–1789. Following is a breakdown of the approximate number of questions for each topic covered on the exam:

- Political Institutions, Political Developments, Behavior, and Public Policy (42 questions)

- Social Developments (30 questions)

- Cultural and Intellectual Developments (18 questions)

- Diplomacy and International Relations (18 questions)

- Economic Developments (12 questions)

History of the United States II: 1865 to the Present

OVERVIEW

- 90 minutes

- 120 multiple-choice questions

Students who take the History of the United States II: 1865 to the Present exam can expect to see questions about topics typically covered in the second semester of a two-semester survey in U.S. history. About 84 of the 120 questions focus on the period 1915–present. The remaining 36 questions cover the period 1865–1914. Following is a breakdown of the approximate number of questions for each topic covered on the exam:

- Political Institutions, Behavior, and Public Policy (42 questions)

- Social Developments (30 questions)

- Cultural and Intellectual Developments (18 questions)

- Diplomacy and International Relations (18 questions)

- Economic Developments (12 questions)

Western Civilization I: Ancient Near East to 1648

OVERVIEW

- 90 minutes

- 120 multiple-choice questions

The Western Civilization I: Ancient Near East to 1648 exam includes questions about topics typically covered in the first semester of a two-semester survey in Western civilization. Among the topics students may see in questions are ancient civilizations (Greece and Rome), the Middle Ages, the Renaissance, the Reformation, and other related topics. Students can expect to answer questions about historical terms, historical figures, maps, and images. Following is a breakdown of the approximate number of questions for each topic covered on the exam:

- Ancient Near East (9–12 questions)
- Ancient Greece and Hellenistic Civilization (18–20 questions)
- Ancient Rome (18–20 questions)
- Medieval History (27–32 questions)
- Renaissance and Reformation (15–20 questions)
- Early Modern Europe, 1560–1648 (12–18 questions)

Western Civilization II: 1648 to the Present

OVERVIEW

- 90 minutes
- 120 multiple-choice questions

The Western Civilization II: 1648 to the Present exam includes questions about topics typically covered in the second semester of a two-semester survey in Western civilization. Among the topics students may see in questions are European history, the Enlightenment, the Industrial Revolution, World War I and World War II, and other related topics. Students can expect to answer questions about historical terms, historical figures, maps, and images. Following is a breakdown of the approximate number of questions for each topic covered on the exam:

- Absolutism and Constitutionalism, 1648–1715 (8–11 questions)
- Competition for Empire and Economic Expansion (4–7 questions)
- The Scientific View of the World (6–8 questions)
- Period of Enlightenment (8–11 questions)
- Revolution and Napoleonic Europe (12–16 questions)
- The Industrial Revolution (8–11 questions)
- Political and Cultural Developments, 1815–1848 (7–10 questions)
- Politics and Diplomacy in the Age of Nationalism, 1850–1914 (9–12 questions)
- Economy, Culture, and Imperialism, 1850–1914 (8–11 questions)
- The First World War and the Russian Revolution (12–14 questions)
- Europe Between the Wars (8–11 questions)
- The Second World War and Contemporary Europe (9–12 questions)

Science and Math

Biology

OVERVIEW

- 90 minutes
- 115 multiple-choice questions

The Biology exam tests students on knowledge typically acquired during a one-year, college-level course in general biology. Students who take the exam can expect to see questions about cells, enzymes, reproduction, heredity, ecology, evolution, and other related topics. Following is a breakdown of the approximate number of questions for each area of biology covered on the exam:

- Molecular and Cellular Biology (38 questions)
- Organismal Biology (39 questions)
- Population Biology (38 questions)

Calculus

OVERVIEW

- 90 minutes (divided into two sections)
- 44 multiple-choice questions

Students who take the Calculus exam can expect to see questions about topics typically covered in a one-semester college calculus class. The first section includes 27 questions, and students have 50 minutes to answer them. The second section has 17 questions, and students have 40 minutes to answer them. About half the questions focus on solving routine calculus problems; the other half require an understanding of calculus concepts and applications. For some questions, students may be required to use an online graphing calculator, which is part of the exam software. Following is a breakdown of the approximate number of questions for each topic covered on the exam:

- Limits and Differential Calculus (26 questions)
- Integral Calculus (18 questions)

Chemistry

OVERVIEW

- 90 minutes
- 75 multiple-choice questions

The Chemistry exam tests students on knowledge typically acquired during a one-year, college-level course in general chemistry. Among the many topics covered on the exam are the states of matter, chemical reactions, kinetics, and atomic theory. Following is a breakdown of the approximate number of questions for each area of chemistry covered on the exam:

- Structure of Matter (15 questions)
- States of Matter (14–15 questions)
- Reaction Types (9 questions)
- Equations and Stoichiometry (7–8 questions)

- Equilibrium (5–6 questions)
- Kinetics (3 questions)
- Thermodynamics (3–4 questions)
- Descriptive Chemistry (10–11 questions)
- Experimental Chemistry (6–7 questions)

College Algebra
OVERVIEW

- 90 minutes
- 60 multiple-choice questions

Students who take the College Algebra exam can expect to see questions about topics typically covered in a one-semester college algebra class. About half the questions focus on solving routine algebra problems; the other half require an understanding of algebraic concepts, skills, and applications. Following is a breakdown of the approximate number of questions for each topic covered on the exam:

- Algebraic Operations (15 questions)
- Equations and Inequalities (15 questions)
- Functions and Their Properties (18 questions)
- Number Systems and Operations (12 questions)

Precalculus
OVERVIEW

- 90 minutes (divided into two sections)
- 48 multiple-choice questions

Students who take the Precalculus exam can expect to see questions about topics typically covered in a first-semester calculus class. The first section includes 25 questions, and students have 50 minutes to answer them. The second section has 23 questions, and students have 40 minutes to answer them. For some questions, students may be required to use an online graphing calculator, which is part of the exam software. Following is a breakdown of the approximate number of questions for each topic covered on the exam:

- Representations of Functions: Symbolic, Graphical, and Tabular (14–15 questions)
- Algebraic Expressions, Equations, and Inequalities (9–10 questions)
- Concepts, Properties, and Operations of Functions (7–8 questions)
- Trigonometry and Its Applications (7–8 questions)
- Analytic Geometry (4–5 questions)
- Functions as Models (4–5 questions)

Business

Financial Accounting

OVERVIEW

- 90 minutes
- 75 multiple-choice questions

Students who take the Financial Accounting exam can expect to encounter material normally covered in a first-semester, college-level financial accounting class including accounting concepts and vocabulary and accounting principles and procedures. In addition, students should be able to apply accounting methods to specific scenarios involving calculations. Following is the approximate number of questions for each of the topics on the test:

- General Accounting Topics (15–23 questions)
- The Income Statement (15–23 questions)
- The Balance Sheet (23–30 questions)
- State of Cash Flows (3–8 questions)
- Miscellaneous (1–3 questions)

Introductory Business Law

OVERVIEW

- 90 minutes
- 100 multiple-choice questions

The Introductory Business Law exam focuses on information that students typically acquire during a one-semester, college-level course in business law. Students may encounter questions about contracts, ethics, product liability, consumer protection as well as American law, legal systems, and procedures. Following is a breakdown of the approximate number of questions for each topic covered on the exam:

- History and Sources of American Law/Constitutional Law (5–10 questions)
- American Legal Systems and Procedures (5–10 questions)
- Contracts (25–35 questions)
- Legal Environment (25–30 questions)
- Torts (10–15 questions)
- Miscellaneous (5–10 questions)

Information Systems and Computer Applications

OVERVIEW

- 90 minutes
- 100 multiple-choice questions

The Information Systems and Computer Applications exam focuses on information that students typically acquire during an introductory information systems and computer applications course.

Students may encounter questions about terminology, basic software, programming concepts, and other related topics. Knowledge of specific products (e.g., a specific word processing program) is not required. Following is a breakdown of the approximate number of questions for each topic covered on the exam:

- Information Systems and Office Application Software in Organizations (25 questions)
- Hardware and Systems Technology (20 questions)
- Information Systems Software Development (15 questions)
- Programming Concepts and Data Management (25 questions)
- Business, Social, and Ethical Implications and Issues (15 questions)

Principles of Management

OVERVIEW

- 90 minutes
- 100 multiple-choice questions

The Principles of Management exam focuses on information that students typically acquire during an introductory course in management. Students may encounter questions about management ideas, techniques, and procedures; problem solving; organizational structures; and other related topics. Following is a breakdown of the approximate number of questions for each topic covered on the exam:

- Functional Aspects of Management (45–55 questions)
- Organization and Human Resources (15–25 questions)
- Operational Aspects of Management (10–20 questions)
- International Management and Contemporary Issues (10–20 questions)

Principles of Marketing

OVERVIEW

- 90 minutes
- 100 multiple-choice questions

Students who take the Principles of Marketing exam can expect to encounter material normally covered in a one-semester, college-level marketing class. Questions may focus on marketing concepts, marketing strategies, consumer behavior, ethics, pricing policies, e-commerce, and other related topics. Following is the approximate number of questions for each of the topics covered on the test:

- Marketing Mix (40–50 questions)
- Target Marketing (22–27 questions)
- Role of Marketing in a Firm (17–24 questions)
- Role of Marketing in Society (8–13 questions)

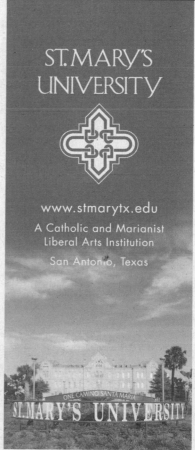

Learn from a National Leader in
Population Health

Jefferson School of Population Health

- **Master of Public Health (MPH); CEPH accredited**
- **PhD in Population Health Sciences**

Online programs
- **Master of Science in Health Policy (MS-HP)**
- **Master of Science in Healthcare Quality and Safety (MS-HQS)**
- **Master of Science in Chronic Care Management (MS-CCM)**
- **Certificates in Public Health, Health Policy, Healthcare Quality and Safety, Chronic Care Management**

Population health – putting health and health care together

215-503-0174
www.jefferson.edu/population_health/ads.cfm

Jefferson.
School of Population Health

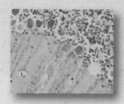

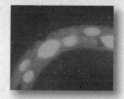

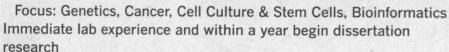
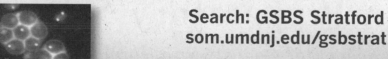
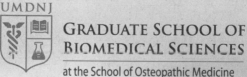

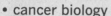

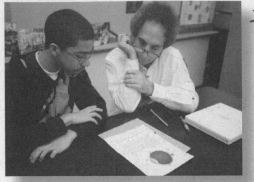

NOTES

NOTES

NOTES

NOTES

NOTES